THE ATTIC NIGHTS
OF AULUS GELLIUS
III

LCL 212

THE ATTIC NIGHTS
OF AULUS GELLIUS

BOOKS XIV–XX

WITH AN ENGLISH TRANSLATION BY
JOHN C. ROLFE

HARVARD UNIVERSITY PRESS
CAMBRIDGE, MASSACHUSETTS
LONDON, ENGLAND

First published 1927
Revised and reprinted 1952
Reprinted 1961, 1967, 1978, 1993

ISBN 0-674-99234-2

Printed in Great Britain by St Edmundsbury Press Ltd,
Bury St Edmunds, Suffolk, on acid-free paper.
Bound by Hunter & Foulis Ltd, Edinburgh, Scotland.

CONTENTS

CAPITULA LIBRI QUARTI DECIMI

CHAPTER HEADINGS OF BOOK XIV

CAPITULA

viii

CHAPTER HEADINGS

CAPITULA

x

CHAPTER HEADINGS

CAPITULA

CAPITULA LIBRI SEXTI DECIMI

xii

CHAPTER HEADINGS

CAPITULA

xiv

CHAPTER HEADINGS

CAPITULA

CAPITULA LIBRI SEPTIMI DECIMI

xvi

CHAPTER HEADINGS

CAPITULA

xviii

CHAPTER HEADINGS

CAPITULA

CAPITULA LIBRI OCTAVI DECIMI

CHAPTER HEADINGS

CAPITULA

CHAPTER HEADINGS

CAPITULA

[1] The lemmata of Book xix are ommited by ω ; they are supplied in
varying forms in ς.

xxiv

CHAPTER HEADINGS

CAPITULA

xxvi

CHAPTER HEADINGS

[1]See critical note, p. xxiv.

CAPITULA

CHAPTER HEADINGS

THE ATTIC NIGHTS
OF AULUS GELLIUS

BOOK XIV

A. GELLII
NOCTIUM ATTICARUM

LIBER QUARTUS DECIMUS

I

Dissertatio Favorini philosophi adversus eos qui Chaldaei appellantur, et ex coetu motibusque siderum et stellarum fata hominum dicturos pollicentur.

1 ADVERSUM istos qui sese "Chaldaeos" seu "ge-
nethliacos" appellant ac de motu deque positu
stellarum dicere posse quae futura sunt profitentur,
audivimus quondam Favorinum philosophum Romae
2 Graece disserentem egregia atque inlustri oratione ;
exercendi autem, non ostentandi, gratia ingenii, an
quod ita serio iudicatoque existimaret, non habeo
dicere. Capita autem locorum argumentorumque
quibus usus est, quod eius meminisse potui, egressus
ibi ex auditione propere adnotavi, eaque fuerunt ad
hanc ferme sententiam : disciplinam istam Chaldaeorum tantae vetustatis non esse quantae videri volunt,
neque eos principes eius auctoresque esse, quos ipsi
ferant, sed id praestigiarum atque offuciarum genus
commentos esse homines aeruscatores et cibum
3 quaestumque ex mendaciis captantes.   Atque eos,

---

[1] Literally, calculators of nativities ; see also note on
i. 9. 6.
[2] p. 44, Marres.

2

THE ATTIC NIGHTS
OF AULUS GELLIUS

BOOK XIV

I

A discourse of the philosopher Favorinus directed against
those who are called Chaldaeans, and who profess to tell
men's fortunes from the conjunction and movements of the
stars and constellations.

AGAINST those who call themselves "Chaldaeans"
or "astrologers,"[1] and profess from the movements
and position of the stars to be able to read the
future, I once at Rome heard the philosopher Favorinus discourse in Greek in admirable and brilliant
language. But whether it was for the purpose of
exercising, not vaunting, his talent, or because he
seriously and sincerely believed what he said, I am
unable to tell; but I promptly jotted down the heads
of the topics and of the arguments which he used,
so far as I could recall them immediately after
leaving the meeting, and they were about to this
effect:[2] That this science of the Chaldaeans was
not of so great antiquity as they would have it
appear; that the founders and authors of it were
not those whom they themselves name, but that
tricks and delusions of that kind were devised by
jugglers and men who made a living and profit from

3

quoniam viderent terrena quaedam inter homines
caelestium rerum sensu atque ductu moveri, quale
est quod oceanus quasi lunae comes cum ea simul
senescit adolescitque, hinc videlicet sibi argumentum
ad suadendum paravisse ut crederemus omnia rerum
humanarum et parva et maxima, tamquam stellis
4 atque sideribus evincta, duci et regi. Esse autem
nimis quam ineptum absurdumque, ut, quoniam
aestus oceani cum lunae curriculo congruit, negotium
quoque alicuius, quod ei forte de aquae ductu cum
rivalibus aut de communi pariete cum vicino apud
iudicem est, ut existimemus, id negotium quasi
5 habena quadam de caelo vinctum gubernari. Quod
etsi vi et ratione quapiam divina fieri potest, nequaquam id tamen censebat in tam brevi exiguoque vitae
spatio quantovis hominis ingenio conprehendi posse
et percipi, set coniectari pauca quaedam, ut verbo
ipsius utar, παχυμερέστερον, nullo scientiae fundo
concepto, sed fusa et vaga et arbitraria, qualis
longinqua oculorum acies est per intervalla media
6 caligantium; tolli enim quod maxime inter deos
atque homines differt, si homines quoque res omnis
7 post futuras praenoscerent. Ipsam deinde siderum
stellarumque observationem, quam esse originem
scientiae suae praedicarent, hautquaquam putabat
8 liquide consistere. " Nam si principes Chaldaei, qui
in patentibus campis colebant, stellarum motus et

---

[1] In a rough and ready, superficial manner.

their lies. And since they saw that some terrestrial
phenomena known to men were caused by the influence and control of the heavenly bodies, as for example the ocean, as though a companion of the moon,
grows old and resumes its youth along with her—from
this, forsooth, they derived an argument for per-
suading us to believe that all human affairs, both the
greatest and the least, as though bound to the stars
and constellations, are influenced and governed by
them. But Favorinus said that it was utterly foolish
and absurd to suppose, because the tide of the ocean
corresponds with the course of the moon, that a suit
at law which one happens to have about an aqueduct
with his neighbours, or with the man next door
about a party wall, is also bound to heaven as if by
a kind of chain and is decided by the stars. But
even if by some divine power and purpose this could
happen, yet he thought that it could by no means
be grasped and understood in such a brief and scant
span of life as ours by any human intellect, but he believed that some few things were conjectured παχυμερέστερον (to use his own term), that is, "somewhat
roughly,"[1] with no sure foundation of knowledge, but
in a loose, random and arbitrary manner, just as when
we look at objects far away with eyes blinded by
their remoteness from us. For the greatest difference between men and gods was removed, if man
also had the power of foreknowing all future events.
Furthermore, he thought that even the observation
of the stars and constellations, which they declared
to be the foundation of their knowledge, was by no
means a matter of certainty. "For if the original
Chaldaeans," said he, "who dwelt in the open plains,
watched the movements and orbits of the stars their

vias et discessiones et coetus intuentes, quid ex his
efficeretur observaverunt, procedat," inquit, "haec
sane disciplina, set sub ea modo inclinatione caeli,
sub qua tunc Chaldaei fuerunt ; non enim potest,"
inquit, "ratio Chaldaeorum observationis manere, si
quis ea uti velit sub diversis caeli regionibus. Nam
quanta," inquit, "partium circulorumque caeli ex
devergentia et convexionibus mundi varietas sit,
9 quis non videt ? Eaedem igitur stellae, per quas
omnia divina humanaque fieri contendunt, sicuti non
usquequaque pruinas aut calores cient, sed mutant et
variant tempestatesque eodem in tempore alibi placi-
das, alibi violentas movent, cur non eventa quoque
rerum ac negotiorum alia efficiunt in Chaldaeis, alia
10 in Gaetulis, alia aput Danuvium, alia aput Nilum ? Per
autem,"[1] inquit, "inconsequens, ipsum quidem corpus et habitum tam profundi aeris sub alio atque alio
caeli curvamine non eundem manere, in hominum
autem negotiis stellas istas opinari idem semper osten-
11 dere, si eas ex quacumque terra conspexeris." Praeterea mirabatur id cuiquam pro percepto liquere, stellas istas quas a Chaldaeis et Babyloniis sive Aegyptiis
observatas ferunt, quas multi "erraticas," Nigidius
"errones" vocat, non esse plures quam volgo diceren-
12 tur ; posse enim fieri existimabat ut et alii quidam
planetes pari potestate essent, sine quibus recta

[1] autem enim, Q ; enim, *Hertz.*

---

[1] Fr. 87, Swoboda ; the reference is to the planets.

separations and conjunctions, and observed their
effects, let this art continue to be practised, but let it
be only under the same inclination of the heavens as
that under which the Chaldaeans then were. For
the system of observation of the Chaldaeans cannot
remain valid, if anyone should wish to apply it
to different regions of the sky. For who does not
see," said he, "how great is the diversity of the
zones and circles of the heavens caused by the
inclination and convexity of the earth? Why then
should not those same stars, by which they maintain
that all human and divine affairs are affected, just as
they do not everywhere arouse cold and heat, but
change and vary the weather, at the same time
causing calm in one place and storm in another—
why should they not, I say, produce one series of
affairs and events in the land of the Chaldaeans,
another among the Gaetulians, another on the
Danube, and still another on the Nile? But," said
he, "it is utterly inconsistent to suppose that the
mass and the condition of this vast height of air
does not remain the same under one or another
region of the heavens, but that in human affairs
those stars always indicate the same thing from
whatever part of the earth you may observe them."
Besides, he expressed his surprise that anyone considered it a certainty that those stars which they
say were observed by the Chaldaeans and Baby-
lonians, or by the Egyptians, which many call
erraticae, or "wandering," but Nigidius called *errones,* or "the wanderers,"[1] are not more numerous
than is commonly assumed; for he thought it might
possibly be the case that there were some other
planets of equal power, without which a correct and

7

atque perpetua observatio perfici non quiret, neque
eos tamen cernere homines possent propter exuper-
13 antiam vel splendoris vel altitudinis. "Nam et
quaedam," inquit, "sidera a quibusdam terris conspiciuntur earumque terrarum hominibus nota sunt; sed
eadem ipsa ex alia omni terra non videntur et sunt
14 aliis omnino ignarissima. Atque uti demus," inquit,
" et has tantummodo stellas et ex una parte terrae
observari debuisse, quae tandem finis observationis
istius fuit et quae tempora satis esse visa sunt
ad percipiendum quid praemonstraret aut coetus
15 stellarum aut circuitus aut transitus? Nam si isto
modo coepta fieri observatio est, ut animadverteretur
quo habitu quaque forma quaque positura stellarum
aliquis nasceretur, tum deinceps ab ineunte vita
fortuna eius et mores et ingenium et circumstantia
rerum negotiorumque et ad postremum finis etiam
vitae spectaretur eaque omnia, ut usu venerant,
litteris mandarentur ac postea longis temporibus,
cum ipsae illae eodem in loco eodemque habitu
forent, eadem ceteris quoque eventura existimarentur,
16 qui eodem[1] illo tempore nati fuissent—si isto,"
inquit, "modo observari coeptum et ex ea observa-
tione conposita quaedam disciplina est, nullo id
17 pacto potest procedere. Dicant enim quot tandem
annis vel potius quot saeculis orbis hic observationis
18 perfici quiverit." Constare quippe inter astrologos
dicebat, stellas istas quas " erraticas " dicerent,

---

[1] eodem *deleted by Skutsch.*

---

[1] That is, the time when the stars were again in the same
position. The point is, that observations made for one man,
even though they came out right, were of no value, because

final observation could not be completed, but that
men could not see them because of their remarkable
brilliance or altitude. "For," said he, "some stars
are visible from certain lands and are known to the
men of those lands; but those same stars are not
visible from every other land and are wholly unknown to other men. And granting," said he, "both
that only these stars ought to be observed, and
that too from one part of the earth, what possible
end was there to such observation, and what
periods of time seemed sufficient for understanding
what the conjunction or the orbits or the transits of
the stars foretold? For if an observation was made in
the beginning in such a manner that it was calculated
under what aspect, arrangement and position of the
stars anyone was born, and if thereafter his fortune
from the beginning of his life, his character, his disposition, the circumstances of his affairs and activities,
and finally also the end of his life were noted, and all
these things as they had actually happened were
committed to writing, and long afterwards, when
the same stars were in the same aspect and position,
it was supposed that those same things would
happen to others who had been born at that same
time;[1] if the first observations were made in that
way," said he, "and from such observations a kind
of science was formed, it can by no means be a
success. For let them tell me in how many years,
pray, or rather in how many ages, the cycle of the
observations could be completed." For he said that
it was agreed among astrologers that those stars
which they call "wandering," which are supposed

of the long time that it took for the stars to reach the same
positions that they had at the time of the earlier observations.

quae esse omnium rerum fatales viderentur, infinito
prope et innumerabili numero annorum ad eundem
locum, cum eodem abitu simul omnes reverti[1]
unde[2] profectae sunt, ut neque ullus observationis
tenor neque memoriae ulla effigies litterarum[3] tanto
19 aevo potuerint edurare. Atque illud etiam cuimodi
esset considerandum putabat, quod aliud stellarum
agmen foret quo primum tempore conciperetur homo
in utero matris, aliud postea cum in decem mensibus
proximis in lucem ederetur, quaerebatque qui conveniret diversam super eodem fieri demonstrationem,
si, ut ipsi putarent, alius atque alius earundem
stellarum situs atque ductus alias atque alias
20 fortunas daret. Sed et nuptiarum tempore, ex
quibus liberi quaererentur, atque ipso etiam illo maris
et feminae iam declarari coitu oportere dicebat certo
quodam et necessario stellarum ordine quales qualique
fortuna homines gignerentur; ac multo etiam ante,
cum[4] pater ipse atque mater nascerentur, ex eorum
genitura debuisse iam tunc prospici quinam olim
futuri essent quos hi creaturi forent; et supra longe
atque longe per infinitum, ut, si disciplina ista fundamento aliquo veritatis nixa est, centesimo usque
abhinc saeculo vel magis primo caeli atque mundi
exordio atque inde iam deinceps continua significatione, quotiens generis auctores eiusdem homines
nascerentur, stellae istae praemonstrare debuerint
qualis qualique fato futurus sit quisquis hodie natus
21 est. "Quo autem," inquit, "pacto credi potest,
uniuscuiusque stellarum formae et positionis sortem

---

[1] reverti (redire, *etc.*) *added by* J. F. Gronov *and others after*
sunt; reverti unde olim omnes, *Skutsch.*

[2] unde *added by Vogel.*

[3] litterarum *deleted by Skutsch.*

to determine the fate of all things, beginning their course together, return to the same place from which they set out only after an innumerable and almost infinite number of years, so that there could be no continuity of observation, and no literary record could endure for so long an epoch. And he thought that this point also ought to be taken into consideration, that one constellation presided at the time when a man was first conceived in his mother's womb, and another one ten months later when he came into the world, and he asked how it was consistent for a different indication to be made about the same person, if, as they themselves thought, a different position and order of the same stars gave different fortunes. But also at the time of marriage, from which children were expected, and at the very union of the husband and wife, he said that it ought to be indicated by a fixed and inevitable position of the stars, with what character and fortune men would be born; and, indeed, long before that, when the father and mother were themselves born, it ought to be foretold even then from their horoscope what offspring they would produce; and far, far back of that, even to infinity, so that, if that science rested on any foundation of truth, a hundred years ago, or rather at the beginning of heaven and earth, and then on in an unbroken series of predictions as long as generation followed generation, those stars ought to have foretold what character and fortune anyone would have who is born to-day. "But how," said he, "can it be believed that the fate and fortune foretold by the form and position of any one of the stars are

---

⁴ ante, cum, *Hertz*; antequam, ω.

atque fortunam uni omnino homini certam destina-
tamque esse eamque formam post longissima saecu-
lorum spatia restitui, si vitae fortunarumque eiusdem
hominis indicia in tam brevibus intervallis per singulos maiorum eius gradus perque infinitum succes-
sionum ordinem tam saepe ac tam multipliciter
eadem ipsa, non eadem stellarum facie denotantur?

22 Quod si id fieri potest eaque diversitas atque varietas
admittitur per omnis antiquitatis gradus ad signifi-
canda eorum hominum qui post nascentur exordia
imparilitas haec turbat observationem omnisque ratio

23 disciplinae confunditur." Iam vero id minime
ferundum censebat, quod non modo casus et eventa
quae evenirent extrinsecus, sed consilia quoque ipsa
hominum et arbitria et varias voluntates adpetitiones-
que et declinationes et fortuitos repentinosque in
levissimis rebus animorum impetus recessusque moveri agitarique desuper e caelo putarent; tamquam
quod forte ire in balneas volueris ac deinde nolueris
atque id rursus volueris, non ex aliqua dispari
variaque animi agitatione, sed ex necessaria quadam
errantium siderum reciprocatione contigerit, ut plane
homines non, quod dicitur, λογικὰ ζῶα, sed ludicra et
ridenda quaedam neurospasta esse videantur, si nihil
sua sponte, nihil arbitratu suo faciunt, sed ducentibus

24 stellis et aurigantibus. "Ac si," inquit, "potuisse
praedici adfirmant Pyrrusne rex an Manius Curius
proelio victurus esset, cur tandem non de alea
quoque ac de calculis et alveolo audent dicere, quis-

fixed and attached to one particular individual, and
that the same position of the stars is restored only
after a long series of years, if the indications of the
same man's life and fortunes in such short intervals,
through the single degrees of his forefathers and
through an infinite order of successions, are so often
and so frequently pointed out as the same, although
the position of the stars is not the same? But if
this can happen, and if this contradiction and variation be admitted through all the epochs of antiquity
in foretelling the origin of those men who are to
be born afterwards, this inequality confounds the
observation and the whole theory of the science
falls to the ground." Moreover, he thought that the
most intolerable thing was their belief that not only
occurrences and events of an external nature, but
even men's very deliberations, their purposes, their
various pleasures, their likes and dislikes, the chance
and sudden attractions and aversions of their feelings on trifling matters, were excited and influenced
from heaven above; for example, if you happened
to wish to go to the baths, and then should change
your mind, and again should decide to go, that all
this happens, not from some shifting and variable
state of mind, but from a fateful ebb and flow of the
planets. Thus men would clearly be seen to be, not
λογικὰ ζῷα, or "reasoning beings," as they are called,
but a species of ludicrous and ridiculous puppets, if
it be true that they do nothing of their own volition
or their own will, but are led and driven by the
stars. "And if," said he, "they affirm that it could
have been foretold whether king Pyrrhus or Manius
Curius was to be victorious in the battle, why,
pray, do they not dare also to predict which of the

nam ibi ludentium vincat? An videlicet magna
sciunt, parva nesciunt, et minora maioribus inper-
25 ceptiora sunt? Sed si magnitudines rerum sibi
vindicant magisque esse perspicuas et facilius com-
prehendi posse dicunt, volo," inquit, "mihi respondeant quid in hac totius mundi contemplatione, prae
tantis naturae operibus, in tam parvis atque brevibus
negotiis fortunisque hominum magnum putent?
26 Atque id velim etiam," inquit, "ut respondeant: si
tam parvum atque rapidum est momentum temporis,
in quo homo nascens fatum accipit, ut in eodem illo
puncto sub eodem circulo caeli plures simul ad
eandem competentiam nasci non queant, et si
idcirco gemini quoque non eadem vitae sorte sunt,
quoniam non eodem temporis puncto editi sunt—
peto," inquit, "respondeant, cursum illum temporis
transvolantis, qui vix cogitatione animi conprehendi
potest, quonam pacto aut consulto adsequi queant
aut ipsi perspicere et reprehendere, cum in tam
praecipiti dierum noctiumque vertigine minima
27 momenta ingentes facere dicant mutationes?" Ad
postremum autem et quid esset quod adversum hoc
dici posset requirebat, quod homines utriusque sexus,
omnium aetatum, diversis stellarum motibus in vitam
editi, regionibus sub quibus geniti sunt longe distantibus, omnes tamen isti, aut hiantibus terris aut
labentibus tectis aut oppidorum expugnationibus aut
eadem in navi fluctu obruti, eodem genere mortis
eodemque ictu temporis universi simul interirent.
28 "Quod scilicet," inquit, "numquam eveniret, si
momenta nascendi singulis adtributa suas unumquid-

players with dice or counters on a board will win?
Or, forsooth, do they know important things, but not
those which are unimportant; and are unimportant
things more difficult to understand than the important? But if they claim knowledge of great
matters and say that they are plainer and easier to
be understood, I should like," said he, "to have
them tell me, in this observation of the whole
world, in comparison with such mighty works of
nature, what they regard as great in the trifling and
brief fortunes and affairs of men. And I should like
to have them answer this question also," said he:
"if the instant in which man at birth is allotted his
destiny is so brief and fleeting, that at that same
moment not more than one can be born with the
same conjunction under the same circle of the
heavens, and if therefore even twins have different
lots in life, since they are not born at the same
instant—I ask them to tell me," said he, "how and
by what plan they are able to overtake the course
of that fleeting moment, which can scarcely be
grasped by one's thoughts, or to detain and examine
it, when in the swift revolution of days and nights
even the briefest moments, as they say, cause great
changes?" Then, finally, he asked what answer
could be made to this argument, that human beings
of both sexes, of all ages, born into the world under
different positions of the stars and in regions widely
separated, nevertheless sometimes all perished together by the same kind of death and at the same
moment, either from an earthquake, or a falling
building, or the sack of a town, or the wreck of the
same ship. "This," said he, "of course would never
happen, if the natal influence assigned to the birth

29 que leges haberent. Quod si quaedam," inquit, "in
hominum morte atque vita etiam diversis temporibus
editorum per stellarum pares quosdam postea con-
ventus paria nonnulla et consimilia posse dicunt
optingere, cur non aliquando possint omnia quoque
paria usu venire, ut existant per huiuscemodi stellarum concursiones et similitudines Socratae simul et
Antisthenae et Platones multi genere, forma, ingenio, moribus, vita omni et morte pari ? Quod
30 nequaquam," inquit, "prorsus fieri potest. Non
igitur hac causa probe uti queunt adversum hominum
31 impares ortus, interitus pares." Illud autem condo-
nare se his dicebat quod non id quoque requireret :
si vitae mortisque hominum rerumque humanarum
omnium tempus et ratio et causa in caelo et apud
stellas foret, quid de muscis aut vermiculis aut
echinis, multis aliis minutissimis terra marique ani-
mantibus dicerent ? An istaec quoque isdem, quibus
homines, legibus nascerentur isdemque itidem ex-
tinguerentur ? ut aut ranunculis quoque et culicibus
nascendi fata sint de caelestium siderum motibus
adtributa aut, si id non putarent, nulla ratio videretur
cur ea siderum vis in hominibus valeret, deficeret in
ceteris.

32 Haec nos sicca et incondita et propemodum ieiuna
oratione adtigimus.[1] Set Favorinus, ut hominis
ingenium fuit utque est Graecae facundiae copia
simul et venustas, latius ea et amoenius et splendidius
et profluentius exequebatur, atque identidem com-

---

[1] adtigimus, *Skutsch* ; adtingimus, *MSS.*

of each of them had its own peculiar conditions. But if," he said, "they answer that even in the life and death of men who are born at different times certain events may happen which are alike and similar, through some similar conjunction of the stars at a later time, why may not sometimes everything become equal, so that through such agreement and similarity of the stars many a Socrates and Antisthenes and Plato may appear, equal in birth, in person, in talent, in character, in their whole life and in their death? But this," said he, "can by no means whatever happen. Therefore they cannot properly use this argument against the inequality of men's births and the similarity of their death." He added that he excused them from this further inquiry: namely, if the time, the manner and the cause of men's life and death, and of all human affairs, were in heaven and with the stars, what would they say of flies, worms, sea urchins, and many other minute animals of land and sea? Were they too born and destroyed under the same laws as men? so that to frogs also and gnats either the same fates are assigned at birth by the movements of the constellations, or, if they do not believe that, there seemed to be no reason why that power of the stars should be effective with men and ineffectual with the other animals.

These remarks I have touched upon in a dry, unadorned, and almost jejune style. But Favorinus, such was the man's talent and such is at once the copiousness and the charm of Greek eloquence, delivered them at greater length and with more charm, brilliance and readiness, and from time to

monebat ut caveremus ne qua nobis isti sycophantae
ad faciendam fidem inreperent, quod viderentur
33 quaedam interdum vera effutire aut spargere. "Non
enim comprehensa," inquit, "neque definita neque
percepta dicunt, sed lubrica atque ambagiosa con-
iectatione nitentes, inter falsa atque vera pedetemptim
quasi per tenebras ingredientes, eunt et aut multa
temptando incidunt repente inprudentes in veritatem
aut ipsorum, qui eos consulunt, multa credulitate
ducente perveniunt callide ad ea quae vera sunt, et
idcirco videntur in praeteritis rebus quam in futuris
veritatem facilius imitari. Ista tamen omnia quae
aut temere aut astute vera dicunt, prae ceteris,"
inquit, "quae mentiuntur, pars ea non sit millesima."
34 Praeter haec autem quae dicentem Favorinum
audivimus, multa etiam memini poetarum veterum
testimonia, quibus huiuscemodi ambages fallaciosae
confutantur. Ex quibus est Pacuvianum illud :

Nám si quae eventúra sunt providéant, aequi-
perént Iovi,

item Accianum illud :

Nihil (inquit) crédo auguribus, qui aúres verbis
dívitant
Aliénas, suas ut aúro locupletént domus.

35 Idem Favorinus, deterrere volens ac depellere
adulescentes a genethliacis istis et quibusdam aliis id
genus, qui prodigiosis artibus futura omnia dicturos
pollicentur, nullo pacto adeundos eos esse consulen-
36 dosque huiuscemodi argumentis concludebat : "Aut

---

[1] v. 407, Ribbeck[3].
[2] v. 169, Ribbeck[3].

time he warned us to take care lest in any way those
sycophants should worm their way into our confidence
by sometimes seeming to stumble upon, and give
utterance to, something true. "For they do not,"
said he, "say anything that is tangible, definite or
comprehensible, but depending upon slippery and
roundabout conjecture, groping with cautious steps
between truth and falsehood, as if walking in the
dark, they go their way. And after making many
attempts they either happen suddenly on the truth
without knowing it, or led by the great credulity of
those who consult them, they get hold by cunning of
something true, and therefore obviously find it easier
to come somewhere near the truth in past events
than in those to come. Yet all the true things
which they say through accident or cunning," said
he, "are not a thousandth part of the falsehoods
which they utter."

But besides these remarks which I heard Favorinus
make, I recall many testimonies of the ancient poets,
by which delusive fallacies of this kind are refuted.
Among these is the following saying of Pacuvius : [1]

Could men divine the future, they'd match Jove.

Also this from Accius, who writes : [2]

I trust the augurs not, who with mere words
Enrich men's ears, to load themselves with gold.

Favorinus too, wishing to deter and turn away
young men from such calculators of nativities and
from certain others of that kind, who profess to
reveal all the future by means of magic arts, concluded with arguments of this sort, to show that they
ought by no means to be resorted to and consulted.

adversa," inquit, "eventura dicunt, aut prospera. Si dicunt prospera et fallunt, miser fies frustra expectando; si adversa dicunt et mentiuntur, miser fies frustra timendo; sin vera respondent eaque sunt non prospera, iam inde ex animo miser fies, antequam e fato fias; si felicia promittunt eaque eventura sunt, tum plane duo erunt incommoda: et expectatio te spei suspensum fatigabit et futurum gaudii fructum spes tibi iam praefloraverit. Nullo igitur pacto utendum est istiusmodi hominibus res futuras praesagientibus."

II

Quem in modum disseruerit Favorinus consultus a me super officio iudicis.

1 Quo primum tempore a praetoribus lectus in iudices sum, ut iudicia quae appellantur "privata" susciperem, libros utriusque linguae de officio iudicis scriptos conquisivi, ut homo adulescens, a poetarum fabulis et a rhetorum epilogis ad iudicandas lites vocatus, rem iudiciariam, quoniam "vocis," ut dicitur, "vivae" penuria erat, ex "mutis," quod aiunt, "magistris" cognoscerem. Atque in dierum quidem diffissionibus conperendinationibusque et aliis quibusdam legitimis ritibus ex ipsa lege Iulia et ex Sabini Masurii et quorundam aliorum iurisperitorum com-
2 mentariis commoniti et adminiculati sumus. In his

---

[1] See note on xii. 13. 1.
[2] A law of Julius Caesar and Augustus regulating criminal processes.

"They predict," said he, "either adverse or prosperous events. If they foretell prosperity and deceive you, you will be made wretched by vain expectations ; if they foretell adversity and lie, you will be made wretched by useless fears. But if they predict truly and the events are unhappy, you will thereby be made wretched by anticipation, before you are fated to be so ; if on the contrary they promise prosperity and it comes to pass, then there will clearly be two disadvantages : the anticipation of your hopes will wear you out with suspense, and hope will in advance have reaped the fruit of your approaching happiness. Therefore there is every reason why you should not resort to men of that kind, who profess knowledge of the future."

II

How Favorinus discoursed when I consulted him about the duty of a judge.

At the time when I was first chosen by the praetors to be one of the judges in charge of the suits which are called "private,"[1] I hunted up books written in both languages on the duty of a judge, in order that, being a young man, called from poets' tales and orators' perorations to preside in court, I might from lack of the "living voice," as they say, gain legal lore from so-called "mute counsellors." And with regard to postponements and delays and some other legal principles I was advised and helped by the Julian Law itself[2] and by the commentaries of Masurius Sabinus[3] and some other jurists.[4] But in

[3] *Jur. Civ.* iii. 3, Bremer.   [4] ii. 2, p. 567, Bremer.

autem, quae existere solent, negotiorum ambagibus
et in ancipiti rationum diversarum circumstantia
nihil quicquam nos huiuscemodi libri iuverunt.

3 Nam, etsi consilia iudicibus ex praesentium causarum
statu capienda sunt, generalia tamen quaedam
praemonita et praecepta sunt, quibus ante causam
praemuniri iudex praepararique ad incertos casus
futurarum difficultatum debeat, sicut illa mihi
tunc accidit inexplicabilis reperiendae sententiae
ambiguitas.

4 Petebatur apud me pecunia, quae dicebatur data
numerataque, sed qui petebat neque tabulis neque
testibus id factum docebat et argumentis admodum

5 exilibus nitebatur. Sed eum constabat virum esse
firme bonum notaeque et expertae fidei et vitae in-
culpatissimae, multaque et inlustria exempla probitatis

6 sinceritatisque eius expromebantur; illum autem
unde petebatur hominem esse non bonae rei vitaque
turpi et sordida convictumque volgo in mendaciis
plenumque esse perfidiarum et fraudum ostendebatur.

7 Is tamen cum suis multis patronis clamitabat probari
apud me debere pecuniam datam consuetis modis,
"expensi latione," "mensae rationibus," "chirogra-
phi exhibitione," "tabularum obsignatione," "testium

8 intercessione," ex quibus omnibus si nulla re probaretur, dimitti iam se sane [1] oportere et adversarium
de calumnia damnari, quod de utriusque autem vita
atque factis diceretur, frustra id fieri atque dici; rem
enim de petenda pecunia apud iudicem privatum
agi, non apud censores de moribus.

---

[1] se sane, *Lion*; se, δ; sane, γ.

---

[1] *i.e.* advanced or loaned by the claimant.

those complicated cases which often come up, and in the perplexity arising from conflicting opinions, such books gave me no aid at all. For although the opinions of judges ought to be formed from the conditions of the cases before them, yet there are certain general principles and precepts by which, before hearing a case, the judge ought to guard and prepare himself against the uncertain event of future difficulties; as, for example, an inexplicable perplexity in coming to an opinion once befell me.

A sum of money was claimed before me, which was said to have been paid and counted out;[1] but the claimant did not show this by documents or witnesses, but relied upon very slender arguments. It was clear, however, that he was a thoroughly good man, of well-known and tested integrity and of blameless life, and many striking instances of his probity and honesty were presented. On the other hand, the man upon whom the claim was made was shown to be of no substance, of base and evil life, often convicted of lying, and full of treachery and fraud. Yet he, along with his numerous advocates, noisily protested that the payment of the money ought to be shown in the usual way, by a "receipt for payment," by a "book of accounts," by "producing a signature," by "a sealed deed," or by the "testimony of witnesses"; and if it could be shown in none of these ways, that he ought surely to be dismissed at once and his accuser found guilty of blackmail. He maintained that the testimony relating to the life and conduct of the two parties was irrelevant; for this was a case of claiming money before a private judge, not a question of morals inquired into by the censors.

9 Tunc ibi amici mei, quos rogaveram in consilium, viri exercitati atque in patrociniis et in operis fori celebres semperque se circumundique distrahentibus causis festinantes, non sedendum diutius ac nihil esse dubium dicebant quin absolvendus foret, quem accepisse pecuniam nulla probatione sollemni docebatur.

10 Sed enim ego homines cum considerabam, alterum fidei, alterum probri plenum spurcissimaeque vitae ac defamatissimae, nequaquam adduci potui ad absol-

11 vendum. Iussi igitur diem diffindi atque inde a subselliis pergo ire ad Favorinum philosophum, quem in eo tempore Romae plurimum sectabar, atque ei de causa ac de hominibus quae apud me dicta fuerant, uti res erat, narro omnia ac peto ut et ipsum illud in quo haerebam, et cetera etiam quae observanda mihi forent in officio iudicis, faceret me ut earum rerum essem prudentior.

12 Tum Favorinus, religione illa cunctationis et sollicitudinis nostrae conprobata: "Id quidem," inquit, "super quo nunc deliberas, videri potest specie tenui parvaque esse. Sed si de omni quoque officio iudicis praeire tibi me vis, nequaquam est vel loci

13 huius vel temporis; est enim disceptatio ista multiiugae et sinuosae quaestionis multaque et anxia

14 cura et circumspicientia indigens. Namque, ut pauca tibi nunc quaestionum capita adtingam, iam omnium primum hoc de iudicis officio quaeritur: si

24

Thereupon some friends of mine, whom I had asked to aid me with their advice, experienced men with a reputation gained in acting as advocates and in the business of the forum, who were always inclined to act in haste because of the suits everywhere demanding attention, declared there was no need of sitting longer and that there was no doubt that the defendant ought to be acquitted, since it could not be shown in any of the usual ways that he had received the money. But when I contemplated the men, one abounding in honesty, the other in baseness and of a most shameful and degraded life, I could not by any means be argued into an acquittal. I therefore ordered a postponement and from the bench I proceeded to go to the philosopher Favorinus, with whom I associated a great deal at Rome at that time. I told him the whole story of the suit and of the men, as it had been related to me, begging that with regard both to the matter about which I was then in doubt, as well as to others which I should have to consider in my position as judge, he should make me a man of greater wisdom in such affairs.

Then Favorinus, after commending my scrupulous hesitation and my conscientiousness said: "The question which you are now considering may seem to be of a trifling and insignificant character. But if you wish me to instruct you as to the full duties of a judge, this is by no means a fit place or time; for such a discussion involves many intricate questions and requires long and anxious attention and consideration. For—to touch at once upon a few leading questions for your benefit—the first query relating to the duty of a judge is this. If a judge

iudex forte id sciat, super qua re apud eum litigatur,
eaque res uni ei, priusquam agi coepta aut in iudi-
cium deducta sit, ex alio quodam negotio casuve [1]
aliquo cognita liquido et comperta sit, neque id
tamen in agenda causa probetur, oporteatne eum
secundum ea quae sciens venit iudicare, an secundum
15 ea quae aguntur? Id etiam," inquit, " quaeri solet,
an deceat atque conveniat iudici causa iam cognita,
si facultas esse videatur conponendi negotii, officio
paulisper iudicis dilato communis amicitiae et quasi
16 pacificatoris partes recipere? Atque illud amplius
ambigi ac dubitari scio, debeatne iudex inter cognos-
cendum ea quae dicto quaesitoque opus est dicere
et quaerere, etiamsi cuius ea dici quaerique interest
neque dicat neque postulet? Patrocinari enim
prorsus hoc esse aiunt, non iudicare.

17 " Praeter haec super ea quoque re dissentitur, an
ex usu exque officio sit iudicis, rem causamque de
qua cognoscit interlocutionibus suis ita exprimere
consignareque, ut ante sententiae tempus, ex iis quae
apud eum in praesens confuse varieque dicuntur, proinde ut quoquo in loco ac tempore movetur, signa
18 et indicia faciat motus atque sensus sui. Nam qui
iudices," inquit, " acres atque celeres videntur, non
aliter existimant rem qua de agitur indagari conpre-

---

[1] casuve, *Cramer*; casuque, *MSS*.

chance to have knowledge of a matter which is
brought to trial before him, and the matter is clearly
known and demonstrated to him alone from some
external circumstance or event, before it has begun
to be argued or brought into court, but nevertheless
the same thing is not proved in the course of the
trial, ought he to decide in accordance with what
he knew beforehand, or according to the evidence
in the case? This question also," said he, "is often
raised, whether it is fitting and proper for a judge,
after a case has been heard, if there seems to be an
opportunity for compromising the dispute, to post-
pone the duty of a judge for a time and take the
part of a common friend and peace-maker, as it
were. And I know that this further is a matter
of doubt and inquiry, whether a judge, when hearing
a suit, ought to mention and ask about the things
which it is for the interest of one of the parties to
the suit to mention and inquire, even if the party in
question neither mentions nor calls for them. For
they say that this is in fact to play the part of an
advocate, not of a judge.

"Besides these questions, there is disagreement
also on this point, whether it is consistent with the
practice and office of a judge by his occasional
remarks so to explain and set forth the matter and
the case which is being tried, that before the time
of his decision, as the result of statements which at
the time are made before him in a confused and
doubtful form, he gives signs and indications of the
emotions and feelings by which he is affected on
each occasion and at every time. For those judges
who give the impression of being keen and quick
think that the matter in dispute cannot be examined

27

hendique posse, nisi is qui iudicat crebris interrogationibus necessariisque interlocutionibus et suos
19 sensus aperiat et litigantium deprehendat.   Contra
autem qui sedatiores et graviores putantur negant
iudicem debere ante sententiam, dum causa utrumque agitatur, quotiens aliqua re proposita motus est,
totiens significare quid sentiat.   Eventurum enim
aiunt, ut, quia pro varietate propositionum argumentorumque alius atque alius motus animi patiendus
est, aliter atque aliter eadem in causa eodemque in
tempore sentire et interloqui videantur.
20   " Sed de his," inquit, " et ceteris huiuscemodi
iudicialis officii tractatibus et nos posthac, cum erit
otium, dicere quid sentiamus conabimur et praecepta
Aelii Tuberonis super officio iudicis, quae nuper-
21 rime legi, recensebimus.   Quod autem ad pecuniam
pertinet quam apud iudicem peti dixisti, suadeo
hercle tibi, utare M. Catonis, prudentissimi viri,
consilio, qui, in oratione quam *Pro L. Turio* contra
Cn. Gellium dixit, ita esse a maioribus traditum
observatumque ait, ut si quod inter duos actum est
neque tabulis neque testibus planum fieri possit,
tum apud iudicem qui de ea re cognosceret, uter
ex his vir melior esset quaereretur et, si pares essent
seu boni pariter seu mali, tum illi unde petitur
22 crederetur ac secundum eum iudicaretur.   In hac

---

[1] *Tempore* evidently refers to the whole period of the
trial ; Favorinus seems to use the word in a double sense,
to emphasize his point.
[2] li., Jordan.

and understood, unless the judge by frequent questions and necessary interruptions makes his own opinion clear and grasps that of the litigants. But, on the other hand, those who have a reputation for calmness and dignity maintain that the judge ought not, before giving his decision and while the case is being pleaded by both parties, to indicate his opinion whenever he is influenced by some argument that is brought forward. For they say that the result will be, since one emotion of the mind after another must be excited by the variety of points and arguments, that such judges will seem to feel and speak differently about the same case and almost at the same time.[1]

"But," said he, "about these and other similar discussions as to the duty of a judge I shall attempt to give you my views later, when we have leisure, and I will repeat the precepts of Aelius Tubero on the subject, which I have read very recently. But so far as concerns the money which you said was claimed before your tribunal, I advise you, by Heaven! to follow the counsel of that shrewdest of men, Marcus Cato; for he, in the speech which he delivered *For Lucius Turius against Gnaeus Gellius*,[2] said that this custom had been handed down and observed by our forefathers, that if a question at issue between two men could not be proved either by documents or witnesses, then the question should be raised before the judge who was trying the case which of the two was the better man, and if they were either equally good or equally bad, that then the one upon whom the claim was made should be believed and the verdict should be given in his favour. But in this case about which you are in

autem causa de qua tu ambigis, optimus est qui
petit, unde petitur deterrimus, et res est inter duos
23 acta sine testibus. Eas igitur et credas ei qui petit,
condemnesque eum de quo petitur, quoniam, sicuti
dicis, duo pares non sunt et qui petit melior est."

24   Hoc quidem mihi tum Favorinus, ut virum philo-
25 sophum decuit, suasit. Sed maius ego altiusque
id esse existimavi quam quod meae aetati et medio-
critati conveniret, ut cognovisse et condemnasse de
moribus, non de probationibus rei gestae viderer;
ut absolverem tamen inducere in animum non quivi
et propterea iuravi, mihi non liquere, atque ita
iudicatu illo solutus sum.

26   Verba ex oratione M. Catonis cuius commeminit
Favorinus, haec sunt: "Atque ego a maioribus
memoria sic accepi: si quis quid alter ab altero
peterent, si ambo pares essent, sive boni sive mali
essent, quod duo res[1] gessissent uti testes non
interessent, illi unde petitur, ei potius credendum
esse. Nunc si sponsionem fecissent[2] Gellius cum
Turio: 'Ni vir melior esset Gellius quam Turius,'
nemo, opinor, tam insanus esset qui iudicaret
meliorem esse Gellium quam Turium; si non melior
Gellius est Turio, potius oportet credi unde petitur."

[1] rei, *Rutgers*; pares, *Skutsch.*
[2] fecisset, NO.

doubt the claimant is a person of the highest
character and the one on whom the claim is made
is the worst of men, and there are no witnesses to
the transaction between the two. So then go and
give credit to the claimant and condemn the one
on whom the claim is made, since, as you say, the
two are not equal and the claimant is the better
man."

This was the advice which Favorinus gave me at
that time, as became a philosopher. But I thought
that I should show more importance and presump-
tion than became my youth and humble merit, if I
appeared to sit in judgment on and condemn a man
from the characters of the disputants rather than
from the evidence in the case ; yet I could not
make up my mind to acquit the defendant, and
accordingly I took oath that the matter was not
clear to me and in that way I was relieved from
rendering a decision.

The words of the speech of Marcus Cato which
Favorinus mentioned are these : "And I have learnt
this from the tradition of our ancestors : if anyone
claim anything from another, and both are equally
either good or bad, provided there are no witnesses
to the transaction between the two, the one from
whom the claim is made ought rather to be credited.
Now, if Gellius had made a wager[1] with Turio on
the issue, 'Provided Gellius were not a better man
than Turio,' no one, I think, would be so mad
as to decide that Gellius is better than Turio ; if
Gellius is not better than Turio, the one from whom
the claim is made ought preferably to be credited."

---

[1] See note on vi. 11. 9.

III

An aemuli offensique inter sese fuerint Xenophon et
Plato.

1 Qui de Xenophontis Platonisque vita et moribus
pleraque omnia exquisitissime scripsere, non afuisse
ab eis motus quosdam tacitos et occultos simultatis
aemulationisque mutuae putaverunt et eius rei
argumenta quaedam coniectaria ex eorum scriptis
2 protulerunt. Ea sunt profecto huiuscemodi: quod
neque a Platone in tot numero libris mentio usquam
facta sit Xenophontis neque item contra ab eo in
suis libris Platonis, quamquam uterque ac maxime
Plato complurium Socratis sectatorum in sermonibus
3 quos scripsit commeminerit. Id etiam esse non
sincerae neque amicae voluntatis indicium credi-
derunt, quod Xenophon inclito illi operi Platonis,
quod de optimo statu reipublicae civitatisque ad-
ministrandae scriptum est, lectis ex eo duobus fere
libris qui primi in volgus exierant, opposuit contra
conscripsitque diversum regiae administrationis
4 genus, quod Παιδείας Κύρου inscriptum est. Eo
facto scriptoque eius usque adeo permotum esse
Platonem ferunt, ut quodam in libro, mentione
Cyri regis habita, retractandi levandique eius operis
gratia, virum quidem Cyrum navum et strenuum
fuisse dixerit, παιδείας δὲ οὐκ ὀρθῶς ἧφθαι τὸ
παράπαν; haec enim verba sunt de Cyro Platonis.
5 Praeterea putant id quoque ad ista, quae dixi,

---

[1] De Legg. 12, p. 694, c.

III

Whether Plato and Xenophon were rivals and not on good
terms with each other.

THOSE who have written most carefully and
thoroughly about the life and character of Xenophon
and Plato have expressed the belief that they were
not free from certain secret and concealed feelings
of enmity and rivalry of each other, and they have
set forth some conjectural evidence of this, drawn
from their writings. These are in fact of this sort:
that Plato in his great number of works nowhere
makes mention of Xenophon, nor, on the other
hand, does Xenophon mention Plato in his writings,
although both men, and in particular Plato in the
dialogues which he wrote, mention many followers
of Socrates. This too they thought was an indication of no sincerely friendly feeling: that Xenophon
in opposition to that celebrated work of Plato, which
he wrote on the best form of constitution and of
governing a city-state, having barely read the two
books of Plato's work which were first made public,
proposed a different mode of government (to wit,
a monarchy) in the work entitled Παιδεία Κύρου, or
The Education of Cyrus. They say that Plato was
so disturbed by that conduct and book of his, that
having made mention of king Cyrus in one of his
own books, in order to criticize and belittle
Xenophon's work he said [1] that Cyrus was indeed
a strong and active man, but " had by no means had
a fitting education "; for these are Plato's words
about Cyrus.

Moreover, they think that this also is added to

accedere : quod Xenophon, in libris quos dictorum
atque factorum Socratis commentarios composuit,
negat Socraten de caeli atque naturae causis
rationibusque umquam disputavisse, ac ne disciplinas
quidem ceteras, quae μαθήματα Graeci appellant,
quae ad bene beateque vivendum non pergerent,
aut attigisse aut comprobasse, idcircoque turpiter
eos mentiri dicit, qui dissertationes istiusmodi
6 Socrati adtribuerent. " Hoc autem," inquiunt,
" Xenophon cum scripsit, Platonem videlicet notat,
in cuius libris Socrates physica et musica et geo-
7 metrica disserit." Sed enim de viris optimis et
gravissimis si credendum hoc aut suspicandum fuit,
causam equidem esse arbitror non obtrectationis nec
invidiae neque de gloria maiore parienda certationis ;
haec enim procul a moribus philosophiae absunt,
in quibus illi duo omnium iudicio excelluerunt.
8 Quae igitur est opinionis istius ratio ? Haec profecto est : aequiperatio ipsa plerumque et parilitas
virtutum inter sese consimilium, etiamsi contentionis
studium et voluntas abest, speciem tamen aemu-
9 lationis creat. Nam cum ingenia quaedam magna
duorum pluriumve in eiusdem rei studio inlustrium
aut pari sunt fama aut proxima, oritur apud diversos
favisores eorum industriae[1] laudisque aestumandae
10 contentio. Tum postea ex alieno certamine ad eos
quoque ipsos contagium certationis adspirat cursusque eorum ad eandem virtutis calcem pergentium,
quando est compar vel ambiguus, in aemulandi

---

[1] inlustriae, *suggested by Hosius.*

---

[1] *Memorabilia*, i.1.11.
[2] For *ambiguus* in this sense see Virg. *Aen.* v. 326.

what I have already said : that Xenophon, in the book which he wrote as records of the sayings and doings of Socrates,[1] asserts that Socrates never discussed the causes and laws of the heavens and of nature, and that he never touched upon or approved the other sciences, called by the Greeks μαθήματα, which did not contribute to a good and happy life ; accordingly, he says that those who have attributed discourses of that kind to Socrates are guilty of a base falsehood.

" But when Xenophon wrote this," they say, " he of course refers to Plato, in whose works Socrates discourses on physics, music and geometry." But if anything of this kind was to be believed, or even suspected, in noble and dignified men, I do not believe that the motive was hostility or envy, or a contest for gaining greater glory ; for such considerations are wholly alien to the character of philosophers, among whom those two were in all men's judgment pre-eminent. What then is the reason for that opinion ? Undoubtedly this : the mere equality and likeness of kindred talents, even though the desire and inclination of contention be absent, nevertheless create an appearance of rivalry. For when two or more men of great intellectual gifts, who have gained distinction in the same pursuit, are of equal or nearly equal fame, then there arises among their various partisans emulation in expressing an estimate of their efforts and merit. Then later, from the contention of others, the contagion of rivalry spreads to the men themselves, and while they are pressing on to the same goal of honour, the race is so even, or almost even,[2] that it comes imperceptibly under a sus-

35

suspiciones non suo, sed faventium studio delabitur.
11 Proinde igitur et Xenophon et Plato, Socraticae amoenitatis duo lumina, certare aemularique inter sese existimati sunt, quia de his apud alios uter esset exuperantior certabatur et quia duae eminentiae, cum simul iunctae in arduum nituntur, simulacrum quoddam contentionis aemulae pariunt.

IV

Quod apte Chrysippus et graphice imaginem Iustitiae modulis coloribusque verborum depinxit.

1 CONDIGNE mehercule et condecore Chrysippus, in librorum qui inscribuntur Περὶ Καλοῦ καὶ Ἡδονῆς primo, os et oculos Iustitiae vultumque eius severis atque venerandis verborum coloribus depinxit.
2 Facit quippe imaginem Iustitiae fierique solitam esse dicit a pictoribus rhetoribusque antiquioribus ad hunc ferme modum : " Forma atque filo virginali, aspectu vehementi et formidabili, luminibus oculorum acribus, neque humilis neque atrocis, sed
3 reverendae cuiusdam tristitiae dignitate." Ex imaginis autem istius significatione intellegi voluit, iudicem, qui Iustitiae antistes est, oportere esse gravem, sanctum, severum, incorruptum, inadulabilem contraque improbos nocentesque inmisericordem atque inexorabilem erectumque et arduum ac potentem, vi et maiestate aequitatis veritatisque terrificum.
4 Verba ipsa Chrysippi de Iustitia scripta haec

---

[1] They were not rivals, but both equally eager to attain "virtue." Thus they seem like competitors in a race, and

picion of rivalry, not from any purpose of their own, but from the zeal of their partisans.[1] So then Xenophon and Plato, two stars of Socrates' charming philosophy, were believed to contend with and rival each other, because others strove to show that one or the other was the superior, and because two eminent characters, when they are labouring side by side for a lofty aim, beget a kind of appearance of rivalry and competition.

IV

That Chrysippus skilfully and vividly represented the likeness of Justice in melodious and picturesque language.

MOST worthily, by Heaven! and most elegantly did Chrysippus, in the first book of his work entitled *On Beauty and Pleasure,* depict the face and eyes of Justice, and her aspect, with austere and noble word-painting. For he represents the figure of Justice, and says that it was usually represented by the painters and orators of old in about the following manner : " Of maidenly form and bearing, with a stern and fearsome countenance, a keen glance of the eye, and a dignity and solemnity which was neither mean nor cruel, but awe-inspiring." From the spirit of this representation he wished it to be understood that the judge, who is the priest of Justice, ought to be dignified, holy, austere, incorruptible, not susceptible to flattery, pitiless and inexorable towards the wicked and guilty, vigorous, lofty, and powerful, terrible by reason of the force and majesty of equity and truth. Chrysippus' own words about Justice

as they run so that you can hardly tell which leads, their partisans insist on regarding them as rivals.

sunt: Παρθένος δὲ εἶναι λέγεται κατὰ σύμβολον τοῦ ἀδιάφθορος εἶναι καὶ μηδαμῶς ἐνδιδόναι τοῖς κακούργοις, μηδὲ προσίεσθαι μήτε τοὺς ἐπιεικεῖς λόγους μήτε παραίτησιν καὶ δέησιν μήτε κολακείαν μήτε ἄλλο μηδὲν τῶν τοιούτων· οἷς ἀκολούθως καὶ σκυθρωπὴ γράφεται καὶ συνεστηκὸς ἔχουσα τὸ πρόσωπον καὶ ἔντονον καὶ δεδορκὸς βλέπουσα, ὥστε τοῖς μὲν ἀδίκοις φόβον ἐμποιεῖν, τοῖς δὲ δικαίοις θάρσος· τοῖς μὲν προσφιλοῦς ὄντος τοῦ τοιούτου προσώπου, τοῖς δὲ ἑτέροις προσάντους.

5 Haec verba Chrysippi eo etiam magis ponenda existimavi, ut prompta ad considerandum iudicandumque sint, quoniam legentibus ea nobis delicatiorum[1] quidam disciplinarum philosophi, Saevitiae imaginem istam esse, non Iustitiae, dixerunt.

V

Lis atque contentio grammaticorum Romae inlustrium enarrata, super casu vocativo vocabuli quod est "egregius."

1 Defessus ego quondam diutina commentatione laxandi levandique animi gratia in Agrippae campo deambulabam. Atque ibi duos forte grammaticos conspicatus non parvi in urbe Roma nominis, certationi eorum acerrimae adfui, cum alter in casu

---

[1] delicatiores, ω; corr. by Stephanus.

---

[1] The *campus Agrippae*, laid out by the famous minister of Augustus, was finished and dedicated by the emperor in

38

are as follows: "She has the title of virgin as a symbol of her purity and an indication that she has never given way to evil-doers, that she has never yielded to soothing words, to prayers and entreaties, to flattery, nor to anything of that kind. Therefore she is properly represented too as stern and dignified, with a serious expression and a keen, steadfast glance, in order that she may inspire fear in the wicked and courage in the good; to the latter, as her friends, she presents a friendly aspect, to the former a stern face."

I thought it the more necessary to quote these words of Chrysippus, in order that they might be before us for consideration and judgment, since, on hearing me read them, some philosophers who are more sentimental in their views called that a representation of Cruelty rather than of Justice.

V

The strife and contention of two eminent grammarians at Rome as to the vocative case of *egregius*.

ONCE upon a time, wearied with constant writing, I was walking in the park of Agrippa[1] for the purpose of relieving and resting my mind. And there, as it chanced, I saw two grammarians of no small repute in the city of Rome, and was a witness of a violent dispute between them, one maintaining

7 B.C. It extended from the line of the *aqua Virgo* on the south at least as far as the modern via S. Claudio on the north, and from the via Lata to the slope of the Quirinal hill, although its eastern boundary is quite uncertain; see Platner, *Topog.*[2], p. 477.

vocativo "vir egregi" dicendum contenderet, alter "vir egregie."

2 Ratio autem eius, qui "egregi" oportere dici censebat, huiuscemodi fuit: "Quaecumque," inquit, "nomina seu vocabula recto casu numero singulari 'us' syllaba finiuntur, in quibus ante ultimam syllabam posita est *i* littera, ea omnia casu vocativo *i* littera terminantur, ut 'Caelius Caeli,' 'modius modi,' 'tertius terti,' 'Accius Acci,' 'Titius Titi' et similia omnia; sic igitur 'egregius,' quoniam 'us' syllaba in casu nominandi finitur eamque syllabam praecedit *i* littera, habere debebit in casu vocandi *i* litteram extremam et idcirco 'egregi,' non 'egregie,' rectius dicetur. Nam 'divus' et 'rivus' et 'clivus' non 'us' syllaba terminantur, sed ea quae per duo *u* scribenda est, propter cuius syllabae sonum declarandum reperta erat nova littera, quae 'digamma' appellabatur."

3 Hoc ubi ille alter audivit, "O," inquit, "egregie grammatice vel, si id mavis, egregissime, dic, oro te, 'inscius' et 'impius' et 'sobrius' et 'ebrius' et 'proprius' et 'propitius' et 'anxius' et 'contrarius,' quae 'us' syllaba finiuntur, in quibus ante ultimam syllabam *i* littera est, quem casum vocandi habent? Me enim pudor et verecundia tenent,

4 pronuntiare ea secundum tuam definitionem." Sed cum ille paulisper opposito horum vocabulorum commotus reticuisset et mox tamen se conlegisset eandemque illam quam definierat regulam retineret

---

[1] The Greek digamma had practically the form of Latin F and the pronunciation of Latin V (the semi-vowel). The Romans used the character to represent the sound of *f*, at first with the addition of the aspirate *h* (as in *fhefhaked*, *C.I.L.* i². 3 and xiv. 4123) and afterwards alone.

that *vir egregi* was the proper form of the vocative
case, the other *vir egregie.*

The argument of the one who thought that we
should say *egregi* was of this sort: "Whatever
nouns or words," said he, "end in the nominative
singular in the syllable *us* preceded by *i*, in the
vocative case terminate in the letter *i*, as *Caelius
Caeli, modius modi, tertius terti, Accius Acci, Titius Titi,*
and the like; so then *egregius,* since it ends in the
syllable *us* in the nominative and the letter *i* precedes that syllable, must in the vocative singular
have *i* for the final letter, and therefore it is correct
to say *egregi,* not *egregie.* For *divus* and *rivus* and
clivus do not end in the syllable *us,* but in that
which ought to be written with two *u*'s, and in order
to indicate that sound a new letter was devised,
which was called the *digamma.*"[1]

When the other heard this, he said: *O egregie
grammatice,* or if you prefer, *egregissime,* tell me, I
pray you, what is the vocative case of *inscius, impius,
sobrius, ebrius, proprius, propitius, anxius,* and *contrarius,* which end in the syllable *us* and have the
letter *i* before the final syllable? For shame and
modesty prevent me from pronouncing them according to your rule." Now the other, overcome by the
accumulation of so many words against him, remained
silent for a time; but then he nevertheless rallied,
and upheld and defended that same rule which he

Since V was used both for the vowel *u* and the semi-vowel *v*,
the emperor Claudius introduced an inverted digamma (Ⅎ),
to represent the latter sound; see Suet. *Claud.* xii. 3 and
(*e.g.*) *C.I.L.* vi. 919. The writing of F for V, to which
Gellius seems to refer, was apparently confined to a few
grammarians; see Cassiodorus, vii. 148. 8 K and Priscian,
ii. 11. 5 K.

et propugnaret diceretque et "proprium" et "pro-
pitium" et "anxium" et "contrarium" itidem in
casu vocativo dicendum, ut "adversarius" et "extrarius" diceretur; "inscium" quoque et "impium"
et "ebrium" et "sobrium" insolentius quidem
paulo, sed rectius per *i* litteram, non per *e,* in eodem
casu pronuntiandum, eaque inter eos contentio
longius duceretur, non arbitratus ego operae pre-
tium esse eadem istaec diutius audire, clamantes
conpugnantesque illos reliqui.

VI

Cuimodi sint quae speciem doctrinarum habeant, sed neque
delectent neque utilia sint; atque inibi de vocabulis
singularum urbium regionumque inmutatis.

1 HOMO nobis familiaris, in litterarum cultu non
ignobilis magnamque aetatis partem in libris versatus "Adiutum," inquit, "ornatumque volo ire
Noctes tuas"; et simul dat mihi librum grandi
volumine doctrinae omnigenus, ut ipse dicebat,
praescatentem, quem sibi elaboratum esse ait ex
multis et variis et remotis lectionibus, ut ex eo
sumerem quantum liberet rerum memoria dignarum.
2 Accipio cupidus et libens, tamquam si copiae cornum
nactus essem, et recondo me penitus, ut sine arbitris
legam.
3 At quae ibi scripta erant, pro Iuppiter, mera
miracula! quo nomine fuerit qui primus "grammaticus" appellatus est; et quot fuerint Pythagorae
nobiles, quot Hippocratae; et cuiusmodi fuisse

had laid down, maintaining that *proprius, propitius, anxius* and *contrarius* ought to have the same form in the vocative case as *adversarius* and *extrarius*; that *inscius* also and *impius* and *ebrius* and *sobrius* were somewhat less commonly, nevertheless more correctly, made to end in that same case in the letter *i* rather than *e*. But as this contest of theirs was likely to be continued for some time, I did not think it worth while to listen to those same arguments any longer, and I left them shouting and wrangling.

VI

Of what kind are the things which have the appearance of learning, but are neither entertaining nor useful; and also of changes in the names of several cities and regions.

A FRIEND of mine, a man not without fame as a student of literature, who had passed a great part of his life among books, said to me: "I should like to aid and adorn your *Nights*," at the same time presenting me with a book of great bulk, overflowing, as he himself put it, with learning of every kind. He said that he had compiled it as the result of wide, varied and abstruse reading, and he invited me to take from it as much as I liked and thought worthy of record. I took the book eagerly and gladly, as if I had got possession of the horn of plenty, and shut myself up in order to read it without interruption.

But what was written there was, by Jove! merely a list of curiosities: the name of the man who was first called a "grammarian"; the number of famous men named Pythagoras and Hippocrates; Homer's

Homerus dicat in Ulixis domo λαύρην; et quam ob causam Telemachus cubans iunctim sibi cubantem Pisistratum non manu adtigerit, sed pedis ictu excitarit; et Euryclia Telemachum quo genere claustri incluserit; et quapropter idem poeta rosam non norit, oleum ex rosa norit. Atque illud etiam scriptum fuit, quae nomina fuerint sociorum Ulixis, qui a Scylla rapti laceratique sunt; utrum ἐν τῇ ἔσω θαλάσσῃ Ulixes erraverit κατ᾽ Ἀρίσταρχον an ἐν τῇ ἔξω κατὰ Κράτητα; item etiam istic scriptum
4 fuit, qui sint apud Homerum versus isopsephi; et quorum ibi nominum παραστιχίς reperiatur; et quis adeo versus sit, qui per singula vocabula singulis syllabis increscat; ac deinde qua ratione dixerit singulas pecudes in singulos annos terna parere; et ex quinque operimentis quibus Achillis clipeus munitus est, quod factum ex auro est summum sit an medium, et praeterea quibus urbibus regionibusque vocabula iam mutata sint, quod Boeotia ante appellata fuerit "Aonia," quod Aegyptus "Aeria," quod Creta quoque eodem nomine "Aeria" dicta sit, quod Attice "Ἀκτή," quod Corinthus "Ephyre," quod Macedonia "Ἠμαθία," quod Thessalia "Αἱμονία," quod Tyros "Sarra," quod Thracia ante "Sithonia"[1] dicta sit, quod Paestum "Ποσειδώνιον."

5 Haec item atque alia multa istiusmodi scripta in eo libro fuerunt.

Quem cum statim properans redderem: "Ὄναιό

---

[1] Sithonia, *Hertz*; Sithon, *MSS.*

---

[1] *Odyss.* xxii. 128, 137.	[2] *Odyss.* xv. 44.
[3] *Odyss.* i. 441.	[4] *Iliad* xxiii. 186.
[5] *Odyss.* xii. 245.	[6] p. 244, Lehrs.

description[1] of the λαυρή, or "narrow passage," in
the house of Ulysses; why Telemachus did not
touch Pisistratus, who was lying beside him, with
his hand, but awakened him by a kick;[2] with what
kind of bolt Euryclia shut in Telemachus;[3] and
why the same poet did not know the rose, but did
know oil made from roses.[4] It also contained the
names of the companions of Ulysses who were seized
and torn to pieces by Scylla;[5] whether the wander-
ings of Ulysses were in the inner sea, as Aristarchus
believed,[6] or in the outer sea, according to Crates.
There was also a list of the isopsephic verses in
Homer;[7] what names in the same writer are given
in the form of an acrostic; what verse it is in which
each word is a syllable longer than the preceding
word;[8] by what rule each head of cattle produces
three offspring each year;[9] of the five layers with
which the shield of Achilles was strengthened,
whether the one made of gold was on top or in the
middle;[10] and besides what regions and cities had
had a change of name, as Boeotia was formerly
called *Aonia,* Egypt *Aeria,* Crete by the same name
Aeria, Attica *Acte,* Corinth *Ephyre,* Macedonia
Emathia, Thessaly *Haemonia,* Tyre *Sarra,* Thrace
Sithonia, Paestum *Poseidonia.*[11]

These things and many others of the same kind
were included in that book.

Hastening to return it to him at once, I said: " I

[7] That is, those whose letters, treated as figures, amounted
to the same sum, thus *Iliad* vii. 264 and 265 = 3498. See
Suet. *Nero* xxxix. 2 and note *a* (*L.C.L.*).

[8] An example is *Iliad* iii. 182, ὦ μάκαρ Ἀτρείδη μοιρηγενὲς
ὀλβιοδαίμων. [9] *Odyss.* iv. 86. [10] *Iliad* xx. 269.

[11] The original name was Ποσειδωνία; Ποσειδώνιον was in
Pallene. Gellius seems to have made a slip. Ποσειδώνιον
means a temple of Poseidon.

σου," inquam, "doctissime virorum, ταύτης τῆς πολυμαθίας et librum hunc opulentissimum recipe, nil prosus ad nostras paupertinas litteras congruentem. Nam meae *Noctes*, quas instructum ornatumque isti, de uno maxime illo versu Homeri quaerunt, quem Socrates prae omnibus semper rebus sibi esse cordi dicebat:

Ὅττι τοι ἐν μεγάροισι κακόν τ᾽ ἀγαθόν τε τέτυκται."

VII

Quod M. Varro Cn. Pompeio, consuli primum designato, commentarium dedit, quem appellavit ipse Εἰσαγωγικόν, de officio senatus habendi.

1 GNAEO POMPEIO consulatus primus cum M. Crasso
2 designatus est. Eum magistratum Pompeius cum initurus foret, quoniam per militiae tempora senatus habendi consulendique,[1] rerum expers urbanarum fuit, M. Varronem, familiarem suum, rogavit uti commentarium faceret Εἰσαγωγικόν—sic enim Varro ipse appellat—, ex quo disceret quid facere dicere-
3 que deberet, cum senatum consuleret. Eum librum commentarium, quem super ea re Pompeio fecerat, perisse Varro ait in litteris quas ad Oppianum

---

[1] senatus . . . consulendique *delcted by C. W. F. Müller*; reliquarumque rerum, *Mommsen*; omninoque rerum, *Mähly*.

---

[1] *Odyss.* iv. 392.
[2] The emphasis is on the last two words. Socrates thought that the chief value of the study of philosophy was its effect

congratulate you, most learned sir, on this display
of encyclopaedic erudition; but take back this
precious volume, which does not have the slightest
connection with my humble writings. For my
Nights, which you wish to assist and adorn, base
their inquiries especially on that one verse of Homer
which Socrates said was above all other things
always dear to him : [1]

> Whate'er of good and ill has come to you at
> home." [2]

VII

*That Marcus Varro presented Gnaeus Pompeius, when he was
consul elect for the first time, with a commentary, which
Varro himself called Εἰσαγωγικός,[3] on the method of
conducting meetings of the senate.*

GNAEUS POMPEIUS was elected consul for the first
time with Marcus Crassus. When he was on the
point of entering upon the office, because of his
long military service he was unacquainted with the
method of convening and consulting the senate,
and of city affairs in general. He therefore asked
his friend Marcus Varro to make him a book of
instructions (Εἰσαγωγικός, as Varro himself termed
it), from which he might learn what he ought to say
and do when he brought a measure before the
House. Varro in letters which he wrote to Op-

on the student's own life and character. Gellius apparently means that he is collecting materials for home
consumption; see Praef. i, *ut liberis meis partae istiusmodi remissiones essent.*

[3] The word means *Introductory.* It was what we should
call a " Handbook of Parliamentary Practice."

dedit, quae sunt in libro *Epistolicarum Quaestionum*
quarto, in quibus litteris, quoniam quae ante scripserat non comparebant, docet rursum multa ad eam
rem ducentia.

4 Primum ibi ponit qui fuerint per quos more
maiorum senatus haberi soleret eosque nominat:
"dictatorem, consules, praetores, tribunos plebi,
interregem, praefectum urbi," neque alii praeter
hos ius fuisse dixit facere senatusconsultum,
quotiensque usus venisset ut omnes isti magistratus
eodem tempore Romae essent, tum quo supra ordine
scripti essent, qui eorum prior aliis esset, ei potis-
5 simum senatus consulendi ius fuisse ait, deinde
extraordinario iure tribunos quoque militares, qui
pro consulibus fuissent, item decemviros, quibus
imperium consulare tum esset,[1] item triumviros
reipublicae constituendae causa creatos ius consulendi senatum habuisse.

6 Postea scripsit de intercessionibus dixitque inter-
cedendi ne senatusconsultum fieret ius fuisse iis
solis qui eadem potestate qua ii qui senatusconsultum facere vellent maioreve essent.

7 Tum adscripsit de locis in quibus senatusconsultum fieri iure posset, docuitque confirmavitque,
nisi in loco per augurem constituto, quod "tem-

---

[1] *I.e.* datum esset *or* datum fuisset, *Mommsen*; tum esset,
MSS.

---

[1] i, p. 195, Bipont.
[2] i, p. 125, Bremer.
[3] From 444 to 384 B.C. military tribunes with consular
authority took the place of the consuls.
[4] The *decemviri legibus scribundis*, who drew up the *Twelve
Tables* in 450 B.C.

pianus, contained in the fourth book of his *Investigations in Epistolary Form,* says[1] that this notebook which he made for Pompey on that subject was lost; and since what he had previously written was no longer in existence, he repeats in those letters a good deal bearing upon the same subject.[2]

First of all, he tells us there by what magistrates the senate was commonly convened according to the usage of our forefathers, naming these : " the dictator, consuls, praetors, tribunes of the commons, interrex, and prefect of the city." No other except these, he said, had the right to pass a decree of the senate, and whenever it happened that all those magistrates were in Rome at the same time, then he says that the first in the order of the list which I have just quoted had the prior right of bringing a matter before the senate ; next, by an exceptional privilege, the military tribunes also who had acted as consuls,[3] and likewise the decemvirs,[4] who in their day had consular authority, and the triumvirs[5] appointed to reorganize the State, had the privilege of bringing measures before the House.

Afterwards he wrote about vetoes, and said that the right to veto a decree of the senate belonged only to those who had the same authority[6] as those who wished to pass the decree, or greater power.

He then added a list of the places in which a decree of the senate might lawfully be made, and he showed and maintained that this was regular only

---

[5] The second triumvirate of Antony, Octavian and Lepidus; cf. iii. 9. 4 and the note.

[6] *Potestate* is used in the technical sense. "The *par potestas* conferred on the colleague of the presiding officer the right to interpose his veto" (Abbott, *Roman Political Institutions,* § 274).

plum" appellaretur, senatusconsultum factum esset, iustum id non fuisse. Propterea et in curia Hostilia et in Pompeia et post in Iulia, cum profana ea loca fuissent, templa esse per augures constituta, ut in iis senatusconsulta more maiorum iusta fieri possent. Inter quae id quoque scriptum reliquit, non omnes aedes sacras templa esse ac ne aedem quidem Vestae templum esse.

8 Post haec deinceps dicit senatusconsultum ante exortum aut post occasum solem factum ratum non fuisse, opus etiam censorium fecisse existimatos per quos eo tempore senatusconsultum factum esset.

9 Docet deinde inibi multa : quibus diebus habere senatum ius non sit ; immolareque hostiam prius auspicarique debere, qui senatum habiturus esset, de rebusque divinis prius quam humanis ad senatum referendum esse ; tum porro referri oportere aut infinite de republica aut de singulis rebus finite ; senatusque consultum fieri duobus modis : aut per discessionem, si consentiretur, aut, si res dubia esset, per singulorum sententias exquisitas ; singulos autem

---

[1] A *templum* (from *temno*) was originally a sacred precinct.
[2] The *curia Hostilia*, on the Comitium (see iv. 5. 1 and note 3), was the earliest senate house, ascribed to Tullus Hostilius, the third king of Rome. It was restored by Sulla in 80 B.C., rebuilt by Faustus Sulla after its destruction by fire in 52 B.C. The *curia Julia* was begun by Caesar in 45 B.C. The *curia Pompei*, in which Caesar was murdered, was built by Pompey in 55 B.C., near his theatre. Whether it was an *exedra* of his colonnade, or a separate building, is uncertain.
[3] The shrine or temple of Vesta, in spite of its sacred character, was not a consecrated *templum*. It was said to

in a place which had been appointed by an augur,
and called a "temple." [1]   Therefore in the Hostilian
Senate House [2] and the Pompeian, and later in the
Julian, since those were unconsecrated places,
"temples" were established by the augurs, in order
that in those places lawful decrees of the senate
might be made according to the usage of our forefathers.   In connection with which he also wrote
this, that not all sacred edifices are temples, and
that not even the shrine of Vesta was a temple. [3]

After this he goes on to say that a decree of
the senate made before sunrise or after sunset was
not valid, and that those through whom a decree of
the senate was made at that time were thought to
have committed an act deserving censure.

Then he gives much instruction on the same
lines: on what days it was not lawful to hold a
meeting of the senate ; that one who was about to
hold a meeting of the senate should first offer up
a victim and take the auspices ; that questions relating to the gods ought to be presented to the
senate before those affecting men ; then further that
resolutions should be presented indefinitely, [4] as affecting the general welfare, or definitely on specific cases ;
that a decree of the senate was made in two ways :
either by division if there was general agreement, or
if the matter was disputed, by calling for the opinion
of each senator ; furthermore the senators ought to

have been built by Numa, and was certainly very ancient.
It was burned and rebuilt several times, the last restora-
tion being in A.D. 196 by Julia Domna, wife of Septimius
Severus.
   [4] That is, in general terms, as in Livy xxii. 1. 5, *cum
(consul) de re publica rettulisset*, *i.e.* " had proposed a general
discussion of the interests of the State."

debere consuli gradatim incipique a consulari gradu.
Ex quo gradu semper quidem antea primum rogari
solitum, qui princeps in senatum lectus esset ; tum
autem, cum haec scriberet, novum morem institutum
refert per ambitionem gratiamque, ut is primus
rogaretur quem rogare vellet qui haberet senatum,
10 dum is tamen ex gradu consulari esset. Praeter
haec de pignore quoque capiendo disserit deque
multa dicenda senatori qui, cum in senatum venire
11 deberet, non adesset. Haec et alia quaedam id
genus in libro quo supra dixi M. Varro epistula ad
Oppianum scripta executus est.

12   Sed quod ait senatusconsultum duobus modis fieri
solere, aut conquisitis sententiis aut per discessionem,
parum convenire videtur cum eo quod Ateius Capito
13 in *Coniectaneis* scriptum reliquit. Nam in libro VIIII.
Tuberonem dicere ait nullum senatusconsultum fieri
posse non discessione facta, quia in omnibus senatus-
consultis, etiam in iis quae per relationem fierent,
discessio esset necessaria, idque ipse Capito verum
esse adfirmat. Sed de hac omni re alio in loco
plenius accuratiusque nos memini scribere.

---

[1] Cf. Suet. *Jul.* xxi.

be asked their opinions in order, beginning with the grade of consul. And in that grade in former times the one to be called upon first was always the one who had first been enrolled in the senate; but at the time when he was writing he said that a new custom had become current, through partiality and a desire to curry favour, of asking first for the opinion of the one whom the presiding officer wished to call upon, provided however that he was of consular rank.[1] Besides this he discoursed about seizure of goods[2] and the imposing of a fine upon a senator who was not present when it was his duty to attend a meeting. These and certain other matters of that kind, first published in the book of which I spoke above, Marcus Varro treated in a letter written to Oppianus.

But when he says that a decree of the senate is commonly made in two ways, either by calling for opinions or by division, that does not seem to agree with what Ateius Capito has written in his *Miscellanies*. For in Book VIIII Capito says[3] that Tubero asserts[4] that no decree of the senate could be made without a division, since in all decrees of the senate, even in those which are made by calling for opinions, a division was necessary, and Capito himself declares that this is true. But I recall writing on this whole matter more fully and exactly in another place.[5]

[2] In consequence of the issue of a writ of execution; see Mommsen, *Staatsr.* i. 160, and cf. Suet. *Jul.* xvii. 2.

[3] Frag. 3, Huschke; 5, Bremer.

[4] Frag. 1, Huschke; *De Off. Sen.* 1, Bremer.

[5] iii. 18.

VIII

Quaesitum esse dissensumque an praefectus Latinarum causa creatus ius senatus convocandi consulendique habeat.

1 PRAEFECTUM urbi Latinarum causa relictum senatum habere posse Iunius negat, quoniam ne senator quidem sit neque ius habeat sententiae dicendae, cum ex ea aetate praefectus fiat quae non sit sena-
2 toria. M. autem Varro in quarto *Epistolicarum Quaestionum* et Ateius Capito in *Coniectaneorum* VIII., ius esse praefecto senatus habendi dicunt ; deque ea re adsensum esse Capito Varronem[1] Tuberoni contra sententiam Iunii refert : " Nam et tribunis," inquit, " plebis senatus habendi ius erat, quamquam senatores non essent ante Atinium plebiscitum."

[1] Capito Varronem, *Hertz* ; capitonem, *ω*.

---

[1] Frag. 10, Huschke ; id., Bremer.
[2] The *feriae Latinae* were held on the Alban Mount in April at a date set by the consuls. Since the consuls must be present at the celebration, they appointed a *praefectus urbi* to take their place in Rome. Under the empire he was called *praefectus urbi feriarum Latinarum*, to distinguish him from the *praefectus urbi* instituted by Augustus (Suet. *Aug.* xxxvii). Since a *praefectus* had the powers of the officer or officers in whose place he was appointed, Varro and Capito are right in theory ; but since very young men were often appointed

VIII

Inquiry and difference of opinion as to whether the praefect appointed for the Latin Festival has the right of convening and consulting the senate.

JUNIUS declares[1] that the praefect left in charge of the city because of the Latin Festival[2] may not hold a meeting of the senate, since he is neither a senator nor has he the right of expressing his opinion, because he is made praefect at an age when he is not eligible to the senate. But Marcus Varro in the fourth book of his *Investigations in Epistolary Form*[3] and Ateius Capito in the ninth of his *Miscellanies*[4] assert that the praefect has the right to convene the senate, and Capito declares that Varro agrees on this point with Tubero, contrary to the view of Junius : " For the tribunes of the commons also," says Capito,[5] " had the right of convening the senate although before the bill of Atinius[6] they were not senators."

---

to the office (Suet. *Nero*, vii. 2 ; S.H.A. *vita Marci*, iv, etc.), Junius may have been right as to the actual practice.

[3] p. 196, Bipont.
[4] Frag. 4, Huschke ; id., Bremer.
[5] *De Off. Sen.* 2, Bremer.
[6] The date of this bill is not known.

BOOK XV

LIBER QUINTUS DECIMUS

I

Quod in Quinti Claudii Annalibus *scriptum est lignum alumine oblitum non ardere.*

1 DECLAMAVERAT Antonius Iulianus rhetor, praeterquam semper alias, tum vero nimium quantum de-
lectabiliter et feliciter. Sunt enim ferme scholasticae
istae declamationes eiusdem hominis eiusdemque fa-
2 cundiae, non eiusdem tamen cotidie felicitatis. Nos
ergo familiares eius circumfusi undique eum prosequebamur domum, cum inde subeuntes montem Cispium
conspicimus insulam quandam occupatam igni multis
arduisque tabulatis editam et propinqua iam omnia
3 flagrare vasto incendio. Tum quispiam ibi ex comi-
tibus Iuliani : " Magni," inquit, "reditus urbanorum
praediorum, sed pericula sunt longe maxima. Si
quid autem posset remedii fore, ut ne tam adsidue
domus Romae arderent, venum hercle dedissem res
4 rusticas et urbicas emissem." Atque illi Iulianus
laeta, ut mos eius fuit, inter fabulandum venustate :
"Si *Annalem*," inquit, "undevicensimum Q. Claudi le-
gisses, optumi et sincerissimi scriptoris, docuisset te
profecto Archelaus, regis Mitridati praefectus, qua
medella quaque sollertia ignem defenderes, ut ne

BOOK XV

I

That it is written in the Annals *of Quintus Claudius that
wood smeared with alum does not burn.*

THE rhetorician Antonius Julianus, besides holding
forth on many other occasions, had once declaimed
with marvellous charm and felicity. For such
scholastic declamations generally show the character-
istics of the same man and the same eloquence, but
nevertheless are not every day equally happy.
We friends of his therefore thronged about him on
all sides and were escorting him home, when, as
we were on our way up the Cispian Hill, we saw
that a block of houses, built high with many stories,
had caught fire, and that now all the neighbouring
buildings were burning in a mighty conflagration.
Then some one of Julianus' companions said:
" The income from city property is great, but the
dangers are far greater. But if some remedy
could be devised to prevent houses in Rome from
so constantly catching fire, by Jove! I would sell
my country property and buy in the city." And
Julianus replied to him in his usual happy and
graceful style: " If you had read the nineteenth
book of the *Annals* of Quintus Claudius, that excellent and faithful writer, you would surely have
learned from Archelaus, a praefect of king Mithridates, by what method and by what skill you might
prevent fires, so that no wooden building of yours

59

ulla tua aedificatio e ligno correpta atque insinuata flammis arderet."

5 Percontatus ego sum quid esset illud mirum
6 Quadrigarii. Repetit : " In eo igitur libro scriptum inveni, cum obpugnaret L. Sulla in terra Attica Piraeum et contra Archelaus regis Mitridati praefectus ex eo oppido propugnaret, turrim ligneam defendendi gratia structam, cum ex omni latere circumplexa igni foret, ardere non quisse, quod alumine ab Archelao oblita fuisset."
7 Verba Quadrigarii ex eo libro haec sunt : " Cum Sulla conatus[1] esset tempore[2] magno, eduxit copias, ut Archelai turrim unam quam ille interposuit ligneam incenderet. Venit, accessit, ligna subdidit, submovit Graecos, ignem admovit; satis sunt diu conati, numquam quiverunt incendere, ita Archelaus omnem materiam obleverat alumine, quod Sulla atque milites mirabantur, et postquam non succendit,[3] reduxit copias."

II

Quod Plato in libris quos *De Legibus* composuit largiores laetioresque in conviviis invitatiunculas vini non inutiles esse existimavit.

1 Ex insula Creta quispiam aetatem Athenis agens Platonicum sese philosophum dicebat et viderier ges-
2 tibat. Erat autem nihili homo et nugator atque in

---

[1] cunctatus, *sugg. by Hosius.*　　[2] opere, *Lipsius.*
[3] succendit, *ω* ; successit, *Damsté.*

would burn, even though caught and penetrated by the flames."

I inquired what this marvel of Quadrigarius [1] was. He rejoined: "In that book then I found it recorded, that when Lucius Sulla attacked the Piraeus in the land of Attica, and Archelaus, praefect of king Mithridates, was defending it against him, Sulla was unable to burn a wooden tower constructed for purposes of defence, although it had been surrounded with fire on every side, because Archelaus had smeared it with alum."

The words of Quadrigarius in that book are as follows: [2] "When Sulla had exerted himself for a long time, he led out his troops in order to set fire to a single wooden tower which Archelaus had interposed. He came, he drew near, he put wood under it, he beat off the Greeks, he applied fire; though they tried for a considerable time, they were never able to set it on fire, so thoroughly had Archelaus covered all the wood with alum. Sulla and his soldiers were amazed at this, and failing in his attempt, the general led back his troops."

II

That Plato in the work which he wrote *On the Laws* expressed the opinion that inducements to drink more abundantly and more merrily at feasts were not without benefit.

A MAN from the island of Crete, who was living in Athens, gave out that he was a Platonic philosopher and desired to pass as one. He was, however, a man of no worth, a trifler, boastful of his command

[1] That is, Quintus Claudius Quadrigarius; see § 4.
[2] Frag. 81, Peter².

Graecae facundiae gloria iactabundus et praeterea
3 vini libidine adusque ludibria ebriosus. Is in conviviis iuvenum, quae agitare Athenis hebdomadibus
lunae sollemne nobis fuit, simulatque modus epulis
factus et utiles delectabilesque sermones coeperant,
tum, silentio ad audiendum petito, loqui coeptabat
atque id genus vili et incondita verborum caterva
hortabatur omnes ad bibendum, idque se facere ex
decreto Platonico praedicabat, tamquam Plato in
libris quos *De Legibus* composuit laudes ebrietatis
copiosissime scripsisset utilemque esse eam bonis ac
fortibus viris censuisset; ac simul inter eiusmodi
orationem crebris et ingentibus poculis ingenium
omne ingurgitabat, fomitem esse quendam dicens
et ignitabulum ingenii virtutisque, si mens et corpus
hominis vino flagraret.
4 Sed enim Plato in primo et secundo *De Legibus*
non, ut ille nebulo opinabatur, ebrietatem istam
turpissimam quae labefacere et inminuere hominum
mentes solet laudavit, sed hanc largiorem paulo iu-
cundioremque vini invitationem, quae fieret sub quibusdam quasi arbitris et magistris conviviorum sobriis,
5 non inprobavit. Nam et modicis honestisque inter
bibendum remissionibus refici integrarique animos ad
instauranda sobrietatis officia existumavit reddique
eos sensim laetiores atque ad intentiones rursum ca-
piendas fieri habiliores, et simul, si qui penitus in his
adfectionum cupiditatumque errores inessent, quos

---

[1] 9, p. 637, A; 14, p. 647, E.

of Grecian eloquence, besides having a passion for wine which fairly made him a laughing stock. At the entertainments which it was the custom of us young men to hold at Athens at the beginning of each week, as soon as we had finished eating and an instructive and pleasant conversation had begun, this fellow, having called for silence that he might be heard, began to speak, and using a cheap and disordered rabble of words after his usual fashion, urged all to drink ; and this he declared that he did in accordance with the injunction of Plato, maintaining that Plato in his work *On the Laws* had written most eloquently in praise of drunkenness, and had decided that it was beneficial to good and strong men. And at the same time, while he was thus speaking, he drenched such wits as he had with frequent and huge beakers, saying that it was a kind of touchwood and tinder to the intellect and the faculties, if mind and body were inflamed with wine.

However, Plato in the first [1] and second [2] books of his work *On the Laws* did not, as that fool thought, praise that shameful intoxication which is wont to undermine and weaken men's minds, although he did not disapprove of that somewhat more generous and cheerful inspiration of wine which is regulated by some temperate arbiters, so to speak, and presidents of banquets. For he thought that by the proper and moderate relaxation of drinking the mind was refreshed and renewed for resuming the duties of sobriety, and that men were gradually rendered happier and became readier to repeat their efforts. At the same time, if there were deep in their hearts any errors of inclination or desire,

[1] 9, p. 666, A ; 12, p. 671, B.

aliquis pudor reverens concelaret, ea omnia sine gravi periculo, libertate per vinum data detegi et ad corrigendum medendumque fieri oportuniora.

6 Atque hoc etiam Plato ibidem dicit, non defugiendas esse neque respuendas huiuscemodi exercitationes adversum propulsandam vini violentiam neque ullum umquam continentem prorsus ac temperantem satis fideliter visum esse, cuius vita victusque non inter ipsa errorum pericula et in mediis voluptatum 7 inlecebris explorata sit. Nam cui libentiae gratiaeque omnes conviviorum incognitae sint quique illarum omnino expers sit, si eum forte ad participandas eiusmodi voluptates aut voluntas tulerit aut casus induxerit aut necessitas compulerit, deleniri plerumque et capi, neque mentem animumque eius con- 8 sistere, sed vi quadam nova ictum labascere. Congrediendum igitur censuit et, tamquam in acie quadam, cum voluptariis rebus cumque ista vini licentia comminus decernendum, ut adversum eas non fuga simus tuti nec absentia, sed vigore animi et constanti praesentia moderatoque usu temperantiam continentiamque tueamur et calefacto simul refotoque animo, si quid in eo vel frigidae tristitiae vel torpentis verecundiae fuerit, deluamus.

which a kind of reverential shame concealed, he thought that by the frankness engendered by wine all these were disclosed without great danger and became more amenable to correction and cure.

And in the same place Plato says this also: that exercises of this kind [1] for the purpose of resisting the violence of wine, are not to be avoided and shunned, and that no one ever appeared to be altogether self-restrained and temperate whose life and habits had not been tested amid the very dangers of error and in the midst of the enticements of pleasures. For when all the license and attractions of banquets are unknown, and a man is wholly unfamiliar with them, if haply inclination has led him, or chance has induced him, or necessity has compelled him, to take part in pleasures of that kind, then he is as a rule seduced and taken captive, his mind and soul fail to meet the test, but give way, as if attacked by some strange power. Therefore he thought that we ought to meet the issue and contend hand to hand, as in a kind of battle, with pleasure and indulgence in wine, in order that we may not be safe against them by flight or absence, but that by vigour of spirit, by presence of mind, and by moderate use, we may preserve our temperance and self-restraint, and at the same time by warming and refreshing the mind we may free it of whatever frigid austerity or dull bashfulness it may contain.

[1] That is, in the moderate use of wine, explained by *adversum . . . violentiam.*

III

Quid M. Cicero de particula ista senserit scripseritque quae
praeposita est verbis "aufugio" et "aufero"; et an in
verbo "autumo" eadem istaec praepositio esse videri
debeat.

1 Legimus librum M. Ciceronis qui inscriptus est
2 *Orator.* In eo libro Cicero, cum dixisset verba haec
"aufugio" et "aufero" composita quidem esse ex
praepositione "ab" et ex verbis "fugio" et "fero,"
sed eam praepositionem, quo fieret vox pronuntiatu
audituque lenior, versam mutatamque esse in "au"
syllabam coeptumque esse dici "aufugio" et "aufero"
3 pro "abfugio" et "abfero"—cum haec, inquam, ita
dixisset, tum postea ibidem super eadem particula
ita scripsit : "Haec,"[1] inquit, "praepositio praeter
haec duo verba nullo alio in verbo reperietur."
4 Invenimus autem in *Commentario* Nigidiano, verbum "autumo" compositum ex "ab" praepositione
et verbo "aestumo" dictumque intercise "autumo"
quasi "abaestumo," quod significaret "totum
5 aestumo," tamquam "abnumero." Sed, quod sit cum
honore multo dictum P. Nigidii, hominis eruditissimi,
audacius hoc argutiusque esse videtur quam verius.
6 "Autumo" enim non id solum significat, "aestumo,"
sed et "dico" et "opinor" et "censeo," cum quibus
verbis praepositio ista neque cohaerentia vocis neque

[1] quae, *Cic.*

---

[1] *Au* is probably a different preposition from *ab*; see
Archiv. f. lat. Lex. u. Gr., x, p. 480, and xiii, pp. 7 f.
[2] § 158.   [3] Frag. 51, Swoboda.
[4] The derivation of *autumo* is uncertain ; some take the
original meaning to be "divining" and connect it with *avis* ;

III

What Marcus Cicero thought and wrote about the prefix in the verbs *aufugio* and *aufero*; and whether this same preposition is to be seen in the verb *autumo*.

I READ a book of Marcus Cicero's entitled *The Orator*. In that book when Cicero had said that the verbs *aufugio* and *aufero* were indeed formed of the preposition *ab* and the verbs *fugio* and *fero*, but that the preposition, in order that the word might be smoother in pronunciation and sound, was changed and altered into the syllable *au*,[1] and *aufugio* and *aufero* began to be used for *abfugio* and *abfero*; when he had said this, I say, he afterwards in the same work wrote as follows of the same particle :[2] "This preposition," he says, "will be found in no other verb save these two only."

But I have found in the *Commentary* of Nigidius [3] that the verb *autumo* is formed from the preposition *ab* and the verb *aestumo* (estimate) and that *autumo* is a contracted form of *abaestumo*, signifying *totum aestumo*, on the analogy of *abnumero*.[4] But, be it said with great respect for Publius Nigidius, a most learned man, this seems to be rather bold and clever than true. For *autumo* does not only mean " I think," but also " I say," " I am of the opinion," and " I consider," with which verbs that preposition has no connection either in the composition of the

see *T.L.L. s.v.* Walde rejects that derivation in favour of the one from *autem*; cf. Fay, *Class. Quart.* i. (1907) p. 25. Here the original meaning is assumed to be " repeat, assert," and in fact *autumo* and *itero* are sometimes synonymous. The development of the meanings of *autumo* was doubtless influenced by *aestumo*, which has the same suffix.

7 significatione sententiae convenit. Praeterea vir acerrimae in studio litterarum diligentiae M. Tullius non sola esse haec duo verba dixisset, si reperiri 8 posset ullum tertium. Sed illud magis inspici quaerique dignum est, versane sit et mutata " ab " praepositio in " au " syllabam propter lenitatem vocis, an potius " au " particula sua sit propria origine et proinde ut pleraeque aliae praepositiones a Graecis, ita haec quoque inde accepta sit; sicuti est in illo versu Homeri :

Αὐέρυσαν μὲν πρῶτα καὶ ἔσφαξαν καὶ ἔδειραν,

et :

Ἄβρομοι, αὐίαχοι.

IV

Historia de Ventidio Basso, ignobili homine, quem primum de Parthis triumphasse memoriae traditum est.

1 IN sermonibus nuper fuit seniorum hominum et eruditorum, multos in vetere memoria altissimum dignitatis gradum ascendisse ignobilissimos prius 2 homines et despicatissimos. Nihil adeo de quoquam tantae admirationi fuit, quantae fuerunt quae de 3 Ventidio Basso scripta sunt : eum Picentem fuisse genere et loco humili ; et matrem eius a Pompeio

---

[1] See note 1, p. 66 ; it is not "taken from the Greeks."
[2] *Iliad* i. 459.   [3] *Iliad* xiii. 41

68

word or in the expression of its meaning.   Besides,
Marcus Tullius, a man of unwearied industry in the
pursuit of letters, would not have said that these
were the only two verbs containing *au*, if any third
example could be found.   But the following point
is more worthy of examination and investigation,
whether the preposition *ab* is altered and changed
into the syllable *au* for the sake of making the
pronunciation smoother, or whether more properly
the particle *au* has its own origin, and just as many
other prepositions were taken from the Greeks, so
this one also is derived from that source.[1]   As in that
verse of Homer :[2]

> First bent them back (αὐέρυσαν), then slew and
>   flayed the beasts ;

and :[3]

> Loud-shouting (αὐίαχοι), noisy.[4]

IV

The story of Ventidius Bassus, a man of obscure birth, who
is reported to have been the first to celebrate a triumph
over the Parthians.

It was lately remarked in the conversation of
certain old and learned men that in ancient times
many persons of most obscure birth, who were
previously held in great contempt, had risen to the
highest grade of dignity.   Nothing that was said
about anyone, however, excited so much wonder as
the story recorded of Ventidius Bassus.   He was
born in Picenum in a humble station, and with his
mother was taken prisoner by Pompeius Strabo,

[4] Or, in silence, noiseless ; see L. and S. *s.vv.*

Strabone, Pompei Magni patre, bello sociali, quo
Asculanos subegit, captam cum ipso esse ; mox trium-
phante Pompeio Strabone eum quoque puerum inter
ceteros ante currum imperatoris sinu matris vectum
esse ; post, cum adolevisset, victum sibi aegre quaesisse eumque sordide invenisse comparandis [1] mulis
et vehiculis, quae magistratibus qui sortiti provincias
forent praebenda publice conduxisset. In isto
quaestu notum esse coepisse C. Caesari et cum eo
profectum esse in Gallias. Tum, quia in ea provincia satis naviter versatus esset et deinceps civili
bello mandata sibi pleraque inpigre et strenue
fecisset, non modo in amicitiam Caesaris, sed ex ea
in amplissimum quoque ordinem pervenisse ; mox
tribunum quoque plebi ac deinde praetorem creatum
atque in eo tempore iudicatum esse a senatu hostem
cum M. Antonio ; post vero coniunctis partibus [2] non
pristinam tantum dignitatem reciperasse, sed ponti-
ficatum ac deinde consulatum quoque adeptum esse,
eamque rem tam intoleranter tulisse populum Romanum, qui Ventidium Bassum meminerat curandis
mulis victitasse, ut vulgo per vias urbis versiculi
proscriberentur :

[1] conquirendis, *Damsté, but cf. Suet. Jul.* lxxv. 3 *; Calig.*
xxvii. 1.
[2] patribus, ω; *corr.* in ς : coniunctum patribus, *Hertz.*

---

[1] 90–89 B.C. War was waged by the Italian allies against
Rome. After a bitter contest, in which 300,000 men are said
to have perished, the Romans were victorious, but by the

father of Pompey the Great, in the Social War,[1] in the course of which Strabo subdued the Aesculani.[2] Afterwards, when Pompeius Strabo triumphed, the boy also was carried in his mother's arms amid the rest of the captives before the general's chariot. Later, when he had grown up, he worked hard to gain a livelihood, resorting to the humble calling of a buyer of mules and carriages, which he had contracted with the State to furnish to the magistrates who had been allotted provinces. In that occupation he made the acquaintance of Gaius Caesar and went with him to the Gallic provinces. Then, because he had shown commendable energy in that province, and later during the civil war had executed numerous commissions with promptness and vigour, he not only gained Caesar's friendship, but because of it rose even to the highest rank. Afterwards he was also made tribune of the commons, and then praetor, and at that time he was declared a public enemy by the senate along with Mark Antony. Afterwards, however, when the parties were united, he not only recovered his former rank, but gained first the pontificate and then the consulship.[3] At this the Roman people, who remembered that Ventidius Bassus had made a living by taking care of mules, were so indignant that these verses[4] were posted everywhere about the streets of the city:

lex Plautia Papiria granted nearly all the demands of the allies, including the franchise.

[2] Aesculum was the capital of the Picenates, one of the seven peoples who made up the allies.

[3] 43 B.C.

[4] p. 331, 7, Bährens; cf. Virg. *Catal.* x., believed by some to refer to Ventidius Bassus, but probably wrongly. See *Virgil, L.C.L.,* ii., p. 499, n. 2.

Concúrrite omnes aúgures, harúspices!
Porténtum inusitátum conflatúm est recens;
Nam múlas qui fricábat, consul fáctus est.

4   Eundem Bassum Suetonius Tranquillus praepositum esse a M. Antonio provinciis orientalibus Parthosque in Syriam introrumpentis tribus ab eo proelis fusos scribit, eumque primum omnium de Parthis triumphasse et morte obita publico funere sepultum esse.

V

Verbum " profligo " a plerisque dici inproprie insciteque.

1   Sicut alia verba pleraque, ignoratione et inscitia improbe dicentium quae non intellegant, deflexa ac depravata sunt a ratione recta et consuetudine, ita huius quoque verbi, quod est " profligo," significatio
2   versa et corrupta est.   Nam cum ab adfligendo et ad perniciem interitumque deducendo inclinatum id tractumque sit, semperque eo verbo qui diligenter locuti sunt ita usi sint, ut "profligare" dicerent "prodigere" et "deperdere" "profligatasque res" quasi "proflictas" et "perditas" appellarent, nunc audio aedificia et templa et alia fere multa quae prope absoluta adfectaque sunt "in profligato" esse
3   dici ipsaque esse iam "profligata." Quapropter urbanissime respondisse praetorem, non indoctum virum, barunculo[1] cuidam ex advocatorum turba, Sulpicius Apollinaris in quadam epistula scriptum

---

[1] barunculo, *Heraeus* (*see T.LL. s.v.*); baruasculo, ω; barbasculo, S. and early edd.; barbariusculo, *Madvig.*

---

[1] Frag. 210, Reiff.

Assemble, soothsayers and augurs all!
A portent strange has taken place of late;
For he who curried mules is consul now.

Suetonius Tranquillus writes[1] that this same
Bassus was put in charge of the eastern provinces by
Mark Antony, and that when the Parthians invaded
Syria he routed them in three battles;[2] that he was
the first of all to celebrate a triumph over the
Parthians, and was honoured when he died with a
public funeral.

V

*That the verb profligo is used by many improperly and
ignorantly.*

Just as many other words, through the ignorance
and stupidity of those who speak badly what they
do not understand, are diverted and turned aside
from their proper and usual meaning, so too has
the signification of the verb *profligo* been changed
and perverted. For while it is taken over and
derived from *adfligo*, in the sense of "bring to ruin
and destruction," and while all who have been
careful in their diction have always used the word
to express "waste" and "destroy," calling things
that were cast down and destroyed *res profligatae*, I
now hear that buildings, temples, and many other
things that are almost complete and finished are
said to be *in profligato* and the things themselves
profligata. Therefore that was a very witty reply, as
Sulpicius Apollinaris has recorded in one of his
Letters, which a praetor, a man not without learning,
made to a simpleton among a crowd of advocates.

[2] 39 and 38 B.C.

4 reliquit. " Nam cum ille," inquit, " rabula audaculus
ita postulasset verbaque ita fecisset : ' Omnia, vir
clarissime, negotia de quibus te cogniturum esse
hodie dixisti diligentia et velocitate tua profligata
sunt, unum id solum relictum est, de quo, rogo,
audias,' tum praetor satis ridicule : ' An illa negotia
de quibus iam cognovisse me dicis profligata sint
equidem nescio ; hoc autem negotium quod in te
incidit, procul dubio, sive id audiam sive non audiam,
profligatum est.' ' "

5 Quod significare autem volunt qui " profligatum "
dicunt, hi qui Latine locuti sunt non " profligatum,"
sed " adfectum " dixerunt, sicuti M. Cicero in ora-
6 tione, quam habuit *De Provinciis Consularibus.* Eius
verba haec sunt : " Bellum adfectum videmus et,
7 vere ut dicam, paene confectum." Item infra : " Nam
ipse Caesar quid est quod [1] in ea [2] provincia com-
morari velit, nisi ut ea quae per eum adfecta sunt,
8 perfecta reipublicae tradat ? " Idem Cicero in
Oeconomico : " Cum vero adfecta iam prope aestate
uvas a sole mitescere tempus est."

VI

In libro M. Ciceronis *De Gloria* secundo manifestum erratum,
in ea parte in qua scriptum est super Hectore et Aiace.

1   IN libro M. Tulli, qui est secundus *De Gloria,*
manifestus error est non magnae rei, quem errorem

----

[1] est cur, *Cic.*   [2] ea, *omitted by MSS. of Cic.*

" For," said he, " when that impudent prater had
made a request in these terms : ' All the business,
renowned sir, about which you said that you would
take cognizance to-day, because of your diligence
and promptness is done (*profligata sunt*) ; one matter
only remains, to which I beg you to give attention.'
Then the praetor wittily enough replied : ' Whether
the affairs of which you say that I have taken
cognizance are done (*profligata*), I do not know ; but
this business which has fallen into your hands is
undoubtedly done for (*profligatum est*), whether I
hear it or not.'"

But to indicate what those wish to express who
use *profligatum* in the sense of " nearly done," those
who have spoken good Latin used, not *profligatum*,
but *adfectum*, as for example Marcus Cicero, in the
speech which he delivered *About the Consular Provinces*.
His words are as follows :[1] " We see the war near-
ing its end (*adfectum*) and, to tell the truth, all but
finished."   Also further on :[2] " For why should
Caesar himself wish to remain longer in that province,
except that he may turn over to the State, completed,
the tasks which he has nearly finished (*adfecta sunt*) ? "
Cicero also says in the *Oeconomicus* :[3] " When indeed,
as summer is already well nigh ended (*adfecta*), it is
time for the grapes to ripen in the sun."

VI

An evident mistake in the second book of Cicero *On Glory*,
in the place where he has written about Hector and Ajax.

IN Cicero's second book *On Glory* there is an
evident mistake, of no great importance—a mistake

---

[1] § 19.   [2] § 29.   [3] Frag. 21, p. 978, Orelli[2].

esse possit cognoscere non aliquis eruditorum, sed qui
2 tantum legerit Ὁμήρου τὸ Η΄. Quamobrem non tam
id mirabamur errasse in ea re M. Tullium, quam
non esse animadversum hoc postea correctumque vel
ab ipso vel a Tirone, liberto eius, diligentissimo
3 homine et librorum patroni sui studiosissimo. Ita
enim scriptum in eo libro est: " Apud eundem
poetam Aiax cum Hectore congrediens depugnandi
causa agit ut sepeliatur, si sit forte victus, declarat-
que se velle ut suum tumulum multis etiam post
saeculis praetereuntes sic loquantur :

> Hic situs est vitae iampridem lumina linquens,
> Qui quondam Hectoreo perculsus concidit ense.
> Fabitur haec aliquis, mea semper gloria vivet.

4   Huius autem sententiae versus, quos Cicero in
linguam Latinam vertit, non Aiax apud Homerum
dicit neque Aiax agit ut sepeliatur, sed Hector dicit
et Hector de sepultura agit, priusquam sciat an Aiax
secum depugnandi causa congressurus sit.

VII

Observatum esse in senibus quod annum fere aetatis tertium
    et sexagesimum agant aut laboribus aut interitu aut clade
    aliqua insignitum ; atque inibi super eadem observatione
    exemplum adpositum epistulae divi Augusti ad Gaium
    filium.

1   OBSERVATUM in multa hominum memoria exper-
tumque est, senioribus plerisque omnibus sexagesimum

---

[1] II., frag. 1, p. 989, Orelli[2].   [2] *Iliad* vii. 89.
[3] Gaius and Lucius Caesar were sons of Agrippa and
Julia, and grandsons of Augustus (see *Gaium nepotem*, § 3).

which it does not require a man of learning to
detect, but merely one who has read the seventh
book of Homer. Therefore I am not so much
surprised that Marcus Tullius erred in that matter,
as that it was not noticed later and corrected either
by Cicero himself or by Tiro, his freedman, a most
careful man, who gave great attention to his patron's
books. Now, in that book the following passage
occurs : [1] " The same poet says that Ajax, when about
to engage with Hector in combat, arranges for his
burial in case he should chance to be defeated,
declaring that he wishes that those who pass his
tomb even after many ages should thus speak : [2]

Here lies a man of life's light long bereft,
Who slain by Hector's sword fell long ago.
This, one shall say ; my glory ne'er shall die."

But the verses to this purport, which Cicero has
turned into the Latin tongue, Ajax does not utter in
Homer, nor is it Ajax who plans his burial, but Hector
speaks the lines and arranges for burial, before he
knows whether Ajax will meet him in combat.

VII

It has been observed of old men, that the sixty-third year of
their life is marked as a rule by troubles, by death, or by
some disaster ; and an example apropos of this observation
is taken from a letter from the deified Augustus to his son
Gaius. [3]

IT has been observed during a long period of
human recollection, and found to be true, that for
almost all old men the sixty-third year of their age

Both were adopted by Augustus, and on the death of the
young Marcellus were made *principes iuventutis*, and thus
designated as the successors of Augustus.

tertium vitae annum cum periculo et clade aliqua
venire aut corporis morbique gravioris aut vitae inte-
2 ritus aut animi aegritudinis. Propterea, qui rerum
verborumque istiusmodi studio tenentur eum aetatis
annum appellant κλιμακτηρικόν.

3   Nocte quoque ista proxima superiore, cum librum
Epistularum divi Augusti, quas ad Gaium nepotem
suum scripsit, legeremus duceremurque elegantia
orationis neque morosa neque anxia, sed facili hercle
et simplici, id ipsum in quadam epistula super eodem
anno scriptum offendimus ; eiusque epistula exemplum hoc est:

   " IX. Kal. Octobris.

" Ave, mi Gai, meus asellus iucundissimus, quem
semper medius fidius desidero, cum a me abes.   Set
praecipue diebus talibus, qualis est hodiernus, oculi
mei requirunt meum Gaium, quem, ubicumque hoc
die fuisti, spero laetum et bene valentem celebrasse
quartum et sexagesimum natalem meum.   Nam, ut
vides, κλιμακτῆρα communem seniorum omnium
tertium et sexagesimum annum evasimus.   Deos
autem oro ut mihi quantumcumque superest temporis,
id salvis nobis traducere liceat in statu reipublicae
felicissimo, ἀνδραγαθούντων ὑμῶν καὶ διαδεχομένων
stationem meam."

---

[1] Cf. iii. 10. 9.   [2] p. 155, 18, Wichert.
[3] Sept. 23.

is attended with danger, and with some disaster involving either serious bodily illness, or loss of life, or mental suffering. Therefore those who are engaged in the study of matters and terms of that kind call that period of life the "climacteric."[1]

Night before last, too, when I was reading a volume of letters of the deified Augustus, written to his grandson Gaius, and was led on by the elegance of the style, which was easy and simple, by Heaven! without mannerisms or effort, in one of the letters I ran upon a reference to this very belief about that same year. I give a copy of the letter:[2]

"The ninth day before the Kalends of October.[3]

"Greeting, my dear Gaius, my dearest little donkey,[4] whom, so help me! I constantly miss whenever you are away from me. But especially on such days as to-day my eyes are eager for my Gaius, and wherever you have been to-day, I hope you have celebrated my sixty-fourth birthday in health and happiness. For, as you see, I have passed the climacteric common to all old men, the sixty-third year. And I pray the gods that whatever time is left to me I may pass with you safe and well, with our country in a flourishing condition, while you[5] are playing the man and preparing to succeed to my position."

[4] A term of affection. The *asellus* is an attractive little beast, whatever the reputation of the *asinus*. The *ocellus* of Beroaldus and Damsté's *aucellus* (=*avicellus*, "birdlet"; the usual form is *avicula*, as in ii. 29. 2) are needless changes, particularly in view of Augustus' humorous tendencies; Weiss cites vi. 16. 5, where *asellus* has a different, but hardly more complimentary, meaning.

[5] The plural refers to Gaius and his brother Lucius; see note.

VIII

Locus ex oratione Favoni, veteris oratoris, de cenarum atque luxuriae obprobratione, qua usus est cum legem Liciniam de sumptu minuendo suasit.

1   Cum legeremus orationem veterem Favoni, non indiserti viri, qua oratione . . . totum, ut meminisse possemus odio esse hercle istiusmodi sumptus atque
2 victus, perdidicimus.   Verba haec, quae adposuimus, Favoni sunt : " Praefecti popinae atque luxuriae negant cenam lautam esse, nisi cum lubentissime edis, tum auferatur et alia esca melior atque amplior succenturietur. Is nunc flos cenae habetur inter istos quibus sumptus et fastidium pro facetiis procedit, qui negant ullam avem praeter ficedulam totam comesse oportere ; ceterarum avium atque altilium nisi tantum adponatur, ut a cluniculis inferiore parte [1] saturi fiant, convivium putant inopia sordere, superiorem partem avium atque altilium qui edint, eos palatum parum delicatum [2] habere. Si proportione pergit luxuria crescere, quid relinquitur, nisi ut delibari sibi cenas iubeant, ne edendo defetigentur, quando stratus lectus [3] auro, argento, purpura amplior aliquot hominibus quam dis inmortalibus adornatur ? "

---

[1] Damsté would delete *inferiore parte* and *avium atque altilium*.

[2] *parum delicatum added by Hertz* ; palatum non habere, σ.

[3] lectus *added by Skutsch*.

---

[1] The sense of the lacuna seems to be given in the chapter heading.

[2] *O.R.F.*, p. 207, Meyer[2].

VIII

A passage from a speech of Favonius, an early orator, containing an attack which he made on luxurious entertainments, when he was advocating the Licinian law for lessening extravagance.

WHEN I was reading an old speech of Favonius, a man of no little eloquence, in which [1] . . . I learned the whole of it by heart, in order to be able to remember that such extravagant living is truly hateful. These words which I have added are those of Favonius : [2] "The leaders in gluttony and luxury declare that an entertainment is not elegant, unless, when you are eating with the greatest relish, your plate is removed and a better, richer dainty comes from the reserves. This to-day is thought the very flower of a feast among those with whom extravagance and fastidiousness take the place of elegance ; who say that the whole of no bird ought to be eaten except a fig-pecker ; who think that a dinner is mean and stingy unless so many of the other birds and fatted fowl are provided, that the guests may be satisfied with the rumps and hinder parts ; who believe that those who eat the upper parts of such birds and fowl have no refinement of taste. If luxury continues to increase in its present proportion, what remains but that men should bid someone to eat their dinners for them, in order that they may not fatigue themselves by feeding, when the couch is more profusely adorned with gold, silver and purple for a few mortals than for the immortal gods ? " [3]

[3] The reference is probably to the *lectisternium*, when the images of the gods were placed upon couches and food was set before them by the vii *viri epulones*.

IX

Quod Caecilius poeta "frontem" genere virili non poetice,
sed cum probatione et cum analogia appellavit.

1   VERE ac diserte Caecilius hoc in *Subdititio* scripsit :

Nam hi súnt inimici péssumi, fronte hílaro, corde
trísti,
Quos néque ut adprendas néque uti dimittás scias.

2   Hos ego versus, cum de quodam istiusmodi homine
sermones essent, in circulo forte iuvenum eruditiorum
3   dixi.   Tum de grammaticorum volgo quispiam nobiscum ibi adsistens non sane ignobilis, " Quanta,"
inquit, " licentia audaciaque Caecilius hic fuit, cum
'fronte hilaro,' non 'fronte hilara' dixit et tam
4   inmanem soloecismum nihil veritus est ! "   " Immo,"
inquam, " potius nos et quam audaces et quam
licentes sumus, qui 'frontem' inprobe indocteque
non virili genere dicimus, cum et ratio proportionis,[1]
quae 'analogia' appellatur, et veterum auctoritates
non 'hanc,' sed 'hunc frontem' debere dici suadeant.
5   Quippe M. Cato in primo *Originum* ita scripsit :
'Postridie signis conlatis, aequo fronte, peditatu,
equitibus atque alis cum hostium legionibus pugnavi-
mus.'   'Recto' quoque 'fronte' idem Cato in libro
eodem dicit."
6   At ille semidoctus grammaticus : " Missas," inquit,
" auctoritates facias, quas quidem ut habeas posse
fieri puto, sed rationem dic, quam non habes."

---

[1] pro portione, *Skutsch, comparing Varro, L.L.* x. 3.37.

---

[1] ii. 79, Ribbeck[3].   [2] On analogy see ii. 25.
[3] Frag. 99, Peter[2].   [4] Frag. 100, Peter[2].

IX

That the poet Caecilius used *frons* in the masculine gender, not by poetic license, but properly and by analogy.

CORRECTLY and elegantly did Caecilius write this in his *Changeling* :[1]

> The worst of foes are these, of aspect gay (*fronte hilaro*),
> Gloomy of heart, whom we can neither grasp
> Nor yet let go.

I chanced to quote these lines in a company of well educated young men, when we were speaking of a man of that kind. Thereupon one of a throng of grammarians who stood there with us, a man of no little repute, said : " What license and boldness Caecilius showed here in saying *fronte hilaro* and not *fronte hilara,* and in not shrinking from so dreadful a solecism." " Nay," said I, " it is rather we who are as bold and free as possible in improperly and ignorantly failing to use *frons* in the masculine gender, when both the principle of regularity which is called analogy[2] and the authority of earlier writers indicate that we ought to say, not *hanc frontem,* but *hunc frontem.* Indeed, Marcus Cato in the first book of his *Origins* wrote as follows :[3] 'On the following day in open combat, with straight front (*aequo fronte*) we fought with the enemy's legions with foot, horse and wings.' Also Cato again says[4] *recto fronte* in the same book."

But that half-educated grammarian said : " Away with your authorities, which I think you may perhaps have, but give me a reason, which you do not

7 Atque ego his eius verbis, ut tum ferebat aetas, inritatior, "Audi," inquam, "mi magister, rationem falsam quidem, sed quam redarguere falsam esse tu
8 non queas. Omnia," inquam, "vocabula tribus litteris finita quibus ' frons ' finitur, generis masculini sunt, si in genetivo quoque casu eadem syllaba
9 finiantur, ut 'mons,' 'fons,' 'pons,' 'frons.' " At ille contra renidens: "Audi," inquit, "discipule, plura alia consimilia, quae non sint generis mascu-
10 lini." Petebant ibi omnes ut vel unum statim diceret. Sed cum homo voltum intorqueret et non hisceret et colores mutaret, tum ego intercessi et "Vade," inquam, "nunc et habeto ad requirendum triginta dies; postquam inveneris, repetes nos."
11 Atque ita hominem nulli rei ad indagandum vocabulum, quo rescinderet finitionem fictam, dimisimus.

X

De voluntario et admirando interitu virginum Milesiarum.

1 PLUTARCHUS in librorum quos Περὶ Ψυχῆς inscripsit primo, cum de morbis dissereret in animos hominum incidentibus, virgines [1] dixit Milesii nominis fere quot tum in ea civitate erant repente sine ulla evidenti causa voluntatem cepisse obeundae mortis ac
2 deinde plurimas vitam suspendio amisisse. Id cum accideret in dies crebrius neque animis earum mori perseverantium medicina adhiberi quiret, decrevisse Milesios ut virgines quae corporibus suspensis de-

---

[1] virginem, δ; virginum, *Hertz.*

---

[1] Nouns of the third declension ending in s preceded by a consonant are regularly feminine. The four excep-

84

have." Then I, somewhat irritated by those words
of his, as was natural at my time of life: "Listen,"
said I, "my dear sir, to a reason that may be false,
but which you cannot prove to be false. All words,"
said I, "ending in the three letters in which *frons* ends
are of the masculine gender, if they end in the same
syllable in the genitive case also, as *mons, fons, pons,
frons*."[1] But he replied with a laugh: "Hear,
young scholar, several other similar words which are
not of the masculine gender." Then all begged him
at once to name just one. But when the man was
screwing up his face, could not open his lips, and
changed colour, then I broke in, saying: "Go now
and take thirty days to hunt one up; when you
have found it, meet us again." And thus we sent
off this worthless fellow to hunt up a word with
which to break down the rule which I had made.

X

About the strange suicides of the maids of Miletus.

PLUTARCH in the first book of his work *On the Soul*,[2]
discussing disorders which affect the human mind,
has told us that almost all the maidens of the
Milesian nation suddenly without any apparent
cause conceived a desire to die, and thereupon many
of them hanged themselves. When this happened
more frequently every day, and no remedy had any
effect on their resolve to die, the Milesians passed a
decree that all those maidens who committed suicide

tions are *mons, fons, dens*, and *pons; frons* is usually
feminine.
  [2] vii. p. 20, Bern.

mortuae forent, ut hae omnes nudae, cum eodem
laqueo quo essent praevinctae efferrentur.   Post id
decretum virgines voluntariam mortem non petisse
pudore solo deterritas tam inhonesti funeris.

XI

Verba senatusconsulti de exigendis urbe Roma philosophis ;
  item verba edicti censorum, quo inprobati et coerciti sunt
  qui disciplinam rhetoricam instituere et exercere Romae
  coeperant.

1   C. FANNIO STRABONE, M. Valerio Messala coss.
senatusconsultum de philosophis et de rhetoribus
Latinis[1] factum est : " M. Pomponius praetor senatum consuluit.   Quod verba facta sunt de philosophis
et de rhetoribus, de ea re ita censuerunt, ut M.
Pomponius praetor animadverteret curaretque, uti
ei[2] e republica fideque sua videretur, uti Romae ne
essent."

2   Aliquot deinde annis post id senatusconsultum Cn.
Domitius Ahenobarbus et L. Licinius Crassus censores de coercendis rhetoribus Latinis ita edixerunt : " Renuntiatum est nobis esse homines, qui
novum genus disciplinae instituerunt, ad quos iu-
ventus in ludum conveniat ; eos sibi nomen inpo-
suisse Latinos rhetoras ; ibi homines adulescentulos

────────────

[1] Latinis *deleted by Pighius, comparing Suetonius, De
Rhet.* 1.
[2] ut si ei, *Suet. De Rhet.* 1.

────────────

[1] 161 B.C.
[2] *Fontes Iuris Rom.*, p. 157 ; cf. Suetonius, *De Rhet.* 1 (ii.
p. 434, *L.C.L.*).

by hanging should be carried to the grave naked, along with the same rope by which they had destroyed themselves. After that decree the maidens ceased to seek a voluntary death, deterred by the mere shame of so disgraceful a burial.

XI

The words of a decree of the senate on expelling philosophers from the city of Rome; also the words of the edict of the censors by which those were rebuked and restrained who had begun to establish and practise the art of rhetoric at Rome.

IN the consulship of Gaius Fannius Strabo and Marcus Valerius Messala [1] the following decree of the senate was passed regarding Latin speaking philosophers and rhetoricians: [2] "The praetor Marcus Pomponius laid a proposition before the senate. As the result of a discussion about philosophers and rhetoricians, the senate decreed that Marcus Pomponius, the praetor, should take heed and provide, in whatever way seemed to him in accord with the interests of the State and his oath of office, that they should not remain in Rome."

Then some years [3] after that decree of the senate Gnaeus Domitius Ahenobarbus and Lucius Licinius Crassus the censors issued the following edict for restraining the Latin rhetoricians: [4] "It has been reported to us that there be men who have introduced a new kind of training, and that our young men frequent their schools; that these men have assumed the title of Latin rhetoricians, and that

[3] 92 B.C.
[4] *F.I.R.*, p. 215; Suetonius ii, p. 434 f. *L.C.L.*

dies totos desidere. Maiores nostri quae liberos suos discere et quos in ludos itare vellent instituerunt. Haec nova, quae praeter consuetudinem ac morem maiorum fiunt, neque placent neque recta videntur. Quapropter et his qui eos ludos habent, et his qui eo venire consuerunt, visum est faciundum, ut ostenderemus nostram sententiam, nobis non placere."

3 Neque illis solum temporibus, nimis rudibus necdum Graeca disciplina expolitis, philosophi ex urbe
4 Roma pulsi sunt, verum etiam Domitiano imperante senatusconsulto eiecti atque urbe et Italia interdicti
5 sunt. Qua tempestate Epictetus quoque philosophus propter id senatusconsultum Nicopolim Roma decessit.

XII

Locus ex oratione Gracchi de parsimonia ac de pudicitia sua memoratissimus.

1 C. Gracchus cum ex Sardinia rediit, orationem ad
2 populum in contione habuit. Ea verba haec sunt : " Versatus sum," inquit, "in provincia, quomodo ex usu vestro existimabam esse, non quomodo ambitioni meae conducere arbitrabar. Nulla apud me fuit popina, neque pueri eximia facie stabant, et in convivio liberi vestri modestius erant quam apud prin-

---

[1] A.D. 89.
[2] The celebrated tribune of 123 and 122 B.C. He was famous as an orator ; cf. i. 11. 10 ff.

young men spend whole days with them in idleness.
Our forefathers determined what they wished their
children to learn and what schools they desired them
to attend. These innovations in the customs and
principles of our forefathers neither please us nor
seem proper. Therefore it seems necessary to make
our opinion known, both to those who have such
schools and to those who are in the habit of attend-
ing them, that they are displeasing to us."

And it was not only in those times, which were
somewhat rude and not yet refined by Greek
training, that philosophers were driven from the
city of Rome, but even in the reign of Domitian[1]
by a decree of the senate they were driven from
the city and forbidden Italy. And it was at that
time that the philosopher Epictetus also withdrew
from Rome to Nicopolis because of that senatorial
decree.

XII

A highly memorable passage from a speech of Gracchus,
regarding his frugality and continence.

When Gaius Gracchus[2] returned from Sardinia,
he delivered a speech to an assembly of the people
in the following words:[3] "I conducted myself in
my province," said he, "as I thought would be to
your advantage, not as I believed would contribute
to my own ambitions. There was no tavern at my
establishment, nor did slaves of conspicuous beauty
wait upon me, and at an entertainment of mine your
sons were treated with more modesty than at their

---

[3] *O.R.F.*, p. 231, Meyer[2].

3 cipia." Post deinde haec dicit: " Ita versatus sum
in provincia, uti nemo posset vere dicere assem aut
eo plus in muneribus me accepisse, aut mea opera
quemquam sumptum fecisse. Biennium fui in provincia ; si ulla meretrix domum meam introivit aut
cuiusquam servulus propter me sollicitatus est, omnium
nationum postremissimum nequissimumque existi-
matote. Cum a servis eorum tam caste me habue-
rim, inde poteritis considerare quomodo me putetis
4 cum liberis vestris vixisse." Atque ibi ex intervallo :
" Itaque," inquit, " Quirites, cum Romam profectus
sum, zonas quas plenas argenti extuli, eas ex provincia inanes retuli. Alii vini amphoras quas plenas
tulerunt, eas argento repletas domum reporta-
verunt."

XIII

De verbis inopinatis, quae utroqueversum dicuntur et a
grammaticis "communia" vocantur.

1 " Utor " et " vereor " et " consolor " communia
verba sunt ac dici utroqueversus possunt : " vereor
te " et " vereor abs te," id est " tu me vereris " ; " utor
te " et " utor abs te," id est " tu me uteris " ; [1] " hortor
te " et " hortor abs te," id est " tu me hortaris " ;
" consolor te " et " consolor abs te," id est " tu me
consolaris " ; " testor " quoque et " interpretor "
2 significatione reciproca dicuntur. Sunt autem verba

---

[1] id . . . uteris, σ ; id (pro id, Q) factum, ω.

general's tent." Later on he continues as follows:
"I so conducted myself in my province that no
one could truly say that I received a penny, or more
than that,[1] by way of present, or that anyone was
put to expense on my account. I spent two years
in my province; if any courtesan entered my house
or anyone's slave was bribed on my account, consider me the lowest and basest of mankind. Since
I conducted myself so continently towards their
slaves, you may judge from that on what terms I
lived with your sons." Then after an interval he
goes on: "Accordingly, fellow citizens, when I
left for Rome, I brought back empty from the
province the purses which I took there full of
money. Others have brought home overflowing
with money the jars which they took to their
province filled with wine."

XIII

Of some unusual words, which are used in either voice and
are called by the grammarians "common."

Utor, vereor, hortor and *consolor* are "common"
verbs and can be used either way: "I respect you"
and "I am respected by you," that is, "you respect
me"; "I use you" and "I am used by you," that
is, "you use me"; "I exhort you" and "I am
exhorted by you," that is, "you exhort me"; "I
console you" and "I am consoled by you," that is,
"you console me." *Testor* too and *interpretor* are
used in a reciprocal sense. But all these words are

---

[1] One is reminded of the story of the politician who
declared that he had never received a penny in bribes, but
that it was as well to say nothing about thousand dollar bills.

haec omnia ex altera parte inusitata, et an dicta
sint in eam quoque partem quaeri solet.

3   Afranius in *Consobrinis*:

> Em istó parentum est víta vilis líberis,
> Ubi málunt metui, quám vereri se áb suis.

Hic " vereri " ex ea parte dictum est quae est non
4 usitatior.   Novius in *Lignaria* verbum quod est
" utitur " ex contraria parte dicit:

> Quía supellex múlta quae non útitur, emitúr
> tamen,

5 id est "quae usui non est." M. Cato in quinta
Origine: " Exercitum," inquit, " suum pransum,
paratum, cohortatum eduxit foras atque instruxit."

6 " Consolor " quoque in partem alteram, praeterquam
dici solitum est, scriptum invenimus in epistula
Q. Metelli, quam, cum in exilio esset, ad Cn. et
ad L. Domitios dedit. " At cum animum," inquit,
" vestrum erga me video, vehementer consolor et
fides virtusque vestra mihi ante oculos versatur."

7 " Testata " itidem et " interpretata " eadem ratione
dixit M. Tullius in primo libro *De Divinatione*, ut
" testor " " interpretor"que verba communia videri

8 debeant. Sallustius quoque eodem modo: " dilargitis proscriptorum bonis " dicit, tamquam verbum
" largior " sit ex verbis communibus.

9   " Veritum " autem, sicut " puditum " et " pigi-

---

unusual in the second of these meanings, and it is
a matter of inquiry whether they are ever so used.
Afranius in *The Cousins* says:[1]

> Lo! there his children hold a sire's life cheap,
> Where rather feared than honoured (*vereri*) he
>   would be.

Here *vereor* is used in its less common sense. Novius
also in the *Wood-dealer* uses the word *utor* with a
passive meaning:[2]

> Since a deal of gear is bought which is not used
>   (*utitur*).

That is, "which is not to be used." Marcus Cato
in the fifth book of his *Origins* has this:[3] "He led
forth his army, fed, ready, and encouraged (*cohortatum*), and drew it up in order of battle." We
find *consolor* also used in a different sense from the
one which it commonly has, in a letter of Quintus
Metellus, which he wrote during his exile to Gnaeus
and Lucius Domitius. "But," he says, "when I
realize your feeling towards me, I am very greatly
consoled (*consolor*); and your loyalty and worth are
brought before my eyes." Marcus Tullius used
testata and *interpretata* in the same manner in the
first book of his work *On Divination*,[4] so that *testor*
and *interpretor* ought also to be considered to be
"common" verbs. Sallust too in a similar way
says:[5] "The goods of the proscribed having been
given away (*dilargitis*)," indicating that *largior* is one
of the "common" verbs.

Moreover, we see that *veritum*, like *puditum* and

---

[3] Frag. 101, Peter².   [4] § 87 and § 53
[5] *Hist*. i. 49, Maur.

tum," non personaliter per infinitum modum dictum
esse, non a vetustioribus tantum videmus, sed a M.
quoque Tullio in secundo *De Finibus.* "Primum,"
inquit, "Aristippi Cyrenaicorumque omnium, quos
non est veritum in ea voluptate quae maxima dul-
cedine sensum moveret summum bonum ponere."

10 "Dignor" quoque et "veneror" et "confiteor"
et "testor" habita sunt in verbis communibus. Sic
illa in Vergilio dicta sunt:

Coniugio, Anchisa, Veneris dignate superbo,

et:

cursusque dabit venerata secundos.

11 "Confessi" autem "aeris," de quo facta confessio
est, in *XII. Tabulis* scriptum est his verbis: "Aeris
confessi rebusque iure[1] iudicatis XXX. dies iusti
sunto." Item ex isdem tabulis id quoque est.
"Qui se sierit testarier libripensve fuerit, ni testimonium fariatur, inprobus intestabilisque esto."

[1] iure, *cf.* **xx**. i. 45; *omitted here by* ω.

---

[1] That is, without having a particular person or thing as its
subject.
[2] § 39.
[3] *i.e.* who did not scruple.

pigitum, is used impersonally and indefinitely,[1] not only by the earlier writers, but also by Marcus Tullius in the second book of his *De Finibus.*[2] "First (I will refute)," says he, "the view of Aristippus and of all the Cyrenaic philosophers, to whom it caused no fear [3] (*veritum est*) to assign the highest good to that pleasure which affects the senses with greatest delight."

Dignor, too, *veneror, confiteor* and *testor* are treated as "common" verbs. Thus we find in Virgil :[4]

Of wedlock high with Venus worthy deemed (*dignate*),

and [5]

Revered in prayer (*venerata*), shall grant a voyage safe.

Moreover, *confessi aeris,* meaning a debt of which admission is made, is written in the *Twelve Tables* in these words :[6] "For an admitted debt, when the matter has been taken into court, let the respite be thirty days." Also in those same *Tables* we find this :[7] "Whoever shall allow himself to be summoned as a witness or shall act as a balance-holder,[8] if he does not give his testimony, let him be regarded as dishonoured and incapable of giving testimony in the future."

---

[4] *Aen.* iii. 475.   [5] *Aen.* iii. 460.
[6] iii. 1.   [7] viii. 22.
[8] That is, in a symbolic sale, when the purchaser touched a balance with a coin. See note on v. 19. 3 (vol. i., p. 436).

XIV

Quod Metellus Numidicus figuram orationis novam ex orationibus Graecis mutuatus est.

1 Aput Q. Metellum Numidicum in libro accusationis *In Valerium Messalam* tertio nove dictum esse
2 adnotavimus. Verba ex oratione eius haec sunt: "Cum sese sciret in tantum crimen venisse atque socios ad senatum questum flentes venisse, sese pe-
3 cunias maximas exactos esse." "Sese[1] pecunias," inquit, "maximas[2] exactos esse" pro eo quod est: "pecunias a se esse[3] maximas exactas."
4 Id nobis videbatur Graeca figura dictum; Graeci enim dicunt: εἰσεπράξατό με ἀργύριον, id significat "exegit me pecuniam." Quod si id dici potest, etiam "exactus esse aliqui pecuniam" dici potest,
5 Caeciliusque eadem figura in *Hypobolimaeo Aeschino* usus videtur:

Ego illúd minus nihilo éxigor portórium,

id est "nihilominus exigitur de me portorium."

XV

"Passis' velis" et "passis manibus" dixisse veteres non a verbo suo, quod est "patior," sed ab alieno, quod est "pando."

1 Ab eo quod est "pando" "passum" veteres dixerunt, non "pansum," et cum "ex" praeposi-

---

[1] Sese *added by Hertz.*   [2] maximas *added by Carrio.*
[3] a se esse, *Hertz*; esse, *Q*; a se, *ω.*

XIV

That Metellus Numidicus borrowed a new form of expression
from Greek usage.

In Quintus Metellus Numidicus, in the third book
of his *Accusation of Valerius Messala*, I have made
note of a novel expression. The words of his speech
are as follows:[1] "When he knew that he had
incurred so grave an accusation, and that our allies
had come to the senate in tears, to make complaint
that they had been exacted enormous sums of
money (*pecunias maximas exactos esse*)." He says
"that they had been exacted enormous sums of
money," instead of "that enormous sums of money
had been exacted from them."

This seemed to me an imitation of a Greek idiom;
for the Greeks say: εἰσεπράξατό με ἀργύριον, meaning
"he exacted me money." But if this can be said,
so too can "one is exacted money," and Caecilius
seems to have used that form of expression in his
Supposititious Aeschinus:[2]

Yet I the customs-fee exacted am.

That is to say, "yet the customs-fee is exacted from
me."

XV

That the early writers used *passis velis* and *passis manibus*,
not from the verb *patior*, to which the participle belongs,
but from *pando*, to which it does not belong.

From the verb *pando* the ancients made *passum*,
not *pansum*, and with the preposition *ex* they formed

[1] *O.R.F.*, p. 276, Meyer[2].   [2] v. 92, Ribbeck[3].

2 tione "expassum," non "expansum." Caecilius in
Synaristosis:

> Herí vero prospéxisse eum se ex tégulis,
> Haec núntiasse et flámmeum expassúm domi

3 "Capillo" quoque esse mulier "passo" dicitur,
quasi porrecto et expanso, et "passis manibus"
et "velis passis" dicimus, quod significat diductis
4 atque distentis. Itaque Plautus in *Milite Glorioso,*
a littera in *e* mutata per compositi vocabuli morem,
"dispessis" dicit pro eo, quod est "dispassis":

> Credo égo istoc exempló tibi esse péreundum[1]
> extra pórtam,
> Dispéssis manibus pátibulum cum habébis.

XVI

De novo genere interitus Crotoniensis Milonis.

1 MILO Crotoniensis, athleta inlustris, quem in
chronicis scriptum est Olympiade LXII[2] primum
coronatum esse, exitum habuit e vita miserandum
2 et mirandum. Cum iam natu grandis artem athle-
ticam desisset iterque faceret forte solus in locis
Italiae silvestribus, quercum vidit proxime viam
3 patulis in parte media rimis hiantem. Tum experiri,
credo, etiam tunc volens an ullae sibi reliquae vires

---

[1] pereundum, *best MSS. of Plaut.*; eundum, ω.
[2] lxii. primum, *Lübbert*; prima, ω; plurima, *Damsté.*

---

[1] v. 197, Ribbeck[3].

expassum, not *expansum*. Caecilius in the *Fellow-breakfasters* says:[1]

> That yesterday he'd looked in from the roof,
> Had this announced, and straight the veil[2] was
>   spread (*expassum*).

A woman too is said to be *capillo passo*, or "with disordered hair," when it is hanging down and loosened, and we say *passis manibus* and *velis passis* of hands and sails stretched out and spread. Therefore Plautus in his *Braggart Captain*, changing an *a* into an *e*, as is usual in compound words, uses *dispessis* for *dispassis* in these lines:[3]

> Methinks you thus must die without the gate,
> When you shall hold the cross with hands out-
>   stretched (*dispessis*).

XVI

Of the singular death of Milo of Croton.[4]

MILO of Croton, a famous athlete, who was first crowned at the sixty-second Olympiad,[5] as the chronicles record, ended his life in a strange and lamentable manner. When he was already advanced in age and had given up the athletic art, he chanced to be journeying alone in a wooded part of Italy. Near the road he saw an oak tree, the middle of which gaped with wide cracks. Then wishing, I suppose, to try whether he still had any strength left,

[2] The flame-coloured (yellow) bridal veil.
[3] 359. Cf. iv. 17. 8 ; *a* became *e* before two consonants, *i* before a single one, except *r*. .
[4] The same story is told by Strabo, vi. 1. 12 (iii, p. 45, *L.C.L.*).   [5] 532 B.C.

adessent, inmissis in cavernas arboris digitis, diducere et rescindere quercum conatus est. Ac mediam
4 quidem partem [1] discidit divellitque ; quercus autem
in duas diducta partis, cum ille, quasi perfecto quod
erat conixus, manus laxasset, cessante vi rediit
in naturam manibusque eius retentis inclusisque
stricta denuo et cohaesa, dilacerandum hominem
feris praebuit.

XVII

Quam ob causam nobiles pueri Atheniensium tibiis canere
desierint, cum patrium istum morem canendi haberent.

1 ALCIBIADES Atheniensis, cum apud avunculum
Periclen puer artibus ac disciplinis liberalibus
erudiretur et arcessi Pericles Antigenidam tibicinem
iussisset, ut eum canere tibiis, quod honestissimum
tum videbatur, doceret, traditas sibi tibias, cum ad os
adhibuisset inflassetque, pudefactus oris deformitate
2 abiecit infregitque. Ea res cum percrebuisset,
omnium tum Atheniensium consensu disciplina
3 tibiis canendi desita est. Scriptum hoc in *Con-
mentario* Pamphilae nono et vicesimo.

[1] partem *deleted by Ranchinus.*

he put his fingers into the hollows of the tree and
tried to rend apart and split the oak.   And in fact
he did tear asunder and divide the middle part;
but when the oak was thus split into two parts, and
he relaxed his hold as if he had accomplished his
attempt, the tree returned to its natural position
when the pressure ceased, and catching and holding
his hands as it came together and united, it kept
the man there, to be torn to pieces by wild beasts.

XVII

Why young men of noble rank at Athens gave up playing
the pipes, although it was one of their native customs.

ALCIBIADES the Athenian in his boyhood was being
trained in the liberal arts and sciences at the home
of his uncle, Pericles; and Pericles had ordered
Antigenides, a player on the pipes, to be sent for,
to teach the boy to play on that instrument, which
was then considered a great accomplishment.   But
when the pipes were handed to him and he had put
them to his lips and blown, disgusted at the ugly
distortion of his face, he threw them away and broke
them in two.   When this matter was noised abroad,
by the universal consent of the Athenians of that
time the art of playing the pipes was given up.   This
story is told in the twenty-ninth book of the
Commentary of Pamphila.[1]

[1] *F.H.G.* iii. 521. 9.

XVIII

Quod pugna belli civilis victoriaque Gai Caesaris, quam vicit in Pharsaliis campis, nuntiata praedictaque est per cuiuspiam sacerdotis[1] vaticinium eodem ipso die in Italia Patavi.

1 Quo C. Caesar et Cn. Pompeius die per civile bellum signis conlatis in Thessalia conflixerunt, res accidit Patavi in transpadana Italia memorari digna.

2 Cornelius quidam sacerdos, et nobilis et sacerdotii religionibus venerandus et castitate vitae sanctus, repente mota mente conspicere se procul dixit pugnam acerrimam pugnari, ac deinde alios cedere, alios urgere, caedem, fugam, tela volantia, instaurationem pugnae, inpressionem, gemitus, vulnera, proinde ut si ipse in proelio versaretur, coram videre sese vociferatus est ac postea subito exclamavit Caesarem vicisse.

3 Ea Cornelii sacerdotis ariolatio levis tum quidem visa est et vecors. Magnae mox admirationi fuit, quod non modo pugnae dies quae in Thessalia pugnata est, neque proelii exitus qui erat praedictus, idem fuit, sed omnes quoque pugnandi reciprocae vices et ipsa exercituum duorum conflictatio vaticinantis motu atque verbis repraesentata est.

[1] sacerdotis, *scripsi, cf.* §§ 2 *and* 3 (*beginning*); praesagi *or* sagacis, *Hosius*; remigis, ω. *As Madvig long ago pointed out (Adv. Crit.* ii, *p.* 605, *n.* 1), *this is not a question of palaeo-*

XVIII

That the battle which Gaius Caesar fought on the plains of
Pharsalus during the civil war was announced on the
very same day at Patavium in Italy, and his victory
foretold, by the divination of a seer.

On the day that Gaius Caesar and Gnaeus
Pompeius engaged in battle in Thessaly during the
civil war, an event occurred at Patavium in Trans-
padane Italy, which is deserving of record. A priest
called Cornelius, a man of good birth, honoured for
scrupulousness in his office and revered for the
purity of his life, was suddenly seized by a prophetic
inspiration and said that he saw a most furious battle
taking place afar off; then he shouted out, just as
if he were personally taking part in the engagement,
that some were giving way, others pressing on;
that he saw before him carnage, flight, flying
weapons, a renewal of the engagement, an attack,
groans and wounds; and later he suddenly exclaimed
that Caesar was victorious.

At the time the prophecy of the priest Cornelius
seemed unimportant and without meaning. Afterwards, however, it caused great surprise, since not
only the time of the battle which was fought in
Thessaly, and its predicted outcome, were verified,
but all the shifting fortunes of the day and the
very conflict of the two armies were represented
by the gestures and words of the seer.[1]

---

[1] Cf. Plutarch, *Caesar*, 47.

---

graphy, but remigis *was a marginal note, suggested by the story
in* Cic. Div. i. 68, *which somehow made its way into the text.*

XIX

Verba M. Varronis memoria digna ex *Satura*, quae inscribitur Περὶ Ἐδεσμάτων.

1 NON paucissimi sunt in quos potest convenire id
quod M. Varro dicit in Satura quae inscribitur
2 Περὶ Ἐδεσμάτων. Verba haec sunt: "Si, quantum
operae sumpsisti ut tuus pistor bonum faceret
panem, eius duodecimam philosophiae dedisses, ipse
bonus iampridem esses factus. Nunc illum qui
norunt volunt emere milibus centum, te qui novit
nemo centussis."

XX

Notata quaedam de Euripidis poetae genere, vita, moribus
deque eiusdem fine vitae.

1 EURIPIDI poetae matrem Theopompus agrestia
2 olera vendentem victum quaesisse dicit. Patri
autem eius nato illo responsum est a Chaldaeis eum
puerum, cum adolevisset, victorem in certaminibus
3 fore; id ei puero fatum esse. Pater interpretatus
athletam debere esse, roborato exercitatoque filii sui
corpore, Olympiam certaturum eum inter athletas
pueros deduxit. Ac primo quidem in certamen per
ambiguam aetatem receptus non est, post Eleusino
et Theseo certamine pugnavit et coronatus est.

---

[1] Fr. 404, Bücheler.   [2] *F.H.G.* i. 294.
[3] He was too old for the boys' races.
[4] Athletic games in connection with the Eleusinian
mysteries.

XIX

Memorable words of Marcus Varro, from the satire entitled
Περὶ Ἐδεσμάτων.

THERE are not a few to whom that may apply which
is said by Marcus Varro in his satire entitled Περὶ
Ἐδεσμάτων, or *On Eatables.* His words are these:[1]
" If you had given to philosophy a twelfth part of
the effort which you spent in making your baker give
you good bread, you would long since have become
a good man. As it is, those who know him are
willing to buy *him* at a hundred thousand sesterces,
while no one who knows you would take *you* at a
hundred."

XX

Certain facts about the birth, life and character of the poet
Euripides, and about the end of his life.

THEOPOMPUS says[2] that the mother of the poet
Euripides made a living by selling country produce.
Furthermore, when Euripides was born, his father
was assured by the astrologers that the boy, when
he grew up, would be victor in the games; for that
was his destiny. His father, understanding this to
mean that he ought to be an athlete, exercised and
strengthened his son's body and took him to Olympia
to contend among the wrestlers. And at first he
was not admitted to the contest because of his
time of life,[3] but afterwards he engaged in the
Eleusinian[4] and Thesean[5] contests and won crowns.

[5] A festival held at Athens in the autumn in the month
Pyanepsion, in honour of Theseus.

4 Mox a corporis cura ad excolendi animi studium
transgressus, auditor fuit physici Anaxagorae et Pro-
dici rhetoris, in morali autem philosophia Socratis.
Tragoediam scribere natus annos duodeviginti
5 adortus est. Philochorus refert in insula Salamine
speluncam esse taetram et horridam, quam nos
vidimus, in qua Euripides tragoedias scriptitarit.
6 Mulieres fere omnes in maiorem modum exosus
fuisse dicitur, sive quod natura abhorruit a mulierum
coetu sive quod duas simul uxores habuerat, cum
id decreto ab Atheniensibus facto ius esset, quarum
7 matrimonii pertaedebat. Eius odii in mulieres
Aristophanes quoque meminit ἐν ταῖς προτέραις
Θεσμοφοριαζούσαις in his versibus:

Νῦν οὖν ἀπάσαισιν παραινῶ καὶ λέγω,
Τοῦτον κολάσαι τὸν ἄνδρα πολλῶν οὕνεκα.
Ἄγρια γὰρ ἡμᾶς, ὦ γυναῖκες, δρᾷ κακά,
Ἅτ’ ἐν ἀγρίοισι τοῖς[1] λαχάνοις αὐτὸς τραφείς.

8 Alexander autem Aetolus hos de Euripide versus
composuit:

Ὁ δ’ Ἀναξαγόρου τρόφιμος χαιοῦ στριφνὸς μὲν ἔμοιγε
προσειπεῖν,
Καὶ μισογέλως, καὶ τωθάζειν οὐδὲ παρ’ οἶνον μεμα-
θηκώς,
Ἀλλ’ ὅ τι γράψαι, τοῦτ’ ἂν μέλιτος καὶ Σειρήνων
ἐτετεύχει.

9 Is cum in Macedonia apud Archelaum regem esset
upereturque eo rex familiariter, rediens nocte ab
eius cena, canibus a quodam aemulo inmissis di-

[1] τοῖς omitted by codd. of Aristoph.

[1] F.H.G. i. 412.
[2] These words are probably not part of the quotation.

Later, turning from attention to bodily exercise to the desire of training his mind, he was a pupil of the natural philosopher Anaxagoras and the rhetorician Prodicus, and, in moral philosophy, of Socrates. At the age of eighteen he attempted to write a tragedy. Philochorus relates[1] that there is on the island of Salamis a grim and gloomy cavern,[2] which I myself have seen, in which Euripides wrote tragedies.

He is said to have had an exceeding antipathy towards almost all women, either because he had a natural disinclination to their society, or because he had had two wives at the same time (since that was permitted by a decree passed by the Athenians) and they had made wedlock hateful to him. Aristophanes also notices his antipathy to women in the first edition of the *Thesmophoriazousae* in these verses :[3]

Now then I urge and call on all our sex
This man to punish for his many crimes.
For on us, women, he brings bitter woes,
Himself brought up 'mid bitter garden plants.

But Alexander the Aetolian composed the following lines about Euripides :[4]

The pupil of stout Anaxagoras,
Of churlish speech and gloomy, ne'er has learned
To jest amid the wine ; but what he wrote
Might honey and the Sirens well have known.

When Euripides was in Macedonia at the court of Archelaus, and had become an intimate friend of the king, returning home one night from a dinner with the monarch he was torn by dogs, which were set

---

[3] 453 ff.
[4] *Anal. Alex.* p. 247, Meineke.

laceratus est et ex his vulneribus mors secuta est.
10 Sepulchrum autem eius et memoriam Macedones
eo dignati sunt honore, ut in gloriae quoque loco
praedicarent : οὔποτ᾽ ἂν¹ σὸν μνῆμα, Εὐρίπιδες, ὄλοιτό
που, quod egregius poeta morte obita sepultus in
eorum terra foret. Quamobrem cum legati ad eos
ab Atheniensibus missi petissent ut ossa Athenas
in terram illius patriam permitterent transferri,
maximo consensu Macedones in ea re deneganda
perstiterunt.

XXI

Quod a poetis Iovis filii prudentissimi humanissimique,
Neptuni autem ferocissimi et inhumanissimi traduntur.

1 PRAESTANTISSIMOS virtute, prudentia, viribus² Iovis
filios poetae appellaverunt, ut Aeacum et Minoa
et Sarpedona; ferocissimos et inmanes et alienos ab
omni humanitate, tamquam e mari genitos, Neptuni
filios dixerunt, Cyclopa et Cercyona et Scirona et
Laestrygonas.

XXII

Historia de Sertorio, egregio duce, deque astu eius com-
menticiisque simulamentis quibus ad barbaros milites
continendos conciliandosque sibi utebatur.

1 SERTORIUS, vir acer egregiusque dux, et utendi³
2 regendique exercitus peritus fuit. Is in temporibus

---

¹ ἂν added by Capps.
² viribus, ω ; moribus, Kronenberg.
³ exacuendi or excitandi suggested by Hosius ; dux
educendi, TY.

---

¹ He died in 406 B.C. ; according to another version of the
story it was a band of women who tore him to pieces. Both
108

upon him by a rival of his, and death resulted from
his wounds.[1] The Macedonians treated his tomb
and his memory with such honour that they used to
proclaim : " Never, Euripides, shall thy monument
perish," also by way of self-glorification, because the
distinguished poet had met his death and been
buried in their land. Therefore when envoys, sent
to them by the Athenians, begged that they should
allow his bones to be moved to Athens, his native
land, the Macedonians unanimously persisted in
refusing.

XXI

That by the poets the sons of Jupiter are represented as most
wise and refined, but those of Neptune as very haughty
and rude.

THE poets have called the sons of Jupiter most
excellent in worth, wisdom and strength, for example
Aeacus, Minos and Sarpedon ; the sons of Neptune,
the Cyclops, Cercyon, Sciron, and the Laestrygonians,
they said, were most haughty and cruel, and strangers
to all refinement, as being sprung from the sea.

XXII

A story of the distinguished leader Sertorius ; of his cunning,
and of the clever devices which he used to control and
conciliate his barbarian soldiers.

SERTORIUS, a brave man and a distinguished
general, was skilled in using and commanding an
army. In times of great difficulty he would lie to

tales are of doubtful authenticity ; the one told by Gellius
appears also in Athenaeus xiii. 597, but is denied in verses
preserved in Suidas, s.v. ὑπαίμεκε.

difficillimis et mentiebatur ad milites, si mendacium
prodesset, et litteras compositas pro veris legebat et
somnium simulabat et falsas religiones conferebat, si
quid istae res eum apud militum animos adiuvabant.
3,4 Illud adeo Sertori nobile est: Cerva alba eximiae
pulchritudinis et vivacissimae celeritatis a Lusitano
5 ei quodam dono data est. Hanc sibi oblatam
divinitus et instinctam Dianae numine conloqui
secum monereque et docere quae utilia factu essent,
persuadere omnibus institit ac, si quid durius videbatur quod imperandum militibus foret, a cerva
sese monitum praedicabat. Id cum dixerat, uni-
6 versi, tamquam si deo, libentes parebant. Ea cerva
quodam die, cum incursio esset hostium nuntiata,
festinatione ac tumultu consternata in fugam se
prorupit atque in palude proxima delituit et frustra [1]
7 requisita perisse credita est. Neque multis diebus
post inventam esse cervam Sertorio nuntiatur.
8 Tum qui nuntiaverat iussit tacere, ac ne cui palam
diceret interminatus est, praecepitque ut eam postero
die repente in eum locum in quo ipse cum amicis
esset inmitteret. Admissis deinde amicis postridie,
visum sibi esse ait in quiete cervam quae perisset
ad se reverti et, ut prius consuerat, quod opus esset
9 facto praedicere ; tum servo quod imperaverat
significat, cerva emissa in cubiculum Sertorii intro-
rupit, clamor factus et orta admiratio est.

---

[1] frustra, *Cornelissen* ; postea, *ω*.

his soldiers, if a lie was advantageous, he would read forged letters for genuine ones, feign dreams, and resort to fictitious omens, if such devices helped him to keep up the spirits of his soldiers. The following story about Sertorius is particularly well known : A white hind of remarkable beauty, agility and swiftness was given him as a present by a man of Lusitania. He tried to convince everyone that the animal had been given him by the gods, and that inspired by the divine power of Diana, it talked with him, and showed and indicated what it was expedient to do ; and if any command which he felt obliged to give his soldiers seemed unusually difficult, he declared that he had been advised by the hind. When he said that, all willingly rendered obedience, as if to a god. One day, when an advance of the enemy had been reported, the hind, alarmed by the hurry and confusion, took to flight and hid in a neighbouring marsh, and after being sought for in vain was believed to have perished. Not many days later, word was brought to Sertorius that the hind had been found. Then he bade the one who had brought the news to keep silence, threatening him with punishment in case he revealed the matter to anyone ; and he ordered him suddenly on the following day to let the animal into the place where he himself was with his friends. Then, next day, having called in his friends, he said that he had dreamed that the lost hind had returned to him, and after its usual manner had told him what ought to be done. Thereupon he signed to the slave to do what he had ordered ; the hind was let loose and burst into Sertorius' room, amid shouts of amazement.

Eaque hominum barbarorum credulitas Sertorio
10 in magnis rebus magno usui fuit. Memoria prodita
est, ex his nationibus quae cum Sertorio faciebant,
cum multis proeliis superatus esset, neminem
umquam ab eo descivisse, quamquam id genus
hominum esset mobilíssimum.

XXIII

De aetatibus historicorum nobilium, Hellanici, Herodoti, Thucydidis.

1 HELLANICUS, Herodotus, Thucydides, historiae
scriptores, in isdem fere temporibus laude ingenti
floruerunt et non nimis longe distantibus fuerunt
2 aetatibus. Nam Hellanicus initio belli Pelopon-
nesiaci fuisse quinque et sexaginta annos natus
videtur, Herodotus tres et quinquaginta, Thucydides
quadraginta. Scriptum est hoc in libro undecimo
Pamphilae.

XXIV

Quid Vulcacius Sedigitus, in libro quem *De Poetis* scripsit, de comicis Latinis iudicarit.

1 SEDIGITUS in libro quem scripsit *De Poetis,* quid
de his sentiat qui comoedias fecerunt, et quem ex
omnibus praestare ceteris putet, ac deinceps quo
quemque in loco et honore ponat, his versibus suis
demonstrat:

Multós incertos cértare hanc rem vídimus,
Palmám poetae cómico cui déferant.
Eum méo iudicio errórem dissolvám tibi,
Ut, cóntra si quis séntiat, nihil séntiat.

---

[1] In 413 B.C.

This credulity of the barbarians was very helpful to Sertorius in important matters. It is recorded that of those tribes which acted with Sertorius, although he was defeated in many battles, not one ever deserted him, although that race of men is most inconstant.

XXIII

Of the age of the famous historians, Hellanicus, Herodotus and Thucydides.

HELLANICUS, Herodotus, and Thucydides, writers of history, enjoyed great glory at almost the same time, and did not differ very greatly in age. For Hellanicus seems to have been sixty-five years old at the beginning of the Peloponnesian war,[1] Herodotus fifty-three, Thucydides forty. This is stated in the eleventh book of Pamphila.[2]

XXIV

Vulcacius Sedigitus' canon of the Latin writers of comedy, from the book which he wrote *On Poets*.

SEDIGITUS, in the book which he wrote *On Poets*, shows in the following verses of his[3] what he thought of those who wrote comedies, which one he thinks surpasses all the rest, and then what rank and honour he gives to each of them:

This question many doubtfully dispute,
Which comic poet they'd award the palm.
This doubt my judgment shall for you resolve;
If any differ from me, senseless he.

[2] *F.H.G.* iii. 521. 7 ; cf. xv. 17. 3, above.
[3] Frag. 1, Bährens.

Caecílio palmam Státio do mímico.
Plautús secundus fácile exuperat céteros.
Dein Naévius, qui férvet, pretio in tértiost.
Si erít, quod quarto détur, dabitur Lícinio.
Post ínsequi Licínium facio Atílium.
In séxto consequétur hos Teréntius,
Turpílius septimúm, Trabea octavum óptinet,
Nonó loco esse fácile facio Lúscium.
Decimum áddo causa antíquitatis Énnium.

XXV

De verbis quibusdam novis, quae in Gnaei Mati *Mimiambis*
offenderamus.

1   CN. MATIUS, vir eruditus, in *Mimiambis* suis non
absurde neque absone finxit "recentatur" pro eo,
quod Graeci dicunt ἀνανεοῦται, id est "denuo nascitur
atque iterum fit recens." Versus, in quibus hoc
verbum est, hi sunt:

Iam iam albicascit Phoebus et recentatur
Commune lumen hominibus[1] voluptatis.[2]

2   Idem Matius in isdem *Mimiambis* edulcare dicit,
quod est 'dulcius reddere,' in his versibus:

Quapropter edulcare convenit vitam
Curasque acerbas sensibus gubernare.

[1] do mimico, *J. Gronor*; do cominico, x²; do comico, *No.*
ii, x².
[2] et voluptatis, ω.

---

[1] The principle on which the ranking was done is a disputed question—the amount of originality, that of πάθος, and

First place I give Caecilius Statius.
Plautus holds second rank without a peer;
Then Naevius third, for passion and for fire.
If fourth there be, be he Licinius.
I place Atilius next, after Licinius.
These let Terentius follow, sixth in rank.
Turpilius seventh, Trabea eighth place holds.
Ninth palm I gladly give to Luscius,
To Ennius tenth, as bard of long ago.[1]

XXV

Of certain new words which I had met in the *Mimiambics* of
Gnaeus Matius.

GNAEUS MATIUS, a learned man, in his *Mimiambics*
properly and fitly coined the word *recentatur* for the
idea expressed by the Greek ἀναιεοῦται, that is "it
is born again and is again made new." The lines in
which the word occurs are these:[2]

E'en now doth Phoebus gleam, again is born
   (*recentatur*)
The common light to joys of mortal men.

Matius too, in the same *Mimiambics*, says *edulcare*,
meaning "to sweeten," in these lines:[3]

And therefore it is fit to sweeten (*edulcare*) life,
And bitter cares with wisdom to control.

personal feeling have been suggested. Vulcacius lived about
130 B.C. He is cited by Suetonius, *v. Ter.* ii, iv, v (*L.C.L.* ii,
pp. 456, 458, 462).
   [2] Frag. 9, Bährens.
   [3] Frag. 10, Bährens.

XXVI

Quibus verbis Aristoteles philosophus definierit syllogismum ;
eiusque definitionis interpretamentum verbis Latinis
factum.

1 ARISTOTELES, quid "syllogismus" esset, his versibus
definivit : Λόγος, ἐν   τεθέντων τινῶν, ἕτερόν τι τῶν
2 κειμένων ἐξ ἀνάγκης συμβαίνει διὰ τῶν κειμένων. Eius
definitionis non videbatur habere incommode inter-
pretatio facta hoc modo : "Syllogismus est oratio, in
qua, consensis quibusdam et concessis, aliud quid
quam quae concessa sunt, per ea quae concessa
sunt, necessario conficitur."

XXVII

Quid sint "comitia calata," quid "curiata," quid "centuriata," quid "tributa," quid "concilium "; atque inibi
quaedam eiusdemmodi.

1 IN libro Laelii Felicis *Ad Q. Mucium* primo
scriptum est Labeonem scribere "calata" comitia
esse quae pro conlegio pontificum habentur, aut
2 regis aut flaminum inaugurandorum causa. Eorum
autem alia esse "curiata," alia "centuriata "; "curiata" per lictorem curiatum "calari," id est "con-
vocari," "centuriata " per cornicinem.

---

[1] *Topic.* i. 1, p. 100. 25.
[2] *Frag.* 1 ff., i. p. 70, Bremer.

XXVI

In what words the philosopher Aristotle defined a syllogism;
and an interpretation of his definition in Latin terms.

ARISTOTLE defines a syllogism in these lines:[1] "A
sentence in which, granted certain premises, something else than these premises necessarily follows as
the result of these premises." The following interpretation of this definition seemed to me fairly
good: "A syllogism is a sentence in which, certain
things being granted and accepted, something else
than that which was granted is necessarily established
through what was granted."

XXVII

The meaning of *comitia calata*, *curiata*, *centuriata*, and
tributa, and of *concilium*, and other related matters of the
same kind.

IN the first book of the work of Laelius Felix
addressed *To Quintus Mucius* it is said[2] that Labeo
wrote[3] that the *comitia calata*, or "convoked
assembly," was held on behalf of the college of
pontiffs for the purpose of installing the king[4] or
the flamens. Of these assemblies some were those
" of the curies ", others those " of the centuries ";
the former were called together (*calari* being used
in the sense of " convoke ") by the curiate lictor,
the latter by a hornblower.

[3] Frag. 22, Huschke; inc. 187, Bremer.
[4] That is, the *rex sacrorum*; see note on x. 15. 21.

3   Isdem comitiis, quae "calata" appellari diximus,
et sacrorum detestatio et testamenta fieri solebant.
Tria enim genera testamentorum fuisse accepimus:
unum, quod calatis comitiis in populi contione fieret,
alterum in procinctu, cum viri ad proelium faciendum
in aciem vocabantur, tertium per familiae emancipa-
tionem, cui aes et libra adhiberetur.

4   In eodem Laeli Felicis libro haec scripta sunt:
"Is qui non[1] universum populum, sed partem
aliquam adesse iubet, non 'comitia,' sed 'concilium'
edicere debet.   Tribuni autem neque advocant
patricios neque ad eos referre ulla de re possunt.
Ita ne 'leges' quidem proprie, sed 'plebisscita'
appellantur quae tribunis plebis ferentibus accepta
sunt, quibus rogationibus ante patricii non tene-
bantur, donec Q. Hortensius dictator legem tulit, ut
eo iure quod plebs statuisset omnes Quirites teneren-

5   tur."   Item n eodem libro hoc scriptum est: "Cum
ex generibus hominum suffragium feratur, 'curiata'
comitia esse, cum ex censu et aetate 'centuriata,'
cum ex regionibus et locis, 'tributa'; centuriata
autem comitia intra pomerium fieri nefas esse, quia
exercitum extra urbem imperari oporteat, intra
urbem imperari ius non sit.   Propterea centuriata

---

[1] non ut, *Q.*

---

[1] See Mommsen, *Staatsr.* iii, p. 307, n. 2.
[2] See note on xv. 13. 11.   [3] In 287 B.C.
[4] The *comitia curiata* were organized on the basis of the
thirty *curiae* of the three original Roman tribes.   These

In that same assembly, which we have said was
called *calata*, or " convoked," wills were customarily
made and sacrifices annulled. For we learn that
there were three kinds of wills : one which was
made in the " convoked assembly " before the collected people, a second on the battle-field,[1] when the
men were called into line for the purpose of fighting,
a third the symbolic sale of a householder's property
by means of the coin and balance.[2]

In the same book of Laelius Felix this is written :
" One who orders a part of the people to assemble,
but not all the people, ought to announce a council
rather than an assembly. Moreover, tribunes do
not summon the patricians, nor may they refer any
question to them. Therefore bills which are passed
on the initiative of the tribunes of the commons are
properly called *plebiscita*, or 'decrees of the commons,' rather than 'laws.' In former times the
patricians were not bound by such decrees until the
dictator Quintus Hortensius passed a law, providing
that all the Quirites should be bound by whatever
enactment the commons should pass." [3] It is also
written in the same book : " When voting is done
according to families of men,[4] the assembly is called
' curiate ' ; when it is according to property and age,
' centuriate ' ; when according to regions and locali-
ties, ' tribal.' Further it impious for the assembly
of the centuries to be held within the pomerium,
because the army must be summoned outside of the
city, and it is not lawful for it to be summoned
within the city. Therefore it was customary for the

curiae included the patrician *gentes*, which, before the time
of the military assembly (*comitia centuriata*) attributed to
Servius Tullius, alone had the full rights of citizenship.

in campo Martio haberi exercitumque imperari
praesidii causa solitum, quoniam populus esset in
suffragiis ferendis occupatus."

XXVIII

Quod erravit Cornelius Nepos, cum scripsit Ciceronem tres
et viginti annos natum causam pro Sexto Roscio dixisse.

1 CORNELIUS NEPOS et rerum memoriae non indiligens
et M. Ciceronis ut qui maxime amicus familiaris
2 fuit. Atque is tamen, in primo librorum quos de
vita illius composuit, errasse videtur, cum eum
scripsit tres et viginti annos natum primum causam
iudicii publici egisse Sextumque Roscium parricidii
3 reum defendisse. Dinumeratis quippe annis a Q.
Caepione et Q. Serrano, quibus consulibus ante diem
tertium Nonas Ianuar. M. Cicero natus est, ad M.
Tullium et Cn. Dolabellam quibus consulibus causam
privatam *Pro Quinctio* apud Aquilium Gallum iudicem
dixit, sex et viginti anni reperiuntur. Neque
dubium est quin post annum quam *Pro Quinctio*
dixerat, Sex. Roscium reum parricidii defenderit,
annos iam septem atque viginti natus, L. Sulla
Felice II. Q. Metello Pio consulibus.
4 In qua re etiam Fenestellam errasse Pedianus
Asconius animadvertit, quod eum scripserit sexto
vicesimo aetatis anno pro Sex. Roscio dixisse.
5 Longior autem Nepotis quam Fenestellae error est,
nisi quis vult in animum inducere Nepotem, studio

---

[1] Frag. 1, Peter[2].   [2] January 3, 106 B.C.
[3] p. xv, Kiessling and Schöll.   [4] Frag. 17, Peter[2].

assembly of the centuries to be held in the field of Mars, and the army to be summoned there for purposes of defence while the people were busy casting their votes."

XXVIII

That Cornelius Nepos was in error when he wrote that Cicero defended Sextus Roscius at the age of twenty-three.

CORNELIUS NEPOS was a careful student of records and one of Marcus Cicero's most intimate friends. Yet in the first book of his *Life of Cicero* he seems to have erred in writing[1] that Cicero made his first plea in a public trial at the age of twenty-three years, defending Sextus Roscius, who was charged with murder. For if we count the years from Quintus Caepio and Quintus Serranus, in whose consulship Cicero was born on the third day before the Nones of January,[2] to Marcus Tullius and Gnaeus Dolabella, in whose consulate he pleaded a private case *In Defence of Quinctius* before Aquilius Gallus as judge, the result is twenty-six years. And there is no doubt that he defended Sextus Roscius on a charge of murder the year after he spoke *In Defence of Quinctius*; that is, at the age of twenty-seven, in the consulship of Lucius Sulla Felix and Metellus Pius, the former for a second time.

Asconius Pedianus has noted[3] that Fenestella also made a mistake in regard to this matter, in writing[4] that he pleaded for Sextus Roscius in the twenty-sixth year of his age. But the mistake of Nepos is greater than that of Fenestella, unless anyone is inclined to believe that Nepos, led by a

amoris et amicitiae adductum, amplificandae admirationis gratia quadriennium suppressisse, ut M. Cicero orationem florentissimam dixisse *Pro Roscio* admodum adulescens videretur.

6 Illud adeo ab utriusque oratoris studiosis animadversum et scriptum est, quod Demosthenes et Cicero pari aetate inlustrissimas primas[1] orationes in causis[2] dixerunt, alter Κατὰ 'Ανδροτίωνος et Κατὰ Τιμοκράτους septem et viginti annos natus, alter anno minor *Pro P. Quinctio* septimoque et vicesimo *Pro Sex. Roscio.*

7 Vixerunt quoque non nimis numerum annorum diversum; alter tres et sexaginta annos, Demosthenes sexaginta.

XXIX

Quali figura orationis et quam nova L. Piso annalium scriptor usus sit.

1 DUAE istae in loquendo figurae notae satis usitataeque sunt : " mihi nomen est Iulius " et " mihi nomen

2 est Iulio "; tertiam figuram novam hercle repperi apud Pisonem in secundo *Annalium.* Verba Pisonis haec sunt: " L. Tarquinium, collegam suum, quia Tarquinio nomine esset, metuere ; eumque orat uti sua voluntate Roma concedat." " Quia Tarquinio," inquit, " nomine esset " ; hoc proinde est, tamquam si ego dicam : " mihi nomen est Iulium."

---

[1] primas *suggested by Hosius, omitted in* ω.
[2] causis privatis, *Hertz.*

feeling of friendship and regard, suppressed four years in order to increase our admiration of Cicero, by making it appear that he delivered his brilliant speech *In Defence of Roscius* when he was a very young man.

This also has been noted and recorded by the admirers of both orators, that Demosthenes and Cicero delivered their first brilliant speeches in the courts at the same age, the former *Against Androtion* and *Against Timocrates* at the age of twenty-seven, the latter when a year younger *In Defence of Quinctius* and at twenty-seven *In Defence of Sextus Roscius.* Also, the number of years which they lived did not differ very greatly; Cicero died at sixty-three, Demosthenes at sixty.[1]

XXIX

A new form of expression used by Lucius Piso, the writer of annals.

The two following modes of saying "my name is Julius" are common and familiar: *mihi nomen est Iulius* and *mihi nomen est Iulio.* I have actually found a third, and new, form in Piso, in the second book of his *Annals.* His words are these:[2] "They feared his colleague, Lucius Tarquinius, because he had the Tarquinian name; and he begged him to leave Rome of his own free will." [3] "Because," says he, "he had the Tarquinian name"; this is as if I should say *mihi nomen est Iulium,* or "I have the Julian name."

XXX

Vehiculum quod "petorritum" appellatur, cuiatis linguae
vocabulum sit, Graecae an Gallicae.

1 Qui ab alio genere vitae detriti iam et retorridi
ad litterarum disciplinas serius adeunt, si forte idem
sunt garruli natura et subargutuli, oppido quam fiunt
2 in litterarum ostentatione inepti et frivoli. Quod
genus profecto ille homo est, qui de "petorritis"
3 nuper argutissimas nugas dixit. Nam cum quaereretur, "petorritum" quali forma vehiculum cuiatis-
que linguae vocabulum esset, et faciem vehiculi
ementitus est longe alienam falsamque et vocabulum
Graecum[1] esse dixit atque adsignificare volucres
rotas interpretatus est, commutataque una littera
"petorritum" esse dictum volebat quasi "petorro-
4 tum"; scriptum etiam hoc esse a Valerio Probo
contendit.
5 Ego, cum Probi multos admodum *Commentationum*
libros adquisierim, neque scriptum in his inveni nec
usquam alioqui Probum scripsisse credo; "petorri-
6 tum" enim est non ex Graecia dimidiatum, sed
totum Transalpibus;[2] nam est vox Gallica. Id
7 scriptum est in libro M. Varronis quarto decimo
Rerum Divinarum, quo in loco Varro, cum de "petor-
rito" dixisset, esse id verbum Gallicum, "lanceam"
quoque dixit non Latinum, set Hispanicum verbum
esse.

---

[1] semigraecum, *Damsté.*
[2] *For* Transalpibus *cf. Pliny, N.H.* iii. 124 (*Heraeus*);
totum ortum trans Alpibus, *Hertz ;* totum transalpinum, *J.
Gronov.*

---

[1] Making a hybrid word, from πέτομαι, "fly," and *rota*.
See crit. note 1.
[2] Frag. 108, Agahd.

XXX

Whether the word *petorritum*, applied to a vehicle, is Greek
or Gallic.

THOSE who approach the study of letters late in
life, after they are worn out and exhausted by some
other occupation, particularly if they are garrulous
and of only moderate keenness, make themselves
exceedingly ridiculous and silly by displaying their
would-be knowledge. To this class that man surely
belongs, who lately talked fine-spun nonsense about
petorrita, or "four-wheeled wagons." For when the
question was asked, what form of vehicle the *petorritum* was, and from what language the word came,
he falsely described a form of vehicle very unlike
the real one; he also declared that the name was
Greek and interpreted it as meaning "flying wheels," [1]
maintaining that *petorritum* was formed by the change
of a single letter from *petorrotum*, and that this form
was actually used by Valerius Probus.

When I had got together many copies of the
Commentaries of Probus, I did not find that spelling
in them, and I do not believe that Probus used it
anywhere else. For *petorritum* is not a hybrid word
derived in part from the Greek, but the entire word
belongs to the people across the Alps; for it is a
Gallic word. It is found in the fourteenth book of
Marcus Varro's *Divine Antiquities*, where Varro, speaking of *petorritum*, says [2] that it is a Gallic term. [3] He
also says that *lancea*, or "lance," is not a Latin, but a
Spanish word.

[3] Gellius is right; *petorrita*, like several other words
connected with horses and carriages, is borrowed from the
Gallic. In Celtic, as also in Oscan and Umbrian, Latin *qu* is
represented by *p*; hence *petor* or *petora* = *quattuor*.

XXXI

Quae verba legaverint Rodii ad hostium ducem Demetrium,
cum ab eo obsiderentur, super illa incluta Ialysi imagine.

1 RODUM insulam celebritatis antiquissimae oppidum-
que in ea pulcherrimum ornatissimumque obsidebat
obpugnabatque Demetrius, dux aetatis suae inclutus,
cui a peritia disciplinaque faciendi obsidii machina-
rumque sollertia ad capienda oppida repertarum
2 cognomentum Πολιορκητής fuit. Tum ibi in obsidione aedes quasdam publice factas, quae extra urbis
muros cum parvo praesidio erant, adgredi et vastare
atque absumere igni parabat.
3 In eis aedibus erat memoratissima illa imago Ialysi, Protogenis manu facta, inlustris pictoris, cuius
operis pulchritudinem praestantiamque ira percitus
4 Rodiis invidebat. Mittunt Rodii ad Demetrium
legatos cum his verbis: "Quae, malum," inquiunt,
"ratiost ut tu imaginem istam velis incendio aedium
facto disperdere? Nam si nos omnes superaveris et
oppidum hoc totum ceperis, imagine quoque illa
integra et incolumi per victoriam potieris; sin vero
nos vincere obsidendo nequiveris, petimus consideres
ne turpe tibi sit, quia non potueris bello Rodios vin-
5 cere, bellum cum Protogene mortuo gessisse." Hoc
ubi ex legatis audivit, obpugnatione desita et imagini
et civitati pepercit.

---

[1] Grandson of Helios, the Sungod, and brother of Lindus
and Cameirus, with whom he possessed the island of Rhodes.
The city of Ialysus on that island was named from him as its
founder.
[2] A famous painter of Caunus in Caria, a contemporary of

XXXI

A message sent by the Rhodians about the celebrated picture of Ialysus to Demetrius, leader of the enemy, at the time when they were besieged by him.

THE island of Rhodes, of ancient fame, and the fairest and richest town in it were besieged and assaulted by Demetrius, a famous general of his time, who was surnamed Πολιορκητής, or "the taker of cities," from his skill and training in conducting sieges and the cleverness of the engines which he devised for the capture of towns. On that occasion he was preparing in the course of the siege to attack, pillage and burn a public building without the walls of the town, which had only a weak garrison.

In this building was that famous picture of Ialysus,[1] the work of Protogenes,[2] the distinguished painter; and incited by anger against them, Demetrius begrudged the Rhodians the beauty and fame of that work of art. The Rhodians sent envoys to Demetrius with this message: "What on earth is your reason for wishing to set fire to that building and destroy our painting? For if you overcome all of us and take this whole town, through your victory you will gain possession also of that painting, uninjured and entire; but if you are unable to overcome us by your siege, we beg you to take thought lest it bring shame upon you, because you could not conquer the Rhodians in war, to have waged war with the dead Protogenes." Upon hearing this message from the envoys, Demetrius abandoned the siege and spared both the picture and the city.

Apelles, flourished about 332 B.C. See Pliny, *N.H.* xxxv. 101 ff.

BOOK XVI

LIBER SEXTUS DECIMUS

I

Verba Musoni philosophi Graeca, digna atque utilia audiri
observarique ; eiusdemque utilitatis sententia a M. Catone
multis ante annis Numantiae ad equites dicta.

1 ADULESCENTULI cum etiamtum in scholis essemus,
ἐνθυμημάτιον hoc Graecum quod adposui dictum esse
a Musonio philosopho audiebamus et, quoniam vere
atque luculente dictum verbisque est brevibus et rotundis vinctum, perquam libenter memineramus :

2 Ἄν τι πράξῃς καλὸν μετὰ πόνου, ὁ μὲν πόνος οἴχεται, τὸ
δὲ καλὸν μένει· ἄν τι ποιήσῃς αἰσχρὸν μετὰ ἡδονῆς, τὸ
μὲν ἡδὺ οἴχεται, τὸ δὲ αἰσχρὸν μένει.

3 Postea istam ipsam sententiam in Catonis oratione, quam dixit *Numantiae apud Equites,* positam
legimus.   Quae etsi laxioribus paulo longioribusque
verbis comprehensa est praequam illud Graecum
quod diximus, quoniam tamen prior tempore anti-

4 quiorque est, venerabilior videri debet.   Verba ex
oratione haec sunt : " Cogitate cum animis vestris,
si quid vos per laborem recte feceritis, labor ille a
vobis cito recedet, bene factum a vobis, dum vivitis,
non abscedet ; sed si qua per voluptatem nequiter
feceritis, voluptas cito abibit, nequiter factum illud
apud vos semper manebit."

---

[1] p. 273, Peerlkamp.

BOOK XVI

I

A saying of Musonius, the Greek philosopher, which is of practical value and worth hearing and bearing in mind; and a remark of equal value made by Marcus Cato many years before to the knights at Numantia.

WHEN I was still young and a schoolboy, I heard that this Greek sentiment which I have subjoined was uttered by the philosopher Musonius, and since it is a true and brilliant saying, expressed briefly and roundly, I very willingly committed it to memory: [1] "If you accomplish anything noble with toil, the toil passes, but the noble deed endures. If you do anything shameful with pleasure, the pleasure passes, but the shame endures."

Later, I read that same sentiment in the speech of Marcus Cato which he delivered *At Numantia to the Knights.* Although it is expressed somewhat loosely and diffusely compared with the Greek which I have given, yet, since it is prior in time and more ancient, it ought to seem worthy of greater respect. The words in the speech are as follows: [2] "Bear in mind, that if through toil you accomplish a good deed, that toil will quickly pass from you, the good deed will not leave you so long as you live; but if through pleasure you do anything dishonourable, the pleasure will quickly pass away, that dishonourable act will remain with you for ever."

[2] p. 38, 11, Jordan.

131

II

Cuiusmodi sit lex apud dialecticos percontandi disserendique ;
et quae sit eius legis reprehensio.

1 LEGEM esse aiunt disciplinae dialecticae, si de
quapiam re quaeratur disputeturque atque ibi quid
rogere ut respondeas, tum ne amplius quid dicas
quam id solum quod es rogatus aut aias aut neges ;
eamque legem qui non servent, et aut plus aut aliter
quam sunt rogati respondeant, existumantur indoc-
2 tique[1] esse disputandique morem atque rationem
non tenere. Hoc quidem quod dicunt in plerisque
3 disputationibus procul dubio fieri oportet. Inde-
finitus namque inexplicabilisque sermo fiet, nisi
interrogationibus responsionibusque simplicibus fuerit
determinatus.

4 Sed enim esse quaedam videntur, in quibus si
breviter et ad id quod rogatus fueris respondeas,
5 capiare. Nam si quis his verbis interroget : " Postulo
uti respondeas desierisne facere adulterium an non,"
utrumcumque dialectica lege responderis, sive aias seu
neges, haerebis in captione, tamquam si te dicas adul-
6 terum quam si neges ;[2] nam qui facere non desinit,
7 non id necessario etiam fecit. Falsa igitur est
species istius captionis et nequaquam procedere ad
id potest, ut conligi concludique possit eum facere
8 adulterium qui se negaverit facere desisse. Quid
autem legis istius propugnatores in illa captiuncula
facient, in qua haerere eos necessum est, si nihil
amplius quam quod interrogati erunt responderint ?

---

[1] indoctique, *QZON* ; indocti, IIQ[2] ; rudes indoctique *N*[2] ;
indocti inscitieque, *sugg. by Hosius* (*cf.* xix. 8. 12).

[2] tam . . . neges, *σ* ; tamquam si te dicas adulterum
. . . negent, *MSS.*

II

The nature of the rule of the logicians in disputation and declamation, and the defect of that rule.

THEY say that it is a rule of the dialectic art, that if there is inquiry and discussion of any subject, and you are called upon to answer a question which is asked, you should answer the question by a simple "yes" or "no." And those who do not observe that rule, but answer more than they were asked, or differently, are thought to be both uneducated and unobservant of the customs and laws of debate. As a matter of fact this dictum undoubtedly ought to be followed in very many debates. For a discussion will become endless and hopelessly involved, unless it is confined to simple questions and answers.

But there seem to be some discussions in which, if you answer what you are asked briefly and directly, you are caught in a trap. For if anyone should put a question in these words: "I ask you to tell me whether you have given up committing adultery or not," whichever way you answer according to this rule of debate, whether you say "yes" or "no," you will be caught in a dilemma, equally if you should say that you are an adulterer, or should deny it; for one who has not given up a thing has not of necessity ever done it. That then is a deceptive kind of catch-question, and can by no means lead to the inference and conclusion that he commits adultery who says that he has not given up doing it. But what will the defenders of that rule do in that dilemma, in which they must necessarily be caught, if they give a simple answer to the question? For

9 Nam, si ita ego istorum aliquem rogem : " Quicquid
non perdidisti habeasne an non habeas postulo ut
aias aut neges," utrumcumque breviter responderit,
10 capietur. Nam si habere [1] se negaverit quod non
perdidit, colligetur oculos eum non habere, quos
non perdidit ; sin vero habere se dixerit, colligetur
11 habere eum cornua, quae non perdidit. Rectius
igitur cautiusque ita respondebitur : " Quicquid
12 habui, id habeo, si id non perdidi." Sed huiuscemodi responsio non fit ex ea lege quam diximus ;
plus enim, quam quod rogatus est, respondet.
13 Propterea id quoque ad eam legem addi solet, non
esse captiosis interrogationibus respondendum.

III

Quanam ratione effici dixerit Erasistratus medicus, si cibus
forte deerit, ut tolerari aliquantisper inedia possit et
tolerari fames ; verbaque ipsa Erasistrati super ea re
scripta.

1 CUM Favorino Romae dies plerumque totos eramus
tenebatque animos nostros homo ille fandi dul-
cissimus atque eum, quoquo iret, quasi ex lingua
prorsum eius capti [2] prosequebamur ; ita sermonibus
2 usquequaque amoenissimis demulcebat. Tum ad
quendam aegrum cum isset visere nosque cum eo
una introissemus multaque ad medicos, qui tum
forte istic erant, valitudinis eius gratia oratione
Graeca dixisset, " Ac ne hoc quidem mirum," inquit,
" videri debet, quod, cum antehac semper edundi

----

[1] si non habere, *ω* ; non *deleted by Gruppe.*

if I should ask any one of them: "Do you, or do you not, have what you have not lost? I demand the answer 'yes' or no,'" whichever way he replies briefly, he will be caught. For if he says that he does not have what he has not lost, the conclusion will be drawn that he has no eyes, since he has not lost them; but if he says that he has it, it will be concluded that he has horns, because he has not lost them. Therefore it will be more cautious and more correct to reply as follows: "I have whatever I had, if I have not lost it." But an answer of that kind is not made in accordance with the rule which we have mentioned; for more is answered than was asked. Therefore this proviso also is commonly added to the rule, that one need not answer catch-questions.

III

By what means Erasistratus, the physician, said that one could do for a time without eating, if food chanced to be lacking, and endure hunger; and his own words on that subject.

I often spent whole days in Rome with Favorinus. His delightful conversation held my mind enthralled, and I attended him wherever he went, as if actually taken prisoner by his eloquence; to such a degree did he constantly delight me with his most agreeable discourse. Once when he had gone to visit a sick man, and I had entered with him, having conversed for some time in Greek about the man's illness with the physicians who chanced to be there at the time, he said: "This ought not to seem surprising either, that although previously he was always

---

² apti, *Stephanus.*

fuerit adpetens, nunc post imperatam inediam tridui
3 omnis eius adpetitio pristina elanguerit. Nam quod
Erasistratus scriptum," inquit, " reliquit propemodum verum est : esuritionem faciunt inanes paten-
tesque intestinorum fibrae et cava intus ventris ac
stomachi vacua et hiantia ; quae ubi aut cibo con-
plentur aut inanitate diutina contrahuntur et con-
vent, tunc loco, in quem cibus capitur, vel stipato
vel adducto, voluntas capiendi eius desiderandique
4 restinguitur." Scythas quoque ait eundem Erasistratum dicere, cum sit usus ut famem longius tole-
rent, fasceis ventrem strictissime circumligare. Ea
ventris conpressione esuritionem posse depelli creditum est.
5   Haec tum Favorinus multaque istiusmodi alia
6 adfabilissime dicebat, nos autem postea, cum librum
forte Erasistrati legeremus Διαιρέσεων primum, id
ipsum in eo libro, quod Favorinum audiebamus di-
7 cere, scriptum offendimus. Verba Erasistrati ad
eam rem pertinentia haec sunt : Ἐλογιζόμεθα οὖν
παρὰ τὴν ἰσχυρὰν σύμπτωσιν τῆς κοιλίας εἶναι τὴν
σφόδρα ἀσιτίαν· καὶ γὰρ τοῖς ἐπίπλεον ἀσιτοῦσιν κατὰ
προαίρεσιν ἐν τοῖς πρώτοις χρόνοις ἡ πεῖνα παρακολουθεῖ,
8 ὕστερον δὲ οὐκέτι. Deinde paululum infra : Εἰθισ-
μένοι δέ εἰσιν καὶ οἱ Σκύθαι, ὅταν διά τινα καιρὸν ἀναγ-
κάζωνται ἀσιτεῖν, ζώναις πλατείαις τὴν κοιλίαν διασφίγγειν,
ὡς τῆς πείνης αὐτοὺς ἧττον ἐνοχλούσης· σχεδὸν δὲ καὶ
ὅταν πλήρης κοιλία ᾖ, διὰ τὸ κένωμα ἐν αὐτῇ μηδὲν εἶναι,
διὰ τοῦτο οὐ πεινῶσιν, ὅταν δὲ σφόδρα συμπεπτωκυῖα ᾖ,
κένωμα οὐκ ἔχει.

---

[1] p. 193, Fuchs.

eager for food, now after an enforced fast of three days all his former appetite is lost. For what Erasistratus has written is pretty nearly true," said he, "that the empty and open fibres of the intestines, the hollowness of the belly within and the empty and yawning cavity of the stomach, cause hunger; but when these are either filled with food or are contracted and brought together by continued fasting, then, since the place into which the food is received is either filled or made smaller, the impulse to take food, or to crave it, is destroyed." He declared that Erasistratus also said that the Scythians too, when it was necessary for them to endure protracted hunger, bound a very tight bandage around their bellies. That by such compression of the belly it was believed that hunger could be prevented.

These things and many others of the kind Favorinus said most entertainingly on that occasion; but later, when I chanced to be reading the first book of Erasistratus' *Distinctions,* I found in that book the very passage which I had heard Favorinus quote.[1] The words of Erasistratus on the subject are as follows: "I reasoned therefore that the ability to fast for a long time is caused by strong compression of the belly; for with those who voluntarily fast for a long time, at first hunger ensues, but later it passes away." Then a little later: "And the Scythians also are accustomed, when on any occasion it is necessary to fast, to bind up the belly with broad belts, in the belief that the hunger thus troubles them less; and one may almost say too that when the stomach is full, men feel no hunger for the reason that there is no vacuity in it, and likewise when it is greatly compressed there is no vacuity."

9 In eodem libro Erasistratus vim quandam famis
non tolerabilem, quam Graeci βούλιμον appellant,
in diebus frigidissimis multo facilius accidere ait
quam cum serenum atque placidum est, atque eius
rei causas, cur is morbus in eo plerumque tempore
10 oriatur, nondum sibi esse compertas dicit. Verba
quibus id dicit, haec sunt : Ἄπορον δὲ καὶ δεόμενον
ἐπισκέψεως καὶ ἐπὶ τούτου καὶ ἐπὶ τῶν λοιπῶν βουλι-
μιώντων, διὰ τί ἐν τοῖς ψύχεσιν μᾶλλον τὸ σύμπτωμα
τοῦτο γίνεται ἢ ἐν ταῖς εὐδίαις ;

IV

Quo ritu quibusque verbis fetialis populi Romani bellum in-
dicere solitus sit his quibus populus bellum fieri iusserat ;
et item in quae verba conceptum fuerit iusiurandum de
furtis militaribus sanciendis ; et uti milites scripti intra
praedictum diem in loco certo frequentitarent, causis
quibusdam exceptis, propter quas id iusiurandum remitti
aecum esset.

1 CINCIUS in libro tertio *De Re Militari*, fetialem
populi Romani bellum indicentem hostibus telumque
in agrum eorum iacientem, hisce verbis uti scripsit :
" Quod populus Hermundulus hominesque populi
Hermunduli adversus populum Romanum bellum [1]
fecere deliqueruntque, quodque populus Romanus
cum populo Hermundulo hominibusque Hermundulis
bellum iussit, ob eam rem ego populusque Romanus
populo Hermundulo hominibusque Hermundulis
bellum dico facioque."
2 Item in libro eiusdem Cincii *De Re Militari*

[1] bellum *deleted by H. J. Müller and A. Schmidt.*

---

[1] Frag. 12, Huschke ; 2, Bremer.

In the same book Erasistratus declares that a kind of irresistibly violent hunger, which the Greeks call βούλιμος, or "ox-hunger," is much more apt to be felt on very cold days than when the weather is calm and pleasant, and that the reasons why this disorder prevails especially at such times have not yet become clear to him. The words which he uses are these: "It is unknown and requires investigation, both in reference to the case in question and in that of others who suffer from ' ox-hunger,' why this symptom appears rather on cold days than in warm weather."

IV

In what fashion and in what language the war-herald of the Roman people was accustomed to declare war upon those against whom the people had voted that war should be made; also in what words the oath relating to the prohibition and punishment of theft by the soldiers was couched; and how the soldiers that were enrolled were to appear at an appointed time and place, with some exceptional cases in which they might properly be freed from that oath.

CINCIUS writes in his third book *On Military Science*[1] that the war-herald of the Roman people, when he declared war on the enemy and hurled a spear into their territory, used the following words: " Whereas the Hermundulan people and the men of the Hermundulam people have made war against the Roman people and have transgressed against them, and whereas the Roman people has ordered war with the Hermundulan people and the men of the Hermundulans, therefore I and the Roman people declare and make war with the Hermundulan people and with the men of the Hermundulans."

Also in the fifth book of the same Cincius *On*

quinto ita scriptum est: " Cum dilectus antiquitus
fieret et milites scriberentur, iusiurandum eos tribunus militaris adigebat in verba haec (magistratus
verba):[1] 'C. Laelii C. fili consulis, L. Cornelii P.
fili consulis in exercitu, decemque milia passuum
prope, furtum non facies dolo malo solus neque cum
pluribus pluris nummi argentei in dies singulos;
extraque hastam, hastile, ligna, poma, pabulum,
utrem, follem, faculam si quid ibi inveneris sustulerisve quod tuum non erit, quod pluris nummi
argentei erit, uti tu ad C. Laelium C. filium consulem Luciumve Cornelium P. filium sive quem ad
uter eorum iusserit proferes, aut profitebere in triduo
proximo quidquid inveneris sustulerisve dolo[2] malo,
aut domino suo, cuium id censebis esse, reddes, uti
quod rectum factum esse voles.' "

3 " Militibus autem scriptis, dies praefiniebatur quo
die adessent et citanti consuli responderent; deinde
4 concipiebatur iusiurandum, ut adessent, his additis
exceptionibus: ' Nisi harunce quae causa erit: funus
familiare feriaeve denicales, quae non eius rei causa
in eum diem conlatae sint, quo is eo die minus ibi
esset, morbus sonticus auspiciumve quod sine pia-
culo praeterire non liceat, sacrificiumve anniver-

[1] magistratu (-us, Q[2]) verba, δ; in magistratu verba, OX;
in magistratu, N Π; *deleted by Hertz, see edit. maior*, ii, xci.
[2] dolo, *Aldus*; in dolo, ω.

[1] Frag. 13, Huschke; 2, Bremer.
[2] *feriae denicales* (from *de* and *nex*) are thus described by
Paul. Fest. p. 61, Linds.: *colebantur cum hominis mortui
causa familia purgatur. Graeci enim νέκυν mortuum dicunt.*
[3] See xx. 1. 27. It refers especially to epilepsy, also called
morbus comitialis, or "election disease," because if anyone

Military Science we read the following : [1] " When a
levy was made in ancient times and soldiers were
enrolled, the tribune of the soldiers compelled them
to take an oath in the following words dictated by
the magistrate : ' In the army of the consuls Gaius
Laelius, son of Gaius, and Lucius Cornelius, son of
Publius, and for ten miles around it, you will not
with malice aforethought commit a theft, either
alone or with others, of more than the value of a
silver sesterce in any one day.   And except for one
spear, a spearshaft, wood, fruit, fodder, a bladder,
a purse and a torch, if you find or carry off anything
there which is not your own and is worth more than
one silver sesterce, you will bring it to the consul
Gaius Laelius, son of Gaius, or to the consul Lucius
Cornelius, son of Publius, or to whomsoever either
of them shall appoint, or you will make known
within the next three days whatever you have
found or wrongfully carried off, or you will restore
it to him whom you suppose to be its rightful
owner, as you wish to do what is right.'

" Moreover, when soldiers had been enrolled, a day
was appointed on which they should appear and should
answer to the consul's summons ; then an oath was
taken, binding them to appear, with the addition
of the following exceptions : ' Unless there be any
of the following excuses : a funeral in his family or
purification from a dead body [2] (provided these were
not appointed for that day in order that he might not
appear on that day), a dangerous disease,[3] or an omen
which could not be passed by without expiatory
rites, or an anniversary sacrifice which could not

present was attacked by it, elections, or other public business,
might be postponed ; cf. Suetonius, *Jul.* xlv. 1.

sarium quod recte fieri non possit nisi ipsus eo die
ibi sit, vis hostesve, status condictusve dies cum
hoste ; si cui eorum harunce quae. causa erit, tum se
postridie quam per eas causas licebit, eo die venturum
adiuturumque eum qui eum pagum, vicum, oppi-
dumve delegerit.' "

5 Item in eodem libro verba haec sunt : " Miles cum
die, qui prodictus est, aberat neque excusatus erat,
infrequens notabatur." [1]

6 Item in libro sexto hoc scriptum est : " Alae dictae
exercitus equitum ordines, quod circum legiones
dextra sinistraque tamquam alae in avium corporibus
locabantur. In legione sunt centuriae sexaginta,
manipuli triginta, cohortes decem."

V

"Vestibulum" quid significet ; deque eius vocabuli
rationibus.

1 PLERAQUE sunt vocabula quibus vulgo utimur,
neque tamen liquido scimus quid ea proprie atque
vere significent ; sed incompertam et vulgariam
traditionem rei non exploratae secuti, videmur magis
dicere quod volumus, quam dicimus ; sicuti est
"vestibulum," verbum in sermonibus celebre atque
obvium, non omnibus tamen qui illo facile utuntur
2 satis spectatum. Animadverti enim quosdam haut-

---

[1] notabatur, *J. F. Gronov* ; dabatur, *ω*.

---

[1] Stranger or foreigner was the original meaning of *hostis*.

be properly celebrated unless he himself were present on that day, violence or the attack of enemies, a stated and appointed day with a foreigner[1]; if anyone shall have any of these excuses, then on the day following that on which he is excused for these reasons he shall come and render service to the one who held the levy in that district, village or town.'"

Also in the same book are these words:[2] "When a soldier was absent on the appointed day and had not been excused, he was branded as a deserter."

Also in the sixth book we find this:[3] "The columns of cavalry were called the wings of the army, because they were placed around the legions on the right and on the left, as wings are on the bodies of birds. In a legion there are sixty centuries, thirty maniples, and ten cohorts."

V

The meaning of *vestibulum* and the various derivations proposed for the word.

THERE are numerous words which we use commonly, without however clearly knowing what their proper and exact meaning is; but following an uncertain and vulgar tradition without investigating the matter, we seem to say what we mean rather than say it; an example is *vestibulum* or "vestibule," a word frequently met in conversation, yet not wholly clear to all who readily make use of it. For I have observed that some men who are by

[2] Frag. 14, Huschke; 3, Bremer.
[3] *Id.* 15 and 4.

quaquam indoctos viros opinari "vestibulum" esse
partem domus primorem, quam vulgus "atrium"
3 vocat. C. Aelius Gallus, in libro *De Significatione
Verborum Quae ad Ius Civile Pertinent* secundo, "vestibulum" esse dicit non in ipsis aedibus neque partem
aedium, sed locum ante ianuam domus vacuum, per
quem a via aditus accessusque ad aedis est, cum
dextra sinistraque ianuam tecta saepiunt [1] viae iuncta
atque ipsa ianua procul a via est, area vacanti inter-
sita.
4 Quae porro huic vocabulo ratio sit, quaeri multum
solet; sed quae scripta legi, ea ferme omnia in-
5 concinna atque absurda visa sunt. Quod Sulpicium
autem Apollinarem memini dicere, virum eleganti
scientia ornatum, huiuscemodi est : "'Ve' particula,
sicuti quaedam alia, tum intentionem significat, tum
6 minutionem. Nam 'vetus' et 'vehemens,' alterum
ab aetatis magnitudine compositum elisumque est,
alterum a mentis vi atque impetu dicitur. 'Vescum'
autem, quod ex 've' particula et 'esca' copulatum
est, utriusque diversae significationis vim capit.
7 Aliter enim Lucretius 'vescum' salem dicit ex
edendi intentione, aliter Lucilius 'vescum' appellat
8 cum edendi fastidio. Qui domos igitur amplas antiquitus faciebant, locum ante ianuam vacuum relin-
quebant, qui inter fores domus et viam medius
9 esset. In eo loco, qui dominum eius domus saluta-

---

[1] ianuam tecta saepiunt, *Madvig*; tecta qu(a)e, NOΠQ[2];
tectaque, QZ (*Hosius*); tecte, X; tecta, *Carrio*.

---

[1] Frag. 5, Huschke; 23, Bremer.
[2] Properly syncope ; from *ve + aetas*! On *vehemens* see
note on v. 12. 10 (i, p. 414).
[3] i. 326 ; see v. 12. 10 and note.
[4] v. 602, Marx.

no means without learning think that the vestibule is the front part of the house, which is commonly known as the *atrium*. Gaius Aelius Gallus, in the second book of his work *On the Meaning of Words relating to the Civil Law*, says [1] that the vestibule is not in the house itself, nor is it a part of the house, but is an open place before the door of the house, through which there is approach and access to the house from the street, while on the right and left the door is hemmed in by buildings extended to the street and the door itself is at a distance from the street, separated from it by this vacant space.

Furthermore, it is often inquired what the derivation of this word is; but nearly everything that I have read on the subject has seemed awkward and absurd. But what I recall hearing from Sulpicius Apollinaris, a man of choice learning, is as follows: "The particle *ve*, like some others, is now intensive and now the reverse; for of *vetus* and *vehemens*, the former is made by intensifying the idea of age, with elision,[2] and the latter from the power and force of the mind. But *vescus*, which is formed from the particle *ve* and *esca*, assumes the force of both opposite meanings. For Lucretius [3] uses *vescum salem*, or 'devouring salt,' in one sense, indicating a strong propensity to eat, Lucilius [4] in the other sense, of fastidiousness in eating.[5] Those then in early times who made spacious houses left a vacant place before the entrance, midway between the door of the house and the street. There those who had come to pay their respects to the master of

[5] Munro, on Lucr. i. 326, takes *vescus* in the sense of "slowly eating away" which would correspond with Lucilius' use of the word.

tum venerant, priusquam admitterentur, consistebant
et neque in via stabant, neque intra aedis erant.
10 Ab illa ergo grandis loci consistione et quasi quadam
stabulatione 'vestibula' appellata sunt spatia, sicuti
diximus, grandia ante fores aedium relicta, in quibus
starent qui venissent, priusquam in domum intro-
11 mitterentur.   Meminisse autem debebimus id
vocabulum non semper a veteribus scriptoribus
proprie, sed per quasdam translationes esse dictum,
quae tamen ita sunt factae, ut ab ista de qua diximus
proprietate non longe desciverint, sicut illud in sexto
Vergilii :

> Vestibulum ante ipsum primisque in faucibus
>   Orci
> Luctus et ultrices posuere cubilia Curae :

12 non enim 'vestibulum' priorem[1] partem domus
infernae esse dicit, quod obrepere potest tamquam si
ita dicatur, sed loca duo demonstrat extra Orci fores,
'vestibulum' et 'fauces,' ex quibus 'vestibulum'
appellat ante ipsam quasi domum et ante ipsa Orci
penetralia, 'fauces' autem vocat iter angustum, per
quod ad vestibulum adiretur."

---

[1] primorem, *Damsté, comparing* § 2.

[1] This derivation is correct, but *ve-* is used in the sense of
"apart."
[2] *Aen.* vi. 273.
[3] In the Roman house the term *fauces* was applied to the
passageway leading from the front door into the atrium.   The

the house took their places before they were admitted, standing neither in the street nor within
the house. Therefore from that standing in a large
space, and as it were from a kind of 'standing
place,' the name vestibule was given to the great
places left, as I have said, before the doors of houses,
in which those who had come to call stood, before
they were admitted to the house.[1] But we shall
have to bear in mind that this word was not always
used literally by the early writers, but in various
figurative senses, which however are so formed as
not to differ widely from that proper meaning which
we have mentioned, as for example in the sixth book
of Vergil:[2]

> Before the vestibule, e'en in Hell's very jaws,
> Avenging Cares and Grief have made their beds.

For he does not call the front part of the infernal
dwelling the 'vestibule,' although one might be
misled into thinking it so called, but he designates
two places outside the doors of Orcus, the 'vestibule' and the *fauces*, of which 'vestibule' is
applied to the part as it were before the house
itself and before the private rooms of Orcus, while
fauces designates the narrow passage through which
the vestibule was approached."[3]

---

fauces and the *vestibulum* formed one continuous passageway,
separated by the door, the *fauces* being inside and the *vestibulum* outside ; see *Harv. Stud. Class. Phil.* i. 1 ff. and most
modern handbooks. In § 10 *vestibulum* is correctly defined ;
in § 12 the relative positions of *fauces* and *vestibulum* are
inverted, and both are put "outside the door." The *vestibulum* can properly be said to be "approached" by the
fauces only *from within*. Virgil probably used *fauces* in its
ordinary sense of "jaws."

VI

Hostiae quae dicuntur "bidentes," quid sint et quam ob
causam ita appellatae sint ; superque ea re P. Nigidii et
Iulii Hygini sententiae.

1 REDEUNTES ex[1] Graecia, Brundisium navem ad-
vertimus. Ibi quispiam linguae Latinae litterator,
Roma a Brundisinis accersitus, experiundum sese
2 vulgo dabat. Imus ad eum nos quoque oblectamenti
gratia, erat enim fessus atque languens animus de
3 aestu maris. Legebat barbare insciteque Vergilii
septimum, in quo libro hic versus est :

Centum lanigeras mactabat rite bidentis,

4 et iubebat rogare se si quis quid omnium rerum
5 vellet discere. Tum ego, indocti hominis confi-
dentiam demiratus : "Docesne," inquam, "nos,
6 magister, cur 'bidentes' dicantur?" "'Bidentes,'"
inquit, "oves appellatae, idcircoque lanigeras
7 dixit, ut oves planius demonstraret." "Posthac,"
inquam, "videbimus an oves solae, ut tu ais, bidentes
dicantur et an Pomponius, Atellanarum poeta, in
Gallis Transalpinis erraverit, cum hoc scripsit :

Mars, tíbi factúrum voveo, si umquam rédierit,
Bidénti verre,

[1] ex *added by Hertz.*

---

[1] The result of seasickness ; cf. Plaut. *Rud.* 510, *animc
male fit. Contine, quaeso, caput.*
[2] vii. 93.
[3] An early farce, of Oscan origin, named from the town of
Atella. The *Atellanae* were first given literary form by L.

VI

What the victims are which are called *bidentes,* and why they
were so called ; and the opinions of Publius Nigidius and
Julius Hyginus on that subject.

On my return from Greece I put in at Brundisium.
There a dabbler in the Latin language, who had
been called from Rome by the people of Brundisium,
was offering himself generally to be tested. I also
went to him for the sake of amusement, for my
mind was weary and languid [1] from the tossing of
the sea. He was reading in a barbarous and
ignorant manner from the seventh book of Vergil,
in which this verse occurs : [2]

> An hundred woolly sheep (*bidentes*) he duly
>   slew,

and he invited anyone to ask him anything whatever
which one wished to learn. Then I, marvelling at
the assurance of the ignorant fellow, said : " Will
you tell us, master, why *bidentes* are so called? "
"*Bidentes,*" said he, " means sheep, and he called
them ' woolly,' to show more clearly that they are
sheep." I replied : " We will see later whether
only sheep are called *bidentes,* as you say, and whether
Pomponius, the writer of *Atellanae,*[3] was in error in
his *Transalpine Gauls,* when he wrote this : [4]

> O Mars, if ever I return, I vow
> To sacrifice to thee with two-toothed (*bidenti*)
>   boar.

Pomponius of Bononia (Bologna) and Novius, in the time of
Sulla.
  [4] v. 51, Ribbeck[3].

8 sed nunc ego a te rogavi ecquam scias esse huiusce
9 vocabuli rationem." Atque ille nihil cunctatus, sed
nimium quantum audacter: "Oves," inquit, "'bidentes' dictae, quod duos tantum dentes habeant."
10 "Ubi terrarum, quaeso te," inquam, "duos solos per
naturam dentes habere ovem vidisti? Ostentum
11 enim est et piaculis factis procurandum." Tum ille
permotus mihi et inritatus: "Quaere," inquit, "ea
potius quae e grammatico quaerenda sunt; nam de
12 ovium dentibus opiliones percontantur." Facetias
nebulonis hominis risi et reliqui.

P. autem Nigidius, in libro quem *De Extis* composuit, "bidentes" appellari ait non oves solas, sed
omnes bimas hostias, neque tamen dixit apertius, cur
"bidentes"; sed, quod ultro existumabamus, id
13 scriptum invenimus in commentariis quisbusdam ad
ius pontificum pertinentibus, "bidennes" primo
dictas, *d* littera inmissa, quasi "biennes," tum longo
usu loquendi corruptam vocem esse et ex "bidenni-
bus" "bidentes" factum, quoniam id videbatur esse
dictu facilius leniusque.

14 Hyginus tamen Iulius, qui ius pontificum non
videtur ignorasse, in quarto librorum quos *De Vergilio* fecit, "bidentes" appellari scripsit hostias quae
15 per aetatem duos dentes altiores haberent. Verba
illius ipsa posui: "Quae 'bidens' est," inquit,
"hostia, oportet habeat dentes octo, sed ex his duo
ceteris altiores, per quos appareat ex minore aetate

But now I asked you whether you know the reason for this name." And he, without a moment's hesitation, but with the greatest possible assurance, said: "Sheep are called *bidentes,* because they have only two teeth." "Where on earth, pray," said I, "have you seen a sheep that by nature had only two teeth? For that is a portent and ought to be met with expiatory offerings." Then he, greatly disturbed and angry with me, cried: "Ask rather such questions as ought to be put to a grammarian; for one inquires of shepherds about the teeth of sheep." I laughed at the wit of the blockhead and left him.

Now Publius Nigidius, in the book which he wrote *On Sacrificial Meats,* says[1] that not sheep alone are called *bidentes,* but all victims that are two years old; yet he has not explained clearly why they are called *bidentes.* But I find written in some *Notes on the Pontifical Law*[2] what I had myself thought, that they were first called *bidennes,* that is *biennes* with the insertion of the letter *d*; then by long use in speech the word became changed and from *bidennes* was formed *bidentes,* because the latter seemed easier and less harsh to pronounce.

However, Julius Hyginus, who seems not to have been ignorant of pontifical law, in the fourth book of his work *On Virgil,* wrote[3] that those victims were called *bidentes* which were of such an age that they had two prominent teeth. I quote his own words: "The victim called *bidens* should have eight teeth, but of these two should be more prominent than the rest, to make it plain that they have passed from

[1] Frag. 81, Swoboda.
[2] iii, p. 566, Bremer.
[3] Fr. 3, Fun.

in maiorem transcendisse." Haec Hygini opinio an vera sit, non argui[1] argumentis, sed oculis videri[2] potest.

VII

Quod Laberius verba pleraque licentius petulantiusque finxit; et quod multis item verbis utitur de quibus an sint Latina quaeri solet.

1 LABERIUS, in mimis quos scriptitavit, oppido quam verba finxit praelicenter. Nam et "mendicimo-
2 nium" dicit et "moechimonium" et "adulterionem" "adulteritatemque" pro "adulterio" et "depudi- cavit" pro "stupravit" et "abluvium" pro "diluvio" et, quod in mimo ponit quem *Cophinum* inscripsit,[3]
3 "manuatus est" pro "furatus est" et item in *Fullone* furem "manuarium" appellat:

> manuari (inquit) pudorem perdidisti,

4 multaque alia huiuscemodi novat. Neque non obso- leta quoque et maculantia ex sordidiore vulgi usu ponit, quale est in *Staminariis*:

> Tóllet bona fidé vos Orcus núdas in catómum.

5 Et "elutriare lintea" et "lavandaria" dicit, quae ad lavandum sint data, et:

---

[1] argui, *an addition suggested by Hosius*; argumentis iudicari, *Hertz* (see crit. note 2).
[2] videri, Q; iudicari, ω.
[3] inscripsit, *Nonius* ii, p. 141. 2 (p. 205 Linds.); scripsit, ω.

---

[1] Hyginus' explanation is the accepted one.
[2] v. 150, Ribbeck[3].   [3] *Id.* v. 39.   [4] *Id.* v. 46.
[5] *manuarius*, an adj. from *manus*, "hand" (*e.g. manu- aria mola*, "a hand-mill"). The transition, in the sub-

infancy to a less tender age." Whether this opinion of Hyginus is true or not may be determined by observation without resort to argument.[1]

VII

That Laberius formed many words freely and boldly, and that he even uses numerous words whose Latinity is often questioned.

LABERIUS, in the mimes which he wrote, coined words with the greatest possible freedom. For he said [2] *mendicimonium* for "beggary," *moechimonium*, *adulterio* or *adulteritas* for "adultery," *depudicavit* for "dishonoured," and *abluvium* for *diluvium*, or "deluge"; in the farce which he entitled *The Basket* [3] he uses *manuatus est* for "he stole," and in *The Fuller* [4] he calls a thief *manuarius*,[5] saying:

> Thief (*manuari*), you have lost your shame,

and he makes many other innovations of the same kind. He also used obsolete and obscene words, such as are spoken only by the dregs of the people, as in the *Spinners' Shop* : [6]

> Orcus, in truth, will bear you on his shoulders (*catomum*) [7] nude.

He uses [8] *elutriare* for "washing out" linen, and *lavandaria*, or "wash," of those things which are sent to be washed.

---

stantive, to the meaning "thief" is made easier by *manuarium aes*, "money won at dice," Gell. xviii. 13. 4.

[6] v. 87, Ribbeck[3].

[7] catomum = κατ' ὦμον, *Thes. Ling. Lat. s.v.*

[8] v. 151, Ribbeck[3].

coícior (inquit) in fullónicam,

et :

Quid próperas ? ecquid praécurris, caldónia ? [1]

6 Item in *Restione* "talabarriunculos" dicit, quos vul-
7 gus "talabarriones," item in *Compitalibus*:

malas malaxavi,

8 item in *Cacomnemone* :

Hic est (inquit)
Ílle gurdus, quém ego me abhinc ménses duos ex
África
Vénientem excepísse tibi narrávi,

9 item in mimo, qui inscribitur *Natalicius*,[2] "cippum"
dicit et "obbam" et "camellam" et "pittacium"
et "capitium" :

Induis (inquit) cápitium tunicaé pittacium.

[1] caldonia, MSS. ; Caldonia, *Hosius* ; Calidoniam, *Ribbeck.*
[2] Natalicius, *Fleckeisen* ; nata, L. (.l. X) ΠΧ ; nata, Z[1] ;
Natalia *or* Natta, *Bothe.*

---

[1] *Id.* v. 147. With *fullonicam*, sc. *artem* and see *Archiv
für lat. Lex. u. Gram.* x, p. 240.
[2] There is nothing unusual in the word *fullonica* ; hence
the unusual word must be *conicior* (in this connection).
[3] *Id.* v. 148. Ribbeck's *Calidoniam*, "would'st outstrip
the Calidonian maid ?" *i.e.* Atalanta, makes excellent sense ;
but with that reading we have no odd or unusual word at all.
caldonia, as a common noun, might mean "heater," or bath
attendant (so Weiss), or it might be derived from *calidus* in
the sense of "quick, hasty." There is nothing to indicate
that it is a proper name, as Hosius takes it to be.

He says:[1]

Into the fulling business I am hurled (*coicior*),[2]

and [3]

O heater (*caldonia*), what's your haste? Would'st
aught outstrip?

Also in the *Ropemaker*[4] he applies the term *tala-barriunculi* to those whom the general public call
talabarriones.[5] He writes in the *Compitalia*:[6]

My jaws I've tamed (*malaxavi*),

and in *The Forgetful Man*,[7]

This is that dolt (*gurdus*) who, when two months
ago
From Africa I came, did meet me here,
As I did say.

Also in the farce entitled *Natalicius* he uses[8] *cippus*
for a small column, *obba* for a cup, *camella* for a
bowl,[9] *pittacium* for a flap[10] and *capitium* for a breast-
band; the last-named passage reads:

A breast-band (*capitium*) you put on, the tunic's
flap (*pittacium*).

---

[4] *Id.* v. 79. [5] The meaning is not known.

[6] *Id.* v. 37; *malaxavi*, from the Greek μαλακίζω. It is
clear that the choice of the word is due to the assonance, or
jingle, of *mala malaxavi*.

[7] *Id.* v. 13. [8] *Id.* vv. 60 and 61.

[9] Literally, "a little room," a diminutive of *camera*.

[10] The *T.L.L.* defines *capitium* as *foramen tunicae capiti
aptum*, which seems meaningless with *induis*. The Forcellini-
De Vit makes *capitium* a breast-band (= *strophium?*) and
pittacium, "*plagula, segmentum, quod vesti assuitur*," with
the explanation: "*quod, tamquam pittacium, tunicae adsutum
et adfixum est.*"

10 Praeterea in *Anna Peranna* "gubernium" pro
"gubernatore" et "planum" pro "sycophanta" et
"nanum" pro "pumilione" dicit; quamquam "planum" pro "sycophanta" M. quoque Cicero in
oratione scriptum reliquit, quam *Pro Cluentio* dixit.

11 Atque item, in mimo qui *Saturnalia* inscriptus est,
"botulum" pro "farcimine" appellat et "hominem
12 levennam" pro "levi." Item in *Necyomantia* "cocio-
nem" pervulgate dicit, quem veteres "arillatorem"
dixerunt. Verba Laberi haec sunt:

Duás uxores? hércle hoc plus negóti est, inquit
  cócio;
Séx aedíles víderat.

13 Sed enim, in mimo quem inscripsit *Alexandream*,
eodem quidem quo vulgus, sed probe Latineque usus
est Graeco vocabulo; "emplastrum" enim dixit οὐθε-
τέρως, non genere feminino, ut isti novicii semidocti.
14 Verba ex eo mimo adposui:

Quíd est ius iurandum? émplastrum aeris álieni.

VIII

Quid significet et quid a nostris appellatum sit quod
  "axioma" dialectici dicunt; et quaedam alia quae prima
  in disciplina dialectica traduntur.

1 Cum in disciplinas dialecticas induci atque imbui
vellemus, necessus fuit adire atque cognoscere quas
2 vocant dialectici εἰσαγωγάς. Tum, quia in primo

---

¹ v. 3, Ribbeck³.　　² Greek πλάνος.　　³ § 72.
　　　⁴ v. 80, Ribbeck³.　　⁵ *Id.* v. 63.

Further, in his *Anna Peranna* he uses[1] *gubernius* for pilot, and *planus*[2] for sycophant, and *nanus* for dwarf; but Marcus Cicero also wrote *planus* for sycophant in the speech which he delivered *In Defence of Cluentius.*[3] Moreover Laberius in the farce entitled *The Saturnalia*[4] calls a sausage *botulus* and says *homo levanna* instead of *levis* or "slight." In the *Necyomantia* too he uses the very vulgar expression *cocio* for what our forefathers called *arillator* or "haggler." His words are these:[5]

> Two wives? More trouble this, the haggler (*cocio*) says;
> Six aediles he had seen.[6]

However, in the farce which he called *Alexandrea,* he used[7] the same Greek word which is in common use, but correctly and in good Latin form; for he put *emplastrum* in the neuter, not in the feminine gender, as those half-educated innovators of ours do. I quote the words of that farce:

> What is an oath? A plaster (*emplastrum*) for a debt.

VIII

The meaning of what the logicians call "an axiom," and what it is called by our countrymen; and some other things which belong to the elements of the dialectic art.

WHEN I wished to be introduced to the science of logic and instructed in it, it was necessary to take up and learn what the dialecticians call εἰσαγωγαί or "introductory exercises."[8] Then because at first

---

[6] Referring to the addition by Caesar of two *aediles cereales* to the two *plebei* and two *curules*; see note on x. 6. 3.

[7] *Id.* v. 1.   [8] II. 194, Arn.

περὶ ἀξιωμάτων discendum, quae M. Varro alias " profata," alias "proloquia" appellat, *Commentarium De Proloquiis* L. Aelii, docti hominis, qui magister Varronis fuit, studiose quaesivimus eumque in Pacis
3 bibliotheca repertum legimus. Sed in eo nihil edocenter neque ad instituendum explanate scriptum est, fecisseque videtur eum librum Aelius sui magis admonendi quam aliorum docendi gratia.
4   Redimus igitur necessario ad Graecos libros. Ex quibus accepimus ἀξίωμα esse his verbis definitum : [1]
5 λεκτὸν αὐτοτελὲς ἀπόφαντον ὅσον ἐφ᾽ αὑτῷ. Hoc ego supersedi vertere, quia novis et inconditis vocibus utendum fuit, quas pati aures per insolentiam vix
6 possent. Sed M. Varro in libro *De Lingua Latina* ad Ciceronem quarto vicesimo expeditissime ita finit : " Proloquium est sententia in qua nihil desideratur."
7   Erit autem planius quid istud sit, si exemplum eius dixerimus. Ἀξίωμα igitur, sive id " proloquium " dicere placet, huiuscemodi est : " Hannibal Poenus fuit "; " Scipio Numantiam delevit "; " Milo caedis
8 damnatus est "; "neque bonum est voluptas neque malum "; et omnino quicquid ita dicitur plena atque perfecta verborum sententia, ut id necesse sit aut verum aut falsum esse, id a dialecticis ἀξίωμα appellatum est, a M. Varrone, sicuti dixi, "proloquium," a M. autem Cicerone " pronuntiatum," quo

---

[1] definitum *added by Skutsch.*

---

[1] Fr. 29, G. and S.
[2] Vespasian's Temple of Peace in the Forum Pacis.
[3] p. 54. 19. Fun.
[4] An absolute and self-evident proposition.

I had to learn about axioms, which Marcus Varro calls,[1] now *profata*, or "propositions," and now *proloquia*, or "preliminary statements," I sought diligently for the *Commentary on Proloquia* of Lucius Aelius, a learned man, who was the teacher of Varro; and finding it in the library of Peace,[2] I read it. But I found in it nothing that was written to instruct or to make the matter clear, but Aelius[3] seems to have made that book rather as suggestions for his own use than for the purpose of teaching others.

I therefore of necessity returned to my Greek books. From these I obtained this definition of an axiom: λεκτὸν αὐτοτελὲς ἀπόφαντον ὅσον ἐφ' αὑτῷ.[4] This I forbore to turn into Latin, since it would have been necessary to use new and as yet uncoined words, such as, from their strangeness, the ear could hardly endure. But Marcus Varro in the twenty-fourth book of his *Latin Language*, dedicated to Cicero, thus defines the word very briefly:[5] "A *proloquium* is a statement in which nothing is lacking."

But his definition will be clearer if I give an example. An axiom, then, or a preliminary proposition, if you prefer, is of this kind: "Hannibal was a Carthaginian"; "Scipio destroyed Numantia"; "Milo was found guilty of murder"; "pleasure is neither a good nor an evil"; and in general any saying which is a full and perfect thought, so expressed in words that it is necessarily either true or false, is called by the logicians an "axiom," by Marcus Varro, as I have said, a "proposition," but by Marcus Cicero[6] a *pronuntiatum*, or "pronouncement,"

---

[5] Fr. 29, G. and S.
[6] *Tusc. Disp.* i. 14.

ille tamen vocabulo tantisper uti se adtestatus est,
" quoad melius," inquit, "invenero."

9   Sed quod Graeci συνημμένον ἀξίωμα dicunt, id alii
nostrorum "adiunctum," alii "conexum" dixerunt.
Id "conexum" tale est: "si Plato ambulat, Plato
10 movetur"; "si dies est, sol super terras est." Item
quod illi συμπεπλεγμένον, nos vel "coniunctum" vel
"copulatum" dicimus, quod est eiusdemmodi: "P.
Scipio, Pauli filius, et bis consul fuit et triumphavit
et censura functus est et collega in censura L.
11 Mummi fuit." In omni autem coniuncto si unum
est mendacium, etiamsi cetera vera sunt, totum esse
mendacium dicitur. Nam si ad ea omnia quae de
Scipione illo vera dixi, addidero "et Hannibalem in
Africa superavit," quod est falsum, universa quoque
illa quae coniuncte dicta sunt, propter hoc unum
quod falsum accesserit, quia simul dicentur, vera non
erunt.

12   Est item aliud quod Graeci διεζευγμένον ἀξίωμα, nos
"disiunctum" dicimus. Id huiuscemodi est: "Aut
malum est voluptas aut bonum, aut neque bonum
13 neque malum est." Omnia autem quae disiunguntur
pugnantia esse inter sese oportet, eorumque opposita,
quae ἀντικείμενα Graeci dicunt, ea quoque ipsa inter
se adversa esse. Ex omnibus quae disiunguntur
14 unum esse verum debet, falsa cetera. Quod si aut
nihil omnium verum aut omnia plurave quam unum
vera erunt, aut quae disiuncta sunt non pugnabunt,
aut quae opposita eorum sunt contraria inter sese
non erunt, tunc id disiunctum mendacium est et

---

[1] Literally, " a connected axiom."   See II. 213. Arn.

[2] Aelius Stilo, Fr. 74, p. 75 Fun.

[3] Two connected sentences of which the second follows as
the result of the first.   [4] II. 218. Arn.

a word however which he declared that he used "only until I can find a better one."

But what the Greeks call συνημμένον ἀξίωμα, or "a hypothetical syllogism,"[1] some of our countrymen[2] call *adiunctum*, others *conexum*.[3] The following are examples of this : "If Plato is walking, Plato is moving " ; "if it is day, the sun is above the earth." Also what they call συμπεπλεγμένον, or "a compound proposition," we call *coniunctum* or *copulatum* ; for example : "Publius Scipio, son of Paulus, was twice consul and celebrated a triumph, and held the censorship, and was the colleague of Lucius Mummius in his censorship." But in the whole of a proposition of this kind, if one member is false, even if the rest are true, the whole is said to be false. For if to all those true statements which I have made about that Scipio I add "and he worsted Hannibal in Africa," which is false, all those other statements which are made in conjunction will not be true, because of this one false statement which is made with them.

There is also another form, which the Greeks call διεζευγμένον ἀξίωμα, or "a disjunctive proposition," and we call *disiunctum*. For example : " Pleasure is either good or evil, or it is neither good nor evil."[4] Now all statements which are contrasted ought to be opposed to each other, and their opposites, which the Greeks call ἀντικείμενα, ought also to be opposed. Of all statements which are contrasted, one ought to be true and the rest false. But if none at all of them is true, or if all, or more than one, are true, or if the contrasted things are not at odds, or if those which are opposed to each other are not contrary, then that is a false contrast and is called

appellatur παραδιεζευγμένον, sicuti hoc est, in quo quae
opposita non sunt contraria : " Aut curris aut am-
bulas aut stas." Nam ipsa quidem inter se adversa
sunt, sed opposita eorum non pugnant : "non ambulare" enim et "non stare" et "non currere" contraria inter sese non sunt, quoniam "contraria" ea
dicuntur quae simul vera esse non queunt; possis
enim simul eodemque tempore neque ambulare neque
stare neque currere.

15 Sed hoc iam breve ex dialectica libamentum de-
16 disse nunc satis erit atque id solum addendum ad-
monendumque est, quod huius disciplinae studium
atque cognitio in principiis quidem taetra et asper-
nabilis insuavisque esse et inutilis videri solet, sed,
ubi aliquantum processeris, tum denique et emolu-
mentum eius in animo tuo dilucebit et sequitur
17 quaedam discendi voluptas insatiabilis, cui sane nisi
modum feceris, periculum non mediocre erit ne, ut
plerique alii, tu quoque in illis dialecticae gyris
atque meandris, tamquam apud Sirenios scopulos,
consenescas.

IX

Quid significet verbum in libris veterum creberrime positum
"susque deque."

1 " SUSQUE deque fero " aut " susque deque sum " [1]
aut " susque deque habeo "—his enim omnibus modis

---

[1] aut s.d. sum, *added by Hertz* ; aut s.d. est, *Skutsch.*

παραδιεζευγμένον. For instance, this case, in which the things which are opposed are not contraries: "Either you run or you walk or you stand." These acts are indeed contrasted, but when opposed they are not contrary; for "not to walk" and "not to stand" and "not to run" are not contrary to one another, since those things are called "contraries" which cannot be true at the same time. But you may at once and at the same time neither walk, stand, nor run.

But for the present it will be enough to have given this little taste of logic, and I need only add by way of advice, that the study and knowledge of this science in its rudiments does indeed, as a rule, seem forbidding and contemptible, as well as disagreeable and useless. But when you have made some progress, then finally its advantages will become clear to you, and a kind of insatiable desire for acquiring it will arise; so much so, that if you do not set bounds to it, there will be great danger lest, as many others have done, you should reach a second childhood amid those mazes and meanders of logic, as if among the rocks of the Sirens.

IX

The meaning of the expression *susque deque*, which occurs frequently in the books of early writers.

SUSQUE *deque fero, susque deque sum*, or *susque deque habeo*[1]—for all these forms occur, meaning "it's all

---

[1] Susque deque, "both up and down," is an expression denoting indifference. It occurs without a verb in Cic. *ad Att.* xiv. 6. 1, *de Octavio susque deque*. See Paul. Fest. p. 271 Linds., *susque deque significat plus minusve.*

dicitur—verbum est ex hominum doctorum sermonibus. In poematis quoque et in epistulis veterum
scriptum est plurifariam; sed facilius reperias qui
2 verbum ostentent quam qui intellegant. Ita plerique nostrum quae remotiora verba invenimus dicere
3 ea properamus, non discere. Significat autem "susque
deque ferre" animo aequo esse et quod accidit non
magni pendere atque interdum neglegere et con-
temnere, et propemodum id valet quod dicitur
4 Graece ἀδιαφορεῖν. Laberius in *Compitalibus*:

Núnc tu lentu's, núnc tu susque déque fers;
Matér familias túa in lecto advérsó sedet,
Servós sextantis útitur nefáriis
Verbís.

5 M. Varro in *Sisenna vel De Historia*: "Quod si non
horum omnium similia essent principia ac post-
6 principia, susque deque esset." Lucilius in tertio:

Verum haec ludus ibi susque omnia deque fuerunt,
Susque et deque fuere, inquam, omnia, ludus
iocusque;
Illud opus durum, ut Setinum accessimus finem:
Αἰγίλιποι[1] montes, Aetnae omnes, asperi Athones.

[1] aigilepes, *Marx.*

one to me "—is an expression used in the everyday
language of cultivated men. It occurs frequently
in poems too and in the letters of the early writers;
but you will more readily find persons who flaunt
the phrase than who understand it. So true is it
that many of us hasten to use out-of-the-way words
that we have stumbled upon, but not to learn
their meaning. Now *susque deque ferre* means to
be indifferent and not to lay much stress upon
anything that happens; sometimes it means to
neglect and despise, having about the force of the
Greek word ἀδιαφορεῖν. Laberius says in his *Compitalia*:[1]

> Now you are dull, now 'tis all one to you (*susque
>   deque fers*);
> Your wife sits by you on the marriage bed,[2]
> A penny slave unseemly language dares.

Marcus Varro in his *Sisenna, or On History* says:[3]
"But if all these things did not have similar beginnings and sequels, it would be all one (*susque deque
esset*)." So Lucilius in his third book writes:[4]

> All this was sport, to us it was all one (*susque
>   deque fuerunt*),
> All one it was, I say, all sport and play;
> That was hard toil, when we gained Setia's
>   bourne:
> Goat-traversed heights, Aetnas, rough Athoses.

---

[1] v. 29, Ribbeck[3].

[2] The marriage bed in the early Roman house stood in the
atrium, opposite the door, whence it was called *lectus adversus*; in later times a symbolic bed stood in the same
place.

[3] 256, Riese.   [4] 110 ff., Marx.

X

Quid sint " proletarii," quid " capite censi " ; quid item sit
in *XII. Tabulis* "adsiduus"; et quae eius vocabuli ratio
sit.

1 OTIUM erat quodam die Romae in foro a negotiis
et laeta quaedam celebritas feriarum legebaturque
in consessu forte conplurium Enni liber ex *Annalibus.*
In eo libro versus hi fuerunt :

    Proletarius publicitus scutisque feroque
    Ornatur ferro ; muros urbemque forumque
    Excubiis curant.

2 Tum ibi quaeri coeptum est, quid esset " proletarius."
3 Atque ego, aspiciens quempiam in eo circulo ius
civile callentem, familiarem meum, rogabam ut id
4 verbum nobis enarraret, et cum illic se iuris, non
rei grammaticae peritum esse respondisset, " Eo
maxime," inquam, " te dicere hoc oportet, quando,
5 ut praedicas, peritus iuris es. Nam Q. Ennius
verbum hoc ex *Duodecim Tabulis* vestris accepit,
in quibus, si recte commemini, ita scriptum est :
' Adsiduo vindex adsiduus esto. Proletario iam civi[1]
6 quis volet vindex esto.' Petimus igitur ne *Annalem*
nunc Q. Ennii, sed *Duodecim Tabulas* legi arbitrere

    [1] civi cui, ω ; cui *deleted by Schöll.*

---

[1] *Ann.* 183 ff.   [2] i. 4.
[3] The *vindex* is here one who voluntarily agrees to go
before the magistrate as the representative of the defendant,

X

The meaning of *proletarii* and *capite censi*; also of *adsiduus* in the *Twelve Tables*, and the origin of the word.

ONE day there was a cessation of business in the Forum at Rome, and as the holiday was being joyfully celebrated, it chanced that one of the books of the *Annals* of Ennius was read in an assembly of very many persons. In this book the following lines occurred:[1]

> With shield and savage sword is Proletarius armed
> At public cost; they guard our walls, our mart and town.

Then the question was raised there, what *proletarius* meant. And seeing in that company a man who was skilled in the civil law, a friend of mine, I asked him to explain the word to us; and when he rejoined that he was an expert in civil law and not in grammatical matters, I said: "You in particular ought to explain this, since, as you declare, you are skilled in civil law. For Quintus Ennius took this word from your *Twelve Tables*, in which, if I remember aright, we have the following:[2] 'For a freeholder let the protector[3] be a freeholder. For a proletariate citizen[4] let whoso will be protector.' We therefore ask you to consider that not one of the books of Quintus Ennius' *Annals*, but the *Twelve*

and thereby takes upon himself the action in the stead of the latter (Allen, *Remnants of Early Latin*, p. 85).

[4] The *proletarii* (cf. *proles*) were "child-producers," who made no other contribution to the State; see § 13.

et quid sit in ea lege 'proletarius civis' interpre-
7 tere." "Ego vero," inquit ille, "dicere atque
interpretari hoc deberem, si ius Faunorum et
8 Aboriginum didicissem. Sed enim cum 'proletarii'
et 'adsidui' et 'sanates' et 'vades' et 'subvades'
et 'viginti quinque asses' et 'taliones' furtorumque
quaestio 'cum lance et licio' evanuerint omnisque
illa *Duodecim Tabularum* antiquitas, nisi in legis
actionibus centumviralium causarum lege Aebutia
lata consopita sit, studium scientiamque ego praestare debeo iuris et legum vocumque earum quibus
utimur."

9 Tum forte quadam Iulium Paulum, poetam memoriae nostrae doctissimum, praetereuntem conspeximus.
10 Is a nobis salutatur, rogatusque uti de sententia deque ratione istius vocabuli nos doceret, "Qui in plebe,"
inquit, "Romana tenuissimi pauperrimique erant neque amplius quam mille quingentum aeris in censum
deferebant, 'proletarii' appellati sunt, qui vero nullo
aut perquam parvo aere censebantur, 'capite censi'
vocabantur, extremus autem census capite censorum
11 aeris fuit trecentis septuaginta quinque. Sed quoniam res pecuniaque familiaris obsidis vicem pigneris-
que esse apud rempublicam videbatur amorisque in
patriam fides quaedam in ea firmamentumque erat,
neque proletarii neque capite censi milites, nisi in
tumultu maximo, scribebantur, quia familia pecu-

---

[1] *XII Tab.* i. 4, 5, 10; viii. 2, 4, 15. For *proletarii* see
note, p. 167. The *adsidui* were "permanent settlers," or tax-
payers, belonging to one of the five upper Servian classes.
The *sanates* seem to have been clients or dependents of the
wealthy Roman citizens. *Vades* were sureties, who gave
bail; *subvades*, sub-sureties, who gave security for the bail.
On *viginti quinque asses*, the penalty for an assault, see xx.

Tables are being read, and interpret the meaning of 'proletariate citizen' in that law." "It is true," said he, "that if I had learned the law of the Fauns and Aborigines, I ought to explain and interpret this. But since *proletarii, adsidui, sanates, vades, subvades,* 'twenty-five asses,' 'retaliation,' and trials for theft 'by plate and girdle'[1] have disappeared, and since all the ancient lore of the *Twelve Tables,* except for legal questions before the court of the centumviri, was put to sleep by the Aebutian law,[2] I ought only to exhibit interest in, and knowledge of, the law and statutes and legal terms which we now actually use."

Just then, by some chance, we caught sight of Julius Paulus passing by, the most learned poet within my recollection. We greeted him, and when he was asked to enlighten us as to the meaning and derivation of that word, he said: "Those of the Roman commons who were humblest and of smallest means, and who reported no more than fifteen hundred asses at the census, were called *proletarii,* but those who were rated as having no property at all, or next to none, were termed *capite censi,* or 'counted by head.' And the lowest rating of the *capite censi* was three hundred and seventy-five asses. But since property and money were regarded as a hostage and pledge of loyalty to the State, and since there was in them a kind of guarantee and assurance of patriotism, neither the *proletarii* nor the *capite censi* were enrolled as soldiers except in some time of extraordinary disorder, because they had

1. 12; for *taliones,* xx. 1. 14; and for *cum lance et licio,* note on xi. 18. 9.

2. The date is unknown.

12 niaque his aut tenuis aut nulla esset. Proletariorum
tamen ordo honestior aliquanto et re et nomine
13 quam capite censorum fuit; nam et asperis reipublicae temporibus, cum iuventutis inopia esset, in
militiam tumultuariam legebantur armaque is sumptu
publico praebebantur, et non capitis censione, sed
prosperiore vocabulo a munere officioque prolis
edendae appellati sunt, quod, cum re familiari parva
minus possent rempublicam iuvare, subolis tamen
14 gignendae copia civitatem frequentarent. Capite
censos autem primus C. Marius, ut quidam ferunt
bello Cimbrico, difficillimis reipublicae temporibus,
vel potius, ut Sallustius ait, bello Iugurthino, milites
scripsisse traditur, cum id factum ante in nulla
15 memoria extaret. 'Adsiduus' in *XII. Tabulis* pro
locuplete et facile facienti dictus aut ab assibus,[1]
id est, aere dando, cum id tempora reipublicae
postularent, aut a muneris pro familiari copia
faciendi adsiduitate."

16 Verba autem Sallusti in *Historia Iugurthina* de
C. Mario consule et de capite censis haec sunt:
"Ipse interea milites scribere, non more maiorum
nec ex classibus, sed ut libido cuiusque erat, capite
censos plerosque. Id factum alii inopia bonorum,

---

[1] ab assiduis ω; *corrected in* σ. *Hosius suggests* assariis,
comparing Varro, L.L. viii. 71 ; *Gram. Lat.* i. 76. 3 K.

---

[1] That is, to meet a *tumultus*, "a rebellion" or irregular
warfare. At first used as a military term, *tumultuarius* later
acquired a general sense ; cf. *tumultuario rogo,* " on a hastily
erected pyre," Suet. *Calig.* lix.

[2] i. 4, 10.

[3] *locuples* seems to be derived from *locus,* in the sense of
"land," and the root *ple-* of *pleo* and *plenus.*

[4] Both these derivations are fanciful ; *adsiduus* is connected with *adsideo,* as the grammarian Caper knew

little or no property and money. However, the class of *proletarii* was somewhat more honourable in fact and in name than that of the *capite censi*; for in times of danger to the State, when there was a scarcity of men of military age, they were enrolled for hasty service,[1] and arms were furnished them at public expense. And they were called, not *capite censi*, but by a more auspicious name derived from their duty and function of producing offspring, for although they could not greatly aid the State with what small property they had, yet they added to the population of their country by their power of begetting children. Gaius Marius is said to have been the first, according to some in the war with the Cimbri in a most critical period for our country, or more probably, as Sallust says, in the Jugurthine war, to have enrolled soldiers from the *capite censi*, since such an act was unheard of before that time. *Adsiduus* in the *Twelve Tables*[2] is used of one who is rich and well to do,[3] either because he contributed 'asses' (that is, money) when the exigencies of the State required it, or from his 'assiduity' in making contributions according to the amount of his property."[4]

Now the words of Sallust in the *Jugurthine War* about Gaius Marius and the *capite censi* are these:[5] "He himself in the meantime enrolled soldiers, not according to the classes, or in the manner of our forefathers, but allowing anyone to volunteer, for the most part the lowest class (*capite censos*). Some say that he did this through lack of good men,

(*Gram. Lat.* vii. 108. 5, Keil), and means "a permanent settler."

[5] *Jug.* lxxxvi. 2.

alii per ambitionem consulis memorabant, quod ab
eo genere celebratus auctusque erat, et homini
potentiam quaerenti egentissimus quisque oportunis-
simus."

XI

Historia ex Herodoti libris sumpta de Psyllorum interitu,
qui in Syrtibus Africanis colebant.

1 Gens in Italia Marsorum orta fertur a Circae filio.
2 Propterea Marsis hominibus, quorum dumtaxat
familiae cum externis cognationibus nondum etiam
permixtae corruptaeque sunt, vi quadam genitali
datum ut et serpentium virulentorum domitores
sint et incentionibus herbarumque sucis faciant
medellarum miracula.
3 Hac eadem vi praeditos esse quosdam videmus,
qui "Psylli" vocantur. Quorum super nomine et
genere cum in veteribus litteris quaesissem,[1] in
quarto denique Herodoti libro fabulam de Psyllis
4 hanc invenimus : Psyllos quondam fuisse in terra
Africa conterminos Nasamonibus Austrumque in
finibus eorum quodam in tempore perquam validum
5 ac diutinum flavisse ; eo flatu aquam omnem in locis
6 in quibus colebant exaruisse ; Psyllos, re aquaria
defectos, eam iniuriam graviter Austro suscensuisse
decretumque fecisse, uti armis sumptis ad Austrum,
proinde quasi ad hostem, iure belli res petitum pro-
7 ficiscerentur. Atque ita profectis ventum Austrum

---

[1] quaesissemus, *Kronenberg.*

---

[1] iv. 173.

others because of a desire to curry favour, since that class had given him honour and rank, and as a matter of fact, to one who aspires to power the poorest man is the most helpful."

XI

A story taken from the books of Herodotus about the destruction of the Psylli, who dwelt in the African Syrtes.

THE race of the Marsians in Italy is said to have sprung from the son of Circe. Therefore it was given to the Marsic men, provided their families were not stained through the admixture of foreign alliances, by an inborn hereditary power to be the subduers of poisonous serpents and to perform wonderful cures by incantations and the juices of plants.

We see certain persons called *Psylli* endowed with this same power. And when I had sought in ancient records for information about their name and race, I found at last in the fourth book of Herodotus[1] this story about them: that the Psylli had once been neighbours in the land of Africa of the Nasamones, and that the South Wind at a certain season in their territories blew very long and hard; that because of that gale all the water in the regions which they inhabited dried up; that the Psylli, deprived of their water supply, were grievously incensed at the South Wind because of that injury and voted to take up arms and march against the South Wind as against an enemy, and demand restitution according to the laws of war. And when they had thus set out, the South Wind

magno spiritus agmine venisse obviam eosque universos cum omnibus copiis armisque, cumulis monti-
8 busque harenarum supervectis, operuisse. Eo facto
Psyllos ad unum omnis interisse, itaque eorum fines
a Nasamonibus occupatos.

XII

De his vocabulis quae Cloatius Verus aut satis commode
aut nimis absurde et inlepide ad origines linguae Graecae
redigit.

1 CLOATIUS VERUS in libris quos inscripsit *Verborum
a Graecis Tractorum*, non pauca hercle dicit curiose
et sagaciter conquisita, neque non tamen quaedam
2 futtilia et frivola. "Errare," inquit, "dictum est
ἀπὸ τοῦ ἔρρειν," versumque infert Homeri, in quo
id verbum est:

Ἔρρ' ἐκ νήσου θᾶσσον, ἐλέγχιστε ζωόντων.

3 Item "alucinari" factum scripsit ex eo, quod dicitur
Graece ἀλύειν, unde "elucum" quoque esse dictum
putat, *a* littera in *e* versa, tarditatem quandam animi
et stuporem, qui alucinantibus plerumque usu venit.
4 Item "fascinum" appellatum [1] quasi "bascanum"
et "fascinare" esse quasi "bascinare."
5 Commode haec sane omnia et conducenter. Sed
in libro quarto: "Faenerator," inquit, "appellatus

---

[1] appellatum, *Skutsch*; appellat, ω.

---

[1] Fr. 3, Fun.   [2] *Odyss.* x. 72.
[3] Gk. βασκάνιον.   [4] Gk. βασκαίνω.

came to meet them with a great blast of air, and piling upon them mountainous heaps of sand, buried them all with their entire forces and arms. Through this act the Psylli all perished to a man, and accordingly their territories were occupied by the Nasamones.

XII

Of those words which Cloatius Verus referred to a Greek origin, either quite fittingly or too absurdly and tastelessly.

CLOATIUS VERUS, in the books which he entitled *Words taken from the Greek*, says not a few things indeed which show careful and keen investigation, but also some which are foolish and trifling. "*Errare* (to err)," he says,[1] "is derived from the Greek ἔρρειν," and he quotes a line of Homer in which that word occurs:[2]

Swift wander (ἔρρει) from the isle, most wretched man.

Cloatius also wrote that *alucinari*, or "dream," is derived from the Greek ἀλύειν, or "be distraught," and from this he thinks that the word *elucus* also is taken, with a change of *a* to *e*, meaning a certain sluggishness and stupidity of mind, which commonly comes to dreamy folk. He also derives *fascinum*, or "charm," as if it were *bascanum*,[3] and *fascinare*, as if it were *bascinare*,[4] or "bewitch."

All these are fitting and proper enough. But in his fourth book he says:[5] "*Faenerator* is equivalent to

[5] Fr. I, Fun.

est quasi φαινεράτωρ, ἀπὸ τοῦ φαίνεσθαι ἐπὶ τὸ
χρηστότερον, quoniam id genus hominum [1] speciem
ostentent humanitatis et commodi esse videantur
6 inopibus nummos desiderantibus," idque dixisse ait
Hypsicraten quempiam grammaticum, cuius libri
sane nobiles sunt super his, quae a Graecis accepta
sunt.   Sive hoc autem ipse Cloatius sive nescio quis
alius nebulo effutivit, nihil potest dici insulsius.
7 " Faenerator " enim, sicuti M. Varro in libro tertio
De Sermone Latino scripsit, a faenore est nominatus ; "faenus" autem dictum ait a fetu et quasi
a fetura quadam pecuniae parientis atque incres-
8 centis.   Idcirco et M. Catonem et ceteros aetatis
eius "feneratorem" sine *a* littera pronuntiasse
tradit, sicuti "fetus" ipse et "fecunditas" appellata.

XIII

Quid sit "municipium" et quid a "colonia" differat ; et
quid sint "municipes" quaeque sit eius vocabuli ratio
ac proprietas ; atque inibi, quod divus Hadrianus in senatu
de iure atque vocabulo municipum verba fecit.

1   "Municipes" et "municipia" verba sunt dictu
facilia et usu obvia, et neutiquam reperias qui haec
dicit, quin scire se plane putet quid dicat.   Sed
2 profecto aliud est, atque aliter dicitur.   Quotus
enim fere nostrum est, qui, cum ex colonia populi
Romani sit, non se "municipem" esse et populares

[1] homines, *Skutsch.*

---

[1] Frag. 57, G. and S.
[2] Thurneysen, *T.L.L. s.v. fenus,* thinks this derivation
176

φαινεράτωρ, meaning 'to appear at one's best,' since that class of men present an appearance of kindliness and pretend to be accommodating to poor men who are in need of money"; and he declared that this was stated by Hypsicrates, a grammarian whose books on *Words Borrowed from the Greeks* are very well known. But whether Cloatius himself or some other blockhead gave vent to this nonsense, nothing can be more silly. For *faenerator,* as Marcus Varro wrote in the third book of his *Latin Diction*,[1] "is so called from *faenus,* or 'interest,' but *faenus,*" he says, "is derived from *fetus*,[2] or 'offspring,' and from a birth, as it were, from money, producing and giving increase." Therefore he says that Marcus Cato[3] and others of his time pronounced *fenerator* without the letter *a,* just as *fetus* itself and *fecunditas* were pronounced.

XIII

The meaning of *municipium* and how it differs from *colonia* ; and what *municipes* are and the derivation and proper use of that word ; and also what the deified Hadrian said in the senate about the name and rights of *municipes*.

MUNICIPES and *municipia* are words which are readily spoken and in common use, and you would never find a man who uses them who does not think that he understands perfectly what he is saying. But in fact it is something different, and the meaning is different. For how rarely is one of us found who, coming from a colony of the Roman people, does not say what is far removed from reason and from truth,

is perhaps correct ; we may compare Greek τόκος, which means both "offspring" and "interest."
[3] Frag. inc. 62, Jordan.

suos "municipes" esse dicat, quod est a ratione et
3 a veritate longe aversum? Sic adeo et "municipia"
quid et quo iure sint quantumque a "colonia"
differant ignoramus, existimamusque meliore con-
dicione esse "colonias" quam "municipia."

4 De cuius opinationis tam promiscae erroribus
divus Hadrianus in oratione, quam *De Italicensibus*,
unde ipse ortus fuit, in senatu habuit, peritissime
disseruit mirarique se ostendit quod et ipsi Italicenses et quaedam item alia municipia antiqua, in
quibus Uticenses nominat, cum suis moribus legi-
busque uti possent, in ius coloniarum mutari gesti-
5 verint. Praenestinos autem refert maximo opere a
Tiberio imperatore petisse orasseque ut ex colonia
in municipii statum redigerentur, idque illis Tiberium
pro ferenda gratia tribuisse, quod in eorum finibus
sub ipso oppido ex capitali morbo revaluisset.

6 "Municipes" ergo sunt cives Romani ex municipiis,
legibus suis et suo iure utentes, muneris tantum
cum populo Romano honorari participes, a quo
munere capessendo appellati videntur, nullis aliis
necessitatibus neque ulla populi Romani lege ad-
stricti, nisi in quam populus eorum fundus factus
7 est. Primos autem municipes sine suffragii iure
Caerites esse factos accepimus concessumque illis
ut civitatis Romanae honorem quidem caperent, sed
negotiis tamen atque oneribus vacarent, pro sacris

---

[1] *O.R.F.*[2] p. 608. Italica was a city of Spain on the river
Baetis, opposite Hispalis (Seville). It was founded by Scipio
Africanus the Elder and peopled by his veterans; whence
the name "the Italian city." It was the birthplace of
Trajan and Hadrian.

[2] Such as serving in the legions and not among the auxili-
aries.

[3] For *fundus* cf. xix. 8. 12.

178

namely, that he is *municeps* and that his fellow citizens are *municipes*? So general is the ignorance of what *municipia* are and what rights they have, and how far they differ from a "colony," as well as the belief that *coloniae* are better off than *municipia*.

With regard to the errors in this opinion which is so general the deified Hadrian, in the speech which he delivered in the senate *In Behalf of the Italicenses*,[1] from whom he himself came, discoursed most learnedly, showing his surprise that the Italicenses themselves and also some other ancient *municipia*, among whom he names the citizens of Utica, when they might enjoy their own customs and laws, desired instead to have the rights of colonies. Moreover, he asserts that the citizens of Praeneste earnestly begged and prayed the emperor Tiberius that they might be changed from a colony into the condition of a *municipium*, and that Tiberius granted their request by way of conferring a favour, because in their territory, and near their town itself, he had recovered from a dangerous illness.

Municipes, then, are Roman citizens from free towns, using their own laws and enjoying their own rights, merely sharing with the Roman people an honorary *munus*, or "privilege"[2] (from the enjoyment of which privilege they appear to derive their name), and bound by no other compulsion and no other law of the Roman people, except such as their own citizens have officially ratified.[3] We learn besides that the people of Caere were the first *municipes* without the right of suffrage, and that it was allowed them to assume the honour of Roman citizenship, but yet to be free from service and burdens, in return for receiving and guarding sacred

bello Gallico receptis custoditisque. Hinc "tabulae Caerites" appellatae versa vice, in quas censores referri iubebant quos notae causa suffragiis privabant.

8   Sed "coloniarum" alia necessitudo est; non enim veniunt extrinsecus in civitatem nec suis radicibus nituntur, sed ex civitate quasi propagatae sunt et iura institutaque omnia populi Romani, non sui

9 arbitrii, habent.   Quae tamen condicio, cum sit magis obnoxia et minus libera, potior tamen et praestabilior existimatur propter amplitudinem maiestatemque populi Romani, cuius istae coloniae quasi effigies parvae simulacraque esse quaedam videntur, et simul quia obscura oblitterataque sunt municipiorum iura, quibus uti iam per innotitiam non queunt.

XIV

Quod M. Cato differre dixit "properare" et "festinare"; et quam incommode Verrius Flaccus verbi quod est "festinat" ἔτυμον interpretatus est.

1   "FESTINARE" et "properare" idem significare
2 atque in eandem rem dici videntur.   Sed M. Cato id differre existimat eaque hoc modo divisa—verba sunt ipsius ex oratione, quam *De Suis Virtutibus*

---

¹ Their government was modelled on that of Rome, with a senate (*decuriones*), two chief magistrates (*IIviri iure dicundo*), elected annually, etc.

objects during the war with the Gauls. Hence by contraries those tablets were called *Caerites* on which the censors ordered those to be enrolled whom they deprived of their votes by way of disgrace.

But the relationship of the " colonies " is a different one ; for they do not come into citizenship from without, nor grow from roots of their own, but they are as it were transplanted from the State and have all the laws and institutions of the Roman people, not those of their own choice. This condition, although it is more exposed to control and less free, is nevertheless thought preferable and superior because of the greatness and majesty of the Roman people, of which those colonies seem to be miniatures, as it were, and in a way copies ;[1] and at the same time because the rights of the municipal towns become obscure and invalid, and from ignorance of their existence the townsmen are no longer able to make use of them.

XIV

That Marcus Cato said there was a difference between *properare* and *festinare*, and how inappropriately Verrius Flaccus explained the origin of the latter word.

FESTINARE and *properare* seem to indicate the same thing and to be used of the same thing. But Marcus Cato thinks that there is a difference, and that the difference is this—I quote his own words from the speech which he pronounced *On his Own Merits* :[2]

[2] p. 44. 4, Jordan.

habuit— : "Aliud est 'properare,' aliud 'festinare.'
Qui unum quid mature transigit, is properat; qui
multa simul incipit neque perficit, is festinat."

3 Verrius Flaccus rationem dicere volens differentiae
huius : "'Festinat,'" inquit, "a fando dicitur, quoniam isti ignaviores, qui nihil perficere possunt,
4 plus verborum quam operae habent." Sed id nimis
coactum atque absurdum videtur neque tanti esse
momenti potest prima in utroque verbo littera, ut
propter eam unam tam diversa verba "festinare"
5 et "fari" eadem videri debeant. Commodius autem
propiusque visum est, "festinare" esse quasi "fessum esse." Nam qui multis simul rebus properandis
defessus est, is iam non properat, set festinat.

XV

Quid Theophrastus mirum de perdicibus scriptum reliquerit
et quid Theopompus de leporibus.

1 THEOPHRASTUS, philosophorum peritissimus, omnes
in Paphlagonia perdices bina corda habere dicit,
Theopompus in Bisaltia lepores bina iecora.

---

[1] p. xv, Müller.

"It is one thing to hasten (*properare*), another to hurry (*festinare*). He who finishes some one thing in good season, hastens (*properat*); one who begins many things at the same time but does not finish them, hurries (*festinat*)."

Verrius Flaccus, wishing to explain the nature of this difference, says:[1] "*Festinat* is derived from *for* (to speak), since those idle folk who can accomplish nothing talk more than they act." But that seems too forced and absurd, nor can the first letter of the two words be of such weight that because of it such different words as *festino* and *for* should appear to be the same. But it seems more fitting and closer to explain *festinare* as equivalent to *fessum esse* or "be wearied." For one who tires himself out by hastily attacking many things at once no longer hastens, but hurries.[2]

XV

The strange thing recorded of partridges by Theophrastus and of hares by Theopompus.

THEOPHRASTUS, most expert of philosophers, declares[3] that in Paphlagonia all the partridges have two hearts; Theopompus,[4] that in Bisaltia the hares have two livers each.

---

[2] Both derivations are fanciful. *Festino* is related to *confestim*, but its origin is uncertain.

[3] Frag. 182, Wimmer.   [4] *F.H.G.* i. 301.

XVI

"Agrippas" a partus aegri et inprosperi vitio appellatos;
deque his deabus quae vocantur "Prorsa" et "Postverta."

1 QUORUM in nascendo non caput, sed pedes primi
extiterant, qui partus difficillimus aegerrimusque
habetur, "Agrippae" appellati, vocabulo ab aegri-
2 tudine et pedibus conficto. Esse autem pueros in
utero Varro dicit capite infimo nixos, sursum pedibus
elatis, non ut hominis natura est, sed ut arboris.
3 Nam pedes cruraque arboris ramos appellat, caput
4 stirpem atque caudicem. "Quando igitur," inquit,
"contra naturam forte conversi in pedes, brachiis
plerumque diductis, retineri solent, aegriusque tunc
mulieres enituntur, huius periculi deprecandi gratia
arae statutae sunt Romae duabus Carmentibus,
quarum altera 'Postverta' cognominatast, 'Prorsa'
altera, a recti perversique partus et potestate et
nomine."

XVII

Quae ratio vocabuli sit agri Vaticani.

1 ET agrum Vaticanum et eiusdem agri deum prae-
sidem appellatum acceperamus a vaticiniis quae vi

---

[1] *Ant. Rer. Div.* xiv, frag. 17[b], Agahd.
[2] Carmenta was a birth-goddess, whose festival, the
Carmentalia (or Karmentalia) occurred on Jan. 11 and 15.
The *Carmentes* may originally have been wise women who

XVI

That the name *Agrippa* was given to those whose birth was difficult and unnatural ; and of the goddesses called *Prorsa* and *Postverta*.

THOSE at whose birth the feet appeared first, instead of the head, which is considered the most difficult and dangerous form of parturition, are called *Agrippae,* a word formed from *aegritudo,* or " difficulty," and *pedes* (feet). But Varro says [1] that the position of children in the womb is with the head lowest and the feet raised up, not according to the nature of a man, but of a tree. For he likens the branches of a tree to the feet and legs, and the stock and trunk to the head. " Accordingly," says he, " when they chanced to be turned upon their feet in an unnatural position, since their arms are usually extended they are wont to be held back, and then women give birth with greater difficulty. For the purpose of averting this danger altars were set up at Rome to the two Carmentes,[2] of whom one was called *Postverta,*[3] the other *Prorsa,*[4] named from natural and unnatural births, and their power over them."

XVII

Of the origin of the term *ager Vaticanus.*

WE had been told that the *ager Vaticanus,* or " Vatican region," and the presiding deity of the same place, took their names from the *vaticinia,* or

assisted at births and were later deified (Fowler, *Roman Festivals,* pp 290 ff.).

[3] That is, head foremost.   [4] That is, feet foremost.

atque instinctu eius dei in eo agro fieri solita essent.
2 Sed praeter hanc causam M. Varro in libris *Divinarum* aliam esse tradit istius nominis rationem :
" Nam sicut Aius," inquit, " deus appellatus araque
ei statuta est quae est infima nova via, quod eo in
loco divinitus vox edita erat, ita Vaticanus deus
nominatus penes quem essent vocis humanae initia,
quoniam pueri, simul atque parti sunt, eam primam
vocem edunt quae prima in Vaticano syllabast
idcircoque ' vagire ' dicitur, exprimente verbo sonum
vocis recentis."

XVIII

Lepida quaedam et memoratu et cognitu de parte geometriae
quae ὀπτική appellatur, et item alia quae κανονική, et
tertia itidem quae dicitur μετρική.

1 PARS quaedam geometriae ὀπτική appellatur quae
ad oculos pertinet, pars altera, quae ad auris, κανονική vocatur, qua musici ut fundamento artis suae
2 utuntur. Utraque harum spatiis et intervallis linearum et ratione numerorum constat.
3 Ὀπτική facit multa demiranda id genus, ut in
speculo uno imagines unius rei plures appareant ;
item ut speculum in loco certo positum nihil imaginet, aliorsum translatum faciat imagines ; item si
rectus speculum spectes, imago fiat tua eiusmodi, ut

---

[1] Frag. 20[b], Agahd.

"prophecies," which were wont to be made in that region through the power and inspiration of that god. But in addition to that reason Marcus Varro, in his *Antiquities of the Gods*, states[1] that there is another explanation of the name: "For," says he, "just as Aius was called a god and the altar was erected in his honour which stands at the bottom of the Nova Via, because in that place a voice from heaven was heard, so that god was called *Vaticanus* who controls the beginnings of human speech, since children, as soon as they are born, first utter the sound which forms the first syllable of *Vaticanus*; hence the word *vagire* ('cry'), which represents the sound of a new-born infant's voice."

XVIII

Some interesting and instructive remarks about that part of Geometry which is called "Optics"; of another part called "Harmony," and also of a third called "Metric."

A PART of Geometry which relates to the sight is called ὀπτική or "Optics," another part, relating to the ears, is known as κανονική, or "Harmony," which musicians make use of as the foundation of their art. These are concerned respectively with the spaces and the intervals between lines and with the theory of musical numbers.

Optics effect many surprising things, such as the appearance in one mirror of several images of the same thing; also that a mirror placed in a certain position shows no image, but when moved to another spot gives reflections; also that if you look straight into a mirror, your reflection is such that your head

caput deorsum videatur, pedes sursum. Reddit etiam
causas ea disciplina cur istae quoque visiones fallant,
ut quae in aqua conspiciuntur maiora ad oculos fiant,
quae procul ab oculis sunt, minora.

4 Κανονική autem longitudines et altitudines vocis
emetitur. Longior mensura vocis ῥυθμός dicitur,
5 altior μέλος. Est et alia species κανονικῆς, quae appellatur μετρική, per quam syllabarum longarum et
brevium et mediocrium iunctura et modus congruens
cum principiis geometriae aurium mensura examina-
6 tur. " Sed haec," inquit M. Varro, " aut omnino
non discimus aut prius desistimus quam intellegamus
cur discenda sint. Voluptas autem," inquit, " vel
utilitas talium disciplinarum in postprincipiis existit,
cum perfectae absolutaeque sunt ; in principiis vero
ipsis ineptae et insuaves videntur."

XIX

Sumpta historia ex Herodoti libro super fidicine Arione.

1 CELERI admodum et cohibili oratione vocumque
filo tereti et candido fabulam scripsit Herodotus
2 super fidicine illo Arione. " Vetus," inquit, " et
3 nobilis Arion cantator fidibus fuit. Is loco et oppido

---

[1] The first effect is produced when the surface of a mirror
is divided into numerous smaller mirrors. Pliny, N.H.
xxxiii. 129, describes cups, the interior of which was so
fashioned as to give numerous reflections. The second is
described (e.g.) in Pausanias viii. 37. 7. The third is pro-

appears below and your feet uppermost.[1] This science also gives the reasons for optical illusions, such as the magnifying of objects seen in the water, and the small size of those that are remote from the eye.

Harmony, on the other hand, measures the length and pitch of sounds. The measure of the length of a tone is called ῥυθμός, or "rhythm," of its pitch, μέλος, or "melody." There is also another variety of Harmony which is called μετρική, or "Metric," by which the combination of long and short syllables, and those which are neither long nor short, and the verse measure according to the principles of geometry are examined with the aid of the ears. "But these things," says Marcus Varro,[2] "we either do not learn at all, or we leave off before we know why they ought to be learned. But the pleasure," he says, "and the advantage of such sciences appear in their later study, when they have been completely mastered; but in their mere elements they seem foolish and unattractive."[3]

XIX

A story about the lyre-player Arion, taken from the work of Herodotus.

HERODOTUS has written [4] of the famous lyre-player Arion in terse and vigorous language and in simple and elegant style. "Arion," says he, "in days of old was a celebrated player upon the lyre. The

duced when one looks into a concave mirror from a certain distance. Magic mirrors of various kinds and properties were known in antiquity, as well as divination by means of mirrors. See *Trans. Numis. and Ant. Soc. of Phila.*, 1910, pp. 187 ff.
  [2] p. 337, Bipont.   [3] Cf. xvi. 8. 15 ff.   [4] i. 23.

Methymnaeus, terra atque insula omni Lesbius fuit.
4 Eum Arionem rex Corinthi Periander amicum ama-
5 tumque habuit artis gratia.   Is inde a rege pro-
6 ficiscitur, terras inclutas Siciliam atque Italiam
visere.   Ubi eo venit auresque omnium mentesque
in utriusque terrae urbibus demulsit, in quaestibus
istic et voluptatibus amoribusque hominum fuit.
7 Is tum postea grandi pecunia et re bona multa
8 copiosus Corinthum instituit redire, navem igitur et
navitas, ut notiores amicioresque sibi, Corinthios
9 delegit."   Sed eos Corinthios, homine accepto
navique in altum provecta, praedae pecuniaeque
10 cupidos cepisse consilium de necando Arione.   Tum
illum ibi, pernicie intellecta, pecuniam ceteraque
sua, ut haberent, dedisse, vitam modo sibi ut parce-
11 rent oravisse.   Navitas precum eius harum com-
miseritum esse illactenus ut ei necem adferre per
vim suis manibus temperarent, sed imperavisse ut
12 iam statim coram desiliret praeceps in mare.
" Homo," inquit, " ibi territus, spe omni vitae
perdita, id unum postea oravit, ut priusquam mortem
obpeteret, induere permitterent sua sibi omnia
indumenta et fides capere et canere carmen casus
13 illius sui consolabile.   Feros et inmanes navitas
prolubium tamen audiendi subit ; quod oraverat im-
14 petrat.   Atque ibi mox de more cinctus, amictus,
ornatus stansque in summae puppis foro, carmen
quod ' orthium ' dicitur voce sublatissima cantavit.
15 Ad postrema cantus cum fidibus ornatuque omni,
sicut stabat canebatque, iecit sese procul in pro-

---

[1] 625–585 B.C.

[2] This was a song in such a high key that it could be
reached by few voices. In Aristophanes, *Knights*, 1279
(*L.C.L.* i, p. 247) the ὅρθιος νόμος is played by a
"prince of harpers."

town in which he was born was Methymna, but from
the name of his country and the island as a whole
he was a Lesbian.   This Arion for the sake of his
art was held in friendship and affection by Periander,
king of Corinth.[1]   Later, he left the king, to visit
the famous lands of Sicily and Italy.   On his arrival
there he charmed the ears and minds of all in the
cities of both countries, and there he was enriched
as well as being generally admired and beloved.
Then later, laden with money and with wealth of
all kinds, he determined to return to Corinth,
choosing a Corinthian vessel and crew, as better
known to him and more friendly."   But Herodotus
says that those Corinthians, having received Arion
on board and put to sea, formed the plan of murder-
ing him for the sake of his money.   Then he,
realizing that death was at hand, gave them possession of his money and other goods, but begged that
they should at least spare his life.   The sailors were
moved by his prayers only so far as to refrain from
putting him to death with their own hands, but they
bade him at once, before their eyes, leap headlong
into the sea.   "Then," says Herodotus, "the poor
man, in terror and utterly hopeless of life, finally
made the one request that before meeting his end he
might be allowed to put on all his costume, take his
lyre, and sing a song in consolation of his fate.   The
sailors, though savage and cruel, nevertheless had a
desire to hear him; his request was granted.   Then
afterwards, crowned in the usual way, robed and
adorned, he stood upon the extreme stern and lifting
up his voice on high sang the song called 'orthian.'[2]
Finally, having finished his song, with his lyre and
all his equipment, just as he stood and sang, he

fundum. Navitae, hautquaquam dubitantes quin
perisset, cursum quem facere coeperant tenuerunt.

16 Sed novum et mirum et pium facinus contigit."
Delphinum repente inter undas adnavisse fluitantique
sese homini subdidisse et dorso super fluctus edito
vectavisse incolumique eum corpore et ornatu

17 Taenarum in terram Laconicam devexisse. Tum
Arionem prorsus ex eo loco Corinthum petivisse
talemque Periandro regi, qualis delphino vectus
fuerat, inopinanti sese optulisse eique rem, sicuti

18 acciderat, narravisse. Regem istaec parum credi-
disse, Arionem, quasi falleret, custodiri iussisse,

19 navitas inquisitos, ablegato Arione, dissimulanter
interrogasse ecquid audissent in his locis unde

20 venissent super Arione? Eos dixisse, hominem, cum
inde irent, in terra Italia fuisse eumque illic bene
agitare et studiis delectationibusque urbium florere
atque in gratia pecuniaque magna opulentum fortu-

21 natumque esse. Tum inter haec eorum verba Arionem cum fidibus et indumentis cum quibus se in

22 salum eiaculaverat extitisse, navitas stupefactos

23 convictosque ire infitias non quisse. Eam fabulam
dicere Lesbios et Corinthios atque esse fabulae
argumentum, quod simulacra duo aenea ad Taenarum viserentur, delphinus vehens et homo in-
sidens.

threw himself far out into the deep. The sailors, not doubting in the least that he had perished, held on the course which they had begun. But an unheard of, strange and miraculous thing happened." Herodotus asserts that a dolphin suddenly swam up amid the waves, dove under the floating man, and lifting his back above the flood, carried him and landed him at Taenarum in the Laconian land, with his person and adornment uninjured. Then Arion went from there straight to Corinth and, just as he was when the dolphin carried him, presented himself unexpectedly to king Periander and told him exactly what had occurred. The king did not believe the story but ordered that Arion be imprisoned as an impostor. He hunted up the sailors, and in the absence of Arion craftily questioned them, asking whether they had heard anything of Arion in the places from which they had come. They replied that the man had been in the land of Italy when they left it, that he was doing well there, enjoying the devotion and the pleasures of the cities, and that both in prestige and in money he was rich and fortunate. Then, in the midst of their story, Arion suddenly appeared with his lyre, clad in the garments in which he had thrown himself into the sea; the sailors were amazed and proved guilty, and could not deny their crime. This story is told by the Lesbians and the Corinthians, and in testimony to its truth two brazen images are to be seen near Taenarum, the dolphin carrying the man, who is seated on his back.

BOOK XVII

LIBER SEPTIMUS DECIMUS

I

Quod Gallus Asinius et Largius Licinus sententiam M. Ciceronis reprehenderunt ex oratione quam dixit *Pro M. Caelio*;
et quid adversus homines stolidissimos pro eadem sententia
vere [1] dignéque dici possit.

1 Ut quidam fuerunt monstra hominum, quod de dis
inmortalibus impias falsasque opiniones prodiderunt,
ita nonnulli tam prodigiosi tamque vecordes extite-
runt, in quibus sunt Gallus Asinius et Largius
Licinus, cuius liber etiam fertur infando titulo
Ciceromastix, ut scribere ausi sint M. Ciceronem
parum integre atque inproprie atque inconsiderate
2 locutum.   Atque alia quidem quae reprehenderunt
3 neque dictu neque auditu digna sunt, sed enim hoc,[2]
in quo sibimet ipsi praeter cetera esse visi sunt
verborum pensitatores·subtilissimi, cedo, quale id sit
consideremus.
4   M. Cicero *Pro M. Caelio* ita scribit : " Nam quod
obiectum est de pudicitia quodque omnium accu-
satorum non criminibus, sed vocibus maledictisque
celebratum est, id numquam tam acerbe feret M.
Caelius, ut eum paeniteat non deformem esse
5 natum."   Non existumant verbo proprio esse usum,
quod ait " paeniteat," atque id prope ineptum etiam

---

[1] e re, *Skutsch* ; mere, δ.
[2] in hoc, ω ; in *deleted by Hosius.*

---

[1] § 6.

BOOK XVII

I

That Asinius Gallus and Largius Licinus criticized a saying
of Cicero's in the speech which he delivered *For Marcus
Caelius*; and what may be said with truth and propriety
in defence of that saying, in reply to those most foolish
critics.

JUST as there have been monsters of men who expressed impious and false opinions about the immortal
gods, so there have been some so extravagant and
so ignorant that they have dared to say that Marcus
Cicero spoke without correctness, propriety, or consideration; among these are Asinius Gallus and
Largius Licinus, and the latter's book even bears the
outrageous title of *The Scourge of Cicero*. Now the
other things that they have censured are certainly not
worth hearing or mentioning; but let us consider
the value of this stricture of theirs, in which particularly they are, in their own opinion, very keen
critics of language.

Marcus Cicero in his speech *For Marcus Caelius* [1]
writes as follows: "As to the charge made against his
chastity and published by all his accusers, not in the
form of actual charges, but of gossip and calumnies,
Marcus Caelius will never take that so much to heart,
as to repent that he was not born ugly." They
think that Cicero has not used the proper word in
saying *paeniteat*, or "repent," and they go so far as
to add that it is almost absurd; "for," they say,

6 esse dicunt. "Nam 'paenitere,'" inquiunt, "tum dicere solemus, cum quae ipsi fecimus aut quae de nostra voluntate nostroque consilio facta sunt, ea nobis post incipiunt displicere sententiamque in iis
7 nostram demutamus"; neminem autem recte ita loqui " paenitere sese, quod natus sit " aut " paenitere, quod mortalis sit " aut " quod ex offenso forte vulneratoque corpore dolorem sentiat," quando istiusmodi rerum nec consilium sit nostrum nec arbitrium, sed ea ingratis nostris[1] vi ac necessitate naturae nobis accidant : " Sicut hercle," inquiunt,
8 " non voluntarium fuit M. Caelio, quali forma nasceretur, cuius eum dixit ' non paenitere,' tamquam in ea causa res esset ut rationem caperet paenitendi."
9 Est haec quidem, quam dicunt, verbi huiusce sententia et " paenitere " nisi in voluntariis rebus non probe dicitur, tametsi antiquiores verbo ipso alio quoque modo usitati sunt et " paenitet " ab eo quod est " paene " et " paenuria " dixerunt. Sed id
10 aliorsum pertinet atque alio in loco dicetur. Nunc autem, sub hac eadem significatione quae vulgo nota est, non modo ineptum hoc non est quod M. Cicero dixit, sed festivissimum adeo et facetissi-
11 mum est. Nam cum adversarii et obtrectatores M. Caeli, quoniam erat pulchro corpore, formam eius et faciem in suspiciones inpudicitiae accerserent, inludens Cicero tam absurdam criminationem, quod formam, quam natura fecerat, vitio darent, eodem ipso errore quem inludebat sciens usus est et " non

---

[1] in nostris, *ω*; in *deleted by Carrio.*

---

[1] This promise is not fulfilled.

"we regularly use *paenitere* when things which we ourselves have done, or which have been done in accordance with our wish and design, later begin to displease us and we change our opinion about them." But that no one correctly says that he "repents being born" or "repents being mortal," or "because he feels pain from any chance injury or wound inflicted upon his body"; for in such cases there is no design or choice on our part, but such things happen to us against our will by some necessity or force of nature. "In the same way," they continue, "it was not a matter of choice with Marcus Caelius with what person he was born; yet he says that 'he did not repent this,' as if there were in that circumstance ground for a feeling of repentance."

This is in fact, as they say, the force of that word, and *paenitere* is strictly used of none but voluntary acts, although our forefathers used that same word also in a different sense and connected *paenitet* with the words *paene* (almost) and *paenuria* (want). But that is another question, and will be spoken of in another place.[1] But with regard to the point at issue, giving to *paenitere* this same meaning which is commonly recognized, what Marcus Cicero said is not only not foolish, but in the highest degree elegant and witty. For since the adversaries and detractors of Marcus Caelius, inasmuch as he was of handsome person, made use of his appearance and figure to throw doubt upon his chastity, therefore Cicero, making sport of such an absurd charge as to impute to him as a fault the good looks which nature had given him, has deliberately adopted that very same false charge of which he is making fun, saying: "Marcus Caelius is not sorry

paenitet," inquit, " M. Caelium, non deformem esse natum," ut vel hac ipsa re, quod ita dicebat, obprobraret adversariis ac per facetias ostentaret facere eos deridiculum, quod proinde Caelio formam crimini darent, quasi arbitrium eius fuisset, quali forma nasceretur.

II

Verba quaedam ex Q. Claudi *Annalium* primo cursim in legendo notata.

1 Cum librum veteris scriptoris legebamus, conabamur postea memoriae vegetandae gratia indipisci animo ac recensere quae in eo libro scripta essent in utrasque existimationes laudis aut culpae adnotamentis digna, eratque hoc sane quam utile exercitium ad conciliandas nobis, ubi venisset usus, verborum
2 sententiarumque elegantium recordationes. Velut haec verba ex Q. Claudi primo *Annali*, quae meminisse potui, notavi, quem librum legimus biduo proximo superiore.
3 " Arma," inquit, "plerique abiciunt atque inermi inlatebrant sese." " Inlatebrant" verbum poeticum visum est, sed non absurdum neque asperum.
4 " Ea," inquit, "dum fiunt, Latini subnixo animo ex victoria inerti consilium ineunt." " Subnixo animo " [1] quasi sublimi et supra nixo, verbum bene significans et non fortuitum ; demonstratque animi altitudinem fiduciamque, quoniam quibus innitimur, iis quasi erigimur attollimurque.

---

[1] ex . . . animo, *supplied by Hertz from Nonius* iv, *p.* 405, 29 ; et victoria certi, *Canter.*

---

[1] Frag. 22, Peter[2]. [2] Frag. 13, Peter[2].

for not having been born ugly"; so that by the very
fact of speaking thus he might reproach his accusers
and wittily show that they were doing an absurd
thing in making Caelius' handsome person an accusation against him, just as if the person with which
he was born depended upon his own volition.

II

Certain words from the first book of the *Annals* of Quintus
Claudius, noted in a hasty reading.

WHENEVER I read the book of an early writer, I
tried afterwards, for the purpose of quickening my
memory, to recall and review any passages in the
book which were worthy of note, in the way either
of praise or censure; and I found it an exceedingly
helpful exercise for ensuring my recollection of
elegant words and phrases, whenever need of them
should arise.   For example, in the first book of the
Annals of Quintus Claudius, which I had read on
the preceding two days, I noted these passages:

"The greater number," says he,[1] "threw away
their arms and hid themselves unarmed."   The verb
inlatebrant, for "hid themselves," seemed poetic, but
neither improper nor harsh.

"While these things were going on," he says,[2]
"the Latins, their spirits raised because of their
easy victory, form a plan."   *Subnixo animo* is
significant and carefully chosen expression with the
force of "raised and elevated in spirit"; and
it indicates loftiness and confidence of spirit, since
we are, as it were, raised and lifted up by that upon
which we depend.

5 "Domus," inquit, "suas quemque ire iubet et sua omnia frunisci." "Frunisci"[1] rarius quidem fuit in aetate M. Tulli ac deinceps infra rarissimum, dubitatumque est ab inperitis antiquitatis an Latinum
6 foret. Non modo autem Latinum, sed iucundius amoeniusque etiam verbum est "fruniscor" quam "fruor," et ut "fatiscor" a "fateor," ita "fruniscor"
7 factum est a "fruor." Q. Metellus Numidicus, qui caste pureque lingua usus Latina videtur, in epistula quam exul *Ad Domitios* misit, ita scripsit : "Illi vero omni iure atque honestate interdicti, ego neque aqua neque igni careo et summa gloria fruniscor."
8 Novius, in Atellania quae *Parcus* inscripta est, hoc verbo ita utitur :

Quód magno opere quaésiverunt, íd frunisci nón queunt.
Quí non parsit ápud se, ... frunítus est.

9 "Et Romani," inquit, "multis armis et magno commeatu praedaque ingenti copiantur." "Copiantur"[2] verbum castrense est nec facile id reperias apud civilium causarum oratores, ex eademque figura est qua "lignantur" et "pabulantur" et "aquantur."
10 "Sole," inquit, "occaso." "Sole occaso" non insuavi vetustate est, si quis aurem habeat non sordidam nec proculcatam ; in *Duodecim* autem

---

[1] frunisci, *added by Carrio.*
[2] copiantur, *added by Hertz (Carrio).*

---

[1] Frag. 23, Peter[2].   [2] v. 77, Ribbeck[3].
[3] Frag. 24, Peter[2].   [4] *Id.* 3.   [5] i. 7, 8, 9.

" He bids each one," he says,[1] " go to his own house and enjoy his possessions." *Frunisci*, meaning " enjoy," was somewhat rare in the days of Marcus Tullius and became still rarer after that time, and its Latinity was questioned by those who were unacquainted with our early literature. However, *fruniscor* is not only good Latin, but it is more elegant and pleasing than *fruor*, from which it is formed in the same way as *fatiscor* from *fateor*. Quintus Metellus Numidicus, who is known to have used the Latin tongue with purity and simplicity, in the letter which he sent when in exile *To the Domitii*, wrote as follows : " They indeed were cut off from every right and honour, I lack neither water nor fire and I enjoy (*fruniscor*) the greatest glory." Novius, in his Atellan farce entitled *The Miser*, uses this word : [2]

What eagerly they sought they can't enjoy
(*frunisci*) ;
Who does not spare, enjoys the goods he has.

" And the Romans," says Quadrigarius,[3] " get possession of (*copiantur*) many arms and a great supply of provisions, and enormous booty." *Copiantur* is a soldier's word, and you will not readily find it in the pleaders of civil suits ; it is formed in the same way as *lignantur*, or " gather wood," *pabulantur*, or " forage," and *aquantur*, or " get water."

Quadrigarius uses *sole occaso* for " at sunset." [4] This expression has a flavour of antiquity which is not without charm, if one possesses an ear that is not dull and commonplace ; furthermore the phrase occurs in the *Twelve Tables* in the following passage : [5]

Tabulis verbum hoc ita scriptum est : " Ante meridiem causam coniciunto, cum perorant ambo praesentes. Post meridiem praesenti litem addicito. Si ambo praesentes, sol[1] occasus suprema tempestas esto."

11 " Nos," inquit, "in medium relinquemus." Vulgus " in medio " dicit ; nam vitium esse istuc putat et, si dicas " in medium ponere," id quoque esse soloecon putant ; set probabilius significantiusque sic dici videbitur, si quis ea verba non incuriose introspiciat ; Graece quoque θεῖναι εἰς μέσον, vitium id non est.

12 " Postquam nuntiatum est," inquit, " ut pugnatum esset in Gallos, id civitas graviter tulit." " In Gallos" mundius subtiliusque est quam "cum Gallis" aut " contra Gallos "; nam pinguiora haec obsoletioraque sunt.

13 " Simul," inquit, "forma, factis, eloquentia, dignitate, acrimonia, confidentia pariter praecellebat, ut facile intellegeretur magnum viaticum ex se atque in se ad rempublicam evertendam habere." " Magnum viaticum" pro magna facultate et paratu magno nove positum est, videturque Graecos secutus, qui ἐφόδιον a sumptu viae ad aliarum quoque rerum apparatus traducunt ac saepe ἐφοδίασον pro eo dicunt, quod est " institue" et " instrue."

---

[1] sol, *Hosius, comparing* xiv. 7. 8 ; solis, *Q.*

---

[1] Frag. 25, Peter[2].

[2] The phrase *in medium* has various meanings, according to the context and the verb with which it is used ; cf. Cic. *ad Fam.* xv. 2. 6, *se . . . eam rem numquam in medium propter periculi metum protulisse; Cluent.* 77 ; Virg. *Aen.* v. 401. If the lexicons are to be trusted, *in medium ponere*

"Before midday let them hear the case, with both parties making their pleas in person. After midday, decide the case in favour of the one who is present. If both are present, let sunset be the limit of the proceedings."

"We," says he,[1] "will leave it undecided (*in medium*)." The common people say *in medio*; for they think that *in medium* is an error, and if you should say *in medium ponere* (to make known),[2] they consider that also a solecism; but if anyone examines these words with some care, that expression will seem to him the more correct and the more expressive; moreover in Greek θεῖναι εἰς μέσον is not an error.

"After it was announced," he says,[3] "that a battle had been fought against the Gauls (*in Gallos*), the State was troubled." *In Gallos* is neater and finer than *cum Gallis* or *contra Gallos*; for these are somewhat awkward and out of date.

"At the same time," he says,[4] "he excelled in person, in exploits, in eloquence, in position, in energy, and confidence alike, so that it was easily seen that he possessed from himself and in himself a great equipment (*magnum viaticum*) for overthrowing the republic." *Magnum viaticum* is a novel expression for great ability and great resources, and Claudius seems to have followed the Greeks, who transferred ἐφόδιον from the meaning of "money for a journey" to preparation for other things, and often say ἐφοδίασον for "prepare" and "make ready."

is rare, and the usual expression is *in medio ponere, e.g.* Cic. *Nat. Deor.* i. 13, *ponam in medio sententias philosophorum.*
[3] Frag. 1, Peter[2].   [4] *Id.* 8.

14   "Nam Marcus," inquit, "Manlius, quem Capitolium servasse a Gallis supra ostendi cuiusque operam
cum M. Furio dictatore apud Gallos cumprime
fortem atque exsuperabilem respublica sensit, is et
genere et vi et virtute bellica nemini concedebat."
"Adprime" crebrius est, "cumprime" rarius tra-
ductumque ex eo est, quod "cumprimis" dicebant
pro quod est "inprimis."

15   "Nihil sibi," inquit, "divitias opus esse." Nos
"divitiis" dicimus. Sed vitium hoc orationis nullum
est ac ne id quidem est quod figura dici solet; recta
enim istaec oratio est et veteres conpluscule ita
dixerunt, nec ratio dici potest, cur rectius sit
"divitiis opus esse" quam "divitias," nisi qui
grammaticorum nova instituta ut τεμένων ἱερά ob-
servant.

16   "Nam hac,"[1] inquit, "maxime versatur deorum
iniquitas, quod deteriores sunt incolumiores neque
optimum quemquam inter nos sinunt diurnare."
Inusitate "diurnare" dixit pro "diu vivere," sed
ex ea figuratione est, qua dicimus "perennare."

17   "Cum iis," inquit, "consermonabatur." "Sermonari" rusticius videtur, sed rectius est, "sermocinari" tritius,[2] sed corruptius est.

18   "Sese," inquit, "ne id quoque, quod tum suaderet,
facturum esse." "Ne id quoque" dixit pro "ne id
quidem," infrequens nunc in loquendo, sed in libris
veterum creberrimum.

---

[1] hac *suggested by Hosius*; haec, ω.
[2] tritius, *Hosius*; rectius, ω; crebrius, σ; lectius, *Dziatzko*.

---

[1] Frag. 7, Peter[2].   [2] *Id.* 26.   [3] *Id.* 9.
[4] *Id.* 6.   [5] *Id.* 17.

" For Marcus Manlius," said he,[1] " who, as I have shown above, saved the Capitol from the Gauls, and whose service, along with that of Marcus Furius the dictator, the State found especially (*cumprime*) valiant and irresistible against the Gauls, yielded to no one in race, in strength and in warlike valour." *Adprime* is more frequent for "especially"; *cumprime* is rarer and is derived from the expression *cumprimis* with the force of *inprimis*.

Quadrigarius says[2] that " he has no need for riches (*divitias*)." We use the ablative *divitiis* with *opus*. But this usage of his is not a mistake in grammar, nor is it even what is termed a figure; for it is correct Latin and the early writers quite frequently used that case; moreover, no reason can be given why *divitiis opus esse* is more correct than *divitias*, except by those who look upon the innovations of grammarians as oracular responses.

" For herein especially," says he,[3] " lies the injustice of the gods, that the worst men are the least subject to injury, and that they do not allow the best men to remain long (*diurnare*) with us." His use of *diurnare* for *diu vivere* is unusual, but it is justified by the figure by which we use *perennare* (to last for years).

He says:[4] " He conversed (*consermonabatur*) with them." *Sermonari* seems somewhat rustic, but is more correct; *sermocinari* is more common, but is not such pure Latin.

" That he would not do even that," says he,[5] " which he then advised." He has used *ne id quoque* for *ne id quidem*; the former is not common now in conversation, but is very frequent in the books of the earlier writers.

19 " Tanta," inquit, " sanctitudo fani est, ut numquam quisquam violare sit ausus." " Sanctitas " quoque et " sanctimonia " non minus Latine dicuntur, sed nescio quid maioris dignitatis est verbum

20 " sanctitudo," sicuti M. Cato *In L. Veturium* " duritudinem " quam " duritiam " dicere gravius putavit : " Qui illius," inquit, " impudentiam norat et duritudinem."

21 " Cum tantus," inquit, " arrabo penes Samnites populi Romani esset." " Arrabonem " dixit sescentos obsides et id maluit quam pignus dicere, quoniam vis huius vocabuli in ea sententia gravior acriorque est ; sed nunc " arrabo " in sordidis verbis haberi coeptus ac multo videtur sordidius " arra," quamquam " arra " quoque veteres saepe dixerint et conpluriens Laberius.

22, 23 " Miserrimas," inquit, " vitas exegerunt," et : " hic nimiis in otiis," inquit, " consumptus est." Elegantia utrobique ex multitudine numeri quaesita est.

24 " Cominius," inquit, " qua ascenderat, descendit atque verba Gallis dedit." " Verba Cominium dedisse Gallis " dicit, qui nihil quicquam cuiquam dixerat ; neque eum Galli, qui Capitolium obsidebant, ascendentem aut descendentem [1] viderant. Sed " verba dedit " haut secus posuit quam si tu dicas " latuit atque obrepsit."

25 " Convalles," inquit, " et arboreta magna erant."

---

[1] aut descendentem, σ ; *not in the MSS.*

---

[1] *Id.* 2.   [2] xviii. 8, Jordan.   [3] Frag. 20, Peter[2].
[4] v. 152, Ribbeck[3].   [5] Frag. 27, Peter[2].
[6] *Id.* 28.   [7] Frag. 4, Peter[2].   [8] *Id.* 29.
[9] From earlier *arbos* and *-etum.*

"Such is the sanctity (*sanctitudo*) of the fane," says he,[1] "that no one ever ventured to violate it." *Sanctitas* and *sanctimonia* are equally good Latin, but the word *sanctitudo* somehow has greater dignity, just as Marcus Cato, in his speech *Against Lucius Veturius*, thought it more forcible to use *durituedo* than *duritia*, saying,[2] "Who knew his impudence and hardihood (*durituedinem*)."

"Since the Roman people," says Quadrigarius,[3] "had given such a pledge (*arrabo*) to the Samnites." He applied the term *arrabo* to the six hundred hostages and preferred to use that word rather than *pignus*, since the force of *arrabo* in that connection is weightier and more pointed; but nowadays *arrabo* is beginning to be numbered among vulgar words, and *arra* seems even more so, although the early writers often used *arra*, and Laberius[4] has it several times.

"They have spent most wretched lives (*vitas*)," says Quadrigarius,[5] and,[6] "This man is worn out by too much leisure (*otiis*)." In both cases elegance is sought by the use of the plural number.

"Cominius," says he,[7] "came down the same way he had gone up and so deceived the Gauls." He says that Cominius "gave words to the Gauls," meaning "deceived them," although he had said nothing to anybody; and the Gauls who were besieging the Capitol had seen him neither going up nor coming down. But "he gave words" is used with the meaning of "he escaped the notice of, and circumvented."

Again he says:[8] "There were valleys and great woods (*arboreta*)." *Arboreta* is a less familiar word, *arbusta*[9] the more usual one.

"Arboreta" ignobilius verbum, "arbusta" cele-
bratius.

26 "Putabant," inquit, "eos qui foris atque qui in
arce erant inter se commutationes et consilia facere."
"Commutationes," id est conlationes communica-
tionesque, non usitate dixit, set non hercle inscite
nec ineleganter.

27 Haec ego pauca interim super eo libro, quorum
memoria post lectionem subpetierat, mihi notavi.

III

Verba M. Varronis ex libro quinto et vicesimo *Humanarum,*
quibus contra opinionem volgariam interpretatus est Homeri
versum.

1 IN sermonibus forte quos de temporibus rerum
ad usus hominum repertarum agitabamus, adulescens
quispiam non indoctus sparti quoque usum in terra
Graecia diu incognitum fuisse dixit multisque post
Ilium captum tempestatibus ex terra Hispania ad-
2 vectum. Riserunt hoc ad inludendum ex his, qui
ibi aderant, unus atque alter, male homines litterati,
quod genus ἀγοραίους Graeci appellant, atque eum
qui id dixerat librum legisse Homeri aiebant, cui
versus hic forte deesset:

Καὶ δὴ δοῦρα σέσηπε νεῶν καὶ σπάρτα λέλυνται.

3 Tum ille prorsum inritatus: "Non," inquit, "meo
libro versus iste,[1] sed vobis plane magister defuit, si
creditis in eo versu σπάρτα id significare quod nos

---

[1] iste, *Lion*; ipse, QΠ; se, Z; sed, NOX; ipse, sed,
Longolius.

---

[1] Frag. 5, Peter[2].   [2] *Iliad* ii. 135.

"They thought," says he,[1] "that those who were without and those that were within the citadel were exchanging communications (*commutationes*) and plans" *Commutationes*, meaning "conferences and communications," is not usual, but, by Heaven! is neither erroneous nor inelegant.

These few notes on that book, such things as I remembered after reading it, I have now jotted down for my own use.

III

The words of Marcus Varro in the twenty-fifth book of his *Human Antiquities*, in which he has interpreted a line of Homer contrary to the general opinion.

IT happened in the course of conversations which we carried on about the dates of various inventions for human use, that a young man not without learning observed that the use of *spartum* or "Spanish broom" also was for a long time unknown in the land of Greece and that it was imported from Spain many years after the taking of Ilium. One or two half-educated fellows who were present there, of the class that the Greeks call ἀγοραῖοι, or "haunters of the market-place," laughed in derision of this statement, and declared that the man who had made it had read a copy of Homer which happened to lack the following verse:[2]

And rotted the ship's timbers, loosed the ropes (σπάρτα).

Then the youth, in great vexation, replied: "It was not my book that lacked that line, but you who badly lacked a teacher, if you believe that σπάρτα in that verse means what we call *spartum*, or 'a

4 'spartum' dicimus." Maiorem illi risum subiciunt, neque id desierunt,[1] nisi liber ab eo prolatus esset M. Varronis vicesimus quintus *Humanarum,* in quo de isto Homeri verbo a Varrone ita scriptum est: "Ego σπάρτα apud Homerum non plus 'spartum' significare puto quam σπάρτους, qui dicuntur in agro Thebano nati. In Graecia sparti copia modo coepit esse ex Hispania. Neque ea ipsa facultate usi Liburni; sed hi plerasque naves loris suebant, Graeci magis cannabo et stuppa ceterisque sativis rebus, a 5 quibus σπάρτα appellabant." Quod cum ita Varro dicat, dubito hercle, an posterior syllaba in eo verbo, quod apud Homerum est, acuenda sit, nisi quia voces huiusmodi, cum ex communi significatione in rei certae proprietatem concedunt, diversitate accentuum separantur.

IV

Quid Menander poeta Philemoni poetae dixerit, a quo saepe indigne in certaminibus comoediarum superatus est; et quod saepissime Euripides in tragoedia ab ignobilibus poetis victus est.

1 MENANDER a Philemone, nequaquam pari scriptore, in certaminibus comoediarum ambitu gratiaque et 2 factionibus saepenumero vincebatur. Eum cum forte habuisset obviam, "Quaeso," inquit, "Philemo, bona venia dic mihi, cum me vincis, non erubescis?"

---

[1] desierunt *suggested by Hosius*; destituerunt, Q[1]Z; *the other MSS. have* destiterunt.

rope of Spanish broom.'" They only laughed the louder, and would have continued to do so, had he not produced the twenty-fifth book of Varro's *Human Antiquities*, in which Varro writes as follows of that Homeric word :[1] "I believe that σπάρτα in Homer does not mean *sparta*, or 'Spanish broom,' but rather σπάρτοι, a kind of broom which is said to grow in the Theban territory. In Greece there has only recently been a supply of *spartum*, imported from Spain. The Liburnians did not make use of that material either, but as a rule fastened their ships together with thongs,[2] while the Greeks made more use of hemp, tow, and other cultivated plants (*sativis*), from which ropes got their name of *sparta*." Since Varro says this, I have grave doubts whether the last syllable in the Homeric word ought not to have an acute accent ; unless it be because words of this kind, when they pass from their general meaning to the designation of a particular thing, are distinguished by a difference in accent.

IV

What the poet Menander said to Philemon, by whom he was often undeservedly defeated in contests in comedy ; and that Euripides was very often vanquished in tragedy by obscure poets.

In contests in comedy Menander was often defeated by Philemon, a writer by no means his equal, owing to intrigue, favour, and partisanship. When Menander once happened to meet his rival, he said : "Pray pardon me, Philemon, but really, don't you blush when you defeat me ?"

[1] Frag. 4, Mirsch.
[2] See *sutiles naves*, Plin. *N.H.* xxiv. 65.

3 Euripidem quoque M. Varro ait, cum quinque
et septuaginta tragoedias scripserit, in quinque solis
vicisse, cum eum saepe vincerent aliquot poetae
ignavissimi.

4 Menandrum autem alii centum octo, partim cen-
5 tum novem reliquisse comoedias ferunt. Sed Apollo-
dori, scriptoris celebratissimi, hos de Menandro versus
legimus in libro qui *Chronica* inscriptus est :

> Κηφισιεὺς ὢν ἐκ Διοπείθους πατρός,
> Πρὸς τοῖσιν ἑκατὸν πέντε γράψας δράματα
> Ἐξέλιπε, πεντήκοντα καὶ δυεῖν ἐτῶν.

6 Ex istis tamen centum et quinque omnibus, solis eum
octo vicisse, idem Apollodorus eodem in libro scripsit.

V

Nequaquam esse verum, quod minutis quibusdam rhetoricae
artificibus videatur, M. Ciceronem in libro quem *De
Amicitia* scripsit vitioso argumento usum, ἀμφισβητούμενον
ἀντὶ ὁμολογουμένου posuisse ; totumque id consideratius
tractatum exploratumque.

1 M. CICERO, in dialogo cui titulus est *Laelius* vel
De Amicitia, docere volens amicitiam non spe expec-
tationeque utilitatis neque pretii mercedisque causa
colendam, sed quod ipsa per sese plena virtutis hones-
tatisque sit expetendam diligendamque esse, etiamsi
nihil opis nihilque emolumenti ex ea percipi queat,
hac sententia atque his verbis usus est eaque dicere

---

[1] p. 351, Bipont.
[2] Some MSS. of the Greek *Life* of Euripides give fifteen,
which seems a more probable number for so popular a poet.
Sophocles won eighteen at the City Dionysia alone.

Marcus Varro says [1] that Euripides also, although he wrote seventy-five tragedies, was victor with only five,[2] and was often vanquished by some very poor poets.

Some say that Menander left one hundred and eight comedies, others that the number was a hundred and nine. But we find these words of Apollodorus, a very famous writer, about Menander in his work entitled *Chronica*: [3]

> Cephissia's child, by Diopeithes sired,
> An hundred plays he left and five besides ;
> At fifty-two he died.

Yet Apollodorus also writes in the same book that out of all those hundred and five dramas Menander gained the victory only with eight.

V

That it is by no means true, as some meticulous artists in rhetoric affirm, that Marcus Cicero, in his book *On Friendship*, made use of a faulty argument and postulated "the disputed for the admitted"; with a careful discussion and examination of this whole question.

MARCUS CICERO, in the dialogue entitled *Laelius*, or *On Friendship*, wishes to teach us that friendship ought not to be cultivated in the hope and expectation of advantage, profit, or gain, but that it should be sought and cherished because in itself it is rich in virtue and honour, even though no aid and no advantage can be gained from it. This thought he has expressed in the following words, put into the mouth of Gaius Laelius, a wise man and a very

[3] Frag. 77, p. 358, Jacoby.

facit C. Laelium, sapientem virum, qui Publii Africani
2 fuerat amicissimus : " Quid enim ? Africanus indigens
mei ? Ne [1] ego quidem illius. Sed ego admiratione
quadam virtutis eius, ille vicissim opinione fortasse
nonnulla quam de meis moribus habebat me dilexit ;
auxit benivolentiam consuetudo. Sed quamquam
utilitates multae et magnae consecutae sunt, non
sunt tamen ab earum spe causae diligendi profectae.
Ut enim benefici liberalesque sumus, non ut exigamus
gratiam—neque enim beneficium faeneramur, sed
natura propensi ad liberalitatem sumus—, sic amicitiam non spe mercedis adducti, sed quod omnis eius
fructus in ipso amore inest, expetendam putamus."
3   Hoc cum legeretur in coetu forte hominum doctorum, rhetoricus quidam sophista, utriusque linguae
callens, haut sane ignobilis ex istis acutulis et
minutis doctoribus qui τεχνικοί appellantur, atque in
disserendo tamen non impiger, usum esse existimabat
argumento M. Tullium non probo neque apodictico,
sed eiusdem quaestionis, cuius esset ea ipsa res de qua
quaereretur ; verbisque id vitium Graecis appellat,
quod accepisset ἀμφισβητούμενον ἀντὶ ὁμολογουμένον.
4 " Nam ' beneficos,' " inquit, " et ' liberales ' sumpsit
ad confirmandum id quod de amicitia dicebat, cum
ipsum illud et soleat quaeri et debeat, quisquis
liberaliter et benigne facit, qua mente quoque consilio benignus liberalisque sit ? utrum, quia mutuam

---

[1] minime hercule ! ac ne, *Cic.*

[1] § 30.

dear friend of Publius Africanus : [1] "Well, then, does Africanus need my help? No more do I need his. But I love him because of a certain admiration for his virtues; he in turn has affection for me perhaps because of some opinion which he has formed of my character; and intimacy has increased our attachment. But although many great advantages have resulted, yet the motives for our friendship did not arise from the hope of those advantages. For just as we are kindly and generous, not in order to compel a return—for we do not put favours out at interest, but we are naturally inclined to generosity —just so we think that friendship is to be desired, not because we are led by hope of gain, but because all its fruit is in the affection itself."

When it chanced that these words were read in a company of cultured men, a sophistical rhetorician, skilled in both tongues, a man of some note among those clever and meticulous teachers known as τεχνικοί, or "connoisseurs," who was at the same time not without ability in disputation, expressed the opinion that Marcus Tullius had used an argument which was neither sound nor clear, but one which was of the same uncertainty as the question at issue itself; and he described that fault by Greek words, saying that Cicero had postulated ἀμφισβητούμενον ἀντὶ ὁμολογουμένου, that is, "what was disputed rather than what was admitted."

"For," said he, "he took *benefici*, 'the kindly,' and *liberales*, 'the generous,' to confirm what he said about friendship, although that very question is commonly asked and ought to be asked, with what thought and purpose one who acts liberally and kindly is kind and generous. Whether it is

gratiam speret et eum in quem benignus sit ad
parem curam sui provocet, quod facere plerique
omnes videntur, an, quia natura sit benivolus be-
nignitasque eum per sese ipsa et liberalitas delectet
sine ulla recipiendae gratiae procuratione, quod est
5 omnium ferme rarissimum?" Argumenta autem
censebat aut probabilia esse debere aut perspicua et
minime controversa, idque "apodixin" vocari dicebat,
cum ea quae dubia aut obscura sunt, per ea quae
6 ambigua non sunt inlustrantur. Atque, ut ostenderet
beneficos liberalesque ad id quod de amicitia quaereretur quasi argumentum exemplumve sumi non oportere, "Eodem," inquit, "simulacro eademque rationis
imagine amicitia invicem pro argumento sumi potest,
si quis adfirmet homines beneficos liberalesque esse
debere, non spe aliqua compendii, set amore et
7 studio honestatis. Poterit enim consimiliter ita
dicere: 'Namque, ut amicitiam non spe utilitatis
amplectimur, sic benefici liberalesque non gratiae
8 reciperandae studio esse debemus.' Poterit sane,"
inquit, "ita dicere, sed neque amicitia liberalitati
neque liberalitas amicitiae praebere argumentum
potest, cum de utraque pariter quaeratur."
9 Haec ille rhetoricus artifex dicere quibusdam videbatur perite et scienter, sed videlicet eum vocabula
10 rerum vera ignoravisse. Nam "beneficum et libera-

---

[1] That is, ἀπόδειξις.

because he hopes for a return of the favour, and tries to arouse in the one to whom he is kind a like feeling towards himself, as almost all seem to do ; or because he is by nature kindly, and kindness and generosity gratify him for their own sakes without any thought of a return of the favour, which is as a rule the rarest of all." Furthermore, he thought that arguments ought to be either convincing, or clear and not open to controversy, and he said that the term *apodixis*,[1] or "demonstration," was properly used only when things that are doubtful or obscure are made plain through things about which there is no doubt. And in order that he might show that the kind and generous ought not to be taken as an argument or example for the question about friendship, he said : " By the same comparison and the same appearance of reason, friendship in its turn may be taken as an argument, if one should declare that men ought to be kindly and generous, not from the hope of a return, but from the desire and love of honourable conduct. For he will be able to argue in a very similar manner as follows : ' Now just as we do not embrace friendship through hope of advantage, so we ought not to be generous and kindly with the desire of having the favour returned.' He will indeed," said he, "be able to say this, but friendship cannot furnish an argument for generosity, nor generosity for friendship, since in the case of each there is equally an open question."

It seemed to some that this artist in rhetoric argued cleverly and learnedly, but that as a matter of fact he was ignorant of the true meaning of terms. For Cicero calls a man "kind and generous" in the

lem" Cicero appellat, ita ut philosophi appellandum esse censent, non eum qui, ut ipse ait, beneficia faeneratur, sed qui benigne facit, nulla tacita[1] ratione

11 ad utilitates suas redundante. Non ergo obscuro neque ambiguo argumento usus est, sed certo atque perspicuo, siquidem, qui vere beneficus liberalisque est, qua mente bene aut liberaliter facit non quae-

12 ritur.[2] Aliis enim longe nominibus appellandus est, si, cum talia facit, sui potius quam alterius iuvandi

13 causa facit. Processisset autem argutatori isti fortassean reprehensio, si Cicero ita dixisset : " Ut enim benefice liberaliterque facimus, non ut exigamus gratiam " ; videretur enim benefice facere etiam in non beneficum cadere posse, si id per aliquam circumstantiam fieret, non per ipsam perpetuae be-

14 nignitatis constantiam. Sed cum " beneficos liberalesque " dixerit neque alius modi isti sint quam cuius esse eos supra diximus, " inlotis," quod aiunt, " pedibus " et verbis reprehendit doctissimi viri orationem.

---

[1] citate, *Q* ; citata, *Q*[2] ; citatus, *Hertz.*
[2] quaerit, *Skutsch.*

---

[1] As quoted in § 2.
[2] Cf. i. 9. 8 (vol. i, p. 49) with the note,* and Plautus, *Poen.*

sense that the philosophers believe those words ought to be used: not of one who, as Cicero himself expresses it, puts favours out at interest, but of one who shows kindness without having any secret reason which redounds to his own advantage. Therefore he has used an argument which is not obscure or doubtful, but trustworthy and clear, since if anyone is truly kind and generous, it is not asked with what motive he acts kindly or generously. For he must be called by very different names if, when he does such things, he does them for his own advantage rather than for that of another. Possibly the criticism made by this sophist might have some justification, if Cicero had said :[1] "For as we do some kind and generous action, not in order to compel a return." For it might seem that anyone who was not kindly might happen to do a kind action, if it was done because of some accidental circumstance and not through a fixed habit of constant kindliness. But since Cicero spoke of "kindly and generous people," and meant no other sort than that which we have mentioned before, it is "with unwashed feet,"[2] as the proverb says, and unwashed words that our critic assails the argument of that most learned man.

316, *illotis manibus.* The reference is to washing before handling sacred objects or performing religious rites. *Et verbis* is an addition by Gellius, in the sense of "hasty, inconsiderate language."

VI

Falsum esse, quod Verrius Flaccus, in libro secundo quos *De Obscuris M. Catonis* composuit, de servo recepticio scriptum reliquit.

1 M. Cato Voconiam legem suadens verbis hisce usus est: "Principio vobis mulier magnam dotem adtulit; tum magnam pecuniam recipit, quam in viri potestatem non conmittit, eam pecuniam viro mutuam dat; postea, ubi irata facta est, servum recepticium sectari atque flagitare virum iubet."

2 Quaerebatur, "servus recepticius" quid esset. Libri statim quaesiti allatique sunt Verrii Flacci *De Obscuris Catonis.* In libro secundo scriptum et inventum est, "recepticium servum" dici nequam et nulli pretii, qui, cum venum esset datus, redhibitus

3 ob aliquod vitium receptusque sit. "Propterea," inquit, "servus eiusmodi sectari maritum et flagitare pecuniam iubebatur, ut eo ipso dolor maior et contumelia gravior viro fieret, quod eum servus nihili petendae pecuniae causa conpellaret."

4 Cum pace autem cumque venia istorum, si qui sunt, qui Verrii Flacci auctoritate capiuntur, dictum

5 hoc sit. "Recepticius" enim "servus," in ea re quam dicit Cato, aliud omnino est quam Verrius

6 scripsit. Atque id cuivis facile intellectu est; res enim procul dubio sic est: quando mulier dotem

---

[1] His recommendation of this law is also mentioned by Cicero, *Cato Mai.* 14, who discusses some features of the law in *Verr.* ii. 1. 101 ff. ; see also xx. 1. 23, below. The law, which in general had to do with inheritances, has been the subject of much discussion ; one of its provisions was that no one should make a woman his heir.

[2] p. 54, 5, Jordan.　　　[3] p. xvi, Müller.

VI

That what Verrius Flaccus wrote about *servus recepticius*,
in his second book *On the Obscurities of Marcus Cato*, is
false.

MARCUS CATO, when recommending the Voconian
.law,[1] spoke as follows:[2] " In the beginning the
woman brought you a great dowry; then she holds
back a large sum of money, which she does not entrust
to the control of her husband, but lends it to her
husband. Later, becoming angry with him, she
orders a *servus recepticius*, or 'slave of her own,'
to hound him and demand the money."

The question was asked what was meant by *servus
recepticius*. At once the books of Verrius Flaccus
On the Obscurities of Cato were asked for and produced. In the second book was found the statement[3] that *servus recepticius* was the name applied
to a slave that was worthless and of no value, who,
after being sold, was returned because of some fault
and taken back. "Therefore," says Flaccus, "a
slave of that kind was bidden to hound her husband
and demand the money, in order that the man's
vexation might be greater, and the insult put upon
him still more bitter, for the very reason that a
worthless slave dunned him for the payment of
money."

But with the indulgence and pardon of those, if
such there be, who are influenced by the authority
of Verrius Flaccus, this must be said. That *recepticius servu*s in the case of which Cato is speaking is
something very different from what Verrius wrote.
And this is easy for anyone to understand; for the
situation is undoubtedly this: when the woman

marito dabat, tum quae ex suis bonis retinebat neque
ad virum tramittebat, ea " recipere " dicebatur, sicuti
nunc quoque in venditionibus " recipi" dicuntur,
7 quae excipiuntur neque veneunt. Quo verbo Plautus
quoque in *Trinummo* usus est in hoc versu :

Postículum hoc recépit,[1] cum aedis véndidit,

id est : cum aedis vendidit, particulam quandam
quae post eas aedis erat non vendidit, sed retinuit.
8 Ipse etiam Cato mulierem demonstrare locupletem
volens : " Mulier," inquit, " et magnam dotem dat
et magnam pecuniam recipit," hoc est : et magnam
9 dotem dat et magnam pecuniam retinet. Ex ea
igitur re familiari, quam sibi dote data retinuit,
10 pecuniam viro mutuam dat. Eam pecuniam cum
viro forte irata repetere instituit, adponit ei flagita-
torem " servum recepticium," hoc est proprium
servum suum, quem cum pecunia reliqua receperat
neque dederat doti, sed retinuerat ; non enim servo
mariti imperare hoc mulierem fas erat, sed proprio
suo.
11   Plura dicere quibus hoc nostrum tuear supersedeo ;
ipsa enim sunt per sese evidentia et quod a Verrio
dicitur et a nobis ; quod utrum ergo videbitur cuique
verius, eo utatur.

[1] recepit, *MSS. of Plaut. except A, and of Nonius, p.* 384
(613, Linds.); recipit, ω.

gave the dowry to her husband, what she retained
of her property and did not give over to her
husband she was said to " hold back " (*recipere*), just
as now also at sales those things are said to be
" held back " which are set aside and not sold. This
word Plautus also used in the *Trinummus* in this
line :[1]

> But when he sold the house, this little place
> Behind it he held back (*recepit*).

That is, when he sold the house, he did not sell a
small part which was behind the house, but held it
back. Cato himself too, wishing to describe the
woman as rich, says : " The woman brings a great
dowry and holds back a large sum of money " ; that
is, she gives a great dowry and retains possession
of a large sum of money. From that property then
which she kept for herself after giving her dowry,
she lent money to her husband. When she
happened to be vexed with her husband and determined to demand the money back, she appoints to
demand it from him a *servus recepticius*, that is, a
slave of her very own, whom she had held back
with the rest of the money and had not given as
part of her dowry, but had retained ; for it was not
right for the woman to give such an order to a slave
of her husband, but only to one of her very own.

I forbear to say more in defence of this view of
mine ; for the opinion of Verrius and mine are
before you, each by itself ; anyone therefore may
adopt whichever of the two seems to him the truer.

[1] v. 194.

VII

Verba haec ex Atinia lege: "quod subruptum erit, eius rei
aeterna auctoritas esto," P. Nigidio et Q. Scaevolae visa
esse non minus de praeterito furto quam de futuro cavisse.

1 LEGIS veteris Atiniae verba sunt: "Quod subrup-
2 tum erit, eius rei aeterna auctoritas esto." Quis
aliud putet in hisce verbis quam de tempore tantum
3 futuro legem loqui? Sed Q. Scaevola patrem suum
et Brutum et Manilium, viros adprime doctos, quaesisse ait dubitasseque utrumne in post facta modo
furta lex valeret an etiam in ante facta; quoniam
"subruptum erit" utrumque tempus videretur osten-
dere, tam praeteritum quam futurum.
4 Itaque P. Nigidius, civitatis Romanae doctissimus,
super dubitatione hac eorum scripsit in tertio vicesimo *Grammaticorum Commentariorum.* Atque ipse
quoque idem putat, incertam esse temporis demon-
5 strationem, sed anguste perquam et obscure disserit,
ut signa rerum ponere videas ad subsidium magis
6 memoriae suae quam ad legentium disciplinam. Videbatur tamen hoc dicere, suum verbum et "est" esse
et "erit"; quando per sese ponuntur, habent atque
retinent tempus suum, cum vero praeterito iunguntur,
vim temporis sui amittunt et in praeteritum conten-
7 dunt. Cum enim dico: "in campo est" et "in
comitio est," tempus instans significo; item cum dico

---

[1] Different from the plebiscitum of xiv. 8. 2. The date is
uncertain.
[2] *Fontes Iur. Rom.*, p. 45, 6.
[3] Fr. 3, Huschke; *Iur. Civ.* xvi. 5, Bremer.
[4] *Resp.* 4, Bremer.   [5] *Resp.* 5, Bremer.
[6] *Resp.* 5, Bremer.   [7] Fr. 34, Swoboda.   [8] Cf. xvi. 8. 3.

VII

These words from the Atinian law, "the claim on whatever
   shall be stolen shall be everlasting," seemed to Publius
   Nigidius and Quintus Scaevola to have reference not less
   to a past theft than to a future one.

THE words of the ancient Atinian law [1] are as
follows: [2] "Whatever shall have been stolen, let
the right to claim the thing be everlasting." Who
would suppose that in these words the law referred
to anything else than to future time? But Quintus
Scaevola says [3] that his father [4] and Brutus [5] and
Manilius, [6] exceedingly learned men, inquired and
were in doubt whether the law was valid in cases
of future theft only or also in those already committed in the past; since *subruptum erit* seems to
indicate both times, past as well as future.

Therefore Publius Nigidius, the most learned man
of the Roman State, discussed this uncertainty of
theirs in the twenty-third book of his *Grammatical
Notes.* [7] And he himself too has the same opinion,
that the indication of the time is indefinite, but he
speaks very concisely and obscurely, so that you may
see that he is rather making notes to aid his own
memory than trying to instruct his readers. [8] However, his meaning seems to be that *est* and *erit* are
independent words; when they are used alone,
they have and retain their own tense, but when
they are joined with a past participle, they lose the
force of their own tense, and are transferred to the
past. For when I say *in campo est*, or "he is in
the field," and *in comitio est*, or "he is in the comitium," I refer to the present time; also when I

227

"in campo erit," tempus futurum demonstro; at cum dico: "factum est," "scriptum est," "subruptum est," quamquam "est" verbum temporis est praesentis, confunditur tamen cum praeterito et praesens esse desinit.

8 "Sic igitur," inquit, "etiam istud quod in lege est; si dividas separesque duo verba haec 'subruptum' et 'erit,' ut sic audias 'subruptum erit,'[1] tamquam 'certamen erit' aut 'sacrificium erit,' tum videbitur lex in postfuturum loqui; si vero copulate permixteque dictum intellegas, ut 'subruptum erit' non duo, sed unum verbum sit idque unitum[2] patiendi declinatione sit, tum hoc verbo non minus praeteritum tempus ostenditur quam futurum."

VIII

In sermonibus apud mensam Tauri philosophi quaeri agitarique eiusmodi solita : "cur oleum saepe et facile, vina rarius congelascant, acetum haut fere umquam" et " quod aquae fluviorum fontiumque durentur, mare gelu non duretur."

1 PHILOSOPHUS TAURUS accipiebat nos Athenis cena
2 plerumque ad id diei ubi iam vesperaverat; id enim est tempus istic cenandi. Frequens eius cenae fundus et firmamentum omne erat aula una lentis Aegyptiae et cucurbitae inibi minutim caesae.

---

[1] erit *added by Hertz*; "subruptum," tum "erit," *suggested by Hosius.*
[2] unitum, *Hertz*; unita, ω; unita p. declinatio, *Skutsch.*

---

[1] In Rome the dinner-hour was considerably earlier, usually the ninth hour, or about three o'clock in the afternoon;

say *in campo erit* (he will be in the field), or *in comitio erit* (he will be in the comitium), I indicate future time : but when I say *factum est, scriptum est* or *subruptum est,* although the verb *est* is in the present tense, it is nevertheless united with the past and ceases to be present.

"Similarly then," he says, "with regard also to the wording of the law ; if you divide and separate these two words *subruptum* and *erit,* so that you understand *subruptum erit* as you would *certamen erit,* that is, 'there will be a contest,' or *sacrificium erit* (there will be a sacrifice), then the law will seem to have reference to an act completed in future time ; but if you understand the two words to be united and mingled, so that *subruptum erit* is not two words, but one, and is a single form of the passive inflection, then that word indicates past time no less than future."

VIII

In conversation at the table of the philosopher Taurus questions of this kind were proposed and discussed : "why oil congeals often and readily, wine seldom, vinegar hardly ever," and "that the waters of rivers and springs freeze, while the sea does not."

THE philosopher Taurus at Athens usually entertained us at dinner at the time of day when evening had already come on ; for there that is the time for dining.[1]   The entire basis and foundation of the meal usually consisted of one pot of Egyptian beans, to which were added gourds cut in small pieces.

see Hor. *Epist.* 1. 7. 71 ; Mart. iv. 8. 6.   To-day, too, the dinner-hour is later in Athens than in Rome, although the difference is not so great as in ancient times.

3 Ea quodam die ubi paratis et expectantibus nobis adlata atque inposita mensae est, puerum iubet
4 Taurus oleum in aulam indere.[1] Erat is puer genere Atticus, ad annos maxime natus octo, festi-
5 vissimis aetatis et gentis argutiis scatens. Gutum Samium ore tenus inprudens inanem, tamquam si inesset oleum, adfert convertitque eum et, ut solitum est, circumegit per omnem partem aulae manum :[2]
6 nullum inde ibat oleum. Aspicit puer gutum atrocibus oculis stomachabundus et concussum vehementius
7 iterum in aulam vertit; idque cum omnes sensim atque summissim rideremus, tum puer Graece, et id quidem perquam Attice " μὴ γελᾶτε," inquit, " ἔνι τοὔλαιον· ἀλλ᾽ οὐκ ἴστε, οἷα φρίκη περὶ τὸν ὄρθρον γέγονε
8 τήμερον; κεκρυστάλλωται." " Verbero," inquit ridens Taurus, " nonne is curriculo atque oleum petis ? "

Sed cum puer foras emptum isset, nihil ipse ista mora offensior : " Aula," inquit, " oleo indiget et, ut video, intolerandum fervit ; cohibeamus manus atque interea, quoniam puer nunc admonuit solere oleum congelascere, consideremus cur oleum quidem saepe
9 et facile, set vina rarenter congelascant ? " Atque
10 aspicit me et iubet quid sentiam dicere. Tum ego respondi coniectare me vinum idcirco minus cito congelascere, quod semina quaedam caldoris in sese haberet essetque natura ignitius, ob eamque rem dictum esse ab Homero αἴθοπα οἶνον, non, ut alii putarent, propter colorem.

---

[1] aedere, X, *with erasure of a* ; videre, Q.
[2] manum, ω ; manu *suggested by Hosius.*

---

[1] *Iliad* i. 462, etc.
[2] In Homer this word, from αἶθός, "fire" and ὄψ, "eye," means "fiery-looking" or "sparkling," rather than "fiery."

One day when this dish had been brought and placed upon the table, and we were ready and awaiting the meal, Taurus ordered a slave-boy to pour some oil into the pot. The slave was a boy of Attic birth, at most eight years old, overflowing with the merry wit characteristic of his race and his time of life. He brought an empty Samian flask, from oversight, as he said, supposing there was oil in it, turned it up and, as he usually did, passed it with his hand over all parts of the pot; but no oil came out. The boy, in anger, looked savagely at the flask, shook it violently, and again turned it over the pot; and when we were all quietly and furtively laughing at his actions, he said in Greek, and excellent Attic Greek at that: "Don't laugh; there's oil in it; but don't you know how cold it was this morning; it's congealed." "You rascal," said Taurus with a laugh, "run and fetch some oil."

But when the boy had gone out to buy oil, Taurus, not at all put out by the delay, said: "The pot needs oil, and, as I see, is intolerably hot; let us withhold our hands and meanwhile, since the slave has just told us that oil is in the habit of congealing, let us consider why oil congeals often and readily, but wine rarely." And he looked at me and bade me give my opinion. Then I replied that I inferred that wine congealed less quickly because it had in it certain seeds of heat and was naturally more fiery, and that was why Homer called [1] it αἶθοψ,[2] and not, as some supposed, on account of its colour.

Gellius seems to be wrong so far as Homer is concerned, although some other writers used αἶθοψ in the sense of "fiery," as applied to persons.

11 "Est quidem," inquit Taurus, "ita ut dicis; nam ferme convenit vinum, ubi potum est, calefacere
12 corpora. Sed non secus oleum quoque calorificum est neque minorem vim in corporibus calefaciendis
13 habet. Ad hoc, si istaec quae calidiora sunt difficilius gelu coguntur, congruens est ut quae frigidiora sunt
14 facile cogantur. Acetum autem omnium maxime frigorificum est atque id numquam tamen concrescit.
15 Num igitur magis causa oleo coaguli celerioris in levitate est? Faciliora enim ad coeundum videntur quae levatiora leviioraque sunt."

16 Praeterea id quoque ait quaeri dignum, cur fluviorum et fontium aquae gelu durentur, mare omne incongelabile sit. "Tametsi Herodotus," inquit, "historiae scriptor, contra omnium ferme qui haec quaesiverunt opinionem, scribit mare Bosporicum, quod 'Cimmerium' appellatur, earumque partium mare omne quod 'Scythicum' dicitur, gelu stringi et consistere."

17 Dum haec Taurus, interea puer venerat et aula deferbuerat tempusque esse coeperat edendi et tacendi.

IX

De notis litterarum quae in C. Caesaris epistulis reperiuntur; deque aliis clandestinis litteris ex vetere historia petitis; [1] et quid σκυτάλη sit Laconica.

1 LIBRI sunt epistularum C. Caesaris ad C. Oppium et Balbum Cornelium, qui rebus eius absentis cura-

---

[1] petita, *Skutsch, comparing lemmata of* i. 3; 7; 11.

---

[1] iv. 28 (ii., p. 226, *L.C.L.*).
[2] The Cimmerian Bosphorus, the present Strait of

" It is indeed," says Taurus, " as you say. For it
is well known that wine, when we drink it, warms
the body. But oil is equally calorific and has no
less power of warming the body. Besides, if those
things which are warmer are frozen with greater
difficulty, it follows that those which are colder
freeze more readily. But vinegar is the most
cooling of all things and yet it never freezes. Is
the reason then for the quicker freezing of oil to be
found in its lightness ? For those things seem to
congeal more readily which are lighter and smoother."

Taurus says besides that it is also worth inquiring
why the waters of rivers and streams freeze, while
all the sea is incapable of freezing. " Although
Herodotus," said he, " the writer of history, contrary
to the opinion of almost all who have investigated
these matters, writes [1] that the Bosphoric sea, which
is called Cimmerian,[2] and all that part of the sea
which is termed Scythian,[3] is bound fast by the
cold and brought to a standstill."

While Taurus was thus speaking, the boy had
returned, the pot had cooled off, and the time had
come to eat and hold our peace.

IX

Of the cypher letters which are found in the epistles of
Gaius Caesar, and of other secret forms of writing taken
from ancient history ; and what the Laconian σκυτάλη is.

THERE are volumes of letters of Gaius Caesar
addressed to Gaius Oppius and Cornelius Balbus,

Yenikale, connecting the Palus Maeotis (Sea of Azov) with
the Pontus Euxinus or Black Sea.

[3] Herodotus does not use the term " Scythian Sea," but
says " the sea," referring to the Palus Maeotis and the
Euxine. See the map, *Herod.*, *L.C.L.*, vol. ii.

2 bant. In his epistulis quibusdam in locis inveniun-
tur litterae singulariae sine coagmentis syllabarum,
quas tu putes positas incondite; nam verba ex his
3 litteris confici nulla possunt. Erat autem conven-
tum inter eos clandestinum de commutando situ
litterarum, ut in scripto quidem alia aliae locum et
nomen teneret, sed in legendo locus cuique suus et
4 potestas restitueretur; quaenam vero littera pro qua
scriberetur, ante is, sicuti dixi, conplacebat qui hanc
5 scribendi latebram parabant. Est adeo Probi grammatici commentarius satis curiose factus *De Occulta
Litterarum Significatione in Epistularum C. Caesaris
Scriptura*.[1]
6 Lacedaemonii autem veteres, cum dissimulare et
occultare litteras publice ad imperatores suos missas
volebant, ne, si ab hostibus eae captae[2] forent,
consilia sua noscerentur, epistulas id genus factas
7 mittebant. Surculi duo erant teretes, oblonguli,
pari crassamento eiusdemque longitudinis, derasi
8 atque ornati consimiliter; unus imperatori in bellum
proficiscenti dabatur, alterum domi magistratus cum
9 iure[3] atque cum signo habebant. Quando usus
venerat litterarum secretiorum, circum eum surcu-
lum lorum modicae tenuitatis, longum autem
quantum rei satis erat, conplicabant, volumine
rotundo et simplici, ita uti orae adiunctae undique et
10 cohaerentes lori, quod plicabatur, coirent. Litteras
deinde in eo loro per transversas iuncturarum oras

---

[1] scriptura, *Hertz* ; scriptarum, ω.
[2] hostibus exceptae, ς.
[3] cura, *Madvig* ; loro, *Goettling*.

---

[1] ii. p. 137, Dinter.
[2] See Suet. *Jul.* lvi. 6, who says that Caesar wrote *d* for *a*,
and so on with the other letters.

who had charge of his affairs in his absence. In certain parts of these letters[1] there are found individual characters which are not connected to form syllables, but apparently are written at random ; for no word can be formed from those letters. But a secret agreement had been made between the correspondents about a change in the position of the letters, so that, in writing, one name and position was given to one letter and another to another, but in reading its own place and force was restored to each of them.[2] But which letter was written for which was, as I have already said, agreed upon by those who devised this secret code. There is in fact a commentary of the grammarian Probus, *On the Secret meaning of the Letters appearing in the Epistles of Gaius Caesar*, which is a very careful piece of work.

But the ancient Lacedaemonians, when they wanted to conceal and disguise the public dispatches sent to their generals, in order that, in case they were intercepted by the enemy, their plans might not be known, used to send letters written in the following manner. There were two thin, cylindrical wands of the same thickness and length, smoothed and prepared so as to be exactly alike. One of these was given to the general when he went to war, the other the magistrates kept at home under their control and seal. When the need of more secret communication arose, they bound about the staff a thong of moderate thickness, but long enough for the purpose, in a simple spiral, in such a way that the edges of the thong which was twined around the stick met and were joined throughout. Then they wrote the dispatch on that thong across

versibus a summo ad imum proficiscentibus inscribe-
11 bant; id lorum litteris ita perscriptis revolutum ex
surculo imperatori commenti istius conscio mitte-
12 bant; resolutio autem lori litteras truncas atque
mutilas reddebat membraque earum et apices in
13 partis diversissimas spargebat; propterea, si id
lorum in manus hostium inciderat, nihil quicquam
14 coniectari ex eo scripto quibat; sed ubi ille ad quem
erat missum acceperat, surculo conpari, quem habebat, a [1] capite ad finem, proinde ut debere fieri
sciebat, circumplicabat, atque ita litterae per eundem
ambitum surculi coalescentes rursum coibant inte-
gramque et incorruptam epistulam et facilem legi
15 praestabant. Hoc genus epistulae Lacedaemonii
16 σκυτάλην appellant. Legebamus id quoque in vetere
historia rerum Poenicarum, virum indidem quempiam
inlustrem—sive ille Hasdrubal sive quis alius est non
retineo—epistulam scriptam super rebus arcanis hoc
17 modo abscondisse: pugillaria nova, nondum etiam
cera inlita, accepisse,[2] litteras in lignum incidisse,
postea tabulas, uti solitum est, cera conlevisse easque
tabulas, tamquam non scriptas, cui facturum id prae-
dixerat misisse; eum deinde ceram derasisse litteras-
que incolumes ligno incisas legisse.
18 Est et alia in monumentis rerum Graecarum pro-
funda quaedam et inopinabilis latebra, barbarico
19 astu excogitata. Histiaeus nomine fuit, loco natus
20 in terra Asia non ignobili. Asiam tunc tenebat

---

[1] a *added by Madvig.*
[2] cepisse, *Kronenberg, comparing* xix. 12. 9; *but see Hor.
Serm.* i. 4. 14–15.

---

[1] See note on xiii. 31. 10, and *A.J.P.* xlviii, No. 1.

the connected edges of the joints, with the lines
running from the top to the bottom. When the
letter had been written in this way, the thong was
unrolled from the wand and sent to the general,
who was familiar with the device. But the unroll-
ing of the thong made the letters imperfect and
broken, and their parts and strokes [1] were divided and
separated. Therefore, if the thong fell into the
hands of the enemy, nothing at all could be made
out from the writing; but when the one to whom
the letter was sent had received it, he wound it
around the corresponding staff, which he had, from
the top to the bottom, just as he knew that it ought
to be done, and thus the letters, united by encircling
a similar staff, came together again, rendering the
dispatch entire and undamaged, and easy to read.
This kind of letter the Lacedaemonians called
σκυτάλη. I also read this in an ancient history of
Carthage, that a certain famous man of that country
—whether it was Hasdrubal or another I do not
recall—disguised a letter written about secret
matters in the following way : he took new tablets,
not yet provided with wax, and cut the letters into
the wood. Afterwards he covered the tablet with
wax in the usual way and sent it, apparently without
writing, to one to whom he had previously told his
plan. The recipient then scraped off the wax,
found the letters safe and sound inscribed upon the
wood, and read them.

There is also in the records of Grecian history
another profound and difficult method of conceal-
ment, devised by a barbarian's cunning. He was
called Histiaeus and was born in the land of Asia in
no mean station. At that time king Darius held

21 imperio rex Darius. Is Histiaeus, cum in Persis
apud Darium esset, Aristagorae cuipiam res quasdam
22 occultas nuntiare furtivo scripto volebat. Com-
miniscitur opertum hoc litterarum admirandum.
Servo suo diu oculos aegros habenti capillum ex
capite omni tamquam medendi gratia deradit
caputque eius leve in litterarum formas conpungit.
23 His litteris quae voluerat perscripsit, hominem
postea quoad capillus adolesceret domo continuit.
24 Ubi id factum est, ire ad Aristagoran iubet et "Cum
25 ad eum," inquit, "veneris, mandasse me dicito ut
caput tuum, sicut nuper egomet feci, deradat."
26 Servus, ut imperatum erat, ad Aristagoran venit
27 mandatumque domini adfert. Atque ille id non
esse frustra ratus, quod erat mandatum fecit. Ita
litterae perlatae sunt.

X

Quid de versibus Vergilii Favorinus existumarit, quibus in
describenda flagrantia montis Aetnae Pindarum poetam
secutus est ; conlataque ab eo super eadem re utriusque
carmina et diiudicata.[1]

1   FAVORINUM philosophum, cum in hospitis sui
Antiatem villam aestu anni concessisset nosque ad
eum videndum Roma venissemus, memini super
Pindaro poeta et Vergilio in hunc ferme modum
2 disserere: "Amici," inquit, "familiaresque P.
Vergilii, in his quae de ingenio moribusque eius
memoriae tradiderunt, dicere eum solitum ferunt
3 parere se versus more atque ritu ursino. Namque

---

[1] indiiudicata, δ ; iudicata, *Hertz.*

sway in Asia. This Histiaeus, being in Persia with
Darius, wished to send a confidential message to
a certain Aristagoras in a secret manner. He
devised this remarkable method of concealing a
letter. He shaved all the hair from the head of
a slave of his who had long suffered from weak eyes,
as if for the purpose of treatment. Then he tattooed
the forms of the letters on his smooth head. When
in this way he had written what he wished, he kept
the man at home for a time, until his hair grew out.
When this happened, he ordered him to go to
Aristagoras, adding: "When you come to him, say
that I told him to shave your head, as I did a little
while ago." The slave, as he was bidden, came
to Aristagoras and delivered his master's order.
Aristagoras, thinking that the command must have
some reason, did as he was directed. And thus the
letter reached its destination.

X

What Favorinus thought of the verses of Virgil in which
he imitated the poet Pindar in his description of an
eruption of Mount Aetna; his comparison and evaluation
of the verses of the two poets on the same theme.

I REMEMBER that the philosopher Favorinus, when
he had gone during the hot season to the villa of a
friend of his at Antium, and I had come from Rome
to see him, discoursed in about the following manner
about the poets Pindar and Virgil. "The friends
and intimates of Publius Vergilius," said he, "in the
accounts which they have left us of his talents and
his character, say that he used to declare that he
produced verses after the manner and fashion of a

ut illa bestia fetum ederet ineffigiatum informemque
lambendoque id postea quod ita edidisset confor-
maret et fingeret, proinde ingenii quoque sui partus
recentes rudi esse facie et inperfecta, sed deinceps
tractando colendoque reddere iis se oris et vultus linia-
4 menta.   Hoc virum iudicii subtilissimi ingenue atque
5 vere dixisse, res," inquit, "indicium facit.   Nam
quae reliquit perfecta expolitaque quibusque inposuit
6 census atque dilectus sui supremam manum, omni
poeticae venustatis laude florent; sed quae pro-
crastinata sunt ab eo, ut post recenserentur, et
absolvi, quoniam mors praeverterat, nequiverunt, nequaquam poetarum elegantissimi nomine atque iudicio
7 digna sunt.   Itaque cum morbo obpressus adventare
mortem viderat, petivit oravitque a suis amicissimis
inpense, ut Aeneida, quam nondum satis elimavisset,
adolerent.
8   "In his autem," inquit, "quae videntur retractari
et corrigi debuisse, is maxime locus est qui de monte
Aetna factus est.   Nam cum Pindari, veteris poetae,
carmen quod de natura atque flagrantia montis eius
compositum est, aemulari vellet, eiusmodi sententias
et verba molitus est, ut Pindaro quoque ipso, qui
nimis opima pinguique esse facundia existimatus est,
9 insolentior hoc quidem in loco tumidiorque sit.
Atque uti vosmet ipsos," inquit, "eius quod dico
arbitros faciam, carmen Pindari quod est super
monte Aetna, quantulum est mihi memoriae,
dicam:

---

[1] Cf. Suet. *Vita Verg.* 22 (ii. p. 470, *L.C.L.*).

bear. For he said that as that beast brought forth her young formless and misshapen, and afterwards by licking the young cub gave it form and shape, just so the fresh products of his mind were rude in form and imperfect, but afterwards by working over them and polishing them he gave them a definite form and expression.[1] That this was honestly and truly said by that man of fine taste," said he, "is shown by the result. For the parts that he left perfected and polished, to which his judgment and approval had applied the final hand, enjoy the highest praise for poetical beauty; but those parts which he postponed, with the intention of revising them later, but was unable to finish because he was overtaken by death, are in no way worthy of the fame and taste of the most elegant of poets. It was for that reason, when he was laid low by disease and saw that death was near, that he begged and earnestly besought his best friends to burn the *Aeneid*, which he had not yet sufficiently revised.

"Now among the passages," said Favorinus, "which particularly seem to have needed revision and correction is the one which was composed about Mount Aetna. For wishing to rival the poem which the earlier poet Pindar composed about the nature and eruption of that mountain, he has heaped up such words and expressions that in this passage at least he is more extravagant and bombastic even than Pindar himself, who was thought to have too rich and luxuriant a style. And in order that you yourselves," said he, "may be judges of what I say, I will repeat Pindar's poem about Mount Aetna, so far as I can remember it:[2]

[2] *Pyth.* i. 21 ff.

Τᾶς ἐρεύγονται μὲν ἀπλάτου πυρὸς ἁγνόταται
Ἐκ μυχῶν παγαί· ποταμοὶ δ' ἀμέρσισιν μὲν προχέοντι
    ῥόον καπνοῦ
Αἴθων'· ἀλλ' ἐν ὄρφναισιν πέτρας [1]
Φοίνισσα κυλινδομένα φλὸξ ἐς βαθεῖαν φέρει πόντου
    πλάκα σὺν πατάγῳ.
Κεῖνο δ' Ἀφαίστοιο κρουνοὺς ἑρπετὸν
Δεινοτάτους ἀναπέμπει· τέρας μὲν θαυμάσιον προσιδέσ-
    θαι, θαῦμα δὲ καὶ παρεόντων ἀκοῦσαι.

10 Audite nunc," inquit, "Vergilii versus, quos inchoasse eum verius dixerim, quam fecisse :

Portus ab accessu ventorum inmotus et ingens
Ipse, sed horrificis iuxta tonat Aetna ruinis
Interdumque atram prorumpit ad aethera nubem,
Turbine fumantem piceo et candente favilla,
Adtollitque globos flammarum et sidera lambit ;
Interdum scopulos avulsaque viscera montis
Erigit eructans liquefactaque saxa sub auras
Cum gemitu glomerat fundoque exaestuat imo.

11 Iam principio," inquit, "Pindarus, veritati magis obsecutus, id dixit quod res erat quodque istic usu veniebat quodque oculis videbatur, interdius fumare
12 Aetnam, noctu flammigare ; Vergilius autem, dum in strepitu sonituque verborum conquirendo laborat, utrumque tempus, nulla discretione facta, confudit.
13 Atque ille Graecus quidem fontes imitus [2] ignis eructari et fluere amnes fumi et flammarum fulva et tortuosa volumina in plagas maris ferre, quasi quos-

---

[1] πέτρας *omitted by* ω.   [2] imitus, *Lipsius* ; imitatus, ω.

---

[1] The monster was the giant Typhoeus, or Typhon, who was struck by Zeus' thunder-bolt and buried under Aetna.

Mount Aetna, from whose inmost caves burst forth
The purest fount of unapproachable fire.
By day her rivers roll a lurid stream
Of smoke, while 'mid the gloom of night red flame,
On sweeping, whirleth rocks with crashing din
Far down to the deep sea.   And high aloft
That monster [1] flingeth fearful founts of fire,
A marvel to behold or e'en to hear
From close at hand.

   " Now hear the verses of Virgil, which I may more
truly say that he began than finished : [2]

There lies a port, safe from the winds' approach,
Spacious itself, but Aetna close at hand
Thunders with crashes dire, and now hurls forth
Skyward a dusky cloud with eddies black
And glowing ash, and uplifts balls of flame
And licks the stars ; now spews forth rocks,
The mountain's entrails torn, hurls molten crags
Groaning to heaven, and seethes from depths
      profound.

"Now in the first place," said Favorinus, " Pindar
has more closely followed the truth and has given
a realistic description of what actually happened
there, and what he saw with his own eyes; namely,
that Aetna in the daytime sends forth smoke and
at night fire; but Virgil, labouring to find grand
and sonorous words, confuses the two periods of time
and makes no distinction between them.   Then the
Greek has vividly pictured the streams of fire belched
from the depths and the flowing rivers of smoke, and

---

[2] *Aen.* iii. 570 ff.

243

dam igneos angues, luculente dixit; at hic noster
14 'atram nubem turbine piceo et favilla fumantem'
ῥόον καπνοῦ αἴθωνα interpretari volens, crasse et in-
15 modice congessit, 'globos' quoque 'flammarum,'
quod ille κρουνούς dixerat, duriter et ἀκύρως trans-
16 tulit. Item quod ait : 'sidera lambit,' vacanter hoc
17 etiam," inquit, "accumulavit et inaniter." Neque
non id quoque inenarrabile esse ait et propemodum
insensibile, quod "nubem atram fumare" dixit
18 "turbine piceo et favilla candente." "Non enim
fumare," inquit, "solent neque atra esse quae sunt
candentia; nisi si 'candenti' dixit pervulgate et
inproprie pro ferventi favilla, non pro ignea et
relucenti. Nam 'candens' scilicet a candore dictum,
19 non a calore. Quod 'saxa' autem 'et scopulos
eructari et erigi' eosdemque ipsos statim 'liquefieri
et gemere atque glomerari sub auras' dixit, hoc,"
inquit, "nec a Pindaro scriptum nec umquam fando
auditum et omnium, quae monstra dicuntur, mon-
struosissimum est."

---

[1] Not all modern critics would agree with Favorinus as to
Virgil's last two lines, with their elaborate accommodation
of sound to sense.

the rushing of lurid and spiral volumes of flame into the waters of the sea, like so many fiery serpents; but our poet, attempting to render ῥόον καπνοῦ αἴθωνα, 'a lurid stream of smoke,' has clumsily and diffusely piled up the words *atram nubem turbine piceo et favilla fumantem*, 'a dusky cloud smoking with eddies black and glowing ash,' and what Pindar called κρουνοί, or 'founts,' he has harshly and inaccurately rendered by 'balls of flame.' Likewise when he says *sidera lambit*, 'it licks the stars,' this also," he says, "is a useless and foolish elaboration. And this too is inexplicable and almost incomprehensible, when he speaks of a 'black cloud smoking with eddies black and glowing ash.' For things which glow," said Favorinus, "do not usually smoke nor are they black; unless *candenti* ('glowing') is used vulgarly and inaccurately for hot ashes, instead of those which are fiery and gleaming. For *candens*, of course, is connected with *candor*, or 'whiteness,' not with *calor* ('heat'). But when he says *saxa et scopulos eructari et erigi*, 'that rocks and crags are spewed forth and whirled skyward,' and that these same crags at once *liquefieri et gemere atque glomerari ad auras*, 'are molten and groan and are whirled to heaven,' this," he said, "is what Pindar never wrote and what was never spoken by anyone; and it is the most monstrous of all monstrous descriptions." [1]

XI

Quod Plutarchus in libris *Symposiacis* opinionem Platonis de
habitu atque natura stomachi, fistulaeque eius quae τραχεῖα
dicitur, adversum Erasistratum medicum tutatus est,
auctoritate adhibita antiqui medici Hippocratis.

1 Et Plutarchus et alii quidam docti viri reprehensum esse ab Erasistrato, nobili medico, Platonem
scripsere, quod potum dixit defluere ad pulmonem
eoque satis humectato demanare per eum, quia sit
rimosior, et confluere inde in vesicam, errorisque
istius fuisse Alcaeum ducem, qui in poematis suis
scriberet :

Τέγγε πνεύμονα οἴνῳ· τὸ γὰρ ἄστρον περιτέλλεται,

2 ipsum autem Erasistratum dicere duas esse quasi
canaliculas quasdam vel fistulas easque ab oris fauci-
bus proficisci deorsum, per earumque alteram deduci
delabique in stomachum esculenta omnia et posculenta [1] ex eoque ferri in ventriculum, quae Graece
appellatur ἡ κάτω κοιλία, atque ibi subigi digerique,
ac deinde aridiora ex his recrementa in alvum convenire, quod Graece κόλον dicitur, humidiora per
3 renes in vesicam. Per alteram autem fistulam, quae
Graece nominatur τραχεῖα ἀρτηρία, spiritum a summo
ore in pulmonem atque inde rursum in os et in
4 nares commeare, perque eandem viam vocis quoque

---

[1] posculenta, *Z*, *cf*. iv. 1. 17 ; poculenta (potulenta, NQ), ω.

---

[1] *Sympos.* vii. 1.   [2] p. 194, Fuchs.
[3] *Tim.* 44, p. 91, A ; 31, p. 70, c.   [4] Frag. 39, Bergk[4].
[5] pp. 184 ff. and 194, Fuchs.
[6] The three places referred to are the stomach, the small

XI

That Plutarch in his *Symposiacs* defended the opinion of
Plato about the structure and nature of the stomach, and
of the tube which is called τραχεῖα, against the physician
Erasistratus, urging the authority of the ancient physician
Hippocrates.

BOTH Plutarch[1] and certain other learned men
have written that Plato was criticized by the famous
physician Erasistratus,[2] because he said[3] that drink
went to the lungs and having sufficiently moistened
them, flowed through them, since they are somewhat
porous, and from there passed into the bladder.
They declared that the originator of that error was
Alcaeus, who wrote[4] in his poems :

Wet now the lungs with wine ; the dog-star shines,

but that Erasistratus himself declared[5] that there
were two little canals, so to speak, or pipes, and
that they extended downward from the throat; that
through one of these all food and drink passed and
went into the stomach, and from there were carried
into the belly, which the Greeks call ἡ κάτω κοιλία.
That there it is reduced and digested and then the
drier excrement passes into the bowels, which the
Greeks call κόλον,[6] and the moisture through the
kidneys into the bladder. But through the other
tube, which the Greeks call the τραχεῖα ἀρτηρία, or
" rough windpipe," the breath passes from the lips
into the lungs, and from there goes back into the
mouth and nostrils, and along this same road a
passage for the voice also is made ; and lest drink

intestine and the large intestine. Neither the Greek nor the
Latin terms are always used consistently.

fieri meatum ac, ne potus cibusve aridior, quem
oporteret in stomachum ire, procideret ex ore labere-
turque in eam fistulam per quam spiritus reciprocatur,
eaque offensione intercluderetur animae via, inposi-
tam esse arte quadam et ope naturae inde apud duo
ista foramina, quae dicitur ἐπιγλωττίς, quasi claustra
quaedam mobilia, coniventia vicissim et resurgentia,
5 eamque ἐπιγλωττίδα inter edendum bibendumque
operire atque protegere τὴν τραχεῖαν ἀρτηρίαν, ne
quid ex esca potuve incideret in illud quasi aestu-
antis animae iter; ac propterea nihil humoris influere
in pulmonem ore ipso arteriae communito.

Haec Erasistratus medicus adversum Platonem.
6 Sed Plutarchus in libro[1] *Symposiacorum* auctorem
Platonis sententiae Hippocraten dicit fuisse idemque
esse opinatos et Philistiona Locrum et Dioxippum
Hippocraticum, veteres medicos et nobiles; atque
illam, de qua Erasistratus dixerat, ἐπιγλωττίδα non
idcirco eo in loco constitutam, ne quid ex potu
influeret in arteriam; nam pulmoni quoque fovendo
rigandoque utiles necessariosque humores videri, set
adpositam quasi moderatricem quandam et arbitram
prohibendi admittendive quod ex salutis usu foret,
uti edulia quidem omnia defenderet ab arteria de-
pelleretque in stomachum, potum autem partiretur
inter stomachum et pulmonem et quod ex eo admitti
in pulmonem per arteriam deberet, non rapidum id
neque universum, sed quadam quasi ōbice sustenta-

---

[1] septimo, *Volkmann* ; Symp. vii, *Skutsch.*

---

[1] vii. 1. 3.   [2] Frag. 7, p. 112, Wellmann.

or drier food, which ought to pass into the stomach,
should fall from the mouth and slip into that tube
through which the breath goes back and forth, and
by such an accident the path of the breath should
be cut off, there has been placed at these two open-
ings by a kind of helpful device of nature, a sort of
movable valve which is called the "epiglottis," which
alternately shuts and opens. This epiglottis, while
we are eating and drinking, covers and protects "the
rough windpipe," in order that no particle of food or
drink may fall into that path, so to speak, of the
rising and falling breath; and on that account no
moisture passes into the lungs, since the opening
of the windpipe itself is well protected.

These are the views of the physician Erasistratus,
as opposed to Plato. But Plutarch, in his *Symposiacs*,[1]
says that the originator of Plato's opinion was Hippocrates, and that the same opinion was held by
Philistion of Locris[2] and Dioxippus the pupil of
Hippocrates, famous physicians of the olden time;
also that the epiglottis, of which Erasistratus spoke,
was not placed where it is to prevent anything
that we drank from flowing into the windpipe; for
fluid seems necessary and serviceable for refreshing
and moistening the lungs; but it was placed there
as a kind of controller and arbiter, to exclude or
admit whatever was necessary for the health of the
body; to keep away all foods from the windpipe
and turn them to the stomach, but to divide what is
drunk between the stomach and the lungs. And
that part which ought to be admitted into the lungs
through the windpipe the epiglottis does not let
through rapidly and all at once, but when it has
been checked and held back, as it were by a kind

tum ac repressum sensim paulatimque tramitteret
atque omne reliquum in alteram stomachi fistulam
derivaret.

XII

De materiis infamibus, quas Graeci ἀδόξους appellant, a
Favorino exercendi gratia disputatis.

1 INFAMES materias, sive quis mavult dicere "ino-
pinabiles," quas Graeci ἀδόξους ὑποθέσεις appellant,
et veteres adorti sunt, non sophistae solum, sed
philosophi quoque, et noster Favorinus oppido quam
libens in eas materias se [1] deiciebat,[2] vel ingenio ex-
pergificando ratus idoneas vel exercendis argutiis vel
2 edomandis usu difficultatibus ; sicuti, cum Thersitae
laudes quaesivit et cum febrim quartis diebus recur-
rentem laudavit, lepida sane multa et non facilia in-
ventu in utramque causam dixit eaque scripta in
libris reliquit.
3   Sed in febris laudibus testem etiam Platonem
produxit, quem scripsisse ait qui quartanam passus
convaluerit viresque integras recuperaverit, fidelius
constantiusque postea valiturum. Atque inibi in [3]
isdem laudibus non hercle hac sententiola invenuste
4 lusit : "Versus," inquit, "est longo hominum aevo
probatus :

Ἄλλοτε μητρυιὴ πέλει ἡμέρη, ἄλλοτε μήτηρ.

    [1] se *added by Madvig.*
    [2] deiciebat, T ; dicebat, X ; deicebaυ, ω.
    [3] in *added in* σ.

----

    [1] See Pease, "Things without Honor," *Class. Phil.* xxi. pp.
27 ff.   An example is Erasmus' *Praise of Folly.*
    [2] Frag. 65, Marres.   [3] See note 1, p. 252.

of dam, it allows it to pass gradually and little by little, and turns aside all the remainder into the other tube leading to the stomach.

XII

Of ignoble subjects, called by the Greeks ἄδοξοι, or "un-expected," argued by Favorinus for the sake of practice.

Not only the sophists of old, but the philosophers as well, took up ignoble subjects,[1] or if you prefer, unexpected ones, ἄδοξοι ὑποθέσεις, as the Greeks call them; and our friend Favorinus took a great deal of pleasure in descending to such subjects,[2] either thinking them suitable for stimulating his thoughts or exercising his cleverness or overcoming difficulties by practice. For example, when he attempted to praise Thersites and pronounced a eulogy upon the quartan ague,[3] he said many clever and ingenious things on both topics, which he has left written in his works.

But in his eulogy of fever he even produced Plato as a witness, declaring that the philosopher wrote [4] that one who after suffering from quartan ague got well and recovered his full strength, would afterwards enjoy surer and more constant health. And in that same eulogy he made this quip, which, of a truth, is not ungraceful: "The following lines," he says, "have met with the approval of many generations of men : [5]

> Sometimes a day is like a stepmother,
> And sometimes like a mother.

[4] *Tim.* 10, p. 86 A.   [5] Hesiod, *Works and Days*, 825.

Eo versu significatur, non omni die bene esse posse,
5 sed isto bene atque alio male. Quod cum ita sit,"
inquit, "ut in rebus humanis bene aut male vice
alterna sit, haec biduo medio intervallata febris
quanto est fortunatior, in qua est μία μητρυιά, δύο
μητέρες!"

XIII

"Quin" particula quot qualesque varietates significationis
habeat et quam saepe in veterum scriptis obscura sit.

1 "Quin" particula, quam grammatici coniunction-
em appellant, variis modis sententiisque conectere
2 orationem videtur. Aliter enim dici putatur, cum
quasi increpantes vel interrogantes vel exhortantes
dicimus "quin venis?" "quin legis?" "quin fugis?"
aliter, cum ita confirmamus: "non dubium est, quin
M. Tullius omnium sit eloquentissimus," aliter autem,
cum sic componimus, quod quasi priori videtur contrarium: "non idcirco causas Isocrates non defendit,
quin id utile esse et honestum existumarit"; a quo
3 illa significatio non abhorret, quae est in tertia *Origine*
M. Catonis. "Haut eos," inquit, "eo postremum
4 scribo, quin populi et boni et strenui sient." In
secunda quoque *Origine* M. Cato non longe secus hac
particula usus est: "Neque satis," inquit, "habuit
quod eum in occulto vitiaverat, quin eius famam
prostitueret."

---

[1] Owing to the Roman method of inclusive reckoning, the
quartan ague, occurring on every fourth day, had an interval
of two days; see *Class Phil.* viii. 1 ff.

[2] Frag. 73, Peter².

[3] This rather difficult example I do not find in our
grammars.   [4] *Id.* 36.

The meaning of the verses is that a man cannot fare well every day, but fares well on one day and ill on another. Since it is true," he says, "that in human affairs things are in turn, now good, now bad, how much more fortunate is this fever which has an interval of two days,[1] since it has only one stepmother, but two mothers!"

XIII

How many and what varieties of meaning the particle *quin* has, and that it is often obscure in the earlier literature.

THE particle *quin,* which the grammarians call a conjunction, seems to connect sentences in various ways and with divers meanings. For it seems to have one meaning when we say, as if chiding or questioning or exhorting, *quin venis?* "Why don't you come?" *quin legis?* "Why don't you read?" or *quin fugis?* "Why don't you flee?"; but it has a different meaning when we affirm, for example, that "there is no doubt but that (*quin*) Marcus Tullius is the most eloquent of all men," and still a third, when we add something which seems contradictory to a former statement: "Isocrates did not plead causes, not but that he thought it useful and honourable so to do." In the last of these sentences the meaning is not very different from that which is found in the third book of Marcus Cato's *Origins* :[2] "these I describe last, not but that they are good and valiant peoples."[3] Also in the second book of the *Origins* Marcus Cato has used this particle in a very similar manner:[4] "He did not consider it enough to have slandered him privately, without openly defaming his character."

5 Praeterea animadvertimus Quadrigarium in octavo *Annalium* particula ista usum esse obscurissime. Verba ipsius posuimus : " Romam venit ; vix superat

6 quin triumphus decernatur." Item in sexto *Annali* eiusdem verba haec sunt : " Paene factum est quin

7 castra relinquerent atque cederent hosti." Non me autem praeterit dicere aliquem posse de summo

8 pectore nil esse in his verbis negotii ; nam " quin " utrobique positum pro " ut " planissimumque esse, si ita dicas : " Romam venit ; vix superat, ut triumphus decernatur " ; item alio in loco : " Paene factum est,

9 ut castra relinquerent atque cederent hosti." Sed utantur sane, qui tam expediti sunt, perfugiis commutationum in verbis quae non intelleguntur, utantur tamen, ubi id facere poterunt, verecundius.

10 Hanc particulam de qua dicimus, nisi si quis didicerit compositam copulatamque esse neque vim tantum coniungendi habere, sed certa quadam significatione factam, numquam profecto rationes ac

11 varietates istius comprehensurus est. Quod quia longioris dissertationis est, poterit, cui otium est, reperire hoc in P. Nigidii *Commentariis,* quos *Grammaticos* inscripsit.

---

[1] Frag. 70, Peter[2].
[2] *Quin* = " why not " ; see note 4 below. [3] *Id*. 58.
[4] This translation, which Gellius rightly rejects, neglects the negative in *quin*. Both examples from Quadrigarius might be explained as dubitative questions in the para-

I have noted, besides, that Quadrigarius in the eighth book of his *Annals* has used that particle in a very obscure manner. I quote his exact words:[1] "He came to Rome; he barely succeeds in having a triumph voted."[2] Also in the sixth book of the same writer's *Annals* are these words:[3] "It lacked little but that (*quin*) they should leave their camp and yield to the enemy." Now I am quite well aware that someone may say off-hand that there is no difficulty in these words; for *quin* in both passages is used for *ut*, and the meaning is perfectly plain if you say: "He came to Rome; he with difficulty brought it about that a triumph should be voted";[4] and also in the other passage, "It almost happened that they left their camp and yielded to the enemy." Let those who are so ready find refuge in changing words which they do not understand, but let them do so with more modesty, when the occasion permits.

Only one who has learned that this particle of which we are speaking is a compound and formed of two parts, and that it does not merely have the function of a connective but has a definite meaning of its own,[5] will ever understand its variations in meaning. But because an explanation of these would require a long dissertation, he who has leisure may find it in the *Commentaries* of Publius Nigidius which he entitled *Grammatical*.[6]

tactic form; *e.g.* "Why should not a triumph be granted him?"

[5] *quin* is formed from *qui*, the ablative of the interrogative and relative stem *qui*-, and *-ne*, "not." It is used in both dependent and independent sentences. See Lane, *Lat. Gr.*[2] 1980 ff.

[6] Frag. 52, Swoboda.

XIV

Sententiae ex Publili *Mimis* selectae lepidiores.

1 PUBLILIUS mimos scriptitavit. Dignus habitus est
2 qui subpar Laberio iudicaretur. C. autem Caesarem
ita Laberii maledicentia et adrogantia offendebat, ut
acceptiores sibi esse Publili quam Laberii mimos
praedicaret.
3 Huius Publili sententiae feruntur pleraeque lepidae
et ad communem sermonum usum commendatissimae,
4 ex quibus sunt istae singulis versibus circumscriptae,
quas libitum hercle est adscribere :

> Malum ést consilium quód mutari nón potest.
> Benefícium dando accépit, qui dignó dedit.
> Ferás, non culpes, quód vitari nón potest.
> Cui plús licet, quam pár est, plus vult, quám licet.
> Comés facundus ín via pro véhiculo est.
> Frugálitas miséria est rumorís boni.
> Herédis fletus súb persona rísus est.
> Furór fit laesa saépius patiéntia.
> Inprobe Neptúnum accusat, qui íterum naufragiúm
>   facit.
> Íta amicum habeas pósse ut facile[1] fíeri hunc
>   inimicúm putes.
> Veterém ferendo iniúriam invités novam.
> Numquám periclum síne periclo víncitur.
> Nimium áltercando véritas amíttitur.
> Pars bénefici est, quod pétitur si bellé neges.

---

[1] facile, *Syrus* ; *omitted by* ω *and Macrob.* ii. 7. 11.

---

[1] Meyer, vv. 362, 55, 176, 106, 104, 193, 221, 178, 264, 245,
645, 383, 416, 469. In one instance it has seemed necessary
to use two lines in the English version.

XIV

Neat sayings selected from the *Mimes* of Publilius.

PUBLILIUS wrote mimes. He was thought worthy of being rated about equal to Laberius. But the scurrility and the arrogance of Laberius so offended Gaius Caesar, that he declared that he was better pleased with the mimes of Publilius than with those of Laberius.

Many sayings of this Publilius are current, which are neat and well adapted to the use of ordinary conversation. Among these are the following, consisting of a single line each, which I have indeed taken pleasure in quoting : [1]

Bad is the plan which cannot bear a change.
He gains by giving who has given to worth.
Endure and don't deplore what can't be helped. [2]
Who's given too much, will want more than 's
    allowed. [3]
A witty comrade at your side,
To walk's as easy as to ride.
Frugality is misery in disguise.
Heirs' tears are laughter underneath a mask.
Patience too oft provoked is turned to rage.
He wrongly Neptune blames, who suffers ship-
    wreck twice.
Regard a friend as one who may be foe.
By bearing old wrongs new ones you provoke.
With danger ever danger 's overcome.
'Mid too much wrangling truth is often lost.
Who courteously declines, grants half your suit.

[2] Cf. "What can't be cured must be endured."
[3] Cf. "Give an inch, he'll take an ell."

XV

Quod Carneades Academicus elleboro stomachum purgavit,
scripturus adversus Zenonis Stoici decreta; deque natura
medellaque ellebori candidi et nigri.

1 CARNEADES Academicus, scripturus adversum Stoici
Zenonis libros, superiora corporis elleboro candido
purgavit, ne quid ex corruptis in stomacho humoribus
ad domicilia usque animi redundaret et instantiam
2 vigoremque mentis labefaceret; tanta cura tantoque
apparatu sui vir ingenio praestanti ad refellenda quae
3 scripserat Zeno aggressus; idque cum in historia
Graeca legissem, quod "elleboro candido" scriptum
erat, quid esset quaesivi.

4 Tum comperi duas species ellebori esse discerni-
culo coloris insignes, candidi et nigri; eos autem
colores non in semine ellebori neque in virgultis, sed
in radice dinosci; candido stomachum et ventrem
superiorem vomitionibus purgari; nigro alvum, quae
"inferior" vocatur, dilui, utriusque esse hanc vim,
ut humores noxios in quibus causae morborum sunt
5 extrahant.   Esse autem periculum ne inter causas
morborum, omni corporum via patefacta, ea quoque
ipsa, in quibus causa vivendi est, effluant[1] amissoque
omni naturalis alimoniae fundamento homo exhaustus
intereat.

[1] effluant *suggested by Hosius*; amittantur, *Vahlen* (*cf.* xix.
12. 5); exinaniantur, σ; *omitted by* ω.

---

[1] The small intestine, see note on xvii. 11. 2.
[2] The large intestine.

XV

That Carneades the Academic purged his stomach with
  hellebore when about to write against the dogmas of Zeno
  the Stoic; and of the nature and curative powers of white
  and black hellebore.

WHEN Carneades, the Academic philosopher, was
about to write against the books of the Stoic Zeno,
he cleansed the upper part of his body with white
hellebore, in order that none of the corrupt humours
of his stomach might rise to the abode of his mind
and weaken the power and vigour of his intellect;
with such care and such preparation did this man of
surpassing talent set about refuting what Zeno had
written. When I had read of this in Grecian
history, I inquired what was meant by the term
"white hellebore."

Then I learned that there are two kinds of
hellebore distinguished by a difference in colour,
white and black; but that those colours are distinguished neither in the seed of the hellebore nor
in its plant, but in the root; further, that with
white hellebore the stomach and upper belly[1] are
purged by vomiting; by the black the so-called
lower belly is loosened,[2] and the effect of both is to
remove the noxious humours in which the causes of
diseases are situated. But that there is danger lest,
when every avenue of the body is opened, along
with the causes of disease the juices on which the
principle of life depends should also pass away, and
the man should perish from exhaustion because of
the destruction of the entire foundation of natural
nourishment.

259

6 Set elleborum sumi posse tutissime in insula Anticyra Plinius Secundus in libris *Naturalis Historiae* scripsit. Propterea Livium Drusum, qui tribunus plebi fuit, cum morbum qui "comitialis" dicitur pateretur, Anticyram navigasse et in ea insula elleborum bibisse ait, atque ita morbo liberatum.

7 Praeterea scriptum legimus Gallos in venatibus tinguere elleboro sagittas, quod his ictae, exanimatae ferae teneriores ad epulas fiant; sed propter ellebori contagium vulnera ex sagittis facta circumcidere latius dicuntur.

XVI

Anates Ponticas vim habere venenis digerendis potentem; atque inibi de Mitridati regis in id genus medicamentum sollertia.

1 ANATES Ponticas dicitur edundis vulgo venenis
2 victitare. Scriptum etiam a Lenaeo, Cn. Pompei liberto, Mitridatem illum Ponti regem medicinae rei et remediorum id genus sollertem fuisse solitumque earum sanguinem miscere medicamentis quae digerendis venenis valent, eumque sanguinem vel po-

---

[1] xxv. 52.

[2] There were three places of this name, all celebrated for their hellebore, which was regarded as a cure for insanity. One was in Locris, on the Corinthian Gulf; the second was on the Maliac Gulf at the foot of Mt. Oeta. The third, usually considered the most important, was a town of Phocis on the Corinthian Gulf. See *Thes. Ling. Lat. s.v.*, where Plin. *N.H.* xxv. 52 is assigned to the last-named, in spite of

But Plinius Secundus, in his work *On Natural History*, wrote[1] that hellebore could be taken with the greatest safety in the island of Anticyra.[2] That for this reason Livius Drusus, the former tribune of the commons, when he was suffering from the so-called "election" disease,[3] sailed to Anticyra, drank hellebore in that island, and was thus cured of the ailment.

I have read besides that the Gauls, when hunting, dip their arrows in hellebore, because the wild animals that are struck and killed by arrows thus treated become tenderer for eating; but because of the contagion of the hellebore they are said to cut out a large piece of flesh around the wounds made by the arrows.

XVI

That Pontic ducks have a power which is able to expel poisons; and also of the skill of Mithridates in preparing antidotes.

It is said that the ducks of Pontus commonly live by eating poisons. It was also written by Lenaeus,[4] the freedman of Pompey the Great, that Mithridates, the famous king of Pontus, was skilled in medicine and in antidotes of that kind, and that he was accustomed to mix the blood of these ducks with drugs that have the power of expelling poisons, and that the blood was the very most powerful agency

---

insula. Baumgarten-Crusius, *Suetonius*, refer the reference in *Calig.* xxix to an island, which they do not locate. In Hor. *Ars. Poet.* 300, *tribus Anticyris* may refer to three Anticyras, but is more probably used in a general sense.

[3] See note on xvi. 4. 4.

[4] See Suet. *De G. amm.* xv. (ii, p. 418, *L.C.L.*).

3 tentissimum esse in ea confectione; ipsum autem
regem adsiduo talium medellarum usu a clandestinis
4 epularum insidiis cavisse, quin et scientem quoque
ultro et ostentandi gratia venenum rapidum et velox
saepenumero hausisse, atque id tamen sine noxa
5 fuisse. Quamobrem postea, cum proelio victus in
ultima regni refugisset et mori decrevisset, venena
violentissima festinandae necis causa frustra ex-
6 pertus, suo se ipse gladio transegit. Huius regis
antidotus celebratissima est, quae " Mitridatios "
vocatur.

XVII

Mitridatem, Ponti regem, quinque[1] et viginti gentium
linguis locutum; Quintumque Ennium tria corda habere
sese dixisse, quod tris linguas percalluisset, Graecam,
Oscam, Latinam.

1   QUINTUS ENNIUS tria corda habere sese dicebat,
2 quod loqui Graece et Osce et Latine sciret.   Mitridates autem, Ponti atque Bithyniae rex inclutus, qui
a Cn. Pompeio bello superatus est, quinque[2] et
viginti gentium quas sub dicione habuit linguas
percalluit earumque omnium gentium viris haut
umquam per interpretem conlocutus est, sed ut
quemque ab eo appellari usus fuit, proinde lingua et
oratione ipsius non minus scite quam si gentilis eius
esset locutus est.

[1] duobus, Π; II, ς; duarum, *Pliny and others.*
[2] duarum, ς.

in their preparation; furthermore, that the king himself by the constant use of such remedies guarded against hidden plots at banquets; nay more, that he often voluntarily and wittingly, to show his immunity, drank a swift and rapid poison, which yet did him no harm. Therefore, at a later time, when he had been defeated in battle, and after fleeing to the remotest bounds of his kingdom had resolved to take his own life, having vainly tried the most violent poisons for the purpose of hastening his death, he fell upon his own sword. The most celebrated antidote of this king is the one which is called "Mithridatian."

XVII

That Mithridates, king of Pontus, spoke the languages of twenty-five nations; and that Quintus Ennius said that he had three hearts, because he was proficient in three tongues, Greek, Oscan, and Latin.

QUINTUS ENNIUS used to say that he had three hearts, because he knew how to speak Greek, Oscan, and Latin. But Mithridates, the celebrated king of Pontus and Bithynia, who was overcome in war by Gnaeus Pompeius,[1] was proficient in the languages of the twenty-five races which he held under his sway. He never spoke to the men of all those nations through an interpreter, but whenever it was necessary for him to address any one of them, he used his language and speech with as much skill as if he were his fellow-countryman.

[1] 66–63 B.C.

XVIII

Quod M. Varro C. Sallustium, historiae scriptorem, deprehensum ab Annio Milone in adulterio scribit et loris caesum
pecuniaque data dimissum.

1　　M. VARRO, in litteris atque vita fide homo multa
et gravis, in libro quem inscripsit [1] *Pius aut De Pace*,
C. Sallustium scriptorem seriae illius et severae
orationis, in cuius historia notiones censorias fieri
atque exerceri videmus, in adulterio deprehensum
ab Annio Milone loris bene caesum dicit et, cum
dedisset pecuniam, dimissum.

XIX

Quid Epictetus philosophus dicere solitus sit hominibus
nequam et inpuris, disciplinas philosophiae studiose
tractantibus ; et quae duo verba observanda praeceperit
omnium rerum longe saluberrima. [2]

1　　FAVORINUM ego audivi dicere Epictetum philosophum dixisse plerosque istos, qui philosophari
viderentur, philosophos esse eiuscemodi ἄνευ τοῦ
πράττειν, μέχρι τοῦ λέγειν; id significat "factis procul,
2　verbis tenus." Iam illud est vehementius quod
Arrianus solitum eum dictitare, in libris quos de
dissertationibus eius composuit, scriptum reliquit.
3　"Nam cum," inquit, " animadverterat hominem
pudore amisso, inportuna industria, corruptis mori-

---

[1] scripsit, ω ; *corrected by Burman.*
[2] saluberrima, *Skutsch* ; salubria, ω.

---

[1] p. 256, Riese.

XVIII

The statement of Marcus Varro that Gaius Sallustius, the
writer of history, was taken in adultery by Annius Milo
and was let go only after he had been beaten with thongs
and had paid a sum of money.

MARCUS VARRO, a man of great trustworthiness and
authority in his writings and in his life, in the work
which he entitled *Pius, or On Peace*,[1] says that Gaius
Sallustius, the author of those austere and dignified
works, whom we see in his history writing and acting like a censor, was taken in adultery by Annius
Milo, soundly beaten with thongs, and allowed to
escape only after paying a sum of money.[2]

XIX

What Epictetus the philosopher used to say to worthless and
vile men, who zealously followed the pursuit of philosophy;
and the two words whose remembrance he enjoined as by
far the most salutary in all respects.

I HEARD Favorinus say that the philosopher Epictetus declared[3] that very many of those who pro-
fessed to be philosophers were of the kind ἄνευ τοῦ
πράττειν, μέχρι τοῦ λέγειν, which means " without
deeds, limited to words "; that is, they preached but
did not practise. But that is still more severe which
Arrian, in his work *On the Dissertations of Epictetus*,[4]
has written that this philosopher used to say. " For,"
says Arrian, " when he perceived that a man without
shame, persistent in wickedness, of abandoned

---

[2] On this story see Sallust, *L.C.L.*, p. x.
[3] Frag. 10, p. 410, Schenkl., *L.C.L.* II, p. 452 ff.
[4] ii. 19; cf. Gell. i. 2. 8.

bus, audacem, confidentem lingua ceteraque omnia
praeterquam animam procurantem, istiusmodi hominem cum viderat studia quoque et disciplinas philosophiae contrectare et physica adire et meditari
dialectica multaque id genus theoremata auspicari
sciscitarique, inclamabat deum atque hominum
fidem ac plerumque inter clamandum his eum verbis
increpabat: ' Ἄνθρωπε, ποῦ βάλλεις; σκέψαι εἰ κε-
κάθαρται τὸ ἀγγεῖον· ἂν γὰρ εἰς τὴν οἴησιν αὐτὰ βάλλῃς,
ἀπώλετο· ἢν σαπῇ, οὖρον ἢ ὄξος γένοιτο ἢ εἴ τι τούτων
4 χεῖρον.' " Nil profecto his verbis gravius, nil verius,
quibus declarabat maximus philosophorum, litteras
atque doctrinas philosophiae, cum in hominem
falsum atque degenerem tamquam in vas spurcum
atque pollutum influxissent, verti, mutari, corrumpi
et, quod ipse κυνικώτερον ait, urinam fieri aut si quid
est urina spurcius.

5   Praeterea idem ille Epictetus, quod ex eodem
Favorino audivimus, solitus dicere est duo esse vitia
multo omnium gravissima ac taeterrima, intolerantiam
et incontinentiam, cum aut iniurias quae sunt
ferendae non toleramus neque ferimus, aut a quibus
rebus voluptatibusque nos tenere debemus, non
6 tenemus. " Itaque," inquit, " si quis haec duo verba
cordi habeat eaque sibi imperando atque observando
curet, is erit pleraque inpeccabilis vitamque vivet
tranquillissimam." Verba haec duo dicebat: ἀνέχου
et ἀπέχου.

---

¹ That is, he used some phrase equivalent to *pro deum
atque hominum fidem !* (Heaven help us !).

character, reckless, boastful, and cultivating everything else except his soul—when he saw such a man taking up also the study and pursuit of philosophy, attacking natural history, practising logic and balancing and investigating many problems of that kind, he used to invoke the help[1] of gods and men, and usually amid his exclamations chided the man in these terms: 'O man, where are you storing these things? Consider whether the vessel be clean. For if you take them into your self-conceit, they are lost; if they are spoiled, they become urine or vinegar or something worse, if possible.'" Nothing surely could be weightier, nothing truer than these words, in which the greatest of philosophers declared that the learning and precepts of philosophy, flowing into a base and degenerate man, as if into a soiled and filthy vessel, are turned, altered, spoiled, and as he himself more cynically expresses it, become urine or, if possible, something worse than urine.

Moreover, that same Epictetus, as we also heard from Favorinus, used to say that there were two faults which were by far the worst and most disgusting of all, lack of endurance and lack of self-restraint, when we cannot put up with or bear the wrongs which we ought to endure, or cannot restrain ourselves from actions or pleasures from which we ought to refrain. "Therefore," said he, "if anyone would take these two words to heart and use them for his own guidance and regulation, he will be almost without sin and will lead a very peaceful life. These two words," he said, "are ἀνέχου (bear) and ἀπέχου (forbear)."[2]

[2] The two Greek words, like Eng. "bear and forbear," formed a stock formula.

ATTIC NIGHTS OF AULUS GELLIUS

XX

Verba sumpta ex *Symposio* Platonis, numeris[1] coagmentisque
verborum scite modulateque apta,[2] exercendi gratia in
Latinam orationem versa.

1 *SYMPOSIUM* Platonis apud philosophum Taurum
2 legebatur. Verba illa Pausaniae inter convivas amo-
rem vice sua laudantis, ea verba ita prorsum amavi-
3 mus, ut meminisse etiam studuerimus. Sunt adeo,
quae meminimus, verba haec : Πᾶσα γὰρ πρᾶξις ὧδε
ἔχει· αὐτὴ ἐφ᾽ αὑτῆς πραττομένη οὔτε καλὴ οὔτε αἰσχρά·
οἷον ὃ νῦν ἡμεῖς ποιοῦμεν, ἢ πίνειν ἢ ᾄδειν ἢ διαλέγεσθαι.
οὐκ ἔστι τούτων αὐτὸ καθ᾽ αὑτὸ καλὸν οὐδέν, ἀλλ᾽ ἐν τῇ
πράξει, ὡς ἂν πραχθῇ, τοιοῦτον ἀπέβη· καλῶς μὲν γὰρ
πραττόμενον καὶ ὀρθῶς καλὸν γίγνεται, μὴ ὀρθῶς δὲ
αἰσχρόν· οὕτω δὴ καὶ τὸ ἐρᾶ·, καὶ ὁ Ἔρως οὐ πᾶς ἐστὶν
καλὸς οὐδὲ ἄξιος ἐγκωμιάζεσθαι, ἀλλ᾽ ὁ καλῶς προτρέπων
ἐρᾶν.

4 Haec verba ubi lecta sunt, atque ibi Taurus mihi :
" Heus," inquit, " tu, rhetorisce,"—sic enim me in
principio recens in diatribam acceptum appellitabat,
existimans eloquentiae unius extundendae gratia
Athenas venisse,—" videsne," inquit, " ἐνθύμημα cre-
brum et coruscum et convexum brevibusque et
rotundis numeris cum quadam aequabili circumactione
5 devinctum ? Habesne nobis dicere in libris rhetorum
vestrorum tam apte tamque modulate compositam
orationem ? Sed hos," inquit, "tamen numeros

---

[1] cum numeris *sugg. by Hosius.*
[2] apta, *Lion* ; apteque composita, *Beloe* ; aptique, *ω* ; apta
atque, *Damsté.*

---

[1] *Sympos.* p. 180, E.

XX

A passage taken from the Symposium of Plato, skilful, harmonious and fitting in its rhythm and structure, which for the sake of practice I have turned into the Latin tongue.

THE *Symposium* of Plato was being read before the philosopher Taurus. Those words of Pausanias in which, taking his turn among the banqueters, he eulogizes love, I admired so much that I even resolved to commit them to memory. And the words, if I remember rightly, are as follows:[1] "Every action is of this nature: in and of itself, when done, it is neither good nor bad; for example, what we are now doing, drinking, or singing, or arguing. Not one of these things is in itself good, but it may become so by the way in which it is done. Well and rightly done, it becomes a good action; wrongly done, it becomes shameful. It is the same with love; for not all love is honourable or worthy of praise, but only that which leads us to love worthily."

When these words had been read, thereupon Taurus said to me: "Ho! you young rhetorician"—for so he used to call me in the beginning, when I was first admitted to his class, supposing that I had come to Athens only to work up eloquence [2]—"do you see this syllogism, full of meaning, brilliant, well rounded and constructed in brief and smooth numbers with a kind of symmetrical turn? Can you quote us so apt and so melodiously formed a passage from the works of your rhetoricians? But yet

---

[2] This would seem to imply that Gellius went to Athens on completing his studies in Rome; see Introd. p. xv.

6 censeo videas ὁδοῦ πάρεργον. Ad ipsa enim Platonis
penetralia ipsarumque rerum pondera et dignitates
pergendum est, non ad vocularum eius amoenitatem
nec ad verborum venustates deversitandum."

7 Haec admonitio Tauri de orationis Platonicae
modulis non modo non repressit, sed instrinxit etiam
nos ad elegantiam Graecae orationis verbis Latinis

8 adfectandam ; atque uti quaedam animalium parva et
vilia ad imitandum sunt quas res cumque audierint
viderintve petulantia, proinde nos ea quae in Platonis
oratione demiramur non aemulari quidem, sed lineas
umbrasque facere ausi sumus. Velut ipsum hoc est,

9 quod ex isdem illis verbis eius effinximus : "Omne,"
inquit, "omnino factum sic sese habet ; neque turpe
est, quantum in eo est, neque honestum : velut est,
quas nunc facimus ipsi res, bibere, cantare, disserere.
Nihil namque horum ipsum ex sese honestum est ;
quali cum fieret modo factum est, tale extitit ; si recte
honesteque factum est, tum honestum fit ; sin parum
recte, turpe fit. Sic amare ; sic amor non honestus
omnis neque omnis laude dignus, sed qui facit nos
ut honeste amemus."

I advise you to look upon this rhythm as an incidental feature; for one must penetrate to the inmost depths of Plato's mind and feel the weight and dignity of his subject matter, not be diverted to the charm of his diction or the grace of his expression."

This admonition of Taurus as to Plato's style not only did not deter me, but even encouraged me to try to equal the elegance of the Greek in a Latin rendering; and just as there are small and insignificant animals which through wantonness imitate everything which they have seen or heard, just so I had the assurance, not indeed to rival those qualities which I admired in Plato's style, but to give a shadowy outline of them, such as the following, which I patterned on those very words of his: " Every act, in general," he says, "is of this nature; it is in itself neither base nor honourable; as, for example, the things which we ourselves are now doing, drinking, singing, arguing. For none of these things is honourable in itself, but it becomes so by the manner in which it is done; if it is done rightly and honourably, it is then honourable; but if it is not rightly done, then it is shameful. It is the same with love; thus not every kind of love is honourable, not every kind is deserving of praise, but only that which leads us to love honourably."

XXI

Quibus temporibus post Romam conditam Graeci Romanique
inlustres viri floruerint ante secundum bellum Carthaginien-
sium.

1 Uτ conspectum quendam aetatum antiquissimarum,
item virorum inlustrium qui in his aetatibus nati
fuissent haberemus, ne in sermonibus forte incon-
spectum aliquid super aetate atque vita clariorum
hominum temere diceremus, sicuti sophista ille ἀπαί-
δευτος, qui publice nuper disserens Carneaden philosophum a rege Alexandro, Philippi filio, pecunia
donatum et Panaetium Stoicum cum superiore Afri-
cano vixisse dixit; ut ab istiusmodi, inquam, temporum
aetatumque erroribus caveremus, et excerpebamus
ex libris qui chronici appellantur quibus temporibus
floruissent Graeci simul atque Romani viri, qui vel
ingenio vel imperio nobiles insignesque post conditam Romam fuissent ante secundum bellum Cartha-
giniensium, easque nunc excerptiones nostras variis
diversisque in locis factas cursim digessimus. Neque
enim id nobis negotium fuit, ut acri atque subtili
cura excellentium in utraque gente hominum συγχρο-
νισμούς componeremus, sed ut *Noctes* istae quadamte-

---

[1] Leuze has shown (see Biogr. Note, i. p. xxiv) that,
besides the *Chronica* of Cornelius Nepos, Gellius made use of
Varronian sources, which used a different chronology.
According to the source which he followed, Gellius' dates are
reckoned from 751 (Nepos) or 753 B.C. (Varro) as the date of
the founding of Rome. He does not, however, confuse these
epochs in speaking of the same event. In my notes the
Varronian chronology is followed, except as otherwise indicated ; for full details see the article of Leutze.

[2] Carneades, who was one of the envoys sent from Athens

XXI

The times after the founding of Rome and before the second
war with Carthage at which distinguished Greeks and
Romans flourished.[1]

I wished to have a kind of survey of ancient times,
and also of the famous men who were born in those
days, lest I might in conversation chance to make
some careless remark about the date and life of
celebrated men, as that ignorant sophist did who
lately, in a public lecture, said that Carneades the
philosopher[2] was presented with a sum of money by
king Alexander, son of Philip, and that Panaetius
the Stoic was intimate with the elder Africanus.[3]
In order, I say, to guard against such errors in dates
and periods of time, I made notes from the books
known as *Chronicles*[4] of the times when those Greeks
and Romans flourished who were famous and conspicuous either for talent or for political power,
between the founding of Rome and the second
Punic war.[5] And these excerpts of mine, made in
various and sundry places, I have now put hastily together. For it was not my endeavour with keen
and subtle care to compile a catalogue of the
eminent men of both nations who lived at the same
time, but merely to strew these *Nights* of mine

to Rome in 155 B.C., lived more than a hundred years after
the death of Alexander.

[3] Panaetius, born about 185 B.C., was the teacher and
personal friend of the younger Africanus.

[4] *Chronica* (χρονικά) were chronological lists of historical
events. The *Chronica* of Nepos seem to have given the important dates in foreign, as well as in Roman, history, including mythology.

[5] 218–202 B.C.

nus his quoque historiae flosculis leviter iniectis
2 aspergerentur. Satis autem visum est in hoc con-
mentario de temporibus paucorum hominum dicere,
ex quorum aetatibus de pluribus quoque, quos non
nominaremus, haut difficilis coniectura fieri posset.

3 Incipiemus igitur a Solone claro, quoniam de
Homero et Hesiodo inter omnes fere scriptores
constitit aetatem eos egisse vel isdem fere temporibus vel Homerum aliquanto antiquiorem, utrumque
tamen ante Romam conditam vixisse, Silviis Albae
regnantibus, annis post bellum Troianum, ut Cassius
in primo *Annalium* de Homero atque Hesiodo scriptum reliquit, plus centum atque sexaginta, ante
Romam autem conditam, ut Cornelius Nepos in
primo *Chronico* de Homero dicit, annis circiter
centum et sexaginta.

4 Solonem ergo accepimus, unum ex illo nobili
numero sapientium, leges scripsisse Atheniensium,
Tarquinio Prisco Romae regnante, anno regni eius
5 tricesimo tertio.[1] Servio autem Tullio regnante,
Pisistratus Athenis tyrannus fuit, Solone ante in
exilium voluntarium profecto, quoniam id ei prae-
6 dicenti non creditum est. Postea Pythagoras Samius
in Italiam venit, Tarquini filio regnum optinente, cui
7 cognomentum Superbus fuit, isdemque temporibus

---

[1] *Leuze (Rh. Mus., 1911) on chronological grounds would
read* xxiii. *with T.*

---

[1] After his usual fashion, Gellius tries to present his
material in an entertaining form by introducing the anecdote
of the ignorant sophist, by freedom of treatment, and by
condensation ; also by the arrangement of his matter.
[2] Frag. 8, Peter[2]; *F.H.G.* iii, p. 688.
[3] Frag. 2, Peter[2]. Nepos' date is 910 B.C., that of Cassius
(Hemina), 1024. Both are too late, for literary and archæo-

lightly here and there with a few of these flowers of history.[1]   Moreover, it seemed sufficient in this survey to speak of the dates of a few men, from which it would not be difficult to infer the periods also of many more whom I did not name.

I shall begin, then, with the illustrious Solon; for, as regards Homer and Hesiod, it is agreed by almost all writers, either that they lived at approximately the same period, or that Homer was somewhat the earlier; yet that both lived before the founding of Rome, when the Silvii were ruling in Alba, more than a hundred and sixty years after the Trojan war, as Cassius has written[2] about Homer and Hesiod in the first book of his *Annals*, but about a hundred and sixty years before the founding of Rome, as Cornelius Nepos says of Homer in the first book of his *Chronicles*.[3]

Well then, we are told that Solon, one of the famous sages,[4] drew up laws for the Athenians when Tarquinius Priscus was king at Rome,[5] in the thirty-third year of his reign.[6]   Afterwards, when Servius Tullius was king,[7] Pisistratus was tyrant at Athens, Solon having previously gone into voluntary exile, since he had not been believed when he predicted that tyranny.   Still later, Pythagoras of Samos came to Italy, when the son of Tarquinius was king, he who was surnamed the Proud,[8] and at that same time

---

logical evidence indicate the end of the twelfth century before our era as the time of the Homeric poems.   See *Amer. Journ. of Phil.* xlvi (1925), pp. 26 ff.

[4] About 639–559 B.C.   For the seven sages see vol. i, p. 10, n. 2.

[5] 616–578 B.C., traditional chronology.

[6] See the critical note.

[7] 578–534 B.C.   [8] 534–510 B.C.

occisus est Athenis ab Harmodio et Aristogitonc
Hipparchus, Pisistrati filius, Hippiae tyranni frater.

8 Archilochum autem Nepos Cornelius tradit, Tullo
Hostilio Romae regnante, iam tunc fuisse poematis
clarum et nobilem.

9 Ducentesimo deinde et sexagesimo anno post Romam conditam, aut non longe amplius, victos esse ab
Atheniensibus Persas memoriae traditum est pugnam
illam inclutam Marathoniam, Miltiade duce, qui post
eam victoriam damnatus a populo Atheniensi in vin-

10 culis publicis mortem obiit.   Tum Aeschylus Athenis
tragoediarum poeta celebris fuit.   Romae autem istis
ferme temporibus tribunos et aediles tum primum
per seditionem sibi plebes creavit ac non diu post
Cn. Marcius Coriolanus exagitatus vexatusque   a

11 tribunis plebi ad Vulscos, qui tum hostes erant, a
rep. descivit bellumque populo Romano fecit.

12 Post deinde paucis annis Xerxes rex ab Atheniensibus et pleraque Graecia, Themistocle duce, navali
proelio quod ad Salamina factum est victus fugatus-

13 que est.   Inde anno fere quarto, Menenio Agrippa,
M. Horatio Pulvillo consulibus, bello Veienti apud
fluvium Cremeram Fabii sex et trecenti patricii
cum familiis suis universi ab hostibus circumventi
perierunt.

---

[1] 514 B.C.   [2] Frag. 4, Peter[2].
[3] 673–641 B.C.   [4] Flourished about 650 B.C.
[5] 490 B.C., but Gellius, here following Nepos, puts it in 493.
[6] He lived from 525 to 456 B.C.   [7] 494 B.C.
[8] Leuze suggests that Gellius so arranged his material as
to show that at a time when the Greeks were fighting epoch-
making battles the Romans were warring with comparatively
insignificant Italian peoples.
[9] 480 B.C.   Gellius is here using a Varronian source ;
Nepos' date would be 483.

Hipparchus, son of Pisistratus and brother of the tyrant Hippias, was slain at Athens by Harmodius and Aristogeiton.[1]   And Cornelius Nepos adds[2] that when Tullus Hostilius was king at Rome[3] Archilochus was already illustrious and famous for his poems.[4]

Then, in the two hundred and sixtieth year after the founding of Rome, or not much later, it is recorded that the Persians were vanquished by the Athenians in the famous battle of Marathon under the lead of Militiades,[5] who after that victory was condemned by the Athenians and died in the public prison.   At that time Aeschylus, the tragic poet, flourished at Athens.[6]   In Rome, at about the same time, the commons, as the result of a secession, for the first time elected their own tribunes and aediles;[7] and not much later Gnaeus Marcius Coriolanus, harassed and exasperated by the tribunes of the commons, turned traitor to the republic and joined the Volscians, who were then our enemies,[8] and made war upon the Roman people.

Then a few years later, King Xerxes was beaten and put to flight by the Athenians and a good part of Greece, under the lead of Themistocles, in the sea-fight at Salamis.[9]   About three[10] years afterwards, in the consulship of Menenius Agrippa and Marcus Horatius Pulvillus, during the war with Veii, the patrician Fabii, three hundred and six in number, along with their dependents,[11] were all ambushed at the river Cremera and slain.

[10] That is, in the fourth year; see note on xvii. 12. 5 (p. 252).
[11] Some 4000 in number.   This was in 477 B.C.

14 Iuxta ea tempora Empedocles Agrigentinus in
15 philosophiae naturalis studio floruit. Romae autem
    per eas tempestates decemviros legibus scribundis
    creatos constitit tabulasque ab his primo decem con-
    scriptas, mox alias duas additas.

16 Bellum deinde in terra Graecia maximum Pelo-
    ponnensiacum, quod Thucydides memoriae mandavit,
    coeptum est circa annum fere post conditam Romam
17 trecentesimum vicesimum tertium. Qua tempestate
    Olus Postumius Tubertus dictator Romae fuit, qui
    filium suum, quod contra suum dictum in hostem
    pugnaverat, securi necavit. Hostes tunc populi
18 Romani fuerunt Fidenates atque Aequi. In hoc
    tempore nobiles celebresque erant Sophocles ac
    deinde Euripides tragici poetae et Hippocrates
    medicus et philosophus Democritus, quibus Socrates
    Atheniensis natu quidem posterior fuit, sed quibus-
    dam temporibus isdem vixerunt.

19 Iam deinde, tribunis militaribus consulari imperio
    rempublicam Romae regentibus, ad annum fere con-
    ditae urbis trecentesimum quadragesimum septimum,
    triginta illi tyranni praepositi sunt a Lacedaemoniis
    Atheniensibus et in Sicilia Dionysius superior tyran-
    nidem tenuit, paucisque annis post Socrates Athenis
    capitis damnatus est et in carcere veneno necatus.
20 Set[1] ea fere tempestate Romae M. Furius Camillus

---

[1] set, Q ; *the other MSS. omit* ; et, *Hertz.*

---

[1] Flourished about 450 B.C. In §§ 14–15 Leuze sees the
chronology of Fabius Pictor.

[2] 451 B.C.   [3] 431 B.C.

[4] See note on § 11, above. Here the contrast is still more
marked.

[5] Born 469 B.C.

[6] 407 B.C. They were first chosen in 444, but were com-

278

At about that time Empedocles of Agrigentum was eminent in the domain of natural philosophy.[1] But at Rome at that epoch it is stated that a board of ten was appointed[2] to codify laws, and that at first they compiled ten tables, to which afterwards two more were added.

Then the great Peloponnesian war began in Greece, which Thucydides has handed down to memory, about three hundred and twenty-three years after the founding of Rome.[3] At that time Olus Postumius Tubertus was dictator at Rome, and executed his own son, because he had fought against the enemy contrary to his father's order. The people of Fidenae and the Aequians were then at war with the Roman people.[4] During that period Sophocles, and later Euripides, were famous and renowned as tragic poets, Hippocrates as a physician, and as a philosopher, Democritus; Socrates the Athenian was younger than these,[5] but was in part their contemporary.

Somewhat later, when the military tribunes with consular authority were in power[6] at Rome, about the three hundred and forty-seventh year after the founding of the city, the notorious thirty tyrants were imposed upon the Athenians by the Lacedaemonians, and in Sicily the elder Dionysius was tyrant.[7] A few years later, at Athens, Socrates was condemned to death and executed in prison by means of poison. At about the same time, at Rome,

pelled to resign. From 404 B.C. (407, Nepos) to 367 the series of military tribunes was interrupted by only two consular years. Gellius here records changes in the form of government of Athens, Syracuse and Rome.

[7] 404 B.C.

21 dictator fuit et Veios cepit; ac post non longo tem-
22 pore bellum Senonicum fuit, cum Galli Romam
praeter Capitolium ceperunt.
23   Neque multo postea Eudoxus astrologus in terra
Graecia nobilitatus est Lacedaemoniique ab Athe-
24 niensibus apud Corinthum superati duce Phormione,
et M. Manlius Romae, qui Gallos in obsidione
Capitolii obrepentes per ardua depulerat, convictus
est consilium de regno occupando inisse, damnatus-
que capitis e saxo Tarpeio, ut M. Varro ait, praeceps
datus, ut Cornelius autem Nepos scriptum reliquit,
25 verberando necatus est; eoque ipso anno, qui erat
post reciperatam urbem septimus, Aristotelem philosophum natum esse memoriae mandatum est.
26   Aliquot deinde annis post bellum Senonicum The-
bani Lacedaemonios duce Epaminonda apud Leuctra
27 superaverunt ac brevi post tempore in urbe Roma
lege Licinii Stolonis consules creari etiam ex plebe
coepti, cum antea ius non esset nisi ex patriciis
gentibus fieri consulem.
28   Circa annum deinde urbis conditae quadringente-
simum Philippus, Amyntae filius, Alexandri pater,
regnum Macedoniae adeptus est inque eo tempore
29 Alexander natus est paucisque inde annis post Plato
philosophus ad Dionysium Siciliae tyrannum posteri-
30 orem profectus est; post deinde aliquanto tempore
Philippus apud Chaeroneam proelio magno Athenien-

---

1 390 B.C.; 387, Varro.   2 429 B.C.
3 *Annales* iii, frag. 2 Peter[2]. In 384 B.C.
4 *Chron.*, frag. 5, Peter[2].
5 384 B.C.   6 371 B.C.   7 367 B.C.
8 356 B.C.   9 338 B.C.

Marcus Furius Camillus was dictator and took Veii. Not long afterwards came the war with the Senones, when the Gauls captured Rome with the exception of the Capitol.[1]

Not long after these events the astronomer Eudoxus was famed in the land of Greece, the Lacedaemonians were defeated by the Athenians at Corinth under the lead of Phormio,[2] and at Rome Marcus Manlius, who during the siege of the Capitol had repulsed the Gauls as they were climbing up its steep cliffs, was convicted of having formed the design of making himself king. Marcus Varro says[3] that he was condemned to death and hurled from the Tarpeian rock; but Cornelius Nepos has written[4] that he was scourged to death. In the very same year, which was the seventh after the recovery of the city, it is recorded that the philosopher Aristotle was born.[5]

Next, some years after the war with the Senones, the Thebans defeated the Lacedaemonians at Leuctra[6] under the lead of Epaminondas, and a little later in the city of Rome the law of Licinius Stolo provided for the elections of consuls also from the plebeians,[7] whereas before that time it was not lawful for a consul to be chosen except from the patrician families.

Then, about the four hundredth year after the founding of the city, Philip, son of Amyntas and father of Alexander, became king of Macedonia. At that time Alexander was born,[8] and a few years later the philosopher Plato went to the court of the younger Dionysius, tyrant of Sicily; then some little time afterwards Philip defeated the Athenians in the great battle at Chaeronea.[9] At that time the

31 ses vicit. Tum Demosthenes orator ex eo proelio
salutem fuga quaesivit, cumque id ei quod fugerat
probrose obiceretur, versu illo notissimo elusit :

"'Ανήρ," inquit, " ὁ φεύγων καὶ πάλιν μαχήσεται."

32 Postea Philippus ex insidiis occiditur ; at Alexander
regnum adeptus ad subigendos Persas in Asiam
33 atque in Orientem transgressus est. Alter autem
Alexander, cui cognomentum Molosso fuit, in Italiam
venit, bellum populo Romano facturus—iam enim
fama virtutis felicitatisque Romanae apud exteras
gentes enitescere inceptabat—, sed priusquam
bellum faceret, vita decessit. Eum Molossum, cum
in Italiam transiret, dixisse accepimus se quidem ad
Romanos ire quasi in andronitin, Macedonem ad
34 Persas quasi in gynaeconitin. Postea Macedo
Alexander, pleraque parte orientali subacta, cum
annos undecim regnavisset, obiit mortis diem.
35 Neque haut longe post Aristoteles philosophus et
post aliquanto Demosthenes vita functi sunt isdem-
36 que ferme tempestatibus populus Romanus gravi ac
diutino Samnitium bello conflictatus est consulesque
Tiberius Veturius et Spurius Postumius, in locis
iniquis apud Caudium a Samnitibus circumvallati ac
subiugi missi, turpi foedere facto discesserunt, ob
eamque causam, populi iussu Samnitibus per fetiales
dediti, recepti non sunt.
37 Post annum deinde urbis conditae quadringentesi-
mum fere et septuagesimum bellum cum rege Pyrro

---

[1] Menander, *Monost.* 45.   [2] 336 b.c. Quint. xi. 2. 50
[3] 323 b.c.   [4] 322 b.c.   [5] 322 b.c.   [6] 321 b.c.

orator Demosthenes sought safety in flight from the battlefield, and when he was bitterly taunted with his flight he jestingly replied in the well-known verse :[1]

The man who runs away will fight again.

Later Philip fell victim to a conspiracy; but Alexander, who succeeded him,[2] crossed over into Asia and the Orient, to subdue the Persians. But another Alexander, surnamed Molossus, came into Italy intending to make war on the Roman people —for already the fame of Roman valour and success was beginning to be conspicuous among foreign nations—but he died before beginning the war. We have learned that on his way to Italy that Molossus said that he was going against the Romans as a nation of men, but the Macedonian was going against the Persians as one of women. Later, the Macedonian Alexander, having subdued the greater part of the east, died[3] after a reign of eleven years. Not long after this the philosopher Aristotle ended his life,[4] and a little later, Demosthenes;[5] at about that same time the Roman people engaged in a dangerous and protracted war with the Samnites and the consuls Tiberius Veturius and Spurius Postumius were surrounded by the Samnites in a perilous position near Caudium and being sent under the yoke were allowed to depart only when they had made a shameful treaty;[6] and when for that reason the consuls by vote of the people were surrendered to the Samnites through the fetial priests, they were not accepted.

Then, about four hundred and seventy years after the founding of the city, war was begun with king

38 sumptum est. Ea tempestate Epicurus Atheniensis
39 et Zeno Citiensis philosophi celebres erant, eodemque tempore C. Fabricius Luscinus et Q. Aemilius
Papus censores Romae fuerunt et P. Cornelium
Rufinum, qui bis consul et dictator fuerat, senatu
moverunt; causamque isti notae subscripserunt,
quod eum comperissent argenti facti cenae gratia
decem pondo libras habere.

40   Anno deinde post Romam conditam quadringente-
simo ferme et nonagesimo, consulibus Appio Claudio,
cui cognomentum Caudex fuit, Appii illius Caeci
fratre, et Marco Fulvio Flacco, bellum adversum
41 Poenos primum coeptum est, neque diu post Callimachus, poeta Cyrenensis, Alexandriae apud Ptole-
maeum regem celebratus est.

42   Annis deinde postea paulo pluribus quam viginti,
pace cum Poenis facta, consulibus C.[1] Claudio Cen-
thone, Appii Caeci filio, et M. Sempronio Tuditano,
primus omnium L. Livius poeta fabulas docere Romae
coepit post Sophoclis et Euripidis mortem annis
plus fere centum et sexaginta, post Menandri annis
43 circiter quinquaginta duobus. Claudium et Tudi-
tanum consules secuntur Q. Valerius et C. Mamilius,
quibus natum esse Q. Ennium poetam M. Varro in
primo *De Poetis* libro scripsit eumque, cum septimum
et sexagesimum annum haberet, duodecimum[2] *Annalem* scripsisse, idque ipsum Ennium in eodem libro
dicere.

44   Anno deinde post Romam conditam quingen-

---

[1] C. *added by Hosius.*
[2] duodevicesimum, *Merula*; xxii (*first* x *erased*), *X*; xvii,
L. Müller.

| [1] 280 B.C. | [2] 264 B.C. | [3] 240 B.C. |
| [4] 239 B.C. | [5] p. 259, Bipont. | |

Pyrrhus.[1] At that time Epicurus the Athenian and
Zeno of Citium were famed as philosophers, and at
the same time the censors at Rome, Gaius Fabricius
Luscinus and Quintus Aemilius Papus, expelled
from the senate Publius Cornelius Rufinus, who had
twice been consul and dictator; and they recorded
as the reason for that censure the fact that they
had learned of his using ten pounds' weight of
silverware at a dinner.

Then, in about the four hundred and ninetieth
year after the founding of Rome, when the consuls
were Appius Claudius, surnamed Caudex, brother
of the celebrated Appius the Blind, and Marcus
Fluvius Flaccus, the first war with the Carthaginians
broke out,[2] and not long afterwards Callimachus,
the poet of Cyrene, was famous at the court of
king Ptolemy at Alexandria.

A little more than twenty years later, when peace
had been made with the Carthaginians and the
consuls were C. Claudius Centho, son of Appius the
Blind, and Marcus Sempronius Tuditanus, the poet
Lucius Livius was the very first to put plays upon
the stage at Rome,[3] more than a hundred and sixty
years after the death of Sophocles and Euripides
and about fifty-two years after the death of
Menander. The consuls Claudius and Tuditanus
were followed by Quintus Valerius and Gaius
Mamilius, in whose year the poet Quintus Ennius
was born,[4] as Marcus Varro has written in the first
book of his work *On Poets*;[5] and he adds that at
the age of sixty-seven Ennius had written the
twelfth *Book of the Annals*, and that Ennius himself
says so in that same book.

Five hundred and nineteen years after the found-

tesimo undevicesimo[1] Sp. Carvilius Ruga primus
Romae de amicorum sententia divortium cum uxore
fecit, quod sterila esset iurassetque apud censores,
45 uxorem se liberum quaerundorum[2] causa habere,
eodemque anno Cn. Naevius poeta fabulas apud
populum dedit, quem M. Varro in libro *De Poetis*
primo stipendia fecisse ait bello Poenico primo,
idque ipsum Naevium dicere in eo carmine quod de
eodem bello scripsit. Porcius autem Licinus serius[3]
poeticam Romae coepisse dicit[4] in his versibus :

Poénico belló secundo Músa pinnató gradu
Íntulit se béllicosam in Rómuli gentém feram.

46 Ac deinde annis fere post quindecim bellum ad-
47 versum Poenos sumptum est atque non nimium
longe[5] M. Cato orator in civitate et Plautus poeta
48 in scaena floruerunt ; isdemque temporibus Diogenes
Stoicus et Carneades Academicus et Critolaus Peripateticus ab Atheniensibus ad senatum populi
49 Romani negotii publici gratia legati sunt. Neque
magno intervallo postea Q. Ennius et iuxta Caecilius

---

[1] vicesimo tertio, iv. 3. 2.   [2] quaerundum, iv. 3. 2.
[3] Porcium (Portium, δ ; Portum, X) autem Licinium
servius, ω, *corrected by Torrentius and Carrio.*
[4] dixit, *Hertz* ; Porcium . . . dicere, *Ritschl, Schanz,
Rhein. Mus.* liv. 19.
[5] longe post (cf. § 35), *sugg. by Hosius.*

---

[1] 235 B.C.   In iv. 3 Gellius gave the date as 231, following
a different chronology.   Dionysius of Halicarnassus agrees
with the former (Varronian) chronology.   On the formula
liberum quaerundorum causa see note on iv. 3. 2 (vol. i,
p. 322).
[2] 235 B.C.   [3] p. 259, Bipont.
[4] Frag. 1, Bährens.   [5] 218 B.C.

ing of Rome, Spurius Carvilius Ruga, at the advice
of his friends, was the first Roman to divorce his
wife, on the ground that she was barren and that he
had taken oath before the censors that he married
for the purpose of having children.[1]   In that same
year the poet Naevius exhibited plays to the people,[2]
and Marcus Varro says[3] in the first book of his
work *On Poets* that Naevius served in the first
Punic war and that the poet himself makes that
statement in the poem which he wrote on that
same war.   But Porcius Licinius says[4] in the following verses that Rome was later in taking up the
poetic art :

> In the second Punic war with winged flight
> The Muse to Romulus' warrior nation came.

Then, about fifteen years later, war was begun
with the Carthaginians,[5] and not very long after
that Marcus Cato was famous as a political orator
and Plautus as a dramatic poet ; and at that same
time Diogenes the Stoic, Carneades the Academic,
and Critolaus the Peripatetic were sent by the
Athenians as envoys to the senate of the Roman
people on public business.   Not very long after
this came Quintus Ennius, and then Caecilius and
Terence,[6] and afterwards Pacuvius[7] and when

---

[6] These three poets died respectively in 169, 168 and
159 B.C., before the coming of the envoys to Rome in
155 B.C.   Since Gellius announced the second Punic war
as his limit, Leuze believes that he added this section from
memory.

[7] Pacuvius (220–130 B.C.) was older than Terence, but
outlived him.   Terence's comedies were produced between
166 and 160 B.C. ; he died in 159, but the date of his birth
is uncertain.

et Terentius et subinde et Pacuvius et Pacuvio iam sene Accius clariorque tunc in poematis eorum obtrectandis Lucilius fuit.

50 Sed progressi longius sumus, cum finem proposuerimus adnotatiunculis istis bellum Poenorum secundum.

Pacuvius was already an old man, Accius and then Lucilius, who was still more famous through his criticisms of the poems of his predecessors.

But I have gone too far, since the limit that I set for these little notes was the second Punic war.

BOOK XVIII

LIBER OCTAVUS DECIMUS

I

Disputationes a philosopho Stoico et contra a Peripatetico,
arbitro Favorino, factae ; quaesitumque inter eos quantum
in perficienda vita beata virtus valeret quantumque esset
in his quae dicuntur extranea.

1 FAMILIARES Favorini erant duo quidam non in-
celebres in urbe Roma philosophi.   Eorum fuit unus
2 Peripateticae disciplinae sector, alter Stoicae.   His
quondam ego acriter atque contente pro suis utrim-
que decretis propugnantibus, cum essemus una
omnes Ostiae cum Favorino, interfui.   Ambulaba-
3 mus autem in litore, cum iam advesperasceret,
aestate anni novi.[1]
4   Atque ibi Stoicus censebat et vitam beatam homini virtute animi sola et miseriam summam malitia
sola posse effici, etiamsi cetera bona omnia quae cor-
poralia et externa appellarentur virtuti deessent,
5 malitiae adessent.   Ille contra Peripateticus miseram
quidem vitam vitiis animi et malitia sola fieri concedebat, sed ad conplendos omnes vitae beatae
numeros virtutem solam nequaquam satis esse
existimabat, quoniam et corporis integritas sani-
tasque et honestus modus formae et pecunia familiaris[2] et bona existimatio ceteraque omnia corporis et
fortunae bona necessaria viderentur perficiendae
vitae beatae.

---

[1] nova, *Salmasius* ; novi, *ω* ; molli, *Damsté.*
[2] fortunae et pecuniae reique familiaris,   *Madvig ;* res
familiaris, *Damsté ; but cf.* iii. 17. 1.

BOOK XVIII

I

Discussions held by a Stoic philosopher and in opposition by a Peripatetic, with Favorinus as arbiter; and the question at issue was, how far virtue availed in determining a happy life and to what extent happiness was dependent on what are called external circumstances.

THERE were two friends of Favorinus, philosophers of no little note in the city of Rome; one of them was a follower of the Peripatetic school, the other of the Stoic. I was once present when these men argued ably and vigorously, each for his own beliefs, when we were all with Favorinus at Ostia. And we were walking along the shore in springtime, just as evening was falling.

And on that occasion the Stoic maintained[1] that man could enjoy a happy life only through virtue, and that the greatest wretchedness was due to wickedness only, even though all the other blessings, which are called external, should be lacking to the virtuous man and present with the wicked. The Peripatetic, on the other hand, admitted that a wretched life was due solely to vicious thoughts and wickedness, but he believed that virtue alone was by no means sufficient to round out all the parts of a happy life, since the complete use of one's limbs, good health, a reasonably attractive person, property, good repute, and all the other advantages of body and fortune seemed necessary to make a perfectly happy life.

[1] III. 56, Arn.

6 Reclamabat hoc in loco Stoicus et, tamquam duas ille res diversas poneret, mirabatur, quod, cum essent malitia et virtus duo contraria, vita misera et beata quoque aeque contraria, non servaret in utrisque vim

7 et naturam contrarii et ad miseriam quidem vitae conficiendam satis valere malitiam solam putaret, ad praestandam vero beatam vitam non satis solam esse

8 virtutem diceret. Atque id maxime dissidere neque convenire dicebat, quod qui profiteretur vitam nullo pacto beatam effici posse si virtus sola abesset, idem contra negaret, beatam fieri vitam cum sola virtus adesset, et quem daret haberetque virtuti absenti honorem, eundem petenti atque praesenti adimeret.

9 Tum Peripateticus perquam hercle festive : " Rogo te," inquit, "cum bona venia respondeas an existimes esse vini amphoram, cum abest ab ea unus

10 congius?" "Minime," inquit, " vini amphora dici

11 potest ex qua abest congius." Hoc ubi accepit Peripateticus, " Unus igitur," inquit, "congius amphoram facere dici debebit, quoniam, cum deest ille unus, non fit amphora vini et, cum accessit, fit amphora. Quod si id dicere absurdum est, uno congio solo fieri amphoram, itidem absurdum est una sola virtute vitam fieri beatam dicere, quoniam, cum virtus abest, beata esse vita numquam potest." [1]

12 Tum Favorinus aspiciens Peripateticum, " Est qui-

---

[1] possit, *or* quamquam *for* quoniam, *Skutsch.*

---

[1] Somewhat less than 6 gallons.
[2] A little less than 6 pints.

Here the Stoic made outcry against him, and maintaining that his opponent was advancing two contrary propositions, expressed his surprise that, since wickedness and virtue were two opposites, and a wretched and a happy life were also opposites, he did not preserve in each the force and nature of an opposite, but believed that wickedness alone was sufficient to cause an unhappy life, at the same time declaring that virtue alone was not sufficient to guarantee a happy life. And he said that it was especially inconsistent and contradictory for one who maintained that a life could in no way be made happy if virtue alone were lacking, to deny on the other hand that a life could be happy when virtue alone was present, and thus to take away from virtue when present and demanding it, that honour which he gave and bestowed upon virtue when lacking.

Thereupon the Peripatetic, in truth very wittily, said: "Pray pardon me, and tell me this, whether you think that an amphora[1] of wine from which a congius[2] has been taken, is still an amphora?" "By no means," was the reply, "can that be called an amphora of wine, from which a congius is missing." When the Peripatetic heard this, he retorted: "Then it will have to be said that one congius makes an amphora of wine, since when that one is lacking, it is not an amphora, and when it is added, it becomes an amphora. But if it is absurd to say that an amphora is made from one single congius, it is equally absurd to say that a life is made happy by virtue alone by itself, because when virtue is lacking life can never be happy."

Then Favorinus, turning to the Peripatetic, said:

dem," inquit, " argutiola haec qua de congio vini
usus es exposita in libris; sed, ut scis, captio magis
lepida quam probum aut simile argumentum videri
13 debet. Congius enim, cum deest, efficit quidem ne
sit iustae mensurae amphora; sed cum accedit et
additur, non ille unus facit amphoram, sed supplet.
14 Virtus autem, ut isti dicunt, non accessio neque
supplementum, sed sola ipsa vitae beatae instar est
et propterea beatam vitam sola una, cum adest,
facit."
15 Haec atque alia quaedam minuta magis et nodosa,
tamquam apud arbitrum Favorinum, in suam uterque
16 sententiam conferebant. Sed cum iam prima fax
noctis et densiores esse tenebrae coepissent, prosecuti
Favorinum in domum, ad quam devertebat, dis-
cessimus.

II

Cuiusmodi quaestionum certationibus Saturnalicia ludicra
Athenis agitare soliti simus; atque inibi expressa quaedam
sophismatia et aenigmata oblectatoria.

1 Saturnalia Athenis agitabamus hilare prorsum ac
modeste, non, ut dicitur, " remittentes animum "—
nam " remittere," inquit Musonius, " animum quasi
amittere est "—, sed demulcentes eum paulum atque
2 laxantes iucundis honestisque sermonum inlecta-
tionibus. Conveniebamus autem ad eandem cenam
conplusculi, qui Romani in Graeciam veneramus
quique easdem auditiones eosdemque doctores cole-
3 bamus. Tum qui et cenulam ordine suo curabat,
praemium solvendae quaestionis ponebat librum

---

¹ p. 133, Hense. ² Cf. note on vii. 13. 2.

"This clever turn which you have used about the congius of wine is indeed set forth in the books; but, as you know, it ought to be regarded rather as a neat catch than as an honest or plausible argument. For when a congius is lacking, it indeed causes the amphora not to be of full measure; but when it is added and put in, it alone does not make, but completes, an amphora. But virtue, as the Stoics say, is not an addition or a supplement, but it by itself is the equivalent of a happy life, and therefore it alone makes a happy life, when it is present."

These and some other minute and knotty arguments each advanced in support of his own opinion, before Favorinus as umpire. But when the first night-lights appeared and the darkness grew thicker, we escorted Favorinus to the house where he was putting up; and when he went in, we separated.

II

What kind of questions we used to discuss when spending the Saturnalia at Athens; and some amusing sophistries and enigmas.

WE used to spend the Saturnalia at Athens very merrily yet temperately, not "relaxing our minds," as the saying is—for, as Musonius asserts,[1] to relax the mind is like losing it—but diverting our minds a little and relieving them by the delights of pleasant and improving conversation. Accordingly, a number of us Romans who had come to Greece, and who attended the same lectures and devoted ourselves to the same teachers, met at the same dinner-table. Then the one who was giving the entertainment in his turn,[2] offered as a prize for solving a problem

veteris scriptoris vel Graecum vel Latinum et
coronam e lauro plexam, totidemque res quaerebat
quot homines istic eramus; cumque eas omnis
exposuerat, rem locumque dicendi sors dabat.
4 Quaestio igitur soluta corona et praemio donabatur,
non soluta autem tramittebatur ad eum qui sortito
5 successerat, idque in orbem vice pari servabatur. Si
nemo dissolvebat, corona eius quaestionis deo cuius
6 id festum erat dicabatur. Quaerebantur autem res
huiuscemodi: aut sententia poetae veteris lepide
obscura, non anxie, aut historiae antiquioris requi-
sitio, aut decreti cuiuspiam ex philosophia perperam
invulgati purgatio, aut captionis sophisticae solutio,
aut inopinati rariorisque verbi indagatio, aut tempus
item in verbo perspicuo obscurissimum.
7   Itaque nuper quaesita esse memini numero septem,
quorum prima fuit enarratio horum versuum, qui
sunt in *Saturis* Quinti Enni uno multifariam verbo
concinniter inplicati. Quorum exemplum hoc est:

Nám qui lepidé postulat álterum frustrári,
Quém frustratúr, frustra eum dícit frustra ésse;
Nám si se [1] frústrari quém frustras séntit,
Quí frustratur frustrast, sí non ille frústra est.[2]

8 Secunda quaestio fuit quonam modo audiri atque
accipi deberet, quod Plato, in civitate quam in libris

---

[1] nam si se *suggested by Hosius*; nam qui sese, *MSS.*
[2] ille frustra est, *Skutsch.*

---

[1] vv. 59 ff., Vahlen[2].
[2] Rendered as follows by R. J. E. Tiddy in Gordon, *English
Literature and the Classics*, p. 206: "The man who thinks to
score a pretty score off another, says that he has scored off
him off whom he would score—but he hasn't all the same.
For he who thinks he's scoring, but isn't all the same, is
scored off himself—and so the other scores."

the work of some old Greek or Roman writer and
a crown woven from laurel, and put to us as many
questions as there were guests present. But when
he had put them all, the question which each was to
discuss and the order of speaking were determined
by lot. Then, when a question was correctly answered, the reward was a crown and a prize; if it
was not correctly answered, it was passed on to the
next in the allotment, and this process was repeated
throughout the circle. If no one could answer a
particular question, the crown was dedicated to the
god in whose honour the festival was held. Now
the questions that were proposed were of this kind:
an obscure saying of some early poet, amusing rather
than perplexing; some point in ancient history; the
correction of some tenet of philosophy which was
commonly misinterpreted, the solution of some
sophistical catch, the investigation of a rare and
unusual word, or of an obscure use of the tense of a
verb of plain meaning.

And I recollect that once seven questions were
put, the first of which was an explanation of these
verses in the *Saturae* of Quintus Ennius,[1] in which
one word is very neatly used in many different
senses. They run as follows:

Who tries with craft another to deceive,
Deceives himself, if he says he's deceived
Whom he'd deceive. For if whom you'd deceive
Perceives that he's deceived, the deceiver 'tis
Who is deceived, if t'other's not deceived.[2]

The second question was how it ought to be
understood and interpreted that Plato in the State

suis condidit, κοινὰς τὰς γυναῖκας, id est communes
esse mulieres, censuit et praemia viris fortissimis
summisque bellatoribus posuit saviationes puerorum
9 et puellarum. Tertio in loco hoc quaesitum est, in
quibus verbis captionum istarum fraus esset et quo
pacto distingui resolvique possent : "Quod non
perdidisti, habes ; cornua non perdidisti : habes
igitur cornua," item altera captio : "quod ego sum,
id tu non es ; homo ego sum :[1] homo igitur tu
10 non es." Quaesitum ibi est quae esset huius quoque
sophismatis resolutio : "Cum mentior et mentiri me
11 dico, mentior an verum dico ?" Postea quaestio
istaec fuit, quam ob causam patricii Megalensibus
12 mutitare soliti sint, plebes Cerealibus. Secundum
ea hoc quaesitum est : verbum "verant," quod
significat "vera dicunt," quisnam poetarum veterum
13 dixerit ? Sexta quaestio fuit, "asphodelum" cuiusmodi herba sit, quod Hesiodus in isto versu
posuerit :

Νήπιοι, οὐδὲ ἴσασιν ὅσῳ πλέον ἥμισυ παντὸς
Οὐδ᾽ ὅσον ἐν μαλάχῃ τε καὶ ἀσφοδέλῳ μέγ᾽ ὄνειαρ,

et quid item Hesiodus se dicere sentiat, cum dimi-
14 dium plus esse toto dicit. Postrema quaestionum

---

[1] homo . . . sum *supplied by Hertz* (sed homo sum
igitur, Q).

---

[1] *Rep.*, p. 457, etc. ; 460, 468.
[2] The festival of Magna Mater, on April 4, established in
204 B.C.
[3] The festival of Ceres, on April 19.
[4] *Works and Days*, 40. Cf. Horace, *Odes*, i. 31. 16 :
  me pascunt olivae,
  Me cichorea levesque malvae.
[5] Hesiod means that a simple and frugal life is the best.
He had shared his father's property with his brother Perses ;

which he planned in his books [1] said κοινὰς τὰς γυναῖκας, that is, declared that women "should be common property," and that the rewards of the bravest men and the greatest warriors should be the kisses of boys and maidens. In the third place this was asked, in what words the fallacy of the following catches consisted and how they could be made out and explained : " What you have not lost, that you have. You have not lost horns ; therefore you have horns." Also another catch : " What I am, that you are not. I am a man ; therefore you are not a man." Then it was inquired what was the solution of this sophistry : " When I lie and admit that I lie, do I lie or speak the truth ? " · Afterwards this question was put, why the patricians are in the habit of entertaining one another on the Megalensia,[2] and the plebeians on the Cerealia.[3] Next came this question : " What one of the early poets used the verb *verant*, in the sense of ' they speak the truth ' ? " The sixth question was, what kind of plant the " asphodel " was, which Hesiod mentioned in the following lines : [4]

O fools ! who know not how much half exceeds
    the whole,[5]
Or that the asphodel and mallow make fine food.

And also what Hesiod meant when he said that the half was more than the whole. The last of all the

but Perses went to law and through the partiality of the judges got possession of the whole inheritance. He soon wasted it, and Hesiod, through his thrift, was able to come to his help. Hence the expression became proverbial. Cicero, on seeing a bust of his brother Quintus, who was of short stature, said : " Half of my brother is greater than the whole." (Macrob. *Sat.* ii. 3. 4.)

omnium haec fuit: "Scripserim," "legerim,"
"venerim," cuius temporis verba sint, praeteriti
an futuri an utriusque?

15 Haec ubi ordine quo dixi proposita atque singulis
sorte ductis disputata explanataque sunt, libris
coronisque omnes donati sumus, nisi ob unam

16 quaestionem, quae fuit de verbo "verant." Nemo
enim tum commeminerat, dictum esse a Q. Ennio
id verbum in tertio decimo *Annalium* in isto versu:

> Satin vates verant aetate in agunda?

Corona igitur huius quaestionis deo feriarum istarum
Saturno datast.

III

Quid Aeschines rhetor, in oratione qua Timarchum de
    inpudicitia accusavit, Lacedaemonios statuisse dixerit
    super sententia probatissima, quam inprobatissimus homo
    dixisset.

1 AESCHINES, vel acerrimus prudentissimusque oratorum qui apud contiones Atheniensium floruerunt, in
oratione illa saeva criminosaque et virulenta, qua
Timarchum de inpudicitia graviter insigniterque
accusabat, nobile et inlustre consilium Laedaemoniis
dedisse dicit virum indidem civitatis eiusdem principem, virtute atque aetate magna praeditum.

2 "Populus," inquit, "Lacedaemonius de summa
republica sua, quidnam esset utile et honestum

---

[1] v. 380, Vahlen[2].   [2] *In Timarch.* 180.

questions was this: of what tense the verbs *scrip-serim*, *legerim* and *venerim* are, perfect or future, or both.

When these questions had been put in the order that I have mentioned, and had been discussed and explained by the several guests on whom the lots fell, we were all presented with crowns and books, except for the one question about the verb *verant*. For at the time no one remembered that the word was used by Quintus Ennius in the thirteenth book of his *Annals* in the following line :[1]

> Do seers speak truth (*verant*), predicting life's extent?

Therefore the crown for this question was presented to Saturn, the god of that festival.

III

What the orator Aeschines, in the speech in which he accused Timarchus of unchastity, said that the Lacedae-monians decided about the praiseworthy suggestion of a most unpraiseworthy man.

AESCHINES, the most acute and sagacious of the orators who gained renown in the Athenian assemblies, in that cruel, slanderous and virulent speech in which he severely and directly accused Timarchus of unchastity, says that a man of advanced years and high character, a leader in that State, once gave noble and distinguished counsel to the Lacedaemonians.

"The people of Lacedaemon," he says,[2] "were deliberating as to what was honourable and expedient in a matter of great moment to their State.

3 deliberabat. Tum exurgit sententiae dicendae gratia
homo quispiam turpitudine pristinae vitae diffama-
tissimus, sed lingua tunc atque facundia nimium
4 quanto praestabilis. Consilium quod dabat, quodque oportere fieri suadebat, acceptum ab universis
et conplacitum est futurumque erat ex eius sententia
5 populi decretum. Ibi unus ex illo principum ordine
quos Lacedaemonii, aetatis dignitatisque maiestate,
tamquam arbitros et magistros disciplinae publicae
verebantur, commoto irritatoque animo exilit, et
'Quaenam,' inquit, 'Lacedaemonii, ratio aut quae
tandem spes erit urbem hanc et hanc rempublicam
salvam inexpugnabilemque esse diutius posse, si
huiuscemodi anteactae vitae hominibus consiliariis
utemur? Quod si proba istaec et honesta sententia
est, quaeso vos, non sinamus eandem dehonestari
6 turpissimi auctoris contagio.' Atque ubi hoc dixit,
elegit virum fortitudine atque iustitia praeter alios
praestantem, sed inopi lingua et infacundum, iussitque eum consensu petituque omnium eandem illam
sententiam diserti viri cuimodi posset verbis dicere,
ut nulla prioris mentione habita, scitum atque
decretum populi ex eius unius nomine fieret qui
7 id [1] ipsum denuo dixerat. Atque ita, ut suaserat
8 prudentissimus senex, factum est. Sic bona sententia mansit, turpis auctor mutatus est."

---

[1] qui id, *J. F. Gronov*; quod, ω.

---

[1] Cf. Cic. *De Senectute*, 20, apud Lacedaemonios quidem
ii qui amplissimum magistratum gerunt, ut sunt, sic etiam
nominantur, senes, referring to the γερουσία.

Then there arose, for the purpose of giving his opinion, a man notorious for the baseness of his past life, but at the same time highly eminent for his eloquence and oratory. The advice which he gave, and the course which he said ought to be followed, were approved and accepted by all, and a decree of the people was about to be passed in accordance with his opinion. Thereupon one of that body of leading citizens whom the Lacedaemonians, because of the prestige of their age and rank, reverenced as judges and directors of public policy,[1] sprang up in a spirit of anger and vexation, and said: 'What prospect, Lacedaemonians, or what hope, pray, will there be that this city and this State can longer be secure and invincible, if we follow counsellors whose past life is like that of this man? Even if this advice is honourable and noble, let us not, I pray you, allow it to be disgraced by the pollution of its most shameful author.' And when he had said this, he selected a man conspicuous before all others for his courage and justice, but a poor speaker and without eloquence, and bade him, with the consent and at the request of all, to deliver that opinion of the eloquent man in the best language he could command, in order that, without mention of the former speaker, the vote and decree of the people might be passed under the name of him alone who had last made that proposition. And the action which that most sagacious old man had recommended was taken. So the good advice endured, but its base author was displaced."

IV

Quod Sulpicius Apollinaris praedicantem quendam a sese
uno Sallusti historias intellegi inlusit, quaestione proposita
quid verba ista apud Sallustium significarent: "incertum,
stolidior an vanior."

1 CUM iam adulescentuli Romae praetextam et
puerilem togam mutassemus magistrosque tunc nobis
nosmet ipsi exploratiores quaereremus, in Sandaliario
forte apud librarios fuimus, cum ibi in multorum
hominum coetu Apollinaris Sulpicius, vir in memoria
nostra praeter alios doctus, iactatorem quempiam
et venditatorem Sallustianae lectionis inrisit inlusit-
que genere illo facetissimae dissimulationis, qua
2 Socrates ad sophistas utebatur. Nam cum ille se
unum et unicum lectorem esse enarratoremque
Sallustii diceret neque primam tantum cutem ac
speciem sententiarum, sed sanguinem quoque ipsum
ac medullam verborum eius eruere atque introspicere
penitus praedicaret, tum Apollinaris amplecti vene-
rarique se doctrinas illius dicens: " Per," inquit,
"magister optume, exoptatus mihi nunc venis cum
3 sanguine et medulla Sallusti verborum. Hesterno
enim die quaerebatur ex me quidnam verba haec
eius in quarto *Historiarum* libro de Cn. Lentulo
scripta significent, de quo incertum fuisse ait,
4 stolidiorne esset an vanior," eaque ipsa verba, uti
sunt a Sallustio scripta, dixit: "At Cn. Lentulus
patriciae gentis, collega eius, cui cognomentum

---

[1] *Hist.* iv. 1, Maur.

IV

How Sulpicius Apollinaris made fun of a man who asserted
that he alone understood Sallust's histories, by inquiring
the meaning of these words in Sallust: *incertum, stolidior
an vanior.*

WHEN I was already a young man at Rome, having
laid aside the purple-bordered toga of boyhood, and
was on my own account seeking masters of deeper
knowledge, I happened to be with the booksellers
in Shoemaker's Street at the time when Sulpicius
Apollinaris, the most learned man of all within my
memory, in the presence of a large gathering made
fun of a boastful fellow who was parading his reading of Sallust, and turned him into ridicule with that
kind of witty irony which Socrates used against the
sophists. For when the man declared that he was
the one and only reader and expositor of Sallust,
and openly boasted that he did not merely search
into the outer skin and obvious meaning of his
sentences, but delved into and thoroughly examined
the very blood and marrow of his words, then
Apollinaris, pretending to embrace and venerate his
learning, said: "Most opportunely, my good master,
do you come to me now with the blood and marrow of
Sallust's language. For yesterday I was asked what
in the world those words of his meant which he
wrote in the fourth book of his *Histories* about
Gnaeus Lentulus, of whom he says that it is uncertain whether he was more churlish or more
unreliable"; and he quoted the very words, as
Sallust wrote them:[1] "But Gnaeus Lentulus, his
colleague, surnamed Clodianus, a man of patrician
family—and it is not at all easy to say whether he

Clodiano fuit, perincertum stolidior an vanior, legem
de pecunia quam Sulla emptoribus bonorum re-
miserat exigenda promulgavit."

5   Quaesitum ergo ex se Apollinaris neque id se
dissolvere potuisse adseverabat, quid esset " vanior "
et quid " stolidior," quoniam Sallustius sic ea sepa-
rasse atque opposuisse inter se videretur, tamquam
diversa ac dissimilia nec eiusdem utraque vitii
forent, ac propterea petebat uti se doceret significationes utriusque vocis et origines.

6   Tum ille rictu oris labearumque ductu contemni
a se ostendens et rem de qua quaereretur et
hominem ipsum qui quaereret, " Priscorum," inquit,
" et remotorum ego verborum medullas et sanguinem, sicuti dixi, perspicere et elicere soleo, non
istorum quae proculcata vulgo et protrita sunt.
Ipso illo quippe Cn. Lentulo 'stolidior' est et
'vanior' qui ignorat eiusdem stultitiae esse vani-
7 tatem et stoliditatem." Sed ubi hoc dixit, media
8 ipsa sermonum reliquit et abire coepit. Nos deinde
eum tenebamus urgebamusque, et cumprimis Apollinaris, ut de vocabulorum vel differentia vel, si ei
ita videretur, similitudine plenius apertiusque dissereret et, ut ne sibi invideret discere volenti,
orabat.

9   Atque ille, se iam plane inludi ratus, negotium
10 sibi esse causatur et digreditur. Nos autem postea
ex Apollinari didicimus, " vanos " proprie dici, non
ut vulgus diceret, desipientis aut hebetes aut in-
eptos, sed, ut veterum doctissimi dixissent, men-

was more churlish or more unreliable—proposed a bill for exacting the money which Sulla had remitted to the purchasers of property."

Apollinaris therefore asserted that it was asked of him, and that he had not been able to answer the question, what was meant by *vanior* and what by *stolidior*, since Sallust seemed to have separated the words and contrasted them with each other, as if they were different and unlike and did not both designate the same fault; and therefore he asked that the man would tell him the meaning and origin of the two words.

Then the other, showing by a grin and a grimace that he despised both the subject of the inquiry and the questioner himself, said: "I am accustomed to examine and explain the marrow and blood of ancient and recondite words, as I said, not of those which are in common use and trite. Surely a man is more worthless and stupid than Gnaeus Lentulus himself, if he does not know that *vanitas* and *stoliditas* indicate the same kind of folly." But having said that, he left us in the very midst of our discussion and began to sneak off. Then we laid hold on him and pressed him, and in particular Apollinaris begged him to discourse at greater length and more plainly upon the difference, or, if he preferred, on the similarity of the words, and not to begrudge the information to one who was eager to learn.

Then the fellow, realizing by this time that he was being laughed at, pleaded an engagement and made off. But we afterwards learned from Apollinaris that the term *vani* was properly applied, not as in common parlance to those who were foolish or dull or silly, but, as the most learned of the ancients

daces et infidos et levia inaniaque pro gravibus et veris astutissime componentes; "stolidos" autem vocari non tam stultos et excordes quam taetros[1] et molestos et inlepidos, quos Graeci μοχθηροὺς καὶ 11 φορτικούς dicerent. Etyma quoque harum vocum et origines scriptas esse dicebat in libris Nigidianis.

Quas requisitas ego et repertas cum primarum significationum exemplis, ut commentariis harum *Noctium* inferrem, notavi et intulisse iam me aliquo in loco commentationibus istis existimo.

V

Quod Q. Ennius in septimo *Annali* "quadrupes eques" ac non "quadrupes equus," ut legunt multi, scriptum reliquit.

1 Cum Antonio Iuliano rhetore, viro hercle bono et facundiae florentis, complures adulescentuli, familiares eius, Puteolis aestivarum feriarum ludum et iocum in litteris amoenioribus et in volup-2 tatibus pudicis honestisque agitabamus. Atque ibi tunc Iuliano nuntiatur, ἀναγνώστην quendam, non indoctum hominem, voce admodum scita et canora Ennii *Annales* legere ad populum in theatro. 3 "Eamus," inquit, "auditum nescio quem istum Ennianistam"; hoc enim se ille nomine appellari volebat.

---

[1] castros, Z; stautros, Q; austeros, *Hertz.*

---

[1] Fr. 45, Swoboda. *Vanus* is related to *vacare* and *vacuus*; Eng. "want"; *stolidus* to *stolo,* "dullard," from the root *stel-,* "stand," "be stiff."

had used them, to liars, deceivers, and those who cleverly devised light and empty statements in place of those which were true and earnest. But that those were called *stolidi* who were not so much foolish and witless as austere, churlish and disagreeable, such men as the Greeks called μοχθηροί, "ugly fellows," and φορτικοί, "common" or "vulgar folk." He also said that the roots and derivations of these words were to be found in the books of Nigidius.[1]

Having sought for these words and found them, with examples of their earliest meanings, I made a note of them, in order to include them in the notes contained in these *Nights,* and I think that I have already introduced them somewhere among them.[2]

V

That Quintus Ennius, in the seventh book of his *Annals,* wrote *quadrupes eques,* and not *quadrupes equus,* as many read it.

A NUMBER of us young men, friends of his, were at Puteoli with the rhetorician Antonius Julianus, a fine man in truth and of distinguished eloquence, and we were spending the summer holidays in amusement and gaiety, amid literary diversions and seemly and improving pleasures. And while we were there, word was brought to Julianus that a certain reader, a man not without learning, was reciting the *Annals* of Ennius to the people in the theatre in a very refined and musical voice. "Let us go," said he, "to hear this 'Ennianist,' whoever he may be"; for that was the name by which the man wished to be called.

[2] viii. 14.

4 Quem cum iam inter ingentes clamores legentem invenissemus—legebat autem librum ex *Annalibus* Ennii septimum—, hos eum primum versus perperam pronuntiantem audivimus:

> Denique vi magna quadrupes equus[1] atque elephanti
> Proiciunt sese,

neque multis postea versibus additis, celebrantibus eum laudantibusque omnibus, discessit.

5 Tum Iulianus egrediens e theatro: "Quid vobis," inquit, "de hoc anagnosta et de quadrupede equo videtur? sic enim profecto legit:

> Denique vi magna quadrupes equus atque elephanti
> Proiciunt sese.

6 Ecquid putatis, si magistrum praelectoremque habuisset alicuius aeris,[2] 'quadrupes equus' dicturum fuisse ac non 'quadrupes eques,' quod ab Ennio ita scriptum relictumque esse nemo unus litterarum veterum diligens dubitavit?" Cumque

7 aliquot eorum qui aderant "quadrupes equus" apud suum quisque grammaticum legisse se dicerent et mirarentur quidnam esset "quadrupes eques," "Vellem vos," inquit, "optimi iuvenes, tam accurate Q. Ennium legisse quam P. Vergilius legerat, qui hunc eius versum secutus in *Georgicis* suis 'equitem' pro 'equo' posuit his in versibus:

---

[1] eques, *Vahlen.*   [2] auris, *Damste.*

---

[1] vv. 232 ff. Vahlen[2].   [2] iii. 115.

When at last we had found him reading amid loud applause—and he was reading the seventh book of the *Annals* of Ennius—we first heard him wrongly recite the following lines:[1]

> Then with great force on rush the four-footed
>   horse (*equus*)
> And elephants,

and without adding many more verses, he departed amid the praises and applause of the whole company.

Then Julianus, as he came out of the theatre, said: " What think you of this reader and his four-footed horse? For surely he read it thus:

> Denique vi magna quadrupes equus atque
>   elephanti
> Proiciunt sese.

Do you think that, if he had had a master and instructor worth a penny, he would have said *quadrupes equus* and not *quadrupes eques*? For no one who has given any attention to ancient literature doubts that Ennius left it written in that way." When several of those who were present declared that they had read *quadrupes equus*, each with his own teacher, and wondered what was the meaning of *quadrupes eques*, Julianus rejoined: " I could wish, my worthy young friends, that you had read Quintus Ennius as accurately as did Publius Vergilius, who, imitating this verse of his in *The Georgics*, used *eques* for *equus* in these lines:[2]

313

> Frena Pelethronii Lapithae gyrosque dedere
> Impositi dorso atque equitem docuere sub armis
> Insultare solo et gressus glomerare superbos.

In quo loco equitem, si quis modo non inscite
inepteque argutior sit, nihil potest accipi aliud nisi
8 'equum'; pleraque enim veterum aetas et hominem
equo insidentem et equum cui[1] insideretur 'equi-
9 tem' dixerunt. Propterea 'equitare' etiam, quod
verbum e vocabulo 'equitis' inclinatum est, et
homo equo utens et equus sub homine gradiens
10 dicebatur. Lucilius adeo, vir adprime linguae
Latinae sciens, 'ecum equitare' dicit his versibus:

> Quis hunc currere equum nos atque equitare
> videmus,
> His equitat curritque; oculis equitare videmus;
> Ergo oculis equitat.

11 Sed enim contentus," inquit, "ego his non fui et,
ut non turbidae fidei nec ambiguae, sed ut purae
liquentisque esset, 'equus'ne an 'eques' scriptum
Ennius reliquisset, librum summae atque reverendae
vestutatis, quem fere constabat Lampadionis manu
emendatum, studio pretioque multo unius versus
inspiciendi gratia conduxi et 'eques,' non 'equus,'
scriptum in eo versu inveni."

---

[1] cui, *Skutsch* ; qui, ω (quo, π[1]).

---

[1] Julianus gave this meaning to *equitem*, but the modern
editors give it the usual one of "horseman."

[2] vv. 1284 ff. Marx, who reads *ecum* for *equum*.

[3] Similar sophistries were indulged in by Chrysippus (*Diog.
Laert.* vii. 180 ff.) and other philosophers. See Marx *ad loc.*

[4] C. Octavius Lampadio edited the *Bellum Punicum* of

Thessalian Lapiths, high on horses' back,
Gave us the bit and circling course, and taught
The horse,[1] full armed, to gallop o'er the
    plain
And round his paces proud.

In this passage, unless one is foolishly and sillily captious, *equitem* can be taken in no other sense than that of 'horse,' for many of the early writers called the man who sat upon a horse *eques* and also the horse on which he sat. Hence *equitare* also, which is derived from the word *eques, equitis,* was said both of the man who rode the horse and of the horse which carried the man. Lucilius, indeed, a man conspicuous for his command of the Latin language, says *equum equitare* in these lines:[2]

With what we see the courser run and trot,
With this he runs and trots. Now, 'tis with
    eyes
We see him trot; hence with his eyes he
    trots.[3]

"But," said Apollinaris, "I was not content with these examples, and in order that it might not appear uncertain and doubtful, but clear and evident, whether Ennius wrote *equus* or *eques,* I procured at great trouble and expense, for the sake of examining one line, a copy of heavy and venerable antiquity, which it was almost certain had been edited by the hand of Lampadio;[4] and in that copy I found *eques* and not *equus* written in that line."

Naevius and divided the poem into seven books; see Suet. *Gr.* ii. (*L. C. L.* ii, p. 399). Apparently he also edited Ennius.

315

12 Hoc tum nobis Iulianus et multa alia lucide simul et adfabiliter dixit. Sed eadem ipsa post etiam in pervulgatis commentariis scripta offendimus.

VI

Quod Aelius Melissus, in libro cui titulum fecit *De Loquendi Proprietate*, quem, cum ederet, cornum esse copiae dicebat, rem scripsit neque dictu neque auditu dignam, cum differre "matronam" et "matrem familias" existimavit differentia longe vanissima.

1 AELIUS MELISSUS in nostra memoria fuit Romae summi quidem loci inter grammaticos id[1] temporis; sed maiore in litteris erat iactantia et σοφιστείᾳ
2 quam opera. Is praeter alia quae scripsit compluria, librum composuit, ut tum videbatur cum
3 est editus, doctrinae inclutae. Ei libro titulus est ingentis cuiusdam inlecebrae ad legendum; scriptus quippe est *De Loquendi Proprietate*. Quis adeo existimet loqui se recte atque proprie posse, nisi illas Melissi proprietates perdidicerit?
4 Ex eo libro verba haec sunt: "'Matrona' est quae semel peperit, quae saepius, 'mater familias'; sicuti sus quae semel peperit, 'porcetra,' quae
5 saepius, 'scrofa.'" Utrum autem hoc de matrona ac de matrefamilias Melissus excogitaverit ipse et coniectaverit, an scriptum ab alio quo legerit,
6 hariolis profecto est opus. Nam de "porcetra"

---

[1] id, *Falster;* et, γ ; s ; (= sed), δ ; sui, *Damsté.*

This at the time Julianus explained to us, along with other problems, clearly and courteously. But afterwards I ran upon the very same remarks in some very well-known handbooks.

VI

That Aelius Melissus, in the book to which he gave the title *On Correctness of Speech*, and which on its publication he called a horn of plenty, wrote something that deserves neither to be said nor heard, when he expressed the opinion that *matrona* and *mater familias* differ in meaning, thus making a distinction that is wholly groundless.

WITHIN my memory Aelius Melissus held the highest rank among the grammarians of his day at Rome; but in literary criticism he showed greater boastfulness and sophistry than real merit. Besides many other works which he wrote, he made a book which at the time when it was issued seemed to be one of remarkable learning. The title of the book was designed to be especially attractive to readers, for it was called *Correct Language*. Who, then, would suppose that he could speak correctly or with propriety unless he had learned those rules of Melissus?

From that book I take these words: " *Matrona*, ' a matron,' is a woman who has given birth once; she who has done so more than once is called *mater familias*, ' mother of a family '; just so a sow which has had one litter is called *porcetra*; one which has had more, *scrofa*." But to decide whether Melissus thought out this distinction between *matrona* and *mater familias* and that it was his own conjecture, or whether he read what someone else had written, surely requires soothsayers. For with regard to

habet sane auctorem Pomponium in Atellania, quae
7 hoc eodem vocabulo inscripta est; sed "matronam"
non esse appellatam nisi quae semel peperit, neque
"matrem familias" nisi quae saepius, nullis veterum
8 scriptorum auctoritatibus confirmari potest. Enim-
vero illud impendio probabilius est quod idonei
vocum antiquarum enarratores tradiderunt, "matronam" dictam esse proprie quae in matrimonium
cum viro convenisset, quoad in eo matrimonio
maneret, etiamsi liberi nondum nati forent, dic-
tamque ita esse a matris nomine, non adepto iam,
sed cum spe et omine mox adipiscendi, unde ipsum
9 quoque "matrimonium" dicitur, "matrem" autem
"familias" appellatam esse eam solam quae in
mariti manu mancipioque aut in eius in cuius
maritus manu mancipioque esset, quoniam non in
matrimonium tantum, sed in familiam quoque mariti et in sui heredis locum venisset.

VII

Quem in modum Favorinus tractaverit intempestivum
   quendam[1] de verborum ambiguitatibus quaerentem;[2]
   atque ibi, quot significationes capiat "contio."

1   Domitio, homini docto celebrique in urbe Roma
grammatico, cui cognomentum "Insano" factum

----

[1] Favorinum tractaverit intempestivus quidam, *J. Gronov*;
Domitius Favorinum tr. intempestive quaedam, *Boot.*
[2] querentem, *Damsté.*

----

[1] p. 295, Ribbeck[3].

porcetra he has, it is true, the authority of Pomponius in the Atellan farce which bears that very title;[1] but that "matron" was applied only to a woman who had given birth once, and "mother of a family" only to one who had done so more than once, can be proved by the authority of no ancient writer. Indeed, that seems much more probable which competent interpreters of ancient terms have written, that "matron" was properly applied to one who had contracted a marriage with a man, so long as she remained in that state, even though children were not yet born to them; and that she was so called from the word *mater*, or "mother," a state which she had not yet attained, but which she had the hope and promise of attaining later. *Matrimonium* itself, or "marriage," has the same derivation; but that woman only is called "mother of the household"[2] who is in the power and possession of her husband, or in the power and possession of the one under whose authority her husband is; since she had come, not only into a state of wedlock, but also into the family of her husband and into the position of his heir.

VII

How Favorinus treated a man who made an unseasonable inquiry about words of ambiguous meaning; and in that connection the different meanings of the word *contio*.

DOMITIUS was a learned and famous grammarian in the city of Rome, who was given the surname

[2] *Mater familias* is the feminine equivalent of *pater familias*. The latter was "father of the household" in authority, although he was not the actual father of all its members. In *C.I.L.* vi. 1035, Julia, wife of Septimius Severus, is called *mater Augusti nostri et castrorum et senatus et patriae*.

2 est, quoniam erat natura intractabilior et morosior,
ei Domitio Favorinus noster cum forte apud fanum
Carmentis obviam venisset atque ego cum Favorino
essem, "Quaeso," inquit, "te, magister, dicas mihi
num erravi quod, cum vellem δημηγορίας Latine
dicere, 'contiones' dixi? Dubito quippe et requiro
an veterum eorum qui electius locuti sunt pro verbis
3 et oratione dixerit quis 'contionem.'" Tum Domitius voce atque vultu atrociore "Nulla," inquit,
"prorsus bonae salutis spes reliqua est, cum vos
quoque, philosophorum inlustrissimi, nihil iam aliud
quam verba auctoritatesque verborum cordi habetis.
Mittam autem librum tibi, in quo id reperias quod
quaeris. Ego enim grammaticus vitae iam atque
morum disciplinas quaero, vos philosophi mera estis,
ut M. Cato ait, 'mortualia'; glosaria namque con-
ligitis et lexidia, res taetras et inanes et frivolas,
tamquam mulierum voces praeficarum. Atque
utinam," inquit, "muti omnes homines essemus!
minus improbitas instrumenti haberet."

4 Cumque digressi essemus, "Non tempestive,"
inquit Favorinus, "hunc hominem accessimus.
Videtur enim mihi ἐπισήμως μαίνεσθαι. Scitote,"
inquit, "tamen intemperiem istam quae μελαγχολία
dicitur, non parvis nec abiectis ingeniis accidere,
ἀλλὰ εἶναι σχεδόν τι τὸ πάθος τοῦτο ἡρωϊκόν et veritates
plerumque fortiter dicere, sed respectum non habere
μήτε καιροῦ μήτε μέτρου. Vel ipsum hoc quale
existimatis quod nunc de philosophis dixit? Nonne,

---

[1] *Contio*, from *coventio* (= *conventio*) meant first an assembly,
then a speech to an assembly, and finally the place of meeting. It is used in the sense of a speech by Cicero, Caesar,
and other good writers.

[2] Frag. incert. 19, Jordan.

Insanus, or "The Madman," because he was by
nature rather difficult and churlish. When our
friend Favorinus, in my company, chanced to have
met this Domitius at the temple of Carmentis,
Favorinus said: "I pray you, master, tell me
whether I was in error in saying *contiones,* when
I wanted to turn δημηγορίαι into Latin; for I am
in doubt and should be glad to be informed whether
any of the men of old who spoke with special
elegance used *contio* of words and of a speech."[1]
Then Domitius, with excited voice and expression,
replied: "There is absolutely no hope left of
anything good, when even you distinguished
philosophers care for nothing save words and the
authority for words. But I will send you a book, in
which you will find what you ask. For I, a grammarian, am inquiring into the conduct of life and
manners, while you philosophers are nothing but
mortualia, or 'winding sheets,' as Marcus Cato says:[2]
for you collect glossaries and word-lists, filthy, foolish,
trifling things, like the dirges of female hired
mourners. And I could wish," said he, "that all we
mortals were dumb! for then dishonesty would lack
its chief instrument."

When we had left him, Favorinus said: "We
approached this man at an unseasonable time. For
he seems to me to be clearly mad. Know, however,"
said he, "that the disorder which is called μελαγχολία, or 'melancholia,' does not attack small or
contemptible minds, but it is in a way a kind of
heroic affliction and its victims often speak the truth
boldly, but without regard to time or moderation.
For example, what think you of this which he just
said of philosophers? If Antisthenes or Diogenes

si id Antisthenes aut Diogenes dixisset, dignum
memoria visum esset?"

5   Misit autem paulo post Favorino librum quem
promiserat—Verri, opinor, Flacci erat—, in quo
scripta ad hoc genus quaestionis pertinentia haec
fuerunt: "senatum" dici et pro loco et pro hominibus, "civitatem" et pro loco et oppido et pro
iure quoque omnium [1] et pro hominum multitudine,
"tribus" quoque et "decurias" dici et pro loco et
pro iure et pro hominibus, "contionem" autem tria
6 significare: locum suggestumque unde verba fierent,
7 sicut M. Tullius in oratione quae inscripta est
Contra Contionem Q. Metelli: "Escendi," inquit, "in
8 contionem; concursus est populi factus"; item
significare coetum populi adsistentis, sicuti idem
M. Tullius in *Oratore* ait: "Contiones saepe ex-
clamare vidi, cum apte verba cecidissent. Etenim [2]
expectant aures, ut verbis conligetur sententia";
item orationem ipsam quae ad populum diceretur.

Exempla [3] in eo libro scripta non erant.   Sed
nos postea Favorino desideranti harum omnium
significationum monumenta apud Ciceronem, sicut
supra scripsi, et apud elegantissimos veterum reperta
9 exhibuimus; id autem quod potissimum expetebat,
"contionem" esse dictam pro verbis et oratione,
docui titulo Tulliani libri, qui a M. Cicerone inscriptus est *Contra Contionem Q. Metelli,* quo nihil

---

[1] civium, *Otho;* Quiritium, *Skutsch;* omnium *deleted by*
Vassis.
[2] id enim, *Cic.*   [3] exempla illa *suggested by Hosius.*

---

[1] Festus, p. xvi, Müller.
[2] Frag. 4, p. 946, Orelli.   [3] § 168.

had said it, would it not have seemed worthy of remembrance?"

But a little later Domitius sent Favorinus the book which he had promised—I think it was one by Verrius Flaccus—in which the following was written with regard to questions of that kind:[1] that *senatus* (senate) was used both of a place and of persons; *civitas* (state) of a situation and a town, also of the rights of a community, and of a body of men; further that *tribus* (tribes) and *decuriae* (decuries) designated places, privileges and persons, and that *contio* had three meanings: the place and tribunal from which speaking was done, as Marcus Tullius in his speech, *In Reply to the Address of Quintus Metellus*, says:[2] "I mounted the tribunal (*contionem*); the people assembled." It also signifies an assembly of the people gathered together, since the same Marcus Tullius says in his *Orator*:[3] "I have often heard audiences (*contiones*) cry out, when words ended in a proper rhythm; for the ears expect the thought to be expressed in harmonious words." It likewise designated the speech itself which was made to the people.[4]

Examples of these uses were not given in that book. But afterwards I found and showed to Favorinus at his request instances of all these meanings in Cicero, as I remarked above, and in the most elegant of the early writers; but that which he especially desired, an example of *contio* used for words and of a speech, I pointed out in the title of a book by Cicero, which he had called *In Reply to the Address of Quintus Metellus*; for there *Contionem*

---

[4] See note 1, p. 320. Gellius has given the meanings in the wrong order.

profecto significatur aliud quam ipsa quae a Metello
dicta est oratio.

VIII

Ὁμοιοτέλευτα et ὁμοιόπτωτα atque alia id genus quae orna-
menta orationis putantur inepta esse et puerilia, Lucili
quoque versibus declarari.

1 Ὁμοιοτέλευτα et ἰσοκατάληκτα et πάρισα et ὁμοιόπτωτα ceteraque huiusmodi scitamenta, quae isti
apirocali qui se Isocratios videri volunt in conlo-
candis verbis immodice faciunt et rancide, quam
sint insubida et inertia et puerilia facetissime hercle
2 significat in quinto *Saturarum* Lucilius. Nam ubi
est cum amico conquestus, quod ad se aegrotum
non viseret, haec ibidem addit festiviter:

Quo me habeam pacto, tametsi non quaeris, docebo,
Quando in eo numero mansi[1] quo in maxima
non[2] est
Pars hominum . . .
Ut perisse velis quem visere nolueris, cum
Debueris. Hoc "nolueris" et "debueris" te
Si minus delectat (quod atechnon)[3] et Isocratium[4]
hoc
σκληρῶδες que simul totum ac si συμμειρακιῶδες,[5]
Non operam perdo, si tu hic.

[1] mansi, ω ; mansti, *Nannius, Hosius.*
[2] non, ω ; nunc, *Scaliger, Hosius.*
[3] atechnon or atexnon, ω ; ἄτεχνον, *Hosius.*
[4] Isocratium, *Scaliger* ; eissocratium, δ ; *the other MSS.*
have eisocratium.
[5] Lerodesque . . . miraciodes, *Marx.*

---

[1] vv. 181 ff.. Marx.
[2] The poet has been ill, but still lives; cf. *abiit ad plures,*
Petron. 42.

surely means nothing else than the speech itself
which was delivered by Metellus.

VIII

That ὁμοιοτέλευτα, ὁμοιόπτωτα, and other devices of the kind
which are considered ornaments of style, are silly and
puerile, is indicated, among other places, in some verses of
Lucilius.

Lucilius in the fifth book of his *Satires* shows, and
indeed most wittily, how silly, useless, and puerile
are ὁμοιοτέλευτα, or "words of the same ending,"
ἰσοκατάληκτα, or "words of the same sound," πάρισα,
or "words exactly balanced," ὁμοιόπτωτα, or "words
of the same case," and other niceties of that kind
which those foolish pedants who wish to appear to
be followers of Isocrates use in their compositions
without moderation or taste. For having complained
to a friend because he did not come to see him when
he was ill, he adds these merry words:[1]

> Although you do not ask me how I am,
> I'll tell you, since with those I still abide
> Who of all mortals are the lesser part [2] . . .
> You are the slacker friend [3] who'd wish him dead
> Whom you'd not visit though it was your debit.
> But if you chide this "visit" joined with "debit"
> ('Twas writ by chance), if you detest it all,
> This silly, puerile, Isocratic [4] stuff,
> I'll waste no time on you,[5] since such you are.[6]

[3] Marx suggests *Tu cessator malus, talis amicus* as the
sense of the lacuna.
[4] The *homoioteleuta* of Isocrates are mentioned, among
others, by Cicero, *Orator*, 38.
[5] That is, in deleting the jingle.
[6] Such a friend as he has described.

IX

Quid significet apud M. Catonem verbum "insecenda"
quodque "insecenda" potius legendum sit quam, quod
plerique existimat, "insequenda."

1 In libro vetere, in quo erat oratio M. Catonis
De Ptolemaeo contra Thermum, sic scriptum fuit:
"Sed si omnia dolo fecit, omnia avaritiae atque
pecuniae causa fecit, eiusmodi scelera nefaria, quae
neque fando neque legendo audivimus, supplicium
pro factis dare oportet." . . .

2 "Insecenda"[1] quid esset quaeri coeptum. Tum
ex his qui aderant alter litterator fuit, alter litteras
sciens, id est alter docens, doctus alter. Hi duo

3 inter sese dissentiebant. Et grammaticus quidem
contendebat, "insequenda" scribendum esse;[2]
"'insequenda' enim scribi," inquit, "debet,[3] non
'insecenda,' quoniam 'insequens' significat . . .
traditumque esse 'inseque' quasi 'perge dicere'
et 'insequere' itaque ab Ennio scriptum in his
versibus:

Inseque, Musa, manu Romanorum induperator
Quod quisque in bello gessit cum rege Philippo."

4 Alter autem ille eruditior, nihil mendum, sed
recte atque integre scriptum esse perseverabat et
Velio Longo, non homini indocto, fidem esse ha-

---

[1] insecenda *must have occurred in the lacuna.*
[2] insequenda . . . esse *added by Hertz.*
[3] debet *added by Carrio.*

---

[1] p. 42. 6, Jordan.

IX

The meaning of the word *insecenda* in Marcus Cato; and that *insecenda* ought to be read rather than *insequenda*, which many prefer.

IN an old book, containing the speech of Marcus Cato *On Ptolemy against Thermus*, were these words:[1] "But if he did everything craftily, everything for the sake of avarice and pelf, such abominable crimes as we have never heard of or read of, he ought to suffer punishment for his acts. . . ."

The question was raised what *insecenda* meant. Of those who were present at the time there was one who was a dabbler in literature and another who was versed in it; that is to say, one was teaching the subject, the other was learned in it.[2] These two disagreed with each other, the grammarian maintaining that *insequenda* ought to be written: "For," said he, "*insequenda* should be written, not *insecenda*, since *insequens* means . . . and *inseque* has come down to us in the sense of 'proceed to say,' and accordingly *insequor* was written by Ennius in the following verses:[3]

Proceed, O Muse, when Rome with Philip warred,
To tell the valorous deeds our leaders wrought."

But the other, more learned, man declared that there was no mistake, but that it was written correctly and properly, and that we ought to trust Velius Longus, a man not without learning, who

---

[2] On the distinction between *litterator* and *litteratus* see Suet. *Gram.* iv. (ii, p. 401 f. *L.C.L.*).

[3] *Ann.* 326 f., Vahlen[2], who reads *insece*.

bendam, qui in commentario quod fecisset *De Usu Antiquae Lectionis* scripserit non "inseque" apud Ennium legendum, sed "insece"; ideoque a veteribus, quas "narrationes" dicimus, "insectiones" esse appellatas; Varronem quoque versum hunc Plauti de *Menaechmis:*

Nihilo[1] minus esse videtur séctius quam sómnia,

sic enarrasse: "nihilo magis narranda esse quam si ea essent somnia." Haec illi inter se certabant.

5 Ego arbitror et a M. Catone "insecenda" et a Q. Ennio "insece" scriptum sine *u* littera. Offendi enim in bibliotheca Patrensi librum verae vetustatis Livii Andronici, qui inscriptus est Ὀδύσσεια, in quo erat versus primus cum hoc verbo sine *u* littera :

Virum mihi, Camena, insece versutum,

factus ex illo Homeri versu :

Ἄνδρα μοι ἔννεπε, Μοῦσα, πολύτροπον.

6 Illic igitur aetatis et fidei magnae libro credo. Nam, quod in versu Plautino est : "sectius quam somnia,"
7 nihil in alteras partes argumenti habet. Etiamsi veteres autem non "inseque," sed "insece" dixerunt, credo, quia erat lenius leviusque, tamen eius-
8 dem sententiae verbum videtur. Nam et "sequo" et "sequor" et item "secta" et "sectio" consuetudine loquendi differunt; sed qui penitus inspexerit, origo et ratio utriusque una est.

---

[1] haec nihilo, *Plaut.* minus esse mihi videntur setius, *edd. Plaut.*

[1] v. 1047.

wrote in the commentary which he composed *On the Use of Archaic Terms*, that *inseque* should not be read in Ennius, but *insece*; and that therefore the early writers called what we term *narrationes*, or "tales," *insectiones*; that Varro also explained this verse from the *Menaechmi* of Plautus:[1]

Nihilo minus esse videtur sectius quam somnia,

as follows: "they seem to me no more worth telling than if they were dreams." Such was their discussion.

I think that both Marcus Cato and Quintus Ennius wrote *insecenda* and *insece* without *u*. For in the library at Patrae[2] I found a manuscript of Livius Andronicus of undoubted antiquity, entitled Ὀδύσσεια, in which the first line contained this word without the letter *u*:[3]

Tell me (*insece*), O Muse, about the crafty man,

translated from this line of Homer:[4]

Ἄνδρα μοι ἔννεπε, Μοῦσα, πολύτροπον.

On that point then I trust a book of great age and authority. For the fact that the line of Plautus has *sectius quam somnia* lends no weight to the opposite opinion. However, even if the men of old did say *insece* and not *inseque*, I suppose because it was lighter and smoother, yet the two words seem to have the same meaning. For *sequo* and *sequor* and likewise *secta* and *sectio* differ in the manner of their use, but anyone who examines them closely will find that their derivation and meaning are the same.

---

[2] A city of Achaia, near the entrance to the Corinthian Gulf, modern Patras.
[3] Frag. 1, Bährens.   [4] *Odyss.* i. 1.

9   Doctores quoque et interpretes vocum Graecarum:

$$\text{"Ανδρα μοι “ ἔννεπε,” Μοῦσα}$$

et:

$$\text{“ ”Εσπετε ” νῦν μοι, Μοῦσαι,}$$

dictum putant, quod Latine "inseque" dicitur;
namque in altero ν geminum, in altero σ esse
10 tralatum dicunt. Sed etiam ipsum illud " ἔπη,"
quod significat verba aut versus, non aliunde esse
dictum tradunt quam " ἀπὸ τοῦ ἔπεσθαι καὶ τοῦ
11 εἰπεῖν." Eadem ergo ratione antiqui nostri narrationes sermonesque "insectiones" appellitaverunt.

X

Errare istos qui in exploranda febri venarum pulsus per-
temptari putant, non arteriarum.

1   In Herodis, C. V., villam, quae est in agro Attico,
loco qui appellatur Cephisiae, aquis lucidis et [1]
nemoribus frequentem, aestu anni medio conces-
2 seram. Ibi alvo mihi cita et accedente febri rapida
3 decubueram. Eo Calvisius Taurus philosophus et
alii quidam sectatores eius cum Athenis visendi mei
gratia venissent, medicus, qui tum in his locis re-
pertus adsidebat mihi, narrare Tauro coeperat quid
incommodi paterer et quibus modulis quibusque
4 intervallis accederet febris decederetque. Tum in
eo sermone, cum iam me sinceriore corpusculo
factum diceret, " Potes," inquit Tauro, " tu quoque

---

[1] lucidis et, *Damsté*; educis, *Q*; et lucis et, *σ*; lucis
deleted by Hertz; laetis *suggested by Hosius*.

The teachers also and interpreters of Greek words think that in

$$ἄνδρα μοι ἔννεπε, Μοῦσα,[1]$$

and

$$ἔσπετε νῦν μοι, Μοῦσαι[2],$$

ἔννεπε and ἔσπετε are expressed by the Latin word *inseque;* for they say that in one word the ν is doubled, in the other changed to σ. And they also say that the word ἔπη, which means "words" or "verses," can be derived only ἀπὸ τοῦ ἔπεσθαι καὶ τοῦ εἰπεῖν, that is from "follow" and "say." Therefore for the same reason our forefathers called narrations and discourses *insectiones.*

X

That those persons are in error who think that in testing for fever the pulse of the veins is felt, and not that of the arteries.

IN the midst of the summer's heat I had withdrawn to the country house of Herodes, a man of senatorial rank, at a place in the territory of Attica which is called Cephisia, abounding in clear waters and groves. There I was confined to my bed by an attack of diarrhoea, accompanied by a high fever. When the philosopher Calvisius Taurus, and some others who were disciples of his, had come there from Athens to visit me, the physician who had been found there and who was sitting by me at the time, began to tell Taurus what discomfort I suffered and with what variations and intervals the fever came and went. Then in the course of the conversation remarking that I was now getting better, he said to Taurus: "You too may satisfy yourself of this, ἐὰν

id ipsum comprehendere, ἐὰν ἅψῃ αὐτοῦ τῆς φλεβός,
quod nostris verbis profecto ita dicitur : ' si attigeris
venam illius.' "

5 Hanc loquendi imperitiam, quod venam pro
arteria dixisset, cum in eo docti homines qui cum
Tauro erant, tamquam in minime utili medico offen-
dissent atque id murmure et vultu ostenderent,
tum ibi Taurus, ut mos eius fuit, satis leniter :
" Certi," inquit, " sumus, vir bone, non ignorare
te quid ' vena' appelletur et quid ' arteria,' quod
venae quidem suapte vi inmobiles sint et sanguinis
tantum demittendi gratia explorentur, arteriae
autem motu atque pulsu suo habitum et modum
6 febrium demonstrent ; sed, ut video, pervulgate
magis quam inscite locutus es ; non enim te solum,
sed alios quoque itidem errantis audivi venam pro
7 arteria dicere. Fac igitur ut experiamur elegan-
tiorem esse te in medendo quam in dicendo, et
cum dis bene volentibus opera tua sistas hunc nobis
sanum atque validum quam citissime."

8 Hoc ego postea cum in medico reprehensum
esse meminissem, existimavi non medico soli, sed
omnibus quoque hominibus liberis liberaliterque
institutis, turpe esse ne ea quidem cognovisse ad
notitiam corporis nostri pertinentia, quae non altius
occultiusque remota sunt et quae natura nobis
tuendae valitudinis causa et in promptu esse et in
propatulo voluerit ; ac propterea, quantum habui
temporis subsicivi, medicinae quoque disciplinae
libros attigi, quos arbitrabar esse idoneos ad do-
cendum, et ex his cum alia pleraque ab isto
humanitatis usu non aliena, tum de venis quoque
et arteriis didicisse videor ad hunc ferme modum :

ἄψῃ αὐτοῦ τῆς φλεβός, which in our language certainly means : *si attigeris venam illius*; that is, 'if you will put your finger on his vein.'"

The learned men who accompanied Taurus were shocked by this careless language in calling an artery a vein, and looking on him as a physician of little value, showed their opinion by their murmurs and expression. Whereupon Taurus, very mildly, as was his way, said : "We feel sure, my good sir, that you are not unaware of the difference between veins and arteries; that the veins have no power of motion and are examined only for the purpose of drawing off blood, but that the arteries by their motion and pulsation show the condition and degree of fever. But, as I see, you spoke rather in common parlance than through ignorance; for I have heard others, as well as you, erroneously use the term 'vein' for 'artery.' Let us then find that you are more skilled in curing diseases than in the use of language, and with the favour of the gods restore this man to us by your art, sound and well, as soon as possible."

Afterwards when I recalled this criticism of the physician, I thought that it was shameful, not only for a physician, but for all cultivated and liberally educated men, not to know even such facts pertaining to the knowledge of our bodies as are not deep and recondite, but which nature, for the purpose of maintaining our health, has allowed to be evident and obvious. Therefore I devoted such spare time as I had to dipping into those books on the art of medicine which I thought were suited to instruct me, and from them I seem to have learned, not only many other things which have to do with human experience, but also concerning veins and arteries what I

9 " Vena " est conceptaculum sanguinis, quod ἀγγεῖον
medici vocant, mixti confusique cum spiritu naturali,
in quo plus sanguinis est, minus spiritus ; " arteria "
est conceptaculum spiritus naturalis mixti confusique cum sanguine, in quo plus spiritus est, minus
10 sanguinis ; σφυγμός autem est intentio motus et
remissio in corde et in arteria naturalis, non arbi-
11 traria. Medicis autem veteribus oratione Graeca
ita definitus est: " Σφυγμός ἐστιν διαστολή τε καὶ
συστολὴ ἀπροαίρετος ἀρτηρίας καὶ καρδίας."

XI

Verba ex carminibus Furi Antiatis inscite a Căesellio Vindice reprehensa ; versusque ipsi in quibus ea verba sunt
  subscripti.

1 Non hercle idem sentio cum Caesellio Vindice,
grammatico, ut mea opinio est, hautquaquam ine-
2 rudito. Verum hoc tamen petulanter insciteque,
quod Furium, veterem poetam, dedecorasse linguam
Latinam scripsit huiuscemodi vocum fictionibus quae
mihi quidem neque abhorrere a poetica facultate
visae sunt neque dictu profatuque ipso taetrae aut
insuaves esse, sicuti sunt quaedam alia ab inlustribus
poetis ficta dure et rancide.
3 Quae reprehendit autem Caesellius Furiana haec
sunt : quod terram in lutum versam " lutescere "
dixerit et tenebras in noctis modum factas " noctescere " et pristinas reciperare vires " virescere," et
quod ventus si[1] mare caerulum crispicans nitefacit
" purpurat " dixerit, et opulentum fieri " opulescere."

  [1] si *suggested by Hosius* ; caerulum cum, *Dziatzko.*
334

may express as follows: A "vein" is a receptacle, or ἀγγεῖον, as the physicians call it, for blood mingled and combined with vital breath, in which the blood predominates and the breath is less. An "artery" is a receptacle for the vital breath mingled and combined with blood, in which there is more breath and less blood. Σφυγμός (pulsation) is the natural and involuntary expansion and contraction in the heart and in the artery. But the ancient Greek physicians defined it thus: "An involuntary dilation or contraction of the pulse and of the heart."

XI

Words from the poems of Furius of Antium which were ignorantly criticised by Caesellius Vindex; a quotation of the very verses which include the words in question.

I CERTAINLY do not agree with Caesellius Vindex, the grammarian, though in my opinion he is by no means without learning. But yet this was a hasty and ignorant statement of his, that the ancient poet Furius of Antium had degraded the Latin language by forming words of a kind which to me did not seem inconsistent with a poet's license nor to be vulgar or unpleasant to speak and utter, as are some others which have been harshly and tastelessly fashioned by distinguished poets.

The expressions of Furius which Caesellius censures are these: that he uses *lutescere* of earth which has turned into mud, *noctescere* of darkness that has arisen like that of night, *virescere* of recovering former strength, describes the wind curling the blue sea and making it shine by *purpurat*, and uses *opulescere* for becoming rich.

4 Versus autem ipsos ex poematis Furianis, in quibus verba haec sunt, subdidi:

Sanguine diluitur tellus, cava terra lutescit.
Omnia noctescunt tenebris caliginis atrae.
Increscunt animi, virescit volnere virtus.
Sicut fulica levis[1] volitat super aequora classis,
Spiritus Eurorum viridis cum purpurat undas.
Quo magis in patriis possint opulescere campis.

XII

Morem istum veteribus nostris fuisse verba patiendi mutare
ac vetere in agendi modum.

1 Id quoque habitum est in oratione facienda elegantiae genus, ut pro verbis habentibus patiendi figuram agentia ponerent ac deinde haec vice inter 2 sese mutua verterent. Iuventius in comoedia:

pallium (inquit) flocci non facio[2] ut splendeat an maculet.[3]

Nonne hoc inpendio venustius gratiusque est 3 quam si diceret "maculetur"? Plautus etiam non dissimiliter:

Quid ést?—Hoc rugat pállium, amíctus non sum cómmode.

---

[1] sic fulica levius, *Beloe.*
[2] non facio, *added by Fleckeisen.*
[3] splendeat an maculet, *Seyffert*: splendean, δ Ο Π Χ.

1 have added the very lines from the poems of
Furius in which these words occur : [1]

> Blood floods the world, the deep earth turns to
>   mud (*lutescit*),
> All becomes night (*noctescunt*) with darkness of
>   black gloom.
> Their courage grows, valour 's renewed (*virescit*)
>   by wounds.
> The fleet, like sea-bird, lightly skims the deep,
> The East Wind's breath empurples (*purpurat*) the
>   green surge.
> That on their native plains they may grow rich
>   (*opulescere*).

XII

*That our forefathers had the custom of changing passive verbs
and turning them into active.*

This also used to be regarded as a kind of elegance
in composition, to use active verbs in place of those
which had a passive form and then in turn to
substitute the former for the latter.   Thus Juventius
in a comedy says : [2]

> I care not if my cloak resplendent be, or spot.[3]

Is not this far more graceful and pleasing than if
he said *maculetur*, "if it be spotted"?   Plautus
also says in a similar way : [4]

> What's wrong ?—This cloak doth wrinkle (*rugat*),
>   I'm ill clad.

[1] Frag. 1–6, Bährens.   [2] 5, Ribbeck[3].
[3] The line is corrupt, but with Seyffert's emendation fairly
clear.   [4] Frag. fab. inc. xlv, Götz.

4 Itidem Plautus "pulveret" dicit, quod non pulvere
impleat, set ipsum pulveris plenum sit:

> Exí tu, Dave, age, spárge; mundum hoc ésse
> vestibulúm volo.
> Venús ventura est nóstra, non hoc púlveret.

5 In *Asinaria* quoque "contemples" dicit pro "contempleris":

> Meúm caput contémples, si quidem é re consultás
> tua.

6 Cn. Gellius in *Annalibus:* "Postquam tempestas
7 sedavit, Atherbal taurum immolavit." M. Cato in
Originibus: "Eodem convenae conplures ex agro
8 accessitavere. Eo res eorum auxit." Varro libris
quos ad Marcellum *De Lingua Latina* fecit: "In
priore verbo graves prosodiae, quae fuerunt, manent,
reliquae mutant," "mutant"[1] inquit elegantissime
9 pro "mutantur." Potest etiam id quoque ab eodem
Varrone in septimo *Divinarum* similiter dictum
videri: "Inter duas filias regum quid mutet, inter
10 Antigonam et Tulliam, est animadvertere." Verba
autem patiendi pro agentibus in omnibus ferme-
modum veterum scriptis reperiuntur. Ex quibus
sunt pauca ista, quae nunc meminimus: "muneror
te" pro "munero" et "significor" pro "significo"
et "sacrificor" pro "sacrifico" et "adsentior" pro
"adsentio" et "faeneror" pro "faenero" et "pigneror" pro "pignero" et alia istiusmodi pleraque,
quae, proinde ut in legendo fuerint obvia, nota-
buntur.

---

[1] mutant *added by Carrio.*

---

[1] *Id.* xlvi.   [2] v. 539.   [3] Frag. 30, Peter [2].
[4] *Id.* 20.   [5] Frag. 85, G. and S.
[6] "Elegant" because it balances *manent.*

Also Plautus uses *pulveret*, not of making dusty, but of being dusty : [1]

> Go, sprinkle, slave ;   I'd have this entrance neat.
> My Venus comes, don't let the place show dust (*pulveret*).

In the *Asinaria* he uses *contemples* for *contempleris* : [2]

> Observe (*contemples*) my head, if you'd your interest heed.

Gnaeus Gellius in his *Annals* [3] writes : " After the storm quieted (*sedavit*) Adherbal sacrificed a bull " ; Marcus Cato in his *Origins :* [4] " Many strangers came to that same place from the country.   Therefore their wealth waxed (*auxit*)."   Varro in the books which he wrote *On Latin Diction*, dedicated to Marcellus, said : [5] " In the former word the accents that were grave remain so.   The others change," where *mutant*, " change," is a very elegant expression for *mutantur*, " are changed." [6]   The same expression too seems to be used by Varro in the seventh book of his *Divine Antiquities :* [7] " What a difference (*quid mutet*) there is between princesses may be seen in Antigone and Tullia."   But passive verbs instead of active are found in the writings of almost all the men of the olden time.   A few of these, which I recall now, are the following : *muneror te*, or " I reward you," for *munero ; significor*, or " I indicate," for *significo ; assentior*, or " I assent," for *assentio ; sacrificor*, or " I sacrifice," for *sacrifico ; faeneror*, or " I practise usury," for *faenero ; pigneror*, or " I take as a pledge," for *pignero*, and many others of the same kind, which will be noted as I meet them in reading.

[7] Frag. 1, p. cxlv, Merkel.

XIII

Quali talione Diogenes philosophus usus sit, pertemptatus a
dialectico quodam sophismatio inpudenti.

1 SATURNALIBUS Athenis alea quadam festiva et
2 honesta lusitabamus huiuscemodi : ubi convene-
ramus conplusculi eiusdem studii homines ad la-
vandi tempus, captiones quae " sophismata " appellantur mente agitabamus easque, quasi talos aut
tesserulas, in medium vice sua quisque iaciebamus.
3 Captionis solutae aut parum intellectae praemium
4 poenave erat nummus unus sestertius. Hoc aere
conlecto, quasi manuario, cenula curabatur omnibus
5 qui eum lusum luseramus. Erant autem captiones
ad hoc fere exemplum, tametsi Latina oratione
non satis scite ac paene etiam inlepide exponuntur :
" Quod nix est, hoc grando non est ; nix autem
alba est : grando igitur alba non est." Item aliud
non dissimile : " Quod homo est, non est hoc equus ;
homo autem animal est : equus igitur animal non
6 est." Dicere ergo debebat qui ad sophisma dilu-
endum ac refellendum ritu aleatorio vocatus erat,
in qua parte quoque in verbo captio foret, quid
dari concedique non oporteret ; nisi dixerat, nummo
singulo multabatur. Ea multa cenam iuvabat.
7 Libet autem dicere quam facete Diogenes sophisma id genus, quod supra dixi, a quodam
dialectico ex Platonis diatriba per con umeliam pro-
8 positum, remuneratus sit. Nam cum ita rogasset

XIII

The retort which the philosopher Diogenes made, when he
was challenged by a logician with an impudent sophistry.

At Athens during the Saturnalia we engaged in a
pleasant and improving diversion of this kind : when
a number of us who were interested in the same
study had met at the time of the bath, we discussed
the catch questions which are called "sophisms,"
and each one of us cast them before the company in
his turn, like knuckle-bones or dice. The prize for
solving a problem, or the penalty for failing to
understand it, was a single sestertius. From the
money thus collected, as if it had been won at dice,
a little dinner was provided for all of us who had
taken part in the game. Now the sophisms were
somewhat as follows, although they cannot be
expressed very elegantly in Latin, or even without
clumsiness : "What snow is, that hail is not ;
but snow is white, therefore hail is not white."
A somewhat similar one is this : "What man is, that
a horse is not ; man is an animal, therefore a horse
is not an animal." The one who was called upon by
the throw of the dice to solve and refute the
sophistry was expected to tell in what part of the
proposition and in what word the fallacy consisted,
and what ought not to be granted and conceded ;
if he did not succeed, he was fined one sestertius.
The fine contributed to the dinner.

I must tell you how wittily Diogenes paid back
a sophism of that kind which I have mentioned
above, proposed with insulting intent by a logician
of the Platonic school. For when the logician had

dialecticus: "Quod ego sum, id tu non es?" et
Diogenes adnuisset, atque ille addidisset: "Homo
autem ego sum," cum id quoque adsensus esset,
contra dialecticus ita conclusisset: "Homo igitur tu
non es," "Hoc quidem," inquit Diogenes, "falsum
est, et si verum fieri vis, a me incipe."

XIV

Quid sit numerus "hemiolios," quid "epitritos"; et quod
vocabula ista non facile nostri ausi sunt convertere in
linguam Latinam.

1 FIGURAE quaedam numerorum, quas Graeci certis
nominibus appellant, vocabula in lingua Latina non
2 habent. Sed qui de numeris Latine scripserunt
Graeca ipsa dixerunt, fingere autem nostra, quoniam
3 id absurde futurum erat, noluerunt. Quale enim
fieri nomen posset "hemiolio" numero aut "epitrito"?
4 Est autem "hemiolios" qui numerum aliquem totum
in sese habet dimidiumque eius, ut tres ad duo, quindecim ad decem, triginta ad viginti; "epitritos" est
5 qui habet totum aliquem numerum et eiusdem partem
tertiam, ut quattuor ad tres, duodecim ad novem,
6 quadraginta ad triginta. Haec autem notare me-
minisseque non esse abs re visum est, quoniam
vocabula ista numerorum nisi intelleguntur, rationes
quaedam subtilissimae in libris philosophorum
scriptae percipi non queunt.

asked: "You are not what I am, are you?" and Diogenes had admitted it, he added: "But I am a man." And when Diogenes had assented to that also and the logician had concluded: "Then you are not a man," Diogenes retorted: "That is a lie, but if you want it to be true, begin your proposition with me."

XIV

What the number is which is called *hemiolios* and what *epitritos*; and that our countrymen have not rashly ventured to translate those words into Latin.

CERTAIN numerical figures which the Greeks call by definite terms have no corresponding names in Latin. But those who have written in Latin about numbers have used the Greek expressions and have hesitated to make up Latin equivalents, since that would be absurd. For what name could one give to a number which is said to be *hemiolios* or *epitritos*? But *hemiolios* is a number which contains in itself some other whole number and its half, as three compared with two, fifteen with ten, thirty with twenty; *epitritos* is a number which contains another whole number and its third part, as four compared with three, twelve with nine, forty with thirty. It does not seem out of place to note and to remember these numerical terms; for unless they are understood, some of the most subtle calculations recorded in the writings of the philosophers cannot be comprehended.

XV

Quod M. Varro in herois versibus observaverit rem nimis
anxiae et curiosae observationis.

1 In longis versibus qui "hexametri" vocantur, item
in senariis, animadverterunt metrici primos duos
pedes, item extremos duos, habere singulos posse
integras partes orationis, medios haut umquam posse,
sed constare eos semper ex verbis aut divisis aut
2 mixtis atque confusis. M. etiam Varro in libris
Disciplinarum scripsit, observasse sese in versu
hexametro, quod omnimodo quintus semipes verbum
finiret et quod priores quinque semipedes aeque
magnam vim haberent in efficiendo versu atque alii
posteriores septem, idque ipsum ratione quadam
geometrica fieri disserit.

---

¹ See note on iv. 5. 6 (vol. i, p. 328).
² That is, the first two feet and the last two may consist
of undivided words, but the third and fourth are formed
either of words which are divided, or of parts of different

XV

That Marcus Varro in heroic verse noted a matter demanding very minute and careful observation.

IN the long lines called hexameters, and likewise in senarii,[1] students of metric have observed that the first two feet, and also the last two, may consist each of a single part of speech, but that those between may not, but are always formed of words which are either divided, or combined and run together.[2] Varro in his book *On the Arts* [3] wrote that he had observed in hexameter verse that the fifth half-foot always ends a word,[4] and that the first five half-feet are of equally great importance in making a verse with the following seven ; and he argues that this happens in accordance with a certain geometrical ratio.

words. But that this rule is not invariable was shown by Muretus, *Variae Lectiones*, xi. 6.

[3] Fr. 116, G. and S.

[4] That is, there is a caesura in the fifth foot, according to Varro.

BOOK XIX

LIBER NONUS DECIMUS

I

Responsio cuiusdam philosophi, interrogati quam ob causam
maris tempestate palluerit.[1]

1 NAVIGABAMUS a Cassiopa Brundisium mare Ionium
2 violentum et vastum et iactabundum. Nox deinde
quae diem primum secuta est, in ea fere tota ventus
3 a latere saeviens navem undis compleverat. Tum
postea, complorantibus nostris omnibus atque in
sentina satis agentibus, dies quidem tandem inluxit.
Sed nihil de periculo neque de saevitia venti
remissum, quin turbines etiam crebriores et caelum
atrum et fumigantes globi et figurae quaedam nubium
metuendae quos "typhonas" vocabant, inpendere
inminereque ac depressurae navem videbantur.
4 In eadem fuit philosophus in disciplina Stoica
celebratus, quem ego Athenis cognoveram non parva
virum auctoritate satisque attente discipulos iuvenes
5 continentem. Eum tunc in tantis periculis inque
illo tumultu caeli marisque requirebam oculis, scire
cupiens quonam statu animi et an interritus intre-
6 pidusque esset. Atque ibi hominem conspicimus

---

[1] *Lemmata of Book* xix *omitted in* ω ; *appear in various forms*
i

---

[1] A town in the north-eastern part of Corcyra, also called
Cassiope.
[2] Typhon, according to Hesiod, was a son of Typhoeus

BOOK XIX

I

The reply of a certain philosopher, when he was asked why he turned pale in a storm at sea.

WE were sailing from Cassiopa[1] to Brundisium over the Ionian sea, violent, vast and storm-tossed. During almost the whole of the night which followed our first day a fierce side-wind blew, which had filled our ship with water. Then afterwards, while we were all still lamenting, and working hard at the pumps, day at last dawned. But there was no less danger and no slackening of the violence of the wind; on the contrary, more frequent whirlwinds, a black sky, masses of fog, and a kind of fearful cloud-forms, which they called *typhones*,[2] or "typhoons," seemed to hang over and threaten us, ready to overwhelm the ship.

In our company was an eminent philosopher of the Stoic sect, whom I had known at Athens as a man of no slight importance, holding the young men who were his pupils under very good control. In the midst of the great dangers of that time and that tumult of sea and sky I looked for him, desiring to know in what state of mind he was and whether he was unterrified and courageous. And then I beheld

(see note on xvii. 10. 9) and father of the winds; but by later poets he was identified with Typhos or Typhoeus. His name was given to the violent storms called typhoons.

pavidum et expallidum,[1] ploratus quidem nullos,
sicuti ceteri omnes, nec ullas huiusmodi voces cientem,
sed coloris et voltus turbatione non multum a ceteris
7 differentem. At ubi caelum enituit et deferbuit
mare et ardor ille periculi deflagravit, accedit ad
Stoicum Graecus quispiam dives ex Asia, magno,
ut videbamus, cultu paratuque rerum et familiae,
atque ipse erat multis corporis animique deliciis
8 affluens. Is quasi inludens : "Quid . hoc," inquit,
"est, o philosophe, quod, cum in periculis essemus,
timuisti tu et palluisti? Ego neque timui neque
9 pallui." Et philosophus aliquantum cunctatus an
respondere ei conveniret, "Si quid ego," inquit. "in
tanta violentia tempestatum videor paulum pavefac-
10 tus, non tu istius rei ratione audienda dignus es.
Set tibi sane Aristippus,[2] ille Socratis discipulus, pro
me responderit, qui in simili[3] tempore a simillimo
tui homine interrogatus quare philosophus timeret,
cum ille contra nihil metueret, non eandem esse
causam sibi atque illi respondit, quoniam is quidem
esset non magnopere sollicitus pro anima nequissimi
nebulonis, ipsum autem pro Aristippi anima timere."
11 His tunc verbis Stoicus divitem illum Asiaticum
12 a sese molitus est. Sed postea, cum Brundisium ad-
ventaremus malaciaque esset venti ac maris, percontatus eum sum quaenam illa ratio esset pavoris sui,
quam dicere ei supersedisset a quo fuerat non satis
13 digne compellatus? Atque ille mihi placide et

---

[1] expallidum, *Hosius;* extrilidum, *ω;* exterritum, *J. F.
Gronov;* exalbidum, *Skutsch;* extimidum, *Georges.*

[2] Aristippius, *J. Gronov*; Aristippus, *ω*; *Hertz placed a
lacuna after* ille, *suggesting* egregius Socratis ille *to fill it.*

[3] qui cum in simili, *ω*; qui (in) consimili, suggested by
Hosius.

the man frightened and ghastly pale, not indeed
uttering any lamentations, as all the rest were doing,
nor any outcries of that kind, but in his loss of colour
and distracted expression not differing much from the
others. But when the sky cleared, the sea grew
calm, and the heat of danger cooled, then the Stoic
was approached by a rich Greek from Asia, a man of
elegant apparel, as we saw, and with an abundance
of baggage and many attendants, while he himself
showed signs of a luxurious person and disposition.
This man, in a bantering tone, said : " What does
this mean, Sir philosopher, that when we were in
danger you were afraid and turned pale, while I
neither feared nor changed colour ? " And the
philosopher, after hesitating for a moment about the
propriety of answering him, said : " If in such a
terrible storm I did show a little fear, you are not
worthy to be told the reason for it. But, if you
please, the famous Aristippus, the pupil of Socrates,
shall answer for me,[1] who on being asked on a
similar occasion by a man much like you why he
feared, though a philosopher, while his questioner on
the contrary had no fear, replied that they had not
the same motives, for his questioner need not be
very anxious about the life of a worthless coxcomb,
but he himself feared for the life of an Aristippus."

With these words then the Stoic rid himself of the
rich Asiatic. But later, when we were approaching
Brundisium and sea and sky were calm, I asked him
what the reason for his fear was, which he had
refused to reveal to the man who had improperly
addressed him. And he quietly and courteously
replied : " Since you are desirous of knowing, hear

[1] *Frag. Phil. Graec.* ii. 407.16.

comiter : " Quoniam," inquit, "audiendi cupidus es,
audi quid super isto brevi quidem, sed necessario et
naturali pavore maiores nostri, conditores sectae
Stoicae, senserint, vel potius," inquit, "lege ; nam et
facilius credideris, si legas, et memineris magis."

14 Atque ibi coram ex sarcinula sua librum protulit
Epicteti philosophi quintum Διαλέξεων, quas ab
Arriano digestas congruere scriptis Ζήνωνος et
Chrysippi non dubium est.

15   In eo libro Graeca scilicet oratione scriptam hanc
sententiam legimus : " Visa animi, quas φαντασίας
philosophi appellant, quibus mens hominis prima statim specie accidentis ad animum rei pellitur, non
voluntatis sunt neque arbitrariae, sed vi quadam sua

16 inferunt sese hominibus noscitanda ; probationes
autem, quas συγκαταθέσεις vocant, quibus eadem visa
noscuntur, voluntariae sunt fiuntque hominum

17 arbitratu.   Propterea cum sonus aliquis formidabilis
aut caelo aut ex ruina aut repentinus nescio cuius
periculi nuntius vel quid aliud est [1] eiusmodi factum,
sapientis quoque animum paulisper moveri et contrahi
et pallescere necessum est, non opinione alicuius mali
praecepta, sed quibusdam motibus rapidis et incon-
sultis, officium mentis atque rationis praevertentibus.

18 Mox tamen ille sapiens ibidem τὰς τοιαύτας φαντασίας,
id est visa istaec animi sui terrifica, non adprobat,
hoc est οὐ συγκατατίθεται οὐδὲ προσεπιδοξάζει,[2] sed
abicit respuitque nec ei metuendum esse in his

19 quicquam videtur.   Atque hoc inter insipientis

---

[1] est, J. Gronov ; ex, δ ; γ omits.
[2] Kronenberg transfers οὐδὲ προσεπιδοξάζει to § 20, after
συγκατατίθεται.

---

[1] Frag. 9, p. 408, Schenkl., L.C.L. II. 448 ff.

what our forefathers, the founders of the Stoic sect, thought about that brief but inevitable and natural fear, or rather," said he, " read it, for if you read it, you will be the more ready to believe it and you will remember it better." Thereupon before my eyes he drew from his little bag the fifth book of the *Discourses* of the philosopher Epictetus, which, as arranged by Arrian, undoubtedly agree with the writings of Zeno and Chrysippus.

In that book I read this statement, which of course was written in Greek [1]: " The mental visions, which the philosophers call φαντασίαι or ' phantasies,' by which the mind of man on the very first appearance of an object is impelled to the perception of the object, are neither voluntary nor controlled by the will, but through a certain power of their own they force their recognition upon men ; but the expressions of assent, which they call συγκαταθέσεις, by which these visions are recognized, are voluntary and subject to man's will. Therefore when some terrifying sound, either from heaven or from a falling building or as a sudden announcement of some danger, or anything else of that kind occurs, even the mind of a wise man must necessarily be disturbed, must shrink and feel alarm, not from a preconceived idea of any danger, but from certain swift and unexpected attacks which forestall the power of the mind and of reason. Presently, however, the wise man does not approve ' such phantasies,' that is to say, such terrifying mental visions (to quote the Greek, 'he does not consent to them nor confirm them '), but he rejects and scorns them, nor does he see in them anything that ought to excite fear. And they say that there is this difference between

sapientisque animum differre dicunt, quod insipiens,
qualia sibi esse primo animi sui pulsu visa sunt saeva
et aspera, talia esse vero putat et eadem incepta,
tamquam si iure metuenda sint, sua quoque adsensione
adprobat καὶ προσεπιδοξάζει: hoc enim verbo Stoici,
20 cum super ista re disserunt, utuntur. Sapiens autem,
cum breviter et strictim colore atque vultu motus est,
οὐ συγκατατίθεται, sed statum vigoremque sententiae
suae retinet quam de huiuscemodi visis semper habuit,
ut de minime metuendis, sed fronte falsa et
formidine inani territantibus."
21 Haec Epictetum philosophum ex decretis Stoicorum sensisse atque dixisse, in eo quo dixi libro
legimus adnotandaque esse idcirco existimavimus,
ut rebus forte id genus quibus dixi genus pavescere
sensim et quasi albescere, non insipientis esse
hominis neque ignavi putemus et in eo tamen brevi
motu naturali magis infirmitati cedamus quam quod
esse ea qualia visa sunt censeamus.

II

Ex quinque corporis sensibus duos esse cum beluis maxiem
communes ; quodque turpis et improba est voluptas quae
ex auditu, visu odoratuque procedit, quae vero ex gustu
tactuque est, rerum omnium foedissima est, cum hae duae
bestiarum etiam sint, reliquae hominum tantum.

1 QUINQUE sunt hominum sensus, quos Graeci
αἰσθήσεις appellant, per quos voluptas animo aut

the mind of a foolish man and that of a wise man,
that the foolish man thinks that such ' visions ' are
in fact as dreadful and terrifying as they appear at
the original impact of them on his mind, and by his
assent he approves of such ideas as if they were
rightly to be feared, and ' confirms ' them ; for
προσεπιδοξάζει is the word which the Stoics use in
their discourses on the subject.   But the wise man,
after being affected for a short time and slightly in
his colour and expression, ' does not assent,' but
retains the steadfastness and strength of the opinion
which he has always had about visions of this kind,
namely that they are in no wise to be feared but
excite terror by a false appearance and vain alarms."

That these were the opinions and utterances of
Epictetus the philosopher in accordance with the
beliefs of the Stoics I read in that book which I
have mentioned, and I thought that they ought to
be recorded for this reason, that when things of the
kind which I have named chance to occur, we may
not think that to fear for a time and, as it were, turn
white is the mark of a foolish and weak man, but in
that brief but natural impulse we yield rather to
human weakness than because we believe that those
things are what they seem.

II

That of the five senses of the body two in particular we share
with beasts ; and that pleasure which comes from hearing,
sight and smell is base and reprehensible, but that which
comes from taste and touch is the most shameful of all,
since the last two are felt also by beasts, the others only by
mankind.

MEN have five senses, which the Greeks call
αἰσθήσεις, by which mental or bodily pleasure is

corpori quaeri videtur: gustus, tactus, odoratus, visus, auditus. Ex his omnibus quae inmodice voluptas capitur, ea turpis atque inproba existimatur.

2 Sed enim quae nimia ex gustu atque tactu est, ea voluptas, sicuti sapientes viri censuerunt, omnium rerum foedissima est, eosque maxime qui duabus istis beluinis voluptatibus sese dediderunt, gravissimi vitii vocabulis Graeci appellant vel ἀκρατεῖς vel ἀκολάστους; nos eos vel "incontinentes" dicimus vel "intemperantes": ἀκολάστους enim, si interpretari coactius velis, nimis id verbum insolens erit.

3 Istae autem voluptates duae gustus atque tactus, id est libidines in cibos atque in Venerem prodigae, solae sunt hominibus communes cum beluis et idcirco in pecudum ferorumque animalium numero habetur, quisquis est his ferinis voluptatibus prae-

4 vinctus; ceterae ex tribus aliis sensibus proficiscentes hominum esse tantum propriae videntur.

5 Verba super hac re Aristotelis philosophi adscripsi, ut vel auctoritas clari atque incluti viri tam infamibus nos voluptatibus deterreret: Διὰ τί οἱ κατὰ τὴν τῆς ἁφῆς ἢ γεύσεως ἡδονὴν[1] γιγνομένην, ἂν ὑπερβάλλωσιν, ἀκρατεῖς λέγονται; οἵ τε γὰρ περὶ τὰ ἀφροδίσια ἀκόλαστοι τοιοῦτοι,[2] οἵ τε περὶ τὰς τῆς τροφῆς ἀπολαύσεις· τῶν δὲ κατὰ τὴν τροφήν, ἀπ᾽ ἐνίων μὲν ἐν τῇ γλώττῃ τὸ ἡδύ, ἀπ᾽ ἐνίων δὲ ἐν τῷ λάρυγγι, διὸ καὶ Φιλόξενος γεράνου λάρυγγα[3] εὔχετο ἔχειν· ἢ διὰ τὸ τὰς ἀπὸ τούτων γιγνομένας ἡδονὰς κοινὰς εἶναι ἡμῖν καὶ τοῖς ἄλλοις ζῴοις; ἅτε[4] οὐσῶν κοινῶν,[5] ἀτιμόταταί εἰσι καὶ μάλιστα ἢ μόναι ἐπονείδιστοι, ὡς τὸν[6] ὑπὸ τούτων ἡττώ-

---

[1] ἡδονήν, οὗ ἄν, *Arist.*   [2] τοιοῦτοι *omitted by MSS. of Arist.*
[3] φάρυγγα, *Arist.*   [4] ἅτε οὖν, *Arist.*
[5] οὖσαι κοιναί, *many MSS. of Arist.*   [6] ὥστε τόν, *Arist.*

[1] *Problemata*, xxviii. 7.

evidently sought : taste, touch, smell, sight, hearing.
From all of these the enjoyment of any immoderate
pleasure is regarded as base and reprehensible.   But
excessive pleasure from taste or touch in the opinion
of philosophers is the basest of all things, and those
in particular who have given themselves up to those
two animal pleasures the Greeks call by terms
of the gravest reproach either ἀκρατεῖς or ἀκόλαστοι ;
we call them either *incontinentes* (incontinent) or
intemperantes (intemperate) ; for if you should desire
to have a closer translation of ἀκόλαστοι, the
equivalent will be too unusual.   But those two
pleasures of taste and touch, namely, gluttony and
venery, are the only ones common to man with the
lower animals, and therefore whoever is enslaved to
these beastly pleasures is regarded as in the number
of brutes and beasts ; the remaining pleasures pro-
ceeding from the other three senses seem to be
peculiar to man alone.

   I have added the words of Aristotle the philosopher
on this subject,[1] in order that the authority of that
renowned and illustrious man might turn us from
such shameful pleasures : " Why are they called
incontinent who indulge to excess in the pleasures of
taste and touch ? For both those who are immoderate
in venery and those who are immoderate in the
enjoyment of food are such.   But of the latter, some
find this gratification in the tongue and others in
the throat, and it was for that reason that Philoxenos
prayed to have the throat of a crane.   Is it because
the pleasures derived from such sources are common
to us with the other animals ?   And being thus
common they are the most dishonourable and more
than the other pleasures, or alone, objects of

357

μενον ψέγομεν καὶ ἀκρατῆ καὶ ἀκόλαστον λέγομεν διὰ τὸ
ὑπὸ τῶν χειρίστων ἡδονῶν ἡττᾶσθαι. οὐσῶν δὲ τῶν
αἰσθήσεων πέντε, τὰ ἄλλα ζῷα ἀπὸ τῶν δύο μόνων τῶν
προειρημένων ἥδεται, κατὰ δὲ τὰς ἄλλας ἢ ὅλως οὐχ
6 ἥδεται ἢ κατὰ συμβεβηκὸς τοῦτο πάσχει. Quis igitur
habens aliquid humani pudoris voluptatibus istis
duabus coeundi atque comedendi, quae sunt homini
7 cum sue atque asino communes, gaudeat? Socrates
quidem dicebat multos homines propterea velle
vivere, ut ederent et biberent, se bibere atque esse,
8 ut viveret. Hippocrates autem, divina vir scientia,
de coitu venerio ita existimabat, partem esse quandam morbi taeterrimi, quem nostri "comitialem"
dixerunt; namque ipsius verba haec traduntur: τὴν
συνουσίαν εἶναι μικρὰν ἐπιληψίαν.

III

Quod turpius est frigide laudari quam acerbius vituperari.

1 TURPIUS esse dicebat Favorinus philosophus exigue
atque frigide laudari quam insectanter et graviter
2 vituperari: "Quoniam," inquit, "qui maledicit et
vituperat, quanto id acerbius facit, tam maximo ille
pro inimico et iniquo ducitur et plerumque propterea
fidem non capit. Sed qui infecunde atque ieiune
laudat destitui a causa videtur et amicus quidem
creditur eius quem laudare vult, sed nihil posse
reperire quod iure laudet."

---

[1] See note on xvi. 4. 4.

reproach, so that we censure a man who is addicted to them and call him incontinent and incorrigible because he is enslaved to the meanest of pleasures. Now, there being five senses, the other animals are gratified by the two which have been mentioned only, but from the others they either enjoy no pleasure at all, or they merely experience it incidentally." Who, then, having any human modesty, would take pleasure in those two delights of venery and gluttony, which are common to man with the hog and the ass? Socrates indeed used to say that many men wish to live in order to eat and drink, but that he ate and drank in order to live. Hippocrates, moreover, a man of divine wisdom, believed of venery that it was a part of the horrible disease which our countrymen call *comitialis,* or "the election disease";[1] for these are his very words as they have come down to us : " that coition is a brief epilepsy."

III

Sthat it is more disgraceful to be praised coldly than to be accused bitterly.

FAVORINUS the philosopher used to say that it was more shameful to be praised faintly and coldly than to be censured violently and severely : " For," said he, " the man who reviles and censures you is regarded as unjust and hostile towards you in proportion to the bitterness of his invective, and therefore he is usually not believed. But one who praises grudgingly and faintly seems to lack a theme ; he is regarded as the friend of a man whom he would like to praise but as unable to find anything in him which he can justly commend."

IV

Quamobrem venter repentino timore effluat; quare etiam
ignis urinam lacessat.

1 ARISTOTELIS libri sunt, qui *Problemata Physica* inscribuntur, lepidissimi et elegantiarum omnigenus
2 referti.   In his quaerit quam ob causam eveniat ut
quibus invasit repentinus rei magnae timor, plerum-
3 que alvo statim cita fiant.   Item quaerit cur accidat
ut eum qui propter ignem diutius stetit libido urinae
4 lacessat.   Ac de alvo quidem inter timendum prona
atque praecipiti causam esse dicit quod timor omnis
sit algificus, quem ille appellat ψυχροποιόν,[1] eaque
vi frigoris sanguinem caldoremque omnem de summa
corporis cute cogat penitus et depellat faciatque
simul ut qui timent, sanguine ex ore decedente,
5 pallescant.   " Is autem," inquit, " sanguis et caldor
in intuma coactus movet plerumque alvum et
6 incitat."   De urina celebri, ex igni proximo facta,
verba haec posuit: Τὸ δὲ πῦρ διαχαλᾷ τὸ πεπηγός,[2]
ὥσπερ ἥλιος τὴν χιόνα.

V

Ex Aristotelis libris sumptum quod nivis aqua potui pessima
sit ; et quod ex nive crystallus concreatur.

1   IN Tiburte rus concesseramus hominis amici divitis
aestate anni flagrantissima ego et quidam alii aequales

---

[1] ψυχροποιόν, *not in Arist.*   [2] πεπηγὸς ἐν τῷ σώματι, *Arist.*

---

[1] xxvii. 10; vii. 3.
[2] This is not what Aristotle said, but that water formed

IV

Why the bowels are loosened by sudden terror; also why
fire provokes urine.

THERE is a work of Aristotle, entitled *Physical
Questions*, which is most delightful, and filled with
choice knowledge of all kinds.   In this book he
inquires[1] why it happens that those who are seized
with sudden fear of some great catastrophe commonly
suffer at once from looseness of the bowels.   He
also inquires why it happens that one who has stood
for some time before a fire is overtaken with a desire
to make water.   And he says that the cause of the
loosening and discharge of the bowels because of
fear is due to the fact that all terror is cold-produc-
ing, or ψυχροποιός, as he calls it, and that by the
effect of that cold it drives and expels all the blood
and heat from the surface of the skin and at the
same time causes those who fear to grow pale,
because the blood leaves the face.   " Now this blood
and heat," he says, " being driven inwards, usually
moves the bowels and stimulates them."   For the
frequent urinating caused by nearness to a fire he
gave this reason : " The fire dissolves the solid
matter, as the sun does snow."

V

A statement from the works of Aristotle, that snow-water is
a very bad thing to drink ; and that ice is formed from
snow.[2]

IN the hottest season of the year with some companions and friends of mine who were students of

from ice was unwholesome, see §§ 5 and 9.   See crit. note 1,
p. 362.

et familiares mei, eloquentiae aut philosophiae secta-
2 tores. Erat nobiscum vir bonus ex peripatetica disciplina, bene doctus et Aristotelis unice studiosissimus.
3 Is nos aquam multam ex diluta nive bibentes coerce-
bat severiusque increpabat. Adhibebat nobis auctoritates nobilium medicorum et cumprimis Aristotelis
philosophi, rei omnis humanae peritissimi, qui aquam
nivalem frugibus sane et arboribus fecundam diceret,
sed hominibus potu nimio insalubrem esse tabemque
et morbos sensim atque in diem longam visceribus
inseminare.
4   Haec quidem ille ad nos prudenter et benivole et
adsidue dictitabat. Sed cum bibendae nivis pausa
fieret nulla, promit e bibliotheca Tiburti, quae tunc
in Herculis templo satis commode instructa libris
erat, Aristotelis librum eumque ad nos adfert et
"Huius saltem," inquit, "sapientissimi viri verbis
credite ac desinite valitudinem vestram profligare."
5   In eo libro scriptum fuit deterrimam esse potu
aquam e nive itemque solidius latiusque concretam
esse [1] eam, quam κρύσταλλον Graeci appellant; causa-
6 que ibi adscripta est huiuscemodi: "Quoniam, cum
aqua frigore aeris duratur et coit, necessum est fieri
evaporationem et quandam quasi auram tenuissimam
7 exprimi ex ea et emanare. Id autem," inquit, "in
ea levissimum est quod evaporatur; manet autem
quod est gravius et sordidius et insalubrius, atque

---

[1] esse *deleted by Vogel.*

[1] Frag. 214, Rose.

eloquence or of philosophy, I had withdrawn to the country-place of a rich friend at Tibur. There was with us a good man of the Peripatetic school, well trained and especially devoted to Aristotle. When we drank a good deal of water made of melted snow, he tried to restrain us and rather severely scolded us. He cited us the authority of famous physicians and in particular of the philosopher Aristotle, a man skilled in all human knowledge, who declared that snow-water was indeed helpful to grain and trees, but was a very unwholesome drink for human beings, and that it gradually produced wasting diseases in the body, which made their appearance only after a long time.

This counsel he gave us repeatedly in a spirit of prudence and goodwill. But when the drinking of snow-water went on without interruption, from the library of Tibur, which at that time was in the temple of Hercules and was well supplied with books, he drew out a volume of Aristotle and brought it to us, saying: "At least believe the words of this wisest of men and cease to ruin your health."

In that book it was written[1] that water from snow was very bad to drink, as was also that water which was more solidly and completely congealed, which the Greeks call κρύσταλλος, or "clear ice"; and the following reason was there given for this: "That when water is hardened by the cold air and congeals, it necessarily follows that evaporation takes place and that a kind of very thin vapour, so to speak, is forced from it and comes out of it. But its lightest part," he said, "is that which is evaporated; what remains is heavier and less clean and wholesome,

363

id, pulsu aeris verberatum, in modum coloremque
8 spumae candidae oritur. Sed aliquantum quod est
salubrius difflari atque evaporari ex nive indicium
illud est, quod[1] minor fit illo, quod ante fuerat
quam concresceret."

9 Verba ipsa Aristotelis ex eo libro pauca sumpsi
et adscripsi: Διὰ τί τὰ ἀπὸ χιόνος καὶ κρυστάλλων
ὕδατα φαῦλά ἐστιν; ὅτι παντὸς ὕδατος πηγνυμένου τὸ
λεπτότατον καὶ κουφότατον ἐξατμίζει. σημεῖον δέ, ὅτι
ἔλαττον γίνεται ἢ πρότερον, ὅταν τακῇ παγέν. ἀπελη-
λυθότος οὖν τοῦ ὑγιεινοτάτου, ἀνάγκη ἀεί, τὸ καταλει-
10 πόμενον χεῖρον εἶναι. Hoc ubi legimus, placuit honorem
doctissimo viro haberi Aristoteli. Atque ita postea
ego bellum et odium nivi indixi, alii indutias cum
ea varie factitabant.

VI

Quod pudor sanguinem ad extera diffundit, timor vero
contrahit.

1 In *Problematis* Aristotelis philosophi ita scriptum
est: Διὰ τί οἱ μὲν αἰσχυνόμενοι ἐρυθριῶσιν, οἱ δὲ φοβού-
μενοι ὠχριῶσιν, παραπλησίων τῶν παθῶν ὄντων; ὅτι
τῶν μὲν αἰσχυνομένων διαχεῖται τὸ αἷμα ἐκ τῆς καρδίας
εἰς ἅπαντα τὰ μέρη τοῦ σώματος, ὥστε ἐπιπολάζειν· τοῖς
δὲ φοβηθεῖσιν συντρέχει εἰς τὴν καρδίαν, ὥστε ἐκλείπειν
ἐκ τῶν ἄλλων μερῶν.
2 Hoc ego Athenis cum Tauro nostro legissem

---

[1] quod, *Hertz*; qui, ω.

---

[1] As Hannibal did against the Romans.

and this part, beaten upon by the throbbing of the air, takes on the form and colour of white foam. But that some more wholesome part is forced out and evaporated from the snow is shown by the fact that it becomes less than it was before it congealed."

I have taken a few of Aristotle's own words from that book, and I quote them: " Why is the water made from snow or ice unwholesome ? Because from all water that is frozen the lightest and thinnest part evaporates. And the proof of this is that when it melts after being frozen, its volume is less than before. But since the most wholesome part is gone, it necessarily follows that what is left is less wholesome." After I read this, we decided to pay honour to the learned Aristotle. And so I for my part immediately declared war upon snow and swore hatred against it,[1] while the others made truces with it on various terms.

VI

That shame drives the blood outward, while fear checks it.

In the *Problems* of the philosopher Aristotle is the following passage : [2] " Why do men who are ashamed turn red and those who fear grow pale; although these emotions are similar ? Because the blood of those who feel shame flows from the heart to all parts of the body, and therefore comes to the surface ; but the blood of those who fear rushes to the heart, and consequently leaves all the other parts of the body."

When I had read this at Athens with our friend

[2] Frag. 243, Rose.

percontatusque essem quid de ratione ista reddita
sentiret, "Dixit quidem," inquit, "probe et vere
quid accideret diffuso sanguine aut contracto, sed
3 cur ita fieret non dixit. Adhuc enim quaeri potest
quam ob causam pudor sanguinem diffundat, timor
contrahat, cum sit pudor species timoris atque ita
definiatur : 'timor iustae reprehensionis.' Ita enim
philosophi definiunt : αἰσχύνη ἐστὶν φόβος δικαίου
ψόγου."

VII

Quid sit "obesum"; nonnullaque alia prisca vocabula.

1 IN agro Vaticano Iulius Paulus poeta, vir bonus et
rerum litterarumque veterum inpense doctus, heredi-
olum tenue possidebat. Eo saepe nos ad sese vocabat
et olusculis pomisque satis comiter copioseque in-
2 vitabat. Atque ita molli quodam tempestatis autum-
nae die ego et Iulius Celsinus, cum ad eum cenas-
semus et apud mensam eius audissemus legi Laevi
Alcestin rediremusque in urbem sole iam fere occiduo,
figuras habitusque verborum nove aut insigniter
dictorum in Laeviano illo carmine ruminabamur et,
ut quaeque vox indidem digna animadverti sub-
venerat, qua nos quoque possemus uti, memoriae
mandabamus.
3 Erant autem verba quae tunc suppetebant, huiuscemodi :

Corpore (inquit) pectoreque undique obeso ac
Mente exsensa tardigenuclo
Senio obpressum.

---

[1] This is characteristic of the archaistic period in which
Gellius lived.

Taurus and had asked him what he thought about
that reason which had been assigned, he answered:
"He has told us properly and truly what happens
when the blood is diffused or concentrated, but he
has not told us why this takes place. For the
question may still be asked why it is that shame
diffuses the blood and fear contracts it, when shame
is a kind of fear and is defined by the philosophers
as 'the fear of just censure.' For they say: αἰσχύνη
ἐστὶν φόβος δικαίου ψόγου."

VII

The meaning of *obesus* and of some other early words.

THE poet Julius Paulus, a worthy man, very learned
in early history and letters, inherited a small estate
in the Vatican district. He often invited us there
to visit him and entertained us very pleasantly and
generously with vegetables and fruits. And so one
mild day in autumn, when Julius Celsinus and I had
dined with him, and after hearing the *Alcestis* of
Laevius read at his table were returning to the city
just before sunset, we were ruminating on the
rhetorical figures and the new or striking use of
words in that poem of Laevius', and as each word
occurred that was worthy of notice with reference
to its future use by ourselves,[1] we committed it to
memory.

Now the passages which then came to mind were
of this sort:[2]

Of chest and body wasted (*obeso*) everywhere,
Of mind devoid of sense and slow of pace,
With age o'ercome.

[2] Frag. 8, Bährens.

" Obesum " hic notavimus proprie magis, quam usitate
dictum pro exili atque gracilento ; vulgus enim ἀκύρως
vel κατὰ ἀντίφρασιν " obesum " pro " uberi " atque
4 " pingui " dicit. Item notavimus quod " oblitteram "
5 gentem pro " oblitterata " dixit ; item quod hostis
qui foedera frangerent, " foedifragos," non " foederi-
6 fragos " dixit ; item, quod rubentem auroram " pudo-
ricolorem " appellavit et Memnonem " nocticolorem " ;
7 item, quod " forte " dubitanter et ab eo quod est
" sileo," " silenta loca " dixit et " pulverulenta " et
" pestilenta " et quod " carendum tui est " pro " te "
8 quodque " magno impete " pro " impetu " ; item
9 quod " fortescere " posuit pro " fortem fieri " quodque " dolentiam " pro " dolore " et " avens " pro
10 " libens " ; item " curis intolerantibus " pro " in-
tolerandis," quodque " manciolis," inquit, " tenellis "
pro " manibus " et " quis tam siliceo ? " Item " fiere,"
inquit, " inpendio infit," id est " fieri inpense in-
11 cipit " ; quodque " accipitret " posuit pro " laceret."
12   His nos inter viam verborum Laevianorum ad-
13 notatiunculis oblectabamus. Cetera enim, quae videbantur nimium poetica, ex prosae orationis usu
alieniora praetermisimus ; veluti fuit quod de Nestore
14 ait " trisaeclisenex " et " dulciorelocus iste," quod de
tumidis magnisque fluctibus inquit " multigrumis " et

----

¹ Frag. 9, Bährens.
² A verb formed from *accipiter*, " hawk," meaning " to
tear," as a hawk does its prey.

Here we noticed that *obesus* is used, rather in its proper than in its common signification, to mean slender and lean; for the vulgar use *obesus*, ἀκύρως (improperly), or κατὰ ἀντίφρασιν (by contraries), for *uber* (bulky) and *pinguis* (fat). We also observed[1] that he spoke of an extinct race as *oblittera* instead of *oblitterata*, and that he characterized enemies who broke treaties as *foedifragi*, not *foederifragi*; that he called the blushing Aurora *pudoricolor*, or "shame-coloured" and Memnon, *nocticolor*, or "night-coloured"; also that he used *forte* for "hesitatingly," and said *silenta loca*, or "silent places," from the verb *sileo*; further, that he used *pulverulenta* for "dusty" and *pestilenta* for "pestilent," the genitive case instead of the ablative with *careo*; *magno impete*, or "mighty onset," instead of *impetu*; that he used *fortescere* for *fortem fieri*, or "become brave," *dolentia* for *dolor*, or "sorrow," *avens* for *libens*, or "desirous"; that he spoke of *curae intolerantes*, or "unendurable cares," instead of *intolerandae*, *manciolae tenellae*, or "tender hands," instead of *manus*, and *quis tam siliceo* for "who is of so flinty a heart?" He also says *fiere inpendio infit*, meaning *fieri inpense incipit*, or "the expense begins to be great," and he used *accipetret*[2] for *laceret*, or "rends."

We entertained ourselves on our way with these notes on Laevius' diction. But others we passed over as too poetic and unsuited to use in prose; for example, when he calls Nestor *trisaeclisenex*, or "an old man who had lived three generations" and *dulciorelocus iste*, or "that sweet-mouthed speaker," when he calls great swelling waves *multigruma*, or "great-hillocked," and says that rivers congealed by

15 flumina gelu concreta "tegimine" esse "onychino"
16 dixit, et quae multiplica ludens conposuit, quale illud
   est, quod vituperones suos "subductisupercilicarptores" appellavit.

VIII

Quaestio an "harena," "caelum," "triticum" pluralia
inveniantur; atque inibi de "quadrigis," "inimicitiis,"
nonnullis praeterea vocabulis, an singulari numero com-
periantur.

1   ADULESCENTULUS Romae, priusquam Athenas con-
cederem, quando erat a magistris auditionibusque
obeundis otium, ad Frontonem Cornelium visendi
gratia pergebam sermonibusque eius purissimis bona-
rumque doctrinarum plenis fruebar. Nec umquam
factum est, quotiens eum vidimus loquentemque
audivimus, quin rediremus fere cultiores doctioresque.
2 Veluti fuit illa quodam die sermocinatio illius, levi
quidem de re, sed a Latinae tamen linguae studio
3 non abhorrens. Nam, cum quispiam familiaris eius,
bene eruditus homo et tum poeta inlustris, liberatum
esse se aquae intercutis morbo diceret, quod " harenis
calentibus" esset usus, tum adludens Fronto : " Morbo
quidem," inquit, " cares, sed verbi vitio non cares.
Gaius enim Caesar, ille perpetuus dictator, Cn.
Pompei socer, a quo familia et appellatio Caesarum
deinceps propagata est, vir ingenii praecellentis, ser-
monis praeter alios suae aetatis castissimi, in libris,
quos ad M. Ciceronem *De Analogia* conscripsit,
'harenas' vitiose dici existimat, quod ' harena ' num-

---

the cold have an *onychinum tegimen,* or "an onyx covering"; also his many humorous multiple compounds, as when he calls his detractors[1] *subductisupercilicarptores,* or "carpers with raised eye-brows."

VIII

An inquiry whether *harena, caelum* and *triticum* are found in the plural; also whether *quadrigae, inimicitiae,* and some other words, occur in the singular.

When I was a young man at Rome, before I went to Athens, I often paid a visit to Cornelius Fronto, when I had leisure from my masters and my lectures, and enjoyed his refined conversations, which abounded besides in excellent information. Whenever I saw him and heard him speak, I almost never failed to come away improved and better informed. An example is the following little talk of his, held one day on a trivial subject, it is true, but yet not without importance for the study of the Latin language. For when an intimate friend of his, a learned man and an eminent poet of the day, said that he had been cured of dropsy by the use of hot sand (*calentes harenae*), thereupon Fronto in jesting fashion said: "You are indeed freed of your complaint, but not of the complaint of improper language. For Gaius Caesar, the famous life-dictator and father-in-law of Gnaeus Pompeius, from whom the family and the name of the Caesars are derived, a man of wonderful talent, surpassing all others of his time in the purity of his diction, in the work *On Analogy,* which he dedicated to Marcus Cicero, wrote[2] that *harenae* is an improper term, since *harena* ought never to be

quam multitudinis numero appellanda sit, sicuti neque
4 'caelum' neque 'triticum'; contra autem 'quadrigas,'
etiamsi currus unus, equorum quattuor iunctorum
agmen unum sit, plurativo semper numero dicendas
putat, sicut 'arma'[1] et 'moenia' et 'comitia' et
'inimicitias'—nisi quid contra ea dicis, poetarum
pulcherrime, quo et te purges et non esse id vitium
demonstres."

5 "De 'caelo,'" inquit ille, "et 'tritico' non infitias
eo, quin singulo semper numero dicenda sint, neque
de 'armis' et 'moenibus' et 'comitiis,' quin figura
6 multitudinis perpetua censeantur; videbimus autem
potius[2] de 'inimicitiis' et 'quadrigis.' Ac fortassean
de 'quadrigis' veterum auctoritati concessero, 'inimicitiam' tamen, sicuti 'inscientiam' et 'inpoten-
tiam' et 'iniuriam,' quae ratio est quamobrem C.
Caesar vel dictam esse a veteribus vel dicendam a
nobis non putat, quando Plautus, linguae Latinae
decus, 'deliciam' quoque ἑνικῶς dixerit pro 'deliciis'?

Méa (inquit) voluptas, méa delicia.[3]

'Inimicitiam' autem Q. Ennius in illo memoratissimo
libro dixit:

Eo ego (inquit) ingenio natus sum;
Amicitiam atque inimicitiam in frontem promptam
gero.

---

[1] circa arma, *Q*; castra, arma, *Vogel*.
[2] potius, *Hosius*; post. ω.
[3] meae deliciae, *codd. Plaut.*; mea delicia, *Lindsay*.

---

[1] *Harenae* is used by Virgil, Horace, and Ovid (*e.g.* Hor.
Odes, i. 28. 1; iii. 4. 31; Virg. *Aen.* i. 107); also by Seneca
the philosopher Tacitus, Suetonius (*Aug.* lxxx.) and other
post-Augustan prose-writers and poets.

used in the plural,[1] any more than *caelum* (heaven) and *triticum* (wheat). But on the other hand he thinks that *quadrigae*, even though it be a single chariot, that is, one team of four horses yoked together, ought always to be used in the plural number, like *arma* (arms), *moenia* (walls), *comitia* (election) and *inimicitiae* (hostility)—unless, my finest of poets, you have anything to say in reply, to excuse yourself and show that you have not made an error."

"With regard to *caelum*," said the poet, "and *triticum* I do not deny that they ought always to be used in the singular, nor with regard to *arma*, *moenia* and *comitia*, that their use ought to be confined to the plural; but we will inquire rather about *inimicitiae* and *quadrigae*. And perhaps in the case of *quadrigae* I shall yield to the authority of the early writers: but what reason is there why Caesar should think that *inimicitia* was not used by the ancients, as were *inscientia* (ignorance) and *impotentia* (impotence) and *iniuria* (injury), and ought not to be used by us, when Plautus, that glory of the Latin tongue, even used *delicia* in the singular number instead of *deliciae*? For he says:[2]

O my delight, my darling (*delicia*).

Furthermore Quintus Ennius, in that most famous book of his, said:[3]

Such is my habit; plain upon my brow
Friendship I bear and enmity (*inimicitiam*) to see.

[2] *Poen.* 365.   [3] *Achilles*, 12, p. 120, Vahlen[2].

Sed enim 'harenas' parum Latine dici, quis, oro te,
alius aut scripsit aut dixit? Ac propterea peto ut, si
Gai Caesaris liber prae manibus est, promi iubeas, ut
quam confidenter hoc indicat aestimari a te possit."

7 Tunc, prolato libro *De Analogia* primo, verba
8 haec ex eo pauca memoriae mandavi. Nam, cum
supra dixisset, neque "caelum" neque "triticum"
neque "harenam" multitudinis significationem pati,
"Num tu," inquit, "harum rerum natura accidere
arbitraris quod 'unam terram' ac[1] 'plures terras
et 'urbem' et 'urbes' et 'imperium' et 'imperia'
dicamus, neque 'quadrigas' in unam nominis figuram
redigere neque 'harenam' multitudinis appellatione
convertere possimus?"

9 His deinde verbis lectis ibi[2] Fronto ad illum poetam : "Videturne tibi," inquit, "C. Caesar de statu
verbi contra te satis aperte satisque constanter pro-
10 nuntiasse?" Tunc permotus auctoritate libri poeta :
"Si a Caesare," inquit, "ius provocandi foret, ego
nunc ab hoc Caesaris libro provocassem. Sed quoniam ipse rationem sententiae suae reddere super-
sedit, nos te nunc rogamus ut dicas quam esse
causam vitii putes et in 'quadriga' dicenda et in
11 'harenis.'"[3] Tum Fronto ita respondit : "'Quadrigae' semper, etsi multiiugae non sunt, multitudinis
tamen numero tenentur, quoniam quattuor simul
equi iuncti 'quadrigae,' quasi 'quadriiugae,' vocantur, neque debet prorsus appellatio equorum plurium
12 includi in singularis numeri unitatem." Eandemque
rationem 'harenae'[4] habendam, sed in specie dispari ;
nam cum 'harena' singulari in numero dicta multi-

---

[1] ac plures, *Hertz* ; adplures, δ ; *the other MSS. have* et.
[2] ibi, *Salmasius ;* sibi, ω. [3] harenis, *Carrio* ; harena, ω.
[4] harenae *supplied by Hertz* ; habet arena, *Madvig.*

But pray, who else has written or said that *harenae* is not good Latin? And therefore I beg of you, if Gaius Caesar's book is accessible, that you have it brought, in order that you may judge with how much confidence he makes this statement."

At the time, the first book *On Analogy* being brought, I committed to memory these few words from it; for, first asserting that neither *caelum, triticum,* nor *harena* admitted a plural meaning, Caesar said: "Do you not think that it happens from the nature of these things that we say 'one land' and 'several lands,' 'city' and 'cities,' 'command' and 'commands,' and that we cannot convert *quadrigae* into the form of a singular noun or *harena* into a plural?"

When these words had been read, Fronto said to the poet: "Does it not seem to you that Gaius Caesar has decided against you as to the status of this word with sufficient clearness and force?" Thereupon the poet, greatly impressed by the authority of the book, said: "If it were lawful to appeal from Caesar, I would now appeal from this book of his. But since he has neglected to give the reason for his opinion, I now ask you to tell on what ground you think it an error to say *quadriga* and *harenae.*" Then Fronto replied as follows: "*Quadrigae* is always confined to the plural number, even though there be only one horse, since four horses yoked together are called *quadrigae,* from *quadriiugae,* and certainly a term which designates many horses ought not to be included under the oneness expressed by the singular number. The same reasoning must be applied to *harena,* but in a different form; for since *harena,* though used in the singular number, never-

tudinem tamen et copiam significet minimarum, ex
quibus constat, partium, indocte et inscite ' harenae '
dici videntur, tamquam id vocabulum indigeat
numeri amplitudine, cum ei singulariter dicto[1]
ingenita sit naturalis sui multitudo.   Sed haec ego,"
inquit, " dixi, non ut huius sententiae legisque
fundus subscriptorque fierem, sed ut ne Caesaris,
viri docti, opinionem ἀπαραμύθητον destituerem.
13 Nam cum ' caelum ' semper ἑνικῶς dicatur, ' mare '
et ' terra ' non semper, et ' pulvis,' ' ventus ' et
' fumus ' non semper, cur ' indutias ' et ' caerimonias '
scriptores veteres nonnumquam singulari numero
appellaverunt, ' ferias ' et ' nundinas ' et ' inferias '
et ' exequias ' numquam ?   Cur ' mel ' et ' vinum '
atque id genus cetera numerum multitudinis capiunt,
14 ' lacte '[2] non capiat ?   Quaeri, inquam, ista omnia et
enucleari et extundi ab hominibus negotiosis in
civitate tam occupata non queunt.   Quin his quoque
ipsis quae iam dixi demoratos vos esse video, alicui,
15 opinor, negotio destinatos.   Ite ergo nunc et,
quando forte erit otium, quaerite an ' quadrigam '
et ' harenas ' dixerit e cohorte illa dumtaxat anti-
quiore vel oratorum aliquis vel poetarum, id est
classicus adsiduusque aliquis scriptor, non proletarius."
16   Haec quidem Fronto requirere nos iussit vocabula
non ea re, opinor, quod scripta esse in ullis veterum
libris existumaret, sed ut nobis studium lectitandi in
17 quaerendis rarioribus verbis exerceret.   Quod unum

---

[1] dicto, *Madvig* ; dici, ω.   [2] lac, γ.

[1] The classical form is, of course, *lac. Lacte* and *lact* occur
in early Latin, and the use of *lacte* here is an archaism, which
was not understood by some of the scribes ; see crit. note 2.

theless indicates the multiplicity and abundance of the minute parts of which it consists, *harenae* seems to be an ignorant and improper usage, as if the word needed a plural form, when its collective nature makes it natural for it to be used in the singular. But," said he, "I have said this, not in order to give my authority and signature to this opinion and rule, but that I might not leave the view of that learned man, Caesar, unsupported. For while *caelum*, or 'sky,' is always used in the singular, but *mare*, or 'sea,' and *terra*, or 'land,' not always, and *pulvis*, or 'dust,' *ventus*, or 'wind,' and *fumus*, or 'smoke,' not always, why did the early writers sometimes use *indutiae*, or 'truce,' and *caerimoniae*, or 'ceremony,' in the singular, but never *feriae*, or 'holiday,' *nundinae*, or 'market day,' *inferiae*, or 'offering to the dead,' and *exsequiae*, or 'obsequies'? Why may *mel*, or 'honey,' and *vinum*, or 'wine,' and other words of that kind, be used in the plural, but not *lacte* (milk)?[1] All these questions, I say, cannot be investigated, unravelled, and thrashed out by men of affairs in so busy a city; indeed, I see that you have been delayed even by these matters of which I have spoken, being intent, I suppose, on some business. So go now and inquire, when you chance to have leisure, whether any orator or poet, provided he be of that earlier band—that is to say, any classical or authoritative writer, not one of the common herd—has used *quadriga* or *harenae*."

Now Fronto asked us to look up these words, I think, not because he thought that they were to be found in any books of the early writers, but to rouse in us an interest in reading for the purpose of hunting down rare words. The one, then, which

ergo rarissimum videbatur, invenimus " quadrigam "
numero singulari dictam in libro *Saturarum* M.
18 Varronis, qui inscriptus est *Ecdemeticus*. " Harenas " autem πληθυντικῶς dictas minore studio quaeri-
mus, quia praeter C. Caesarem, quod equidem
meminerim, nemo id doctorum hominum dedit.

IX

Antonii Iuliani in convivio ad quosdam Graecos lepidissima
responsio.

1 ADULESCENS e terra Asia de equestri loco, laetae
indolis moribusque et fortuna bene ornatus et ad
rem musicam facili ingenio ac lubenti, cenam dabat
amicis ac magistris sub urbe in rusculo celebrandae
lucis annuae, quam principem sibi vitae habuerat.
2 Venerat tum nobiscum ad eandem cenam Antonius
Iulianus rhetor, docendis publice iuvenibus magister,
Hispano ore florentisque homo facundiae et rerum
3 litterarumque veterum peritus. Is, ubi eduliis finis
et poculis mox sermonibusque tempus fuit, deside-
ravit exhiberi, quos habere eum adulescentem sciebat, scitissimos utriusque sexus, qui canerent voce
4 et qui psallerent. Ac posteaquam introducti pueri
puellaeque sunt, iucundum in modum 'Ανακρεόντεια
pleraque et Sapphica et poetarum quoque recentium
ἐλεγεῖα quaedam erotica dulcia et venusta cecinerunt.
5 Oblectati autem sumus praeter multa alia versiculis
lepidissimis Anacreontis senis, quos equidem scripsi,
ut interea labor hic vigiliarum et inquies suavitate
paulisper vocum atque modulorum adquiesceret :

---

[1] The plural is used by Ovid, Virgil, and Horace; and by
later poets and prose-writers; *e.g.* Suetonius, *Aug.* lxxx.
(i., p. 246, *L.C.L.*).   [2] Cf. facundia rabida iurgiosaque, § 7.
[3] *Poetae Lyrici Graeci*, iii., p. 298, Bergk[4].

seemed the rarest, *quadriga,* I found used in the singular number in that book of Marcus Varro's *Satires* which is entitled *Ecdemeticus.* But I sought with less interest for an example of the plural *harenae,* because, except Gaius Caesar, no one among learned men has used that form, so far as I can recall.[1]

IX

The very neat reply of Antonius Julianus to certain Greeks at a banquet.

A YOUNG man of equestrian rank from the land of Asia, gifted by nature, well off in manners and fortune, with a taste and talent for music, was celebrating the anniversary of the day on which he began life by giving a dinner to his friends and teachers in a little country place near the city. There had come with us then to that dinner the rhetorician Antonius Julianus, a public teacher of young men, who spoke in the Spanish manner,[2] but was very eloquent, besides being well acquainted with our early literature. When there was an end of eating and drinking, and the time came for conversation, Julianus asked that the singers and lyre-players be produced, the most skilful of both sexes, whom he knew that the young man had at hand. And when the boys and girls were brought in, they sang in a most charming way several odes of Anacreon and Sappho, as well as some erotic elegies of more recent poets that were sweet and graceful. But we were especially pleased with some delightful verses of Anacreon, written in his old age,[3] which I noted down, in order that sometimes the toil and worry of this task of mine might find relief in the sweetness of poetical compositions:

6

Τὸν ἄργυρον τορεύσας,
Ἥφαιστέ, μοι ποίησον
Πανοπλίας μὲν οὐχί,
Τί γὰρ μάχαισι κἀμοί;
Ποτήριον δὲ κοῖλον
Ὅσον δύνῃ βάθυνον,
Καὶ μὴ ¹ ποίει κατ' αὐτὸ
Μήτ' ἄστρα μήτ' ἀμάξας·
Τί Πλειάδων μέλει μοι,
Τί δ' ἀστέρος Βοώτεω;
Ποίησον ἀμπέλους μοι
Καὶ βότρυας κατ' αὐτῶν
Καὶ χρυσέους πατοῦντας
Ὁμοῦ καλῷ Λυαίῳ
Ἔρωτα καὶ Βάθυλλον.

7 Tum Graeci plusculi qui in eo convivio erant,
homines amoeni et nostras quoque litteras haut incuriose docti, Iulianum rhetorem lacessere insectari-
que adorti sunt tamquam prorsus barbarum et
agrestem, qui ortus terra Hispania foret clamatorque
tantum et facundia rabida iurgiosaque esset eiusque
linguae exercitationes doceret quae nullas voluptates nullamque mulcedinem Veneris atque Musae
haberet; saepeque eum percontabantur quid de
Anacreonte ceterisque id genus poetis sentiret et
ecquis nostrorum poetarum tam fluentes carminum
delicias fecisset. "Nisi Catullus," inquiunt, "forte
pauca et Calvus itidem pauca. Nam Laevius inpli-
cata et Hortensius invenusta et Cinna inlepida et
Memmius dura ac deinceps omnes rudia fecerunt
atque absona."

8 Tum ille pro lingua patria, tamquam pro aris et
focis, animo inritato indignabundus: " Cedere equi-

Shaping the silver, Hephaestus,
Make me no panoply, pray;
What do I care for war's combats?
Make me a drinking cup rather,
Deep as you ever can make it;
Carve on it no stars and no wains;
What care I, pray, for the Pleiads,
What for the star of Bootes?
Make vines, and clusters upon them,
Treading them Love and Bathyllus,
Made of pure gold, with Lyaeus.

Then several Greeks who were present at that dinner, men of refinement and not without considerable acquaintance also with our literature, began to attack and assail Julianus the rhetorician as altogether barbarous and rustic, since he was sprung from the land of Spain, was a mere ranter of violent and noisy speech, and taught exercises in a tongue which had no charm and no sweetness of Venus and the Muse; and they asked him more than once what he thought of Anacreon and the other poets of that kind, and whether any of our bards had written such smooth-flowing and delightful poems; "except," said they, "perhaps a few of Catullus and also possibly a few of Calvus; for the compositions of Laevius were involved, those of Hortensius without elegance, of Cinna harsh, of Memmius rude, and in short those of all the poets without polish or melody."

Then Julianus, filled with anger and indignation, spoke as follows in behalf of his mother tongue, as if for his altars and his fires: "I must indeed grant you

<hr>

[1] μοι, *Bergk from Anth. Pal.* xi. 48.

dem," inquit, "vobis debui, ut in tali asotia atque nequitia Alcinum [1] vinceretis et sicut in voluptatibus cultus atque victus, ita in cantilenarum quoque
9 mollitiis [2] anteiretis. Sed ne nos, id est nomen Latinum, tamquam profecto vastos quosdam et insubidos, ἀναφροδισίας condemnetis, permittite mihi, quaeso, operire pallio caput, quod in quadam parum pudica oratione Socraten fecisse aiunt, et audite ac discite nostros quoque antiquiores ante eos quos nominastis poetas amasios ac venerios fuisse."

10 Tum resupinus, capite convelato, voce admodum quam suavi, versus cecinit Valeri Aeditui, veteris poetae, item Porcii Licini et Q. Catuli, quibus mundius, venustius, limatius, tersius,[3] Graecum Latinumve nihil quicquam reperiri puto.

11 Aeditui versus :

Dicere cum conor curam tibi, Pamphila, cordis,
    Quid mi abs te quaeram ? verba labris abeunt,
Per pectus manat subito subido [4] mihi sudor :
    Sic tacitus, subidus, dum pudeo, pereo.

12 Atque item alios versus eiusdem addidit, non hercle minus dulces quam priores :

[1] Alcinum, *Hertz* (*cf. Hor. Ep.* i. 2. 28 *ff.*) ; arcinnum, ω ; Apicium *suggested by Hosius* (*cf. Sen. Ep.* cxx. 19).
[2] mollitiis, *Hertz ;* multis, ω.
[3] tersius, *Salmasius ;* persius, pessius, pressius, *MSS.*
[4] subido *added by Usener ;* stupido, *C. F. W. Müller.*

---

[1] Probably (see crit. note) another form of Alcinous, King of the Phaeacians. He is not represented by Homer as "licentious and base," but that opinion arose at a later time. Cf. Horace, *Epist.* i. 2. 28 ff.
[2] Frag. 1, Bährens.

that in such licentiousness and baseness you would
outdo Alcinus[1] and that as you outstrip us in the
pleasures of adornment and of food, so you do also in
the wantonness of your ditties.   But lest you should
condemn us, that is, the Latin race, as lacking in
Aphrodite's charm, just as if we were barbarous
and ignorant, allow me, I pray, to cover my head
with my cloak (as they say Socrates did when
making somewhat indelicate remarks), and hear
and learn that our forefathers also were lovers and
devoted to Venus before those poets whom you
have named."

Then lying upon his back with veiled head, he
chanted in exceedingly sweet tones some verses of
Valerius Aedituus, an early poet, and also of Porcius
Licinus and Quintus Catulus; and I think that
nothing can be found neater, more graceful, more
polished and more terse than those verses, either in
Greek or in Latin:

The verses of Aedituus are as follows:[2]

> When, Pamphila, I try to tell my love,
> What shall I ask of you?   Words fail my lips,
> A sudden sweat o'erflows my ardent [3] breast;
> Thus fond and silent, I refrain and die.

And he also added other verses of the same poet,
no less sweet than the former ones:[4]

---

[3] *Subidus* occurs only here, and its meaning is not certain
It seems to be connected with the verb *subo*, "burn with
love," but some regard it as the opposite of *insubidus*,
"foolish, stupid," in which case it might be translated
"conscious." The alliteration and assonance in this epigram
are noteworthy.

[4] Frag. 2, Bährens.

Qui faculam praefers, Phileros, quae nil opus
    nobis?
Ibimus sic, lucet pectore flamma satis.
Istam nam potis est vis saeva extinguere venti
    Aut imber caelo candidus[1] praecipitans,
At contra hunc ignem Veneris, nisi si Venus ipsa,
    Nullast quae possit vis alia opprimere.

13 Item dixit versus Porcii Licini hosce:

Custodes ovium tenerae[2] propaginis, agnum,
    Quaeritis ignem? ite huc; quaeritis? ignis
        homost.
Si digito attigero, incendam silvam simul omnem;
    Omne pecus flammast, omnia quae video.

14 Quinti Catuli versus illi fuerunt:

Aufugit mi animus; credo, ut solet, ad Theo-
        timum
Devenit. Sic est: perfugium illud habet.
Qui, si non interdixem, ne illunc fugitivum
    Mitteret ad se intro, sed magis eiceret?
Ibimus quaesitum. Verum, ne ipsi teneamur,
    Formido. Quid ago? Da Venus consilium.

X

Verba haec, " praeter propter," in usu vulgi protrita,[3] etiam
Ennii fuisse.

1 MEMINI me quondam et Celsinum Iulium Numidam
ad Frontonem Cornelium, pedes tunc graviter
aegrum, ire et visere. Atque ubi[4] introducti sumus,
offendimus eum cubantem in scimpodio Graeciensi,

---

[1] concitus, *Bährens.*
[2] teneraeque, *Victorius*; vernae, *Hertz and Unger*; ven-
dere, *ω.*   [3] prodita, *MSS.*

O Phileros, why a torch, that we need not?
Just as we are we'll go, our hearts aflame.
That flame no wild wind's blast can ever quench,
Or rain that falls torrential from the skies;
Venus herself alone can quell her fire,
No other force there is that has such power.

He also recited the following verses of Porcius
Licinus: [1]

O shepherds of the lambs, the ewes' young
  brood,
Seek ye for fire? Come hither; man is fire.
Touch I the wood with finger-tip, it burns;
Your flock's a flame, all I behold is fire.

The verses of Quintus Catulus were these: [2]

My soul has left me; it has fled, methinks,
To Theotimus; he its refuge is.
But what if I should beg that he refuse
The truant to admit, but cast it out?
I'll go to him; but what if I be caught?
What shall I do? Queen Venus, lend me aid.

X

That the words *praeter propter*, which are in common use,
were found also in Ennius.

I REMEMBER that I once went with Julius Celsinus
the Numidian to visit Cornelius Fronto, who was then
seriously ill with the gout. When we arrived and
were admitted, we found him lying on a Greek

---

[1] Frag. 5, Bährens.   [2] Frag. 1, Bährens.

---

[4] ubi, *Salmasius;* ibi, δ; ibi qui, γ; ibi ubi, *Hertz.*

circumundique sedentibus multis doctrina aut genere
2 aut fortuna nobilibus viris. Adsistebant fabri aedium
complures, balneis novis moliendis adhibiti, ostende-
3 bantque depictas in membranulis varias species balnearum. Ex quibus cum elegisset unam formam
speciemque operis,[1] interrogavit quantus esset
pecuniae sumptus[2] ad id totum opus absolvendum.
4 Cumque architectus dixisset necessaria videri esse
sestertia ferme trecenta, unus ex amicis Frontonis :
" Et praeterpropter," inquit, "alia quinquaginta."
5   Tum Fronto, dilatis sermonibus quos habere de
balnearum sumptu institerat, aspiciens ad eum
amicum qui dixerat quinquaginta esse alia praeterpropter necessaria,[3] eum interrogavit quid signifi-
6 caret verbum " praeterpropter." Atque ille amicus :
" Non meum," inquit, " hoc verbum est, sed mul-
7 torum hominum quos loquentis id audias ; quid autem
id verbum significet, non ex me, sed ex grammatico
quaerundum est," ac simul digito demonstrat grammaticum, haud incelebri nomine Romae docentem
unaque ibi[4] sedentem. Tum grammaticus usitati
8 pervulgatique verbi obscuritate motus : " Quaeri-
mus," inquit, " quod honore quaestionis minime
9 dignum est. Nam nescio quid hoc praenimis ple-
beium est et in opificum sermonibus quam in
hominum doctorum[5] notius."
10   At enim Fronto, iam voce atque vultu intentiore :
" Itane," inquit, " magister, dehonestum tibi decul-

---

[1] operis, *Lipsius ;* veris (veneris, X), *MSS. ;* verisimilem,
Damsté.
[2] sumptus, Q ; espectus, Z ; conspectus, γ ; conputus
suggested by Hosius.
[3] necessaria . . . praeterpropter *supplied by Skutsch.*
[4] unaque ibi *supplied by Hosius.*

couch, and sitting around him a large number of men famous for learning, birth or fortune. By his side stood several builders, who had been summoned to construct some new baths and were exhibiting different plans for baths, drawn on little pieces of parchment. When he had selected one plan and specimen of their work, he inquired what the expense would be of completing that entire project. And when the architect had said that it would probably require about three hundred thousand sesterces, one of Fronto's friends said, "And another fifty thousand, more or less (*praeterpropter*)."

Then Fronto, interrupting the conversation which he had begun to hold about the expense of the baths, and looking at the friend who had said that another fifty thousand would be needed *praeterpropter*, asked him what that word meant. And the friend replied: "That word is not my own, for you may hear many men using it; but what the word means you must ask from a grammarian, not from me"; and at the same time he pointed out a grammarian of no little fame as a teacher at Rome, who was sitting there with them. Then the grammarian, surprised by the uncertainty about a familiar and much used word, said: "We inquire about something which does not at all deserve the honour of investigation, for this is some utterly plebeian expression or other, better known in the talk of mechanics than in that of cultivated men."

But Fronto, raising his voice and with a more earnest expression, said: "Sir, does this word seem to you so degraded and utterly faulty, when Marcus

---

[5] in hominum doctorum *supplied by Carrio*.

patumque hoc verbum videtur, quo et M. Cato et
M. Varro et pleraque aetas superior ut necessario
11 et Latino usi sunt?" Atque ibi Iulius Celsinus
admonuit, in tragoedia quoque Enni quae *Iphigenia*
inscripta est, id ipsum de quo quaerebatur scriptum
esse et a grammaticis contaminari magis solitum
12 quam enarrari. Quocirca statim proferri *Iphigeniam*
Q. Enni iubet. In eius tragoediae choro inscriptos
esse hos versus legimus :

> Ótio qui néscit uti
> Plús negoti habét quam cum est negótium in
>   negótio.
> Nám cui quod agat ínstitutumst, níl nisi[1] ne-
>   gótium,
> Íd agit, id[2] studét, ibi mentem atque ánimum
>   delectát suum,
> Ótioso in ótio animus néscit quid velit.[3]
> Hóc idem est; em néque domi nunc nós nec
>   militiaé sumus,
> Ímus huc, hinc ílluc, cum illuc véntum est, ire
>   illínc lubet,
> Íncerte errat ánimus, praeterprópter vitam vívitur.

13   Hoc ibi lectum est, tum deinde Fronto ad grammaticum iam labentem: " Audistine," inquit, " magister optime, Ennium tuum dixisse 'praeterpropter'
et cum sententia quidem tali, quali severissimae
philosophorum esse obiurgationes solent? Petimus
igitur dicas, quoniam de Enniano iam verbo quaeritur, qu sit remotus[4] huiusce versus sensus :

---

[1] nil nisi, *Hertz ;* in illis, δ ; in illo, γ.
[2] id *added by Ribbeck.*
[3] quid agat, quid velit, *Dziatzko.*
[4] remotus, *Hosius ;* motus, ω ; ignotus, *Hertz.*

Cato[1] and Marcus Varro,[2] and the early writers in
general, have used it as necessary and as good
Latin?" And thereupon Julius Celsinus reminded
him that also in the tragedy of Ennius entitled
Iphigenia the very word about which we were inquiring was found, and that it was more frequently
corrupted by the grammarians than explained.
Consequently, he at once asked that the *Iphigenia* of
Quintus Ennius be brought and in a chorus of that
tragedy we read these lines:[3]

That man in truth who knows not leisure's use
More trouble has than one by tasks pursued;
For he who has a task must be performed,
Devotes himself to that with heart and soul;
The idle mind knows not what 'tis it wants.
With us it is the same; for not at home
Are we nor in the field; from place to place
We haste; and once arrived, we would be gone.
Aimless we drift, we live but more or less
    (*praeterpropter*).[4]

When this had been read there, then Fronto said
to the grammarian, who was already wavering:
"Have you heard, most worthy master, that your
Ennius used *praeterpropter*, and that too in an expression of opinion resembling the austerest diatribes
of the philosophers? We beg you then to tell us,
since we are now investigating a word used by
Ennius, what the hidden meaning is in this line:

[1] Frag. inc. 53, Jordan.
[2] p. 340, Bipont. [3] 183, Ribbeck[3].
[4] That is, we exist rather than really live. Cf. Sophocles,
fr. Iphig. τίκτει γὰρ οὐδὲν ἐσθλὸν εἰκαία σχολή, "aimless idleness produces nothing that is good." (Bergk, *De Frag.
Soph.* p. 15.)

Íncerte errat ánimus,praeterprópter vitam vívitur."

14 Et grammaticus sudans multum ac rubens multum, cum id plerique prolixius riderent, exurgit et abiens: "Tibi," inquit, "Fronto, postea uni dicam, ne inscitiores audiant ac discant." Atque ita omnes, relicta ibi quaestione verbi, consurreximus.

XI

Ponit versus Platonis amatorios quos admodum iuvenis lusit, dum tragoediis contendit.

1 CELEBRANTUR duo isti Graeci versiculi multorum-que doctorum hominum memoria dignantur, quod
2 sint lepidissimi et venustissimae brevitatis. Neque adeo pauci sunt veteres scriptores, qui quidem [1] eos Platonis esse philosophi adfirmant, quibus ille adulescens luserit, cum tragoediis quoque eodem tempore faciendis praeluderet:

Τὴν ψυχὴν Ἀγάθωνα φιλῶν ἐπὶ χείλεσιν ἔσχον·
Ἦλθε γὰρ ἡ τλήμων ὡς διαβησομένη.

3 Hoc δίστιχον amicus meus, οὐκ ἄμουσος adulescens, in plures versiculos licentius liberiusque vertit. Qui quoniam mihi quidem visi sunt non esse memoratu indigni, subdidi:

---

[1] qui quidem, *Lion;* quidem, Q; quid, Z; qui, γ.

---

[1] The writing of tragedies as youthful literary exercises

Aimless we drift, we live but more or less."

And the grammarian, in a profuse sweat and blushing deeply, since many of the company were laughing long and loud at this, got up, saying as he left: "I will tell you at a later time, when we are alone, Fronto, in order that ignorant folk may not hear and learn." And so we all rose, leaving the consideration of the word at that point.

XI

He gives some amatory verses of Plato, with which the philosopher amused himself when he was a very young man and was contending for the tragic prize.

HERE are two Greek verses that are famous and deemed worthy of remembrance by many learned men because of their charm and graceful terseness. There are in fact not a few ancient writers who declare that they are the work of the philosopher Plato, with which he amused himself in his youth, while at the same time he was beginning his literary career by writing tragedies.[1]

My soul, when I kissed Agathon, did pass
My lips; as though, poor soul, 'twould leap across.

This distich a friend of mine, a young man no stranger to the Muses, has paraphrased somewhat boldly and freely in a number of lines. And since they seemed to me not undeserving of remembrance, I have added them here:[2]

was not uncommon; see Suet. *Jul.* lvi. 7, and Plin. *Epist.* vii. 4. 2. The lemma is wrong; cf. note 2, p. 360.
  [2] p. 375, Bährens.

4

Cum semihiulco savio
Meo puellum savior
Dulcemque florem spiritus
Duco ex aperto tramite,
Anima male [1] aegra et saucia
Cucurrit ad labeas mihi,
Rictumque in oris pervium
Et labra pueri mollia,
Rimata itineri transitus,
Ut transiliret, nititur.
Tum si morae quid plusculae
Fuisset in coetu osculi,
Amoris igni percita
Transisset et me linqueret
Et mira prorsum res foret,
Ut fierem ad me [2] mortuus,
Ad puerum ut [3] intus viverem.

XII

Dissertatio Herodis Attici super vi et natura doloris suaeque opinionis affirmatio per exemplum indocti rustici, qui cum rubis fructiferas arbores praecidit.

1 HERODEM ATTICUM, consularem virum, Athenis disserentem audivi Graeca oratione, in qua fere omnes memoriae nostrae universos gravitate atque 2 copia et elegantia vocum longe praestitit. Disseruit autem contra ἀπάθειαν Stoicorum, lacessitus a quodam Stoico, tamquam minus sapienter et parum viriliter 3 dolorem ferret ex morte pueri quem amaverat. In

---

[1] male *suggested by Hosius* (*cf. Hor. S.* i. 4. 66) ; mea, *Hertz.*
[2] fierem *and* ad me *transposed by L. Müller.*
[3] ut *added by Scaliger ;* at puerulo intus *suggested by Hosius.*

When with my parted lips my love I kiss,
And quaff the breath's sweet balm from open
    mouth,
Smitten with love my soul mounts to my lips,
And through my love's soft mouth its way would
    take,
Passing the open gateway of the lips.
But if our kiss, delayed, had been prolonged,
By love's fire swayed my soul that way had ta'en,
And left me.   Faith, a wondrous thing it were,
If I should die, but live within my love.

XII

A discourse of Herodes Atticus on the power and nature of
pain, and a confirmation of his view by the example of an
ignorant countryman who cut down fruit-trees along
with thorns.

I ONCE heard Herodes Atticus, the ex-consul,
holding forth at Athens in the Greek language, in
which he far surpassed almost all the men of our
time in distinction, fluency, and elegance of diction.
He was speaking at the time against the ἀπάθεια,
or "lack of feeling" of the Stoics, in consequence
of having been assailed by one of that sect, who
alleged that he did not endure the grief which he
felt at the death of a beloved boy with sufficient

ea dissertione,[1] quantulum memini, huiuscemodi
sensus est : quod nullus usquam homo, qui secundum
naturam sentiret et saperet, adfectionibus istis animi,
quas πάθη appellabat, aegritudinis, cupiditatis,
timoris, irae, voluptatis, carere et vacare totis posset,[2]
atque, si posset etiam obniti ut totis careret, non
fore [3] id melius, quoniam langueret animus et tor-
peret, adfectionum quarundam adminiculis, ut
4 necessaria plurimum temperie privatus. Dicebat
enim sensus istos motusque animi, qui cum inmode-
ratiores sunt vitia fiunt, innexos inplicatosque esse
5 vigoribus quibusdam mentium et alacritatibus, ac
propterea, si omnino omnis eos inperitius convella-
mus, periculum esse ne eis [4] adhaerentes bonas
6 quoque et utiles animi indoles amittamus. Mode-
randos esse igitur et scite considerateque purgandos
censebat, ut ea tantum quae aliena sunt contraque
naturam videntur et cum pernicie adgnata sunt
detrahantur, ne profecto id accidat quod cuipiam
Thraco insipienti et rudi in agro quem emerat
procurando venisse usu fabulast.

7   " Homo Thracus," inquit, " ex ultima barbaria,
ruris colendi insolens, cum in terras cultiores hu-
manioris vitae cupidine commigrasset, fundum mer-
catus est oleo atque vino consitum. Qui cum [5]
nihil admodum super vite aut arbore colenda sciret,
videt forte vicinum rubos alte atque late obortas
excidentem, fraxinos ad summum prope verticem

---

[1] dissertione, ω (cf. Thes. Ling. Lat.); dissertatione,
Beroaldus.
[2] posset rhetor non dolere (dolore) MSS.; rh. non d.
deleted by Carrio.
[3] fore, H. J. Müller; ex re, ω.
[4] ne eis, σ; necis, ω.

wisdom and fortitude. The sense of the discourse, so far as I remember, was as follows: that no man, who felt and thought normally, could be wholly exempt and free from those emotions of the mind, which he called πάθη, caused by sorrow, desire, fear, anger and pleasure; and even if he could so resist them as to be free from them altogether, he would not be better off, since his mind would grow weak and sluggish, being deprived of the support of certain emotions, as of a highly necessary stimulus. For he declared that those feelings and impulses of the mind, though they become faults when excessive, are connected and involved in certain powers and activities of the intellect; and therefore, if we should in our ignorance eradicate them altogether, there would be danger lest we lose also the good and useful qualities of the mind which are connected with them. Therefore he thought that they ought to be regulated, and pruned skilfully and carefully, so that those only should be removed which are unsuitable and unnatural, lest in fact that should happen which once (according to the story) befell an ignorant and rude Thracian in cultivating a field which he had bought.

"When a man of Thrace," said he, "from a remote and barbarous land, and unskilled in agriculture, had moved into a more civilized country, in order to lead a less wild life, he bought a farm planted with olives and vines. Knowing nothing at all about the care of vines or trees, he chanced to see a neighbour cutting down the thorns which had sprung up high and wide, pruning his ash-trees almost to

---

⁵ cum *added by Skutsch.*

deputantem, suboles vitium e radicibus caudicum
super terram fusas revellentem, stolones in pomis
aut in oleis proceros atque derectos amputantem,
acceditque prope et cur tantam ligni atque frondium
8 caedem faceret percontatus est. Et vicinus ita
respondit: 'Ut ager,' inquit, 'mundus purusque
9 fiat, eius arbor atque vitis fecundior.' Discedit
ille a vicino gratias agens et laetus, tamquam adeptus
rei rusticae disciplinam. Tum falcem ibi ac securim
capit: atque ibi homo misere[1] inperitus vites suas
sibi omnis et oleas detruncat comasque arborum
laetissimas uberrimosque vitium palmites decidit et
frutecta atque virgulta simul omnia, pomis frugi-
busque gignendis felicia, cum sentibus et rubis puri-
ficandi agri gratia convellit, mala mercede doctus
audaciam fiduciamque peccandi imitatione falsa
10 eruditus. Sic," inquit, " isti apathiae sectatores,
qui videri se esse tranquillos et intrepidos et inmobiles volunt, dum nihil cupiunt, nihil dolent, nihil
irascuntur, nihil gaudent, omnibus vehementioris
animi officiis amputatis, in torpore ignavae et quasi
enervatae vitae consenescunt."

XIII

Quos "pumiliones" dicimus, Graece νάνους appellari.

1 STABANT forte una in vestibulo Palatii fabulantes
Fronto Cornelius et Festus Postumius et Apollinaris
Sulpicius, atque ego ibi adsistens cum quibusdam

---

[1] miser, ω; *corr. by Hosius (cf.* xiii. 31. 1, *etc.*).

their tops, pulling up the suckers of his vines which had spread over the earth from the main roots, and cutting off the tall straight shoots on his fruit and olive trees. He drew near and asked why the other was making such havoc of his wood and leaves. The neighbour answered; ' In order to make the field clean and neat and the trees and vines more productive.' The Thracian left his neighbour with thanks, rejoicing that he had gained some knowledge of farming. Then he took his sickle and axe; and thereupon in his pitiful ignorance the fellow cuts down all his vines and olives, lopping off the richest branches of the trees and the most fruitful shoots of the vines, and, with the idea of clearing up his place, he pulls up all the shrubs and shoots fit for bearing fruits and crops, along with the brambles and thorns, having learnt assurance at a ruinous price and acquired boldness in error through faulty imitation. Thus it is," said Herodes, "that those disciples of insensibility, wishing to be thought calm, courageous and steadfast because of showing neither desire nor grief, neither wrath nor joy, root out all the more vigorous emotions of the mind, and grow old in the torpor of a sluggish and, as it were, nerveless life."

XIII

That what we call *pumiliones* the Greeks term *νάνοι*.

CORNELIUS FRONTO, Festus Postumius, and Sulpicius Apollinaris chanced to be standing and talking together in the vestibule of the Palace;[1] and I, being near by with some companions, eagerly

---

[1] The palace of the Caesars on the Palatine Hill at Rome.

aliis sermones eorum, quos de litterarum disciplinis
2 habebant, curiosius captabam. Tum Fronto Apollinari: "Fac me," inquit, "oro, magister, ut sim
certus an recte supersederim 'nanos' dicere parva
nimis statura homines maluerimque eos 'pumiliones'
appellare, quoniam hoc scriptum esse in libris
veterum memineram, 'nanos' autem sordidum esse
3 verbum et barbarum credebam?" "Est quidem,"
inquit, "hoc" Apollinaris, "in consuetudine inperiti
vulgi frequens, sed barbarum non est censeturque
linguae Graecae origine; νάνους enim Graeci [1] voca-
verunt brevi atque humili corpore homines paulum
supra terram extantes idque ita dixerunt adhibita
quadam ratione etymologiae cum sententia vocabuli
competente et, si memoria," inquit, "mihi non
labat scriptum hoc est in comoedia Aristophanis,
cui nomen est Ὀλκάδες.[2] Fuisset autem verbum hoc
a te civitate donatum aut in Latinam coloniam
deductum, si tu eo uti dignatus fores, essetque id
inpendio probabilius quam quae a Laberio ignobilia
nimis et sordentia in usum linguae Latinae intro-
missa sunt."
4   Tum Festus Postumius grammatico cuipiam Latino,
Frontonis familiari: "Docuit," inquit, "nos Apollinaris, 'nanos' verbum Graecum esse, tu nos doce,
quoniam[3] de mulis aut eculeis humilioribus vulgo
dicitur, anne Latinum sit et aput quem scriptum
5 reperiatur?" Atque ille grammaticus, homo sane
perquam in noscendis veteribus scriptis exercitus:
"Si piaculum," inquit, "non committitur, praesente

---

[1] Graeci, σ; Graece, ω.
[2] Ὀλκάδες, *Hertz*; ἀκαλες, ω (*or something similar*).
[3] quoniam, *Skutsch*; in quo, ω.

---

[1] That is, a short word for short people. The derivation

listened to their conversations on literary subjects.
Then said Fronto to Apollinaris: "I pray you, Sir,
inform me whether I was right in forbearing to
call men of excessively small stature *nani* and in
preferring the term *pumiliones;* for I remembered
that the latter word appears in the books of early
writers, while I thought that *nani* was vulgar and
barbarous." "It is true," replied Apollinaris, that
the word *nani* is frequent in the language of the
ignorant vulgar; yet it is not barbarous, but is
thought to be of Greek origin; for the Greeks
called men of short and low stature, rising but little
above the ground, νάνοι, or 'dwarfs,' using that word
by the application of a certain etymological principle
corresponding with its meaning,[1] and if my memory
is not at fault," said he, "it occurs in the comedy of
Aristophanes entitled Ὁλκάδες,[2] or *The Cargo Boats.*
But this word would have been given citizenship
by you, or established in a Latin colony, if you had
deigned to use it, and it would be very much more
acceptable than the low and vulgar words which
Laberius introduced into the Latin language."[3]

Thereupon Postumius Festus said to a Latin
grammarian, a friend of Fronto's: "Apollinaris has
told us that *nani* is a Greek word; do you inform
us whether it is good Latin, when it is used, as it
commonly is, of small mules or ponies, and in what
author it is found." And that grammarian, a man
very well versed in knowledge of the early literature,
said: "If I am not committing sacrilege in giving

of νάνος, from which *nani* comes, is uncertain. *Pumilio* is
connected by some with πυγμαλίων, = πυγμαῖος, "thumb-
ing"; cf. Lat. *pugnus*: by others with *puer* and *pubes.*
[2] Frag. 427, Kock.   [3] See xvi. 7.

399

Apollinare, quid de voce ulla Graeca Latinave sentiam dicere, audeo tibi, Feste, quaerenti respondere esse hoc verbum Latinum scriptumque inveniri in poematis Helvi Cinnae, non ignobilis neque indocti poetae," versusque eius ipsos dixit, quos, quoniam memoriae mihi forte aderant, adscripsi :

> At nunc me Genumana per salicta
> Bigis raeda rapit citata nanis.

XIV

Contemporaneos fuisse Caesari et Ciceroni M. Varronem et P. Nigidium, aetatis suae doctissimos Romanos ; et quod Nigidii commentationes propter earum obscuritatem subtilitatemque in vulgus non exeunt.

1   Aetas M. Ciceronis et C. Caesaris praestanti facundia paucos habuit, doctrinarum autem multiformium variarumque artium quibus humanitas erudita est columina habuit M. Varronem et P. Nigidium.
2 Sed Varronis quidem monumenta rerum ac disciplinarum, quae per litteras condidit, in propatulo
3 frequentique usu feruntur, Nigidianae autem commentationes non proinde in volgus exeunt et obscuritas subtilitasque earum tamquam parum utilis
4 derelicta est.   Sicuti sunt quae paulo ante legimus in *Commentariis* eius, quos *Grammaticos* inscripsit, ex [1] quibus quaedam ad demonstrandum scripturae genus exempli gratia sumpsi.
5   Nam, cum de natura atque ordine litterarum dissereret quas grammatici " vocales " appellant, verba

---

[1] ex, *Aldus* ; et, ω.

my opinion of any Greek or Latin word in the
presence of Apollinaris, I venture to reply to your
inquiry, Festus, that the word is Latin and is found
in the poems of Helvius Cinna, a poet neither
obscure nor without learning." And he gave the
verses themselves,[1] which I have added, since I
chanced to remember them:

But now through Genumanian willow groves
The wagon hurries me with dwarf steeds (*bigis
nanis*) twain.

XIV

That Marcus Varro and Publius Nigidius, the most learned
Romans of their time, were contemporaries of Caesar and
Cicero, and that the commentaries of Nigidius, because of
their obscurity and subtlety, did not become popular.

THE time of Marcus Cicero and Gaius Caesar had
few men of surpassing eloquence, but in encyclopaedic learning and in the varied sciences by which
humanity is enobled it possesses two towering figures
in Marcus Varro and Publius Nigidius. Now the
records of knowledge and learning left in written
form by Varro are familiar and in general use, the
observations of Nigidius, however, are not so widely
known, but their obscurity and subtlety have caused
them to be neglected, as of little practical value. As
a specimen I may cite what I read a short time ago
in his work entitled *Grammatical Notes;* from this
book I have made a few extracts, as an example of
the nature of his writings.

When discussing the nature and order of the
letters[2] which the grammarians call *vocales,* or

---

[1] Frag. 1, Bährens.   [2] Properly "sounds."

haec scripsit, quae reliquimus inenarrata ad exercen-
6 dam legentium intentionem : " *A* et *o* semper
principes sunt, *i* et *u* semper subditae, *e* et subit et
praeit; praeit[1] in ' Euripo,' subit in ' Aemilio.' Si
quis putat praeire *u* in his verbis : ' Valerius,' ' Ven-
nonius,' ' Volusius,' aut *i* in his : ' iampridem,' ' iecur,'
' iocus,' ' iucundum,' errabit, quod hae litterae, cum
7 praeeunt, ne vocales quidem sunt." Item ex eodem
libro verba haec sunt : " Inter litteram *n* et *g* est alia
vis, ut in nomine ' anguis' et ' angari' et ' ancorae'
et ' increpat' et ' incurrit' et ' ingenuus.' In omnibus
his non verum *n*, sed adulterinum ponitur. Nam *n*
non esse lingua indicio est ; nam si ea littera esset,
8 lingua palatum tangeret." Alio deinde in loco ita
scriptum : " Graecos non tantae inscitiae arcesso, qui
ov ex *o* et *v* scripserunt, quantae[2] qui *ei* ex *e* et *i* ;
illud enim inopia fecerunt, hoc nulla re subacti."

---

[1] praeit *added by Hertz.*
[2] quantae *added in* σ ; quantae nostri fuerunt, *Hertz.*

---

[1] Frag. 53, Swoboda. [2] They are semi-vowels.
[3] Frag. 54, Swoboda.
[4] This word is cited by the *Thes. Ling. Lat.* from Lucilius
200, Lachmann ; that, however, is a conjecture of Scaliger's
and Marx (262) reads Ancerius, a personal name. The meaning of the word is uncertain. It is perhaps the same as the
Greek ἄγγαρος, " courier," a loan-word of Persian origin.
[5] Pronounced like *ng ;* for example, *angcora.*
[6] Frag. 55, Swoboda. [7] That is, the Romans.
[8] Since the sound of *v* was that of French *u*, German *ü*,
the Greeks were compelled to use *ov* for the long *v*. In
Latin the genuine diphthong *ei* had changed to *ī* before the

"vowels," he wrote the following, which I leave unexplained, in order to test my readers' powers of application :[1] "*A* and *o*," he says, "always stand first in diphthongs, *i* and *u* always second, *e* both follows and precedes ; it precedes in *Euripus*, follows in *Aemilius*. If anyone supposes that *u* precedes in the words *Valerius*, *Vannonius*, and *Volusius*, or that *i* precedes in *iampridem* (long ago), *iecur* (liver), *iocus* (joke), and *iucundus* (agreeable), he will be wrong, for when these letters precede, they are in fact not vowels."[2] These words also are from the same book :[3] "Between the letters *n* and *g* another element is introduced, as in the words *anguis* (snake), *angari*,[4] *ancora* (anchor), *increpat* (chides), *incurrit* (runs upon), and *ingenuus* (free-born). In all these we have, not a true *n*, but a so-called *n adulterinum*.[5] For the tongue shows that it is not an ordinary *n* ; since if it were that sound, the tongue would touch the palate in making it." Then in another place we find this :[6] "I do not charge those Greeks with so great ignorance in writing *ov* (= *ū*) with *o* and *v*, as I do those[7] who wrote *ei* (= *ī*) with *e* and *i* ; for the former the Greeks did from necessity, in the latter case there was no compulsion."[8]

period of our earliest records ; an example is *dīco* for *deico* (cf. δείκνυμι). The spurious diphthong *ei*, which probably was the only_ one known to Nigidius, was introduced to indicate the sound of *ī*, and was not necessary, although, like the tall *I* and the apex (over other vowels) it was convenient.

BOOK XX

LIBER VICESIMUS

I

Disputatio Sex. Caecilii iureconsulti et Favorini philosophi
de legibus *Duodecim Tabularum*.

1 SEXTUS CAECILIUS in disciplina iuris atque in legibus
populi Romani noscendis interpretandisque scientia,
2 usu auctoritateque inlustris fuit.   Ad eum forte in
area Palatina, cum salutationem Caesaris opperiremur,
philosophus Favorinus accessit conlocutusque est,
3 nobis multisque aliis praesentibus.   In illis tunc
eorum sermonibus orta mentiost legum decemvira-
lium, quas decemviri eius rei gratia a populo creati
conposuerunt, in duodecim tabulas conscripserunt.
4   Eas leges cum Sex. Caecilius, inquisitis explora-
tisque multarum urbium legibus, eleganti atque
absoluta brevitate verborum scriptas diceret, "Sit,"[1]
inquit, "hoc" Favorinus, "in pleraque earum legum
parte ita uti dicis; non enim minus cupide tabulas
istas duodecim legi quam illos duodecim libros
Platonis *De Legibus*.   Sed quaedam istic esse anim-
advertuntur aut obscurissima aut durissima[2] aut
lenia contra nimis et remissa aut nequaquam ita, ut
scriptum est, consistentia."

[1] sit, *Beroaldus*; sed, *ω*.
[2] aut durissima, *added by J. Gronov.*

---

[1] That is, Antoninus Pius.
[2] The *Area Palatina* was originally the space bounded on
the west by the *Domus Tiberiana*, or Palace of Tiberius, and
the *Domus Augustana;* as time went on, it must have been
bounded and restricted by other parts of the Imperial Palace.
406

BOOK XX

I

A discussion of the jurist Sextus Caecilius and the philosopher Favorinus about the laws of the *Twelve Tables*.

SEXTUS CAECILIUS was famed for his knowledge, experience and authority in the science of jurisprudence and in understanding and interpreting the laws of the Roman people. It happened that as we were waiting to pay our respects to Caesar,[1] the philosopher Favorinus met and accosted Caecilius in the Palatine square[2] in my presence and that of several others. In the conversation which they carried on at the time mention was made of the laws of the decemvirs, which the board of ten appointed by the people for that purpose wrote and inscribed upon twelve tablets.[3]

When Sextus Caecilius, who had examined and studied the laws of many cities, said that they were drawn up in the most choice and concise terms, Favorinus rejoined: " It may be as you say in the greater part of those laws ; for I read your twelve tables with as eager interest as I did the twelve books of Plato *On the Laws*. But some of them seem to me to be either very obscure or very cruel, or on the other hand too mild and lenient, or by no means to be taken exactly as they are written."

---

[3] These laws were set up in the Forum on ten tablets of bronze in 451 B.C., to which two more tablets were added in 450.

5 "Obscuritates," inquit Sex. Caecilius,"non adsigne-
mus culpae scribentium, sed inscitiae non adsequent-
ium, quamquam hi quoque ipsi, qui quae scripta sunt
6 minus percipiunt culpa vacant. Nam longa aetas
verba atque mores veteres oblitteravit, quibus verbis
moribusque sententia legum conprehensa est. Tre-
centesimo quoque anno post Romam conditam
tabulae conpositae scriptaeque sunt, a quo tempore
ad hunc diem anni esse non longe minus sescenti[1]
7 videntur. Dure autem scriptum esse in istis legibus
quid existimari potest? nisi duram esse legem putas,
quae iudicem arbitrumve iure datum, qui ob rem
iudicandam[2] pecuniam accepisse convictus est,
capite poenitur aut quae furem manifestum ei cui
furtum factum est in servitutem tradit, nocturnum
8 autem furem ius occidendi tribuit. Dic enim,
quaeso, dic, vir sapientiae studiosissime, an aut
iudicis illius perfidiam contra omnia divina atque
humana iusiurandum suum pecunia vendentis aut
furis manifesti intolerandam audaciam aut nocturni
grassatoris insidiosam violentiam non dignam esse
capitis poena existumes?"
9 "Noli," inquit Favorinus, "ex me quaerere quid
ego existumem. Scis enim solitum esse me, pro
disciplina sectae quam colo, inquirere potius quam
10 decernere. Sed non levis existimator neque asper-

---

[1] sexcenti, *J. F. Gronov*; septingenti, *ω*.
[2] iudicandam, *Scioppius* (*cf. Quint.* v. 10. 87; *Tac. Ann.*
iv. 31; *etc.*); dicendam, *ω*. *Heracus suggests that we have a
fusion of* ob rem iudicandum *and* ob ius dicendum *or* ob
falsum testimonium dicendum.

---

[1] The chronology of Nepos; see note on § 3, above, and on
the chapter heading of xvii. 21.
[2] ix. 3. [3] viii. 4. [4] viii. 12.

"As for the obscurities," said Sextus Caecilius, "let us not charge those to the fault of the makers of the laws, but to the ignorance of those who cannot follow their meaning, although they also who do not fully understand what is written may be excused. For long lapse of time has rendered old words and customs obsolete, and it is in the light of those words and customs that the sense of the laws is to be understood. As a matter of fact, the laws were compiled and written in the three hundredth year after the founding of Rome,[1] and from that time until to-day is clearly not less than six hundred years. But what can be looked upon as cruel in those laws? Unless you think a law is cruel which punishes with death a judge or arbiter appointed by law, who has been convicted of taking a bribe for rendering his decision,[2] or which hands over a thief caught in the act to be the slave of the man from whom he stole,[3] and makes it lawful to kill a robber who comes by night.[4] Tell me, I pray, tell me, you deep student of philosophy, whether you think that the perfidy of a juror who sells his oath contrary to all laws, human and divine, or the intolerable audacity of an open theft, or the treacherous violence of a nocturnal footpad, does not deserve the penalty of death?"

"Don't ask me," said Favorinus, "what I think. For you know that, according to the practice of the sect to which I belong,[5] I am accustomed rather to inquire than to decide. But the Roman people is a judge neither insignificant nor contemptible, and

[5] He probably refers to the Pyrronian sceptics, about whose beliefs he wrote a work in ten books ; see xi. 5. 5.

nabilis est populus Romanus, cui delicta quidem
istaec vindicanda, poenae tamen huiuscemodi nimis
durae esse visae sunt; passus enim est leges istas de

11 tam inmodico supplicio situ atque senio emori. Sicut
illud quoque inhumaniter scriptum improbavit, quod,
si homo in ius vocatus, morbo aut aetate aeger ad
ingrediendum invalidus est, 'arcera non sternitur,'
sed ipse aufertur et iumento imponitur atque ex
domo sua ad praetorem in comitium nova funeris
facie effertur. Quam enim ob causam morbo ad-
fectus et ad respondendum pro sese non idoneus,
iumento adhaerens in ius adversario deportatur?

12 Quod vero dixi videri quaedam esse inpendio molliora,
nonne tibi quoque videtur nimis esse dilutum quod ita
de iniuria poenienda scriptum est: 'Si iniuriam
alteri faxsit, viginti quinque aeris poenae sunto'?
Quis enim erit tam inops, quem ab iniuriae faciendae

13 libidine viginti quinque asses deterreant? Itaque
cum eam legem Labeo quoque [1] vester in libris, quos
Ad Duodecim Tabulas conscripsit, non probaret:
'Quidam,' [2] inquit, 'L. Veratius fuit egregie
homo inprobus atque inmani vecordia. Is pro de-
lectamento habebat, os hominis liberi manus suae
palma verberare. Eum servus sequebatur ferens
crumenam plenam assium; ut quemque depalma-
verat, numerari statim secundum *Duodecim Tabulas*
quinque et viginti asses iubebat.' Propterea," in-

---

[1] Labeo quoque, *Huschke*; cum Labeo q., δNO; cum (tum,
Π) quoque Labeo, ΠX.
[2] quidam *added by Carrio; various other suggestions for
partly filling the lacuna before* inquit *have been made.*

---

[1] That is, with a pallet for lying upon.
[2] At that time one of the two chief magistrates, corresponding to the consuls of later times.

while they thought that such crimes ought to be
punished, they yet believed that punishments of
that kind were too severe; for they have allowed
the laws which prescribed such excessive penalties
to die out from disuse and old age.   Just so they
considered it also an inhuman provision, that if a
man has been summoned to court, and being dis-
abled through illness or years is too weak to walk,
'a covered waggon he need not spread';[1] but the
man is carried out and placed upon a beast of burden
and conveyed from his home to the praetor [2] in the
comitium, as if he were a living corpse.   For why
should one who is a prey to illness, and unable to
appear, be haled into court at the demand of his
adversary, clinging to a draught animal?   But as
for my statement that some laws were excessively
lenient, do not you yourself think that law too
lax, which reads as follows with regard to the
penalty for an injury: [3] 'If anyone has inflicted an
injury upon another, let him be fined twenty-five
asses'?   For who will be found so poor that
twenty-five asses would keep him from inflicting an
injury if he desired to?   And therefore your friend
Labeo also, in the work which he wrote *On the
Twelve Tables*,[4] expressing his disapproval of that
law, says: [5] 'One Lucius Veratius was an exceedingly
wicked man and of cruel brutality.   He used to
amuse himself by striking free men in the face with
his open hand.   A slave followed him with a purse
full of asses; as often as he had buffeted anyone, he
ordered twenty-five asses to be counted out at once,
according to the provision of the *Twelve Tables*'

---

[3] viii. 4.   [4] Frag. 25, Hushke; 3, Bremer.
[5] There seems to be a lacuna in the text; see crit. note.

quit, "praetores postea hanc abolescere et relinqui
censuerunt iniuriisque aestumandis recuperatores se

14 daturos edixerunt. Nonnulla autem in istis legibus
ne consistere quidem, sicuti dixi, visa sunt, velut illa
lex talionis, cuius verba, nisi memoria me fallit, haec
sunt : ' Si membrum rupit, ni cum e pacto, talio esto.'

15 Praeter enim ulciscendi acerbitatem ne procedere
quoque executio iustae talionis potest. Nam cui
membrum ab alio ruptum est, si ipsi itidem rumpere
per talionem velit, quaero, an efficere possit rum-
pendi pariter membri aequilibrium? In qua re

16 primum ea difficultas est inexplicabilis. Quid si[1]
membrum," inquit, " alteri inprudens ruperit? Quod
enim inprudentia factum est, retaliari per inpruden-
tiam debet. Ictus quippe fortuitus et consultus non
cadunt sub eiusdem talionis similitudinem. Quonam
igitur modo inprudentem poterit imitari, qui in
exequenda talione non licentiae ius habet, sed in-

17 prudentiae? Sed et si prudens ruperit, nequaquam
patietur aut altius se laedi aut latius. Quod cuiusmodi libra atque mensura caveri possit, non reperio.

18 Quin etiam, si quid plus erit aliterve conmissum, res
fiet ridiculae atrocitatis, ut contraria actio mutuae
talionis oriatur et adolescat infinita quaedam recipro-

19 catio talionum. Nam de inmanitate illa secandi
partiendique humani corporis, si unus ob pecuniam
debitam iudicatus addictusque sit pluribus, non libet

[1] quid si, Q^2 ; qui si, ПZ ; quis in, O ; quis vi, Q ; qui sin,
N ; quis, X.

---

[1] The law reads: *tertiis nundinis partis secanto. Si plus
minusve secuerunt, se fraude esto,* "on the third market day
(*i.e.* after about two weeks ; see note on § 49, below) let them
cut him into pieces. If they have cut more or less (than
their proper share), let it be without prejudice (to them)."

Therefore," he continued, " the praetors afterwards decided that this law was obsolete and invalid and declared that they would appoint arbiters to appraise damages. Again, some things in those laws obviously cannot, as I have said, even be carried out ; for instance, the one referring to retaliation, which reads as follows, if my memory is correct : ' If one has broken another's limb, there shall be retaliation, unless a compromise be made.' Now not to mention the cruelty of the vengeance, the exaction even of a just retaliation is impossible. For if one whose limb has been broken by another wishes to retaliate by breaking a limb of his injurer, can he succeed, pray, in breaking the limb in exactly the same manner ? In this case there first arises this insoluble difficulty. What about one who has broken another's limb unintentionally ? For what has been done unintentionally ought to be retaliated unintentionally. For a chance blow and an intentional one do not fall under the same category of retaliation. How then will it be possible to imitate unintentional action, when in retaliating one has not the right of intention, but of unintention ? But if he break it intentionally, the offender will certainly not allow himself to be injured more deeply or more severely ; but by what weight and measure this can be avoided, I do not understand. Nay more, if retaliation is taken to a greater extent or differently, it will be a matter of absurd cruelty that a counter-action for retaliation should arise and an endless interchange of retaliation take place. But that enormity of cutting and dividing a man's body, if an individual is brought to trial for debt and adjudged to several creditors,[1] I do not care to remember, and I am

meminisse et piget dicere. Quid enim videri potest
efferatius, quid ab hominis ingenio diversius quam
quod membra inopis debitoris acerbissimo[1] laniatu
distrahebantur, sicuti nunc bona venum distra-
huntur ? "

20 Tum Sex. Caecilius amplexus utraque manu
Favorinum, "Tu es," inquit, "unus profecto in
nostra memoria non Graecae modo, sed Romanae
quoque rei peritissimus. Quis enim philosophorum
disciplinae suae leges tam scite atque docte callet
quam leges tu nostras decemvirales percalluisti ?

21 Sed, quaeso tecum tamen, degrediare paulisper
curriculis istis disputationum vestrarum academicis
omissoque studio, quicquid lubitum est arguendi
tuendique, consideres gravius cuiusmodi sint ea

22 quae reprehendisti, nec ideo contemnas legum
istarum antiquitates, quod plerisque ipse[2] iam
populus Romanus uti desiverit. Non enim profecto
ignoras legum oportunitates et medellas pro temporum moribus et pro rerum publicarum generibus ac
pro utilitatum praesentium rationibus proque viti-
orum quibus medendum est fervoribus mutari atque
flecti neque uno statu consistere, quin, ut facies caeli
et maris, ita rerum atque fortunae tempestatibus

23 varientur. Quid salubrius visum est rogatione illa
Stolonis iugerum de numero praefinito ? Quid uti-
lius plebisscito Voconio de coercendis mulierum
hereditatibus ? Quid tam necessarium existimatum
est propulsandae civium luxuriae quam lex Licinia

---

[1] acerbissimo, *Hosius* ; brevissimo, *ω* ; saevissimo, *Bynkers-
hoek.*   [2] ipse, *Hosius* ; ipsis, *ω* ; ipsus, *Boot.*

[1] *Oportunitates* refers to the advantage or assistance which
the laws afford to meet the special needs of defence ; *medellas*,
to the remedies they furnish for the cure of vice and crime.

ashamed to mention it. For what can seem more savage, what more inconsistent with humanity, than for the limbs of a poor debtor to be barbarously butchered and sold, just as to-day his goods are divided and sold ? "

Then Sextus Caecilius, throwing both arms about Favorinus, said : " You are indeed the one man within my memory who is most familiar both with Greek and with Roman lore. For what philosopher is skilled and learned in the laws of his sect to the extent to which you are thoroughly versed in our decemviral legislation ? But yet, I pray you, depart for a little from that academic manner of arguing of yours, and laying aside the passion for attacking or defending anything whatever according to your inclination, consider more seriously what is the nature of the details which you have censured, and do not scorn those ancient laws merely because there are many of them which even the Roman people have now ceased to use. For you surely are not unaware that according to the manners of the times, the conditions of governments, considerations of immediate utility, and the vehemence of the vices which are to be remedied, the advantages and remedies offered by the laws [1] are often changed and modified, and do not remain in the same condition ; on the contrary, like the face of heaven and the sea, they vary according to the seasons of circumstances and of fortune. What seemed more salutary than that law of Stolo limiting the number of acres ? What more expedient than the bill of Voconius regulating the inheritances of women ? What was thought so necessary for checking the luxury of the citizens as the law of Licinius

et Fannia aliaeque item leges sumptuariae? Omnia
tamen haec oblitterata et operta sunt civitatis opu-
24 lentia quasi quibusdam fluctibus exaestuantis. Sed
cur tibi esse visa est inhumana lex omnium mea
quidem sententia humanissima, quae iumentum dari
25 iubet aegro aut seni in ius vocato? Verba sunt
haec de lege ' Si in ius vocat' : ' Si morbus aevitasve
vitium escit, qui in ius vocabit iumentum dato; si
26 nolet, arceram ne sternito.' An tu forte morbum
appellari hic putas aegrotationem gravem cum febri
rapida et quercera, iumentumque dici pecus aliquod
unicum tergo vehens? ac propterea minus fuisse
humanum existumas aegrotum domi suae cubantem
27 iumento inpositum in ius rapi? Hoc, mi Favorine,
nequaquam ita est. Nam morbus in lege ista non
febriculosus neque nimium gravis, sed vitium aliquod
inbecillitatis atque invalentiae demonstratur, non
periculum vitae ostenditur. Ceteroqui morbum
vehementiorem, vim graviter nocendi habentem,
legum istarum scriptores alio in loco, non per se
28 'morbum,' sed 'morbum sonticum' appellant. Iumentum quoque non id solum significat quod nunc
dicitur, sed vectabulum etiam quod a iunctis pecori-
bus trahebatur; veteres[1] nostri 'iumentum' a
29 'iungendo' dixerunt. ' Arcera' autem vocabatur
plaustrum[2] tectum undique et munitum, quasi arca

---

[1] veteres enim, σ.
[2] plaustrum rusticum, *Hertz from Nonius.*

---

[1] The first provision of the law is : *Si in ius vocat, ito,* "if
he summon him to court, let him go." Here the words
"*Si . . . vocat*" are used merely to designate the law.
[2] i. 1, 3.   [3] ii. 2.   [4] See xvi. 4. 4 and the note.

and Fannius and other sumptuary laws? Yet all
these have been wiped out and buried by the wealth
of the State, as if by the waves of a swelling sea.
But why did that law appear to you inhumane
which in my opinion is the most humane of all;
that law, namely, which provides that a beast be
furnished for a sick or aged man who is called into
court? The words of that law, 'if he summon
him to court,'[1] are as follows:[2] 'If disease or age
be a hindrance, let the summoner provide a beast;
if he does not wish, he need not spread a covered
waggon.' Do you by any chance suppose that
morbus (disease) here means a dangerous sickness
with a high fever and ague, and that *iumentum* (beast)
means only one animal, capable of carrying someone
on his back; and is it for that reason that you think
it was inhumane for a man lying sick-a-bed at his
home to be placed upon a beast and hurried off to
court? That is by no means the case, my dear
Favorinus. For *morbus* in that law does not mean
a serious complaint attended with fever, but some
defect of weakness and indisposition, not involving
danger to life. On the contrary, a more severe disorder, having the power of material injury, the
writers of those laws call in another place,[3] not
morbus alone, but *morbus sonticus,* or 'a serious
disease.'[4] *Iumentum* also does not have only the
meaning which it has at present, but it might even
mean a vehicle drawn by yoked animals; for our
forefathers formed *iumentum* from *iungo.* Furthermore *arcera* was the name for a waggon, enclosed
and shut in on all sides like a great chest (*arca*),[5] and

[5] The derivation of *arcera* from *arca* seems to be generally
accepted.

quaedam magna, vestimentis instrata, qua nimis
30 aegri aut senes portari cubantes solebant. Quaenam
tibi igitur acerbitas esse visa est, quod in ius vocato
paupertino homini vel inopi, qui aut pedibus forte
aegris esset aut quo alio casu ingredi non quiret,
plaustrum esse dandum censuerunt? neque insterni
tamen delicate arceram iusserunt, quoniam satis
esset invalido cuimodi vectabulum. Atque id fecerunt, ne causatio ista aegri corporis perpetuam
vocationem daret fidem detractantibus iurisque
31 actiones declinantibus; sed enim insubide.[1]

" Iniurias factas quinque et viginti assibus sanxerunt. Non omnino omnes, mi Favorine, iniurias aere
isto pauco diluerunt, tametsi haec ipsa paucitas assium
grave pondus aeris fuit; nam librariis assibus in ea
32 tempestate populus usus est. Sed iniurias atrociores,
ut de osse fracto, non liberis modo, verum etiam
servis factas, inpensiore damno vindicaverunt, qui-
33 busdam autem iniuriis talionem quoque adposuerunt.
Quam quidem tu talionem, vir optime, iniquius
paulo insectatus es ac ne consistere quidem dixisti
lepida quadam sollertia verborum, quoniam talioni
par non sit talio neque rumpi membrum facile possit
ad alterius rupturae, ut ais tu, 'aequilibrium.'
34 Verumst, mi Favorine, talionem parissimam fieri
difficillime. Sed decemviri minuere atque extinguere
volentes huiuscemodi violentiam pulsandi atque
laedendi talione, eo quoque metu coercendos esse

---

[1] insubide, *Heraeus*; ipsum vide, *ω*; ipse, *Boot*; vide
quod, *σ*.

---

[1] See note on § 11, above.   [2] viii. 3.

strewn with robes, and in it men who were too ill
or old used to be carried lying down.   What cruelty
then does there seem to you to be in deciding that
a waggon ought to be furnished for a poor or needy
man who was called into court, if haply through
lameness or some other mischance he was unable to
walk ; and in not requiring that ' a closed carriage '
be luxuriously strewn,[1] when a conveyance of any
kind was sufficient for the invalid ?   And they made
that decision, in order that the excuse of a diseased
body might not give perpetual immunity to those
who neglected their obligations and put off suits at
law ; but foolishly.

   " They assessed inflicted injuries at twenty-five
asses.   They did not, my dear Favorinus, by any
means compensate all injuries by that trifling sum,
although even that small number of asses meant
a heavy weight of copper ; for the as which the
people then used weighed a pound.   But more cruel
injuries, such as breaking a bone, inflicted not only
on freemen but even on slaves, they punished with
a heavier fine,[2] and for some injuries they even prescribed retaliation.   This very law of retaliation,
my dear sir, you criticized somewhat unfairly, saying
with facetious captiousness that it was impossible
to carry it out, since injury and retaliation could not
be exactly alike, and because it was not easy to
break a limb in such a way as to be an exact
aequilibrium, or ' balance,' as you put it, of the
breaking of the other man's.   It is true, my dear
Favorinus, that to make exact retaliation is very
difficult.   But the Ten, wishing by retaliation to
diminish and abolish such violence as beating and
injuring, thought that men ought to be restrained

homines putaverunt neque eius qui membrum alteri
rupisset et pacisci tamen de talione redimenda
nollet tantam esse habendam rationem arbitrati
sunt, ut an prudens inprudensne rupisset spectandum
putarent aut talionem in eo vel ad amussim aequi-
perarent vel in librili perpenderent; sed potius
eundem animum eundemque impetum in eadem
parte corporis rumpenda, non eundem quoque casum
exigi voluerunt, quoniam modus voluntatis praestari
35 posset, casus ictus non posset.

" Quod si ita est ut dico, et ut ipse aequitatis habitus
demonstrat, taliones illae tuae reciprocae argutiores
36 profectoquam veriores fuerunt. Sed quoniam acerbum
quoque esse hoc genus poenae putas, quae, obsecro te,
ista acerbitas est, si idem fiat in te quod tute in alio
feceris? praesertim cum habeas facultatem paciscendi
et non necesse sit pati talionem, nisi eam tu elegeris.
37 Quod edictum autem praetorum de aestimandis
iniuriis probabilius esse existimas,[1] nolo hoc ignores,
hanc quoque ipsam talionem ad aestimationem
38 iudicis redigi necessario solitam. Nam si reus, qui
depecisci noluerat, iudici talionem imperanti non
parebat, aestimata lite iudex hominem pecuniae
damnabat, atque ita, si reo et pactio gravis et acerba
talio visa fuerat, severitas legis ad pecuniae multam
39 redibat.

" Restat, ut ei quod de sectione partitioneque
que corporis inmanissimum esse tibi visum est
respondeam. Omnibus quidem virtutum generibus

---

[1] existimas, *Huschke*; ex his (iis, *NOX*), ω.

by. the. fear of such a penalty ; and they did not think that so much consideration ought to be had for one who broke another's limb, and refused to compromise by buying off retaliation, as to consider that the question ought to be raised whether he broke it intentionally or not, nor did they make the retaliation in such a case exactly equivalent or weigh it in a balance; but they aimed rather at exacting the same spirit and the same violence in breaking the same part of the body, but not also the same result, since the degree of intention can be determined, but the effect of a chance blow cannot.

" But if this is as I say, and as the condition of fairness itself dictates, those mutual retaliations that you imagined were certainly rather ingenious than real. But since you think that even this kind of punishment is cruel, what cruelty, pray, is there in doing the same thing to you which you have done to another ? especially when you have the opportunity of compromising, and when it is not necessary for you to suffer retaliation unless you choose that alternative. As for your idea that the praetors' edict was preferable in taking cognizance of injuries, I want you to realize this, that this retaliation also was wont of necessity to be subject to the discretion of a judge. For if a defendant, who refused to compromise, did not obey the judge who ordered retaliation, the judge considered the case and fined the man a sum of money ; so that, if the defendant thought the compromise hard and the retaliation cruel, the severity of the law was limited to a fine.

" It remains for me to answer your belief that the cutting and division of a man's body is most inhuman. It was by the exercise and cultivation of

exercendis colendisque populus Romanus e parva
origine ad tantae amplitudinis instar emicuit, sed
omnium maxime atque praecipue fidem coluit
40 sanctamque habuit tam privatim quam publice.   Sic
consules, clarissimos viros, hostibus confirmandae
fidei publicae causa dedidit,[1] sic clientem in fidem
acceptum cariorem haberi quam propinquos tuendum-
que esse contra cognatos censuit, neque peius ullum
facinus existimatum est quam si cui probaretur
41 clientem divisui habuisse.   Hanc autem fidem
maiores nostri non modo in officiorum vicibus, sed in
negotiorum quoque contractibus sanxerunt maxime-
que in pecuniae mutuaticae usu atque commercio;
adimi enim putaverunt subsidium hoc inopiae
temporariae, quo communis omnium vita indiget,
si perfidia debitorum sine gravi poena eluderet.
42 Confessi igitur aeris ac debiti iudicatis triginta dies
sunt dati conquirendae pecuniae causa, quam
43 dissolverent, eosque dies decemviri 'iustos' appellaverunt, velut quoddam iustitium, id est iuris inter
eos quasi interstitionem quandam et cessationem,
44 quibus diebus nihil cum his agi iure posset.
  " Post deinde, nisi dissolverant, ad praetorem vocabantur et ab eo quibus erant iudicati addicebantur,
45 nervo quoque aut compedibus vinciebantur.   Sic enim
sunt, opinor, verba legis : ' Aeris confessi rebusque
iure iudicatis triginta dies iusti sunto.   Post deinde

[1] dedit, *ω* ; *corr. by Daniel.*

---

[1] In the Samnite war, after the battle of the Caudine
Forks in 321 B.C.
[2] iii. 1–4.

all the virtues that the Roman people sprang from
a lowly origin to such a height of greatness, but
most of all and in particular they cultivated integrity
and regarded it as sacred, whether public or private.
Thus for the purpose of vindicating the public
honour it surrendered its consuls, most distinguished
men, to the enemy,[1] thus it maintained that a client
taken under a man's protection should be held dearer
than his relatives and protected against his own
kindred, nor was any crime thought to be worse
than if anyone was convicted of having defrauded
a client. This degree of faith our forefathers
ordained, not only in public functions, but also
in private contracts, and particularly in the use and
interchange of borrowed money ; for they thought
that this aid to temporary need, which is made
necessary by the common intercourse of life, was
lost, if perfidy on the part of debtors escaped with
a slight punishment. Therefore in the case of those
liable for an acknowledged debt thirty days were
allowed for raising the money to satisfy the
obligation, and those days the Ten called 'legitimate,' as if they formed a kind of *moratorium,* that
is to say, a cessation and interruption of judicial
proceedings, during which no legal action could be
taken against them.

"Then later, unless they had paid the debt,
they were summoned before the praetor and
were by him made over to those to whom they
had been adjudged ; and they were also fastened
in the stocks or in fetters. For that, I think,
is the meaning of these words :[2] 'For a con-
fessed debt and for judgment duly pronounced let
thirty days be the legitimate time. Then let there

423

manus iniectio esto, in ius ducito. Ni iudicatum
facit aut quis endo eo in iure vindicit, secum ducito,
vincito aut nervo aut compedibus. Quindecim
pondo ne minore aut si volet maiore vincito. Si
volet suo vivito. Ni suo vivit, qui eum vinctum
habebit, libras farris endo dies dato. Si volet plus
46 dato.' Erat autem ius interea paciscendi ac, nisi
pacti forent, habebantur in vinculis dies sexaginta.
47 Inter eos dies trinis nundinis continuis ad praetorem
in comitium producebantur, quantaeque pecuniae
iudicati essent praedicabatur. Tertiis autem nundinis capite poenas dabant aut trans Tiberim peregre
48 venum ibant. Sed eam capitis poenam sanciendae,
sicuti dixi, fidei gratia horrificam atrocitatis ostentu
novisque terroribus metuendam reddiderunt. Nam
si plures forent, quibus reus esset iudicatus,[1] secare,
si vellent, atque partiri corpus addicti sibi hominis
49 permiserunt. Et quidem verba ipsa legis dicam,
ne existimes invidiam me istam forte formidare:
'Tertiis,' inquit, 'nundinis partis secanto. Si plus
50 minusve secuerunt, se fraude esto.' Nihil profecto
inmitius, nihil inmanius, nisi, ut re ipsa apparet, eo
consilio tanta inmanitas poenae denuntiatast, ne ad

----

[1] adiudicatus, *Skutsch.*

----

[1] F. D. Allen, *Remnants of Early Latin,* p. 86, suggested
that *minore* and *maiore* probably ought to change places.
[2] iii. 5.
[3] The *nundinae,* or market days, came on every ninth day,
reckoned in the Roman fashion. The time between two
market days was the French "huit jours" and our "week."
Tertiis nundinis, counting the one at the beginning of the
period (in the Roman fashion), would be about two weeks
(actually seventeen days).

be a laying on of hands, bring him to court. If he does not satisfy the judgment, or unless someone in the presence of the magistrate intervenes as a surety, let the creditor take him home and fasten him in stocks or in fetters. Let him fasten him with not less than fifteen pounds weight, or if he wish, with more.[1] If the prisoner wishes, he may live at his own expense. If he does not, the creditor shall give him a pound of meal each day. If he wishes, he may give more.' In the meantime the right of compromising the case was allowed,[2] and if they did not compromise it, debtors were confined for sixty days. During that time on three successive market-days[3] they were brought before the praetor and the amount of the judgment against them was announced. But on the third day[4] they were capitally condemned or sent across the Tiber to be sold abroad. But they made this capital punishment horrible by a show of cruelty and fearful by unusual terrors, for the sake, as I have said, of making faith sacred. For if there were several, to whom the debtor had been adjudged, the laws allowed them to cut the man who had been made over to them in pieces, if they wished, and share his body. And indeed I will quote the very words of the law, less haply you should think that I shrink from their odium :[5] 'On the third market day,' it says, 'let them cut him up; if they have cut more or less, let them not be held accountable.' Nothing surely is more merciless, nothing less humane, unless, as is evident on the face of it, such a cruel punishment was threatened in order that they

[4] iii. 6.   [5] iii. 6.

51 eam umquam perveniretur. Addici namque nunc
et vinciri multos videmus, quia vinculorum poenam
52 deterrimi homines contemnunt, dissectum esse
antiquitus neminem equidem legi neque audivi,
quoniam saevitia ista poenae contemni non quitast.
53 An putas, Favorine, si non illa etiam ex *Duodecim
Tabulis* de testimoniis falsis poena abolevisset et si
nunc quoque, ut antea, qui falsum testimonium
dixisse convictus esset, e saxo Tarpeio deiceretur,
mentituros fuisse pro testimonio tam multos quam
videmus? Acerbitas plerumque ulciscendi maleficii
54 bene atque caute vivendi disciplinast. Historia de
Metto Fufetio Albano nobis quoque, non admodum
numero[1] istiusmodi libros lectitantibus, ignota non
est, qui, quoniam pactum atque condictum cum rege
populi Romani perfide ruperat, binis quadrigis
evinctus in diversa nitentibus laceratus est; novum
atque asperum supplicium quis negat? sed, quid
elegantissimus poeta dicat, vide :

at tu dictis, Albane, maneres."

55 Haec taliaque alia ubi Sextus Caecilius, omnibus
qui aderant, ipso quoque Favorino adprobante atque
laudante, disseruit, nuntiatum est Caesarem iam
salutari, et separati sumus.

[1] saepe numero, *Knapp.*

---

[1] viii. 23.
[2] He was the ruler of Alba Longa in the time of Tullus
Hostilius, the third king of Rome (673–641 B.C.).

might never have to resort to it. For nowadays
we see many condemned and bound, because worthless men despise the punishment of bondage; but
I have never read or heard of anyone having been
cut up in ancient days, since the severity of that
law could not be scorned. Or do you suppose,
Favorinus, that if the penalty provided by the
Twelve Tables[1] for false witness had not become obsolete, and if now, as formerly, one who was convicted
of giving false witness was hurled from the Tarpeian
Rock, that we should see so many guilty of lying
on the witness stand? Severity in punishing crime
is often the cause of upright and careful living.
The story of the Alban Mettius Fufetius[2] is not
unknown even to me, although I read few books
of that kind. Since he had treacherously broken
a pact and agreement made with the king of the
Roman people, he was bound to two four-horse
teams and torn asunder as the horses rushed in
opposite directions. Who denies that this is an
unusual and cruel punishment? but see what the
most refined of poets says:[3]

But you, O Alban, should have kept your word."

When Sextus Caecilius had said these and other
things with the approval of all who were present,
including Favorinus himself, it was announced that
Caesar was now receiving, and we separated.

[3] Virg. *Aen.* viii. 643.

II

Vocabulum "siticinum" in M. Catonis oratione quid significet.

1 "SITICINES" scriptum est in oratione M. Catonis, quae scribitur *Ne Imperium sit Veteri, ubi Novus Venerit.* "Siticines," inquit, " et liticines et tubi-
2 cines." Sed Caesellius Vindex in *Conmentariis Lectionum Antiquarum* scire quidem se ait, "liticines" lituo cantare et "tubicines" tuba ; quid istuc autem sit, quo "siticines" cantant, homo ingenuae veritatis
3 scire sese negat. Nos autem in Capitonis Atei *Coniectaneis* invenimus, "siticines" appellatos qui apud "sitos" canere soliti essent, hoc est vita functos et sepultos, eosque habuisse proprium genus tubae, qua canerent, a ceterorum tubicinum differens.

III

Quam ob causam L. Accius poeta in *Pragmaticis* sicinnistas "nebuloso nomine" esse dixerit.

1 Quos "sicinistas" vulgus dicit, qui rectius locuti
2 sunt, "sicinnistas" littera *n* gemina dixerunt. "Sicinnium" enim genus veteris saltationis fuit. Saltabundi autem canebant, quae nunc stantes canunt.
3 Posuit hoc verbum L. Accius poeta in *Pragmaticis* appellarique "sicinnistas" ait "nebuloso nomine," credo propterea "nebuloso," quod, "sicinnium" cur diceretur, obscurum esset.

---

[1] lxix, Jordan.   [2] Frag. 7, Huschke ; 9, Bremer.

II

The meaning of the word *siticines* in a speech of Marcus
Cato's.

The word *siticines* is found in a speech of Marcus
Cato entitled *Let not a Former Official retain his
power, when his Successor arrives.*[1] He speaks of
siticines, liticines and *tubicines.* But Caesellius Vindex,
in his *Notes on Early Words,* declares that he knows
that *liticines* played upon the *lituus,* or "clarion," and
tibicines on the *tuba,* or "trumpet," but, being a man
of conscientious honesty, he says that he does not
know what instrument the *siticines* used. But I have
found in the *Miscellanies* of Ateius Capito[2] that those
were called *siticines* who played in the presence of
those who were "laid away" (*sitos*), that is, who were
dead and buried; and that they had a special kind
of trumpet on which they played, differing from
those of the other trumpeters.

III

Why the poet Lucius Accius in his *Pragmatica* said that
sicinnistae was a "nebulous word."

Those whom the vulgar call *sicinistae,* persons
who speak more accurately have called *sicinnistae*
with a double *n.* For the *sicinnium* was an ancient
form of dance. Moreover, those who now stand and
sing formerly danced as they sang. Lucius Accius
used this word in his *Pragmatica,* and says that
sicinnistae are so called by a "nebulous" (*nebuloso*)
term, using the word "nebulous," I suppose, because the reason for the term *sicinnium* was obscure.

IV

Artificum scaenicorum studium amoremque inhonestum pro-
brosumque esse ; et super ea re verba Aristotelis philosophi adscripta.

1 COMOEDOS quispiam et tragoedos et tibicines dives
adulescens, Tauri philosophi discipulus, ut [1] liberos
homines in deliciis atque in delectamentis habebat.
2 Id genus autem artifices Graece appellantur οἱ περὶ
3 τὸν Διόνυσον τεχνῖται. Eum adulescentem Taurus
a sodalitatibus convictuque hominum scaenicorum
abducere volens, misit ei verba haec ex Aristotelis
libro exscripta, qui Προβλήματα Ἐγκύκλια inscriptus
4 est, iussitque uti ea cotidie lectitaret : Διὰ τί οἱ
Διονυσιακοὶ τεχνῖται ὡς ἐπὶ τὸ πολὺ πονηροί εἰσιν ; ἢ [2]
ὅτι ἥκιστα λόγου καὶ [3] φιλοσοφίας [4] κοινωνοῦσι διὰ
τὸ περὶ τὰς ἀναγκαίας τέχνας τὸ πολὺ μέρος τοῦ βίου
εἶναι, καὶ ὅτι ἐν ἀκρασίαις τὸν πολὺν χρόνον εἰσίν,
ὁτὲ δὲ ἐν ἀπορίαις ; [5] ἀμφότερα δὲ φαυλότητος παρασκευασ-
τικά.

V

Exempla epistularum Alexandri regis et Aristotelis philosophi, ita uti sunt edita ; eaque in linguam Latinam versa.

1 COMMENTATIONUM suarum artiumque quas dis-
cipulis tradebat Aristoteles philosophus, regis
Alexandri magister, duas species habuisse dicitur.
Alia erant, quae nominabat ἐξωτερικά, alia, quae

---

[1] ut added by Vogel.   [2] ἤ, Arist. ; omitted by ω.
[3] καί omitted by Arist   [4] σοφίας, Arist.
[5] τὸ πολὺ τοῦ βίου εἰσίν, τὰ δὲ καὶ ἐν ἀπ., Arist.

IV

That devotion to play-actors, and love of them, was shameful and disgraceful, with a quotation of the words of the philosopher Aristotle on that subject.

A WEALTHY young man, a pupil of the philosopher Taurus, was devoted to, and delighted in, the society of comic and tragic actors and musicians, as if they were freemen. Now in Greek they call artists of that kind οἱ περὶ Διόνυσον τεχνῖται or "craftsmen of Dionysus." Taurus, wishing to wean that youth from the intimacy and companionship of men connected with the stage, sent him these words extracted from the work of Aristotle entitled *Universal Questions*, and bade him read it over every day:[1] "Why are the craftsmen of Dionysus for the most part worthless fellows? Is it because they are least of all familiar with reading and philosophy, since the greater part of their life is given to their essential pursuits and much of their time is spent in intemperance and sometimes in poverty too? For both of these things are incentives to wickedness."

V

Specimens of letters of King Alexander and the philosopher Aristotle, just as they were written; with a rendering of the same into Latin.

THE philosopher Aristotle, the teacher of king Alexander, is said to have had two forms of the lectures and instructions which he delivered to his pupils. One of these was the kind called ἐξωτερικά,

---

[1] *Prob.* xxx. 10 ; frag. 209, Rose.

2 appellabat ἀκροατικά. Ἐξωτερικά dicebantur, quae
ad rhetoricas meditationes facultatemque arguti-
arum civiliumque rerum notitiam conducebant,
3 ἀκροατικά autem vocabantur, in quibus philosophia
remotior subtiliorque agitabatur quaeque ad naturae
contemplationes disceptationesve dialecticas perti-
4 nebant. Huic disciplinae, quam dixi, ἀκροατικῇ
tempus exercendae dabat in Lycio matutinum nec
ad eam quemquam temere admittebat, nisi quorum
ante ingenium et eruditionis elementa atque in
5 discendo studium laboremque explorasset. Illas
vero exotericas auditiones exercitiumque dicendi
eodem in loco vesperi faciebat easque vulgo iuvenibus sine dilectu praebebat, atque eum δειλινὸν
περίπατον appellabat, illum alterum supra ἑωθινόν;
6 utroque enim tempore ambulans disserebat. Líbros
quoque suos, earum omnium rerum conmentarios,
seorsum divisit, ut alii "exoterici" dicerentur,
partim "acroatici."
7 Eos libros generis "acroatici" cum in vulgus
ab eo editos rex Alexander cognovisset atque ea
tempestate armis exercitam[1] omnem prope Asiam
teneret regemque ipsum Darium proeliis et victoriis
urgeret, in illis tamen tantis negotiis litteras ad
Aristotelem misit, non eum recte fecisse, quod
disciplinas acroaticas, quibus ab eo ipse eruditus

---

[1] exercitam, *Carrio* (*cf. Plaut. Epid.* 529, *Skutsch*);
exercitum, ω.

---

[1] *i.e.* esoteric, or inner, for the initiated only. The term was
originally applied to Aristotle's acroatic (or acroamatic) writings, which were not made public, as were his exoteric
Dialogues, but were read to hearers only (cf. ἀκούω) and were
of a strictly scientific character. Except for the fragments of

or "exoteric," the other ἀκροατικά, or "acroatic." [1]
Those were called "exoteric" which gave training
in rhetorical exercises, logical subtlety, and acquaintance with politics; those were called "acroatic" in
which a more profound and recondite philosophy
was discussed, which related to the contemplation
of nature or dialectic discussions. To the practice
of the "acroatic" training which I have mentioned
he devoted the morning hours in the Lyceum,[2] and he
did not ordinarily admit any pupil to it until he had
tested his ability, his elementary knowledge, and his
zeal and devotion to study. The exoteric lectures
and exercises in speaking he held at the same place
in the evening and opened them generally to young
men without distinction. This he called δειλινὸς
περίπατος, or "the evening walk," the other which I
have mentioned above, ἑωθινός, or "the morning
walk";[3] for on both occasions he walked as he
spoke. He also divided his books on all these
subjects into two divisions, calling one set "exoteric,"
the other "acroatic."

When King Alexander knew that he had published
those books of the "acroatic" set, although at that
time the king was keeping almost all of Asia in a state
of panic by his deeds of arms, and was pressing King
Darius himself hard by attacks and victories, yet in
the midst of such urgent affairs he sent a letter to
Aristotle, saying that the philosopher had not done
right in publishing the books and so revealing to the

---

his *Dialogues*, all the works of Aristotle which have come
down to us are of the latter class.

[2] See note on vii. 16. 1 (ii, p. 135).

[3] Hence the term "peripatetics," from περιπατέω, "walk
up and down."

8 foret, libris foras editis involgasset: "Nam qua,"
inquit, "alia re praestare ceteris poterimus, si ea
quae ex te accepimus omnium prosus fient communia? Quippe ego doctrina anteire malim quam
copiis atque opulentiis."

9 Rescripsit ei Aristoteles ad hanc sententiam:
"Acroaticos libros, quos editos quereris et non
proinde ut arcana absconditos, neque editos scito
esse neque non editos, quoniam his solis cognobiles
erunt, qui nos audiverunt."[1]

10 Exempla utrarumque litterarum sumpta ex Andronici philosophi libro subdidi; amavi[2] prosus
in utriusque epistula brevitatis elegantissimae filum
tenuissimum:

11 Ἀλέξανδρος Ἀριστοτέλει εὖ πράττειν.

Οὐκ ὀρθῶς ἐποίησας, ἐκδοὺς τοὺς ἀκροατικοὺς[3] τῶν
λόγων· τίνι γὰρ δὴ διοίσομεν ἡμεῖς τῶν ἄλλων, εἰ καθ'
οὓς ἐπαιδεύθημεν λόγους, οὗτοι πάντων ἔσονται κοινοί;
ἐγὼ δὲ βουλοίμην ἂν ταῖς περὶ τὰ ἄριστα ἐμπειρίαις ἢ
ταῖς δυνάμεσιν διαφέρειν. ἔρρωσο.

12 Ἀριστοτέλης βασιλεῖ Ἀλεξάνδρῳ εὖ πράττειν.

Ἔγραψάς μοι περὶ τῶν ἀκροατικῶν λόγων, οἰόμενος
δεῖν αὐτοὺς φυλάττειν ἐν ἀπορρήτοις. ἴσθι οὖν αὐτοὺς
καὶ ἐκδεδομένους καὶ μὴ ἐκδεδομένους· ξυνετοὶ γάρ εἰσιν
μόνοις τοῖς ἡμῶν ἀκούσασιν. ἔρρωσο, Ἀλέξανδρε
βασιλεῦ.

---

[1] qui . . . audiverunt *added by Hertz.*
[2] amavi *scripsi*; amavi autem, σ; an autem, ω; en
autem, *Rose.* Prosus *seems to call for a preceding verb or
adjective; see my article in Class. Phil.* xvii (1922), 144 *ff.
Otherwise I should prefer the* en autem *of Rose.*
[3] ἀκροαματικούς, *Plut.*

public the acroatic training, in which he himself had been instructed. "For in what other way," said he, "can I excel the rest, if that instruction which I have received from you becomes the common property of all the world? For I would rather be first in learning than in wealth and power."

Aristotle replied to him to this purport: "Know that the acroatic books, which you complain have been made public and not hidden as if they contained secrets, have neither been made public nor hidden, since they can be understood only by those who have heard my lectures."

I have added copies of both letters, taken from the book of the philosopher Andronicus.[1] I was particularly charmed with the slender thread of elegant brevity in the letter of each.

"Alexander to Aristotle, Greeting.

"You have not done right in publishing your acroatic lectures; for wherein, pray, shall I differ from other men, if these lectures, by which I was instructed, become the common property of all? As for me, I should wish to excel in acquaintance with what is noblest, rather than in power. Farewell."

"Aristotle to King Alexander, Greeting.

"You have written to me regarding my acroatic lectures, thinking that I ought to have kept them secret. Know then that they have both been made public and not made public. For they are intelligible only to those who have heard me. Farewell, King Alexander."

[1] Frag. 662, Rose.

13 Hoc ego verbum ξυνετοὶ γάρ εἰσιν quaerens uno itidem verbo dicere, aliud non repperi quam quod est scriptum a M. Catone in sexta *Origine :* " Itaque ego," inquit, " cognobiliorem cognitionem esse arbitror."

VI

Quaesitum atque tractatum utrum siet rectius dicere "habeo curam vestri," an "vestrum."

1 Percontabar Apollinarem Sulpicium, cum eum Romae adulescentulus sectarer, qua ratione diceretur " habeo curam vestri " aut " misereor vestri " et iste casus " vestri " eo in loco quem videretur 2 habere casum rectum. Is hic mihi ita respondit : " Quaeris," inquit, " ex me, quod mihi quoque est iamdiu in perpetua quaestione. Videtur enim non 'vestri' oportere dici, sed 'vestrum,' sicuti Graeci locuntur : ἐπιμελοῦμαι ὑμῶν, κήδομαι ὑμῶν, in quo loco ὑμῶν aptius 'vestrum' dicitur quam 'vestri' et habet casum nominandi, quem tu 'rectum' 3 appellasti, 'vos.'[1] Invenio tamen," inquit, " non paucis in locis 'nostri' atque 'vestri' dictum, non 'nostrum' aut 'vestrum.' L. Sulla *Rerum Gestarum* libro secundo : 'Quod si fieri potest, ut etiam nunc nostri vobis in mentem veniat, nosque magis dignos creditis quibus civibus quam hostibus utamini quique pro vobis potius quam contra vos pugnemus, neque nostro neque maiorum nostrorum immerito[2] 4 nobis id continget.' Terentius in *Phormione :*

[1] vos *added by Hertz.*
[2] immerito, *Madvig* ; merito, ω.

When trying, in the phrase ξυνετοὶ γάρ εἰσιν, to express the word ξυνετοί by a single Latin term, I found nothing better than what is written by Marcus Cato in the sixth book of his *Origins* : [1] " Therefore I think the information is more comprehensible (*cognobilior*)."

VI

It is asked and discussed whether it it is more correct to say *habeo curam vestri,* or *vestrum.*

I ASKED Sulpicius Apollinaris, when I was studying with him at Rome in my youth, on what principle people said *habeo curam, vestri,* or " I have care for you," and *misereor, vestri,* or " I pity you," and what he thought the nominative case of *vestri* was in such connections. Thereupon he answered me as follows : " You ask something of me about which I too have long been in a state of uncertainty. For it seems to me that one ought to say, not *vestri,* but *vestrum,* just as the Greeks say ἐπιμελοῦμαι ὑμῶν and κήδομαι ὑμῶν, where ὑμῶν is translated by *vestrum* more fittingly than by *vestri,* having *vos* for the naming case, or the ' direct ' case, as you called it. Yet in not a few places," said he, " I find *nostri* and *vestri,* not *nostrum* or *vestrum.* Thus Lucius Sulla says, in the second book of his *Autobiography* : [2] " But if it is possible that even now you think of me (*nostri*), and believe me worthy to be your fellow citizen rather than your enemy, and to fight for you rather than against you, this will surely be due to my services and those of my forefathers." Also Terence in the *Phormio* : [3]

[1] Frag. 105, Peter².   [2] Frag. 3, Peter².   [3] v. 172.

Ita plérique ingenió sumus omnes, nóstri nosmet paénitet.

5 Afranius in togata :

Nescío qui nostri míseritust tandém deus.

6 Et Laberius in *Necyomantia :*

Dum diútius retinétur, nostri oblítus est.

7 " Dubium porro," inquit, " non est, quin eodem haec omnia casu dicantur : ' nostri paenitet,' [1] ' nostri oblitus est,' ' nostri misertus est,' quo dicitur : ' mei paenitet,' ' mei misertus est,' ' mei oblitus est.'
8 ' Mei ' autem casus interrogandi est, quem ' genetivum ' grammatici vocant, et ab eo declinatur, quod est ' ego '; huius deinde plurativum est ' nos.' ' Tui ' aeque declinatur ab eo, quod est ' tu '; huius
9 itidem plurativum est ' vos.' Sic namque Plautus declinavit in *Pseudolo* in hisce versibus :

Si ex té tacente fíeri possem cértior,
Ere, quaé miseriae té tam misere mácerent,
Duorúm labori ego hóminum parsissém lubens :
Mei té rogandi et tís [2] respondendí mihi.

' Mei ' enim Plautus hoc in loco non ab eo dixit, quod
10 est ' meus,' sed ab eo, quod est ' ego.' Itaque si dicere velis ' patrem mei ' pro ' patrem meum,' quo Graeci modò τὸν πατέρα μου dicunt, inusitate quidem, sed recte profecto eaque ratione dices, qua Plautus
11 dixit ' labori mei ' pro ' labori meo.' Haec autem ipsa ratio est in numero plurativo, qua Gracchus ' misereri vestrum ' dixit et qua M. Cicero ' contentio

---

[1] nostri paenitet *added by Skutsch.*   [2] tui tis γ.

[1] v. 417, Ribbeck[3].

Of such a nature are we almost all,
That with ourselves (*nostri*) we discontented are.

Afranius wrote in an Italian play : [1]

At last some god or other pitied us (*nostri*).

And Laberius in the *Necyomantia* : [2]

Detained for many days, he us (*nostri*) forgot.

" There is no doubt," said he, " that in all these phrases : ' we are discontented,' ' he forgot us,' ' he pitied us ' (*nostri*), the same case is used as in ' I repent ' (*mei paenitet*), ' he pitied me ' (*mei miseritus est*), ' he forgot me ' (*mei oblitus est*). But *mei* is the case of questioning,[3] which the grammarians call ' genitive,' and comes from *ego ;* and the plural of *ego* is *nos*. *Tui* also is formed from *tu*, and the plural of this is *vos*. For Plautus has thus declined those pronouns in the *Pseudolus*, in the following lines : [4]

O Sir, could I be told without your words
What wretchedness so grievous troubles you,
I would have spared the trouble of two men :
My own (*mei*), of asking you, and yours (*tis = tui*),
　　of answering.

For Plautus here uses *mei*, not from *meus*, but from *ego*. Therefore if you should choose to say *patrem mei* instead of *patrem meum*, as the Greeks say τὸν πατέρα μου, it would be unusual, but surely correct, and on the same principle that Plautus used *labori mei*, ' the trouble of me,' for *labori meo*, ' my trouble.' The same rule applies also in the plural number, where Gracchus said [5] *misereri vestrum* and Marcus

---

[2] v. 62, Ribbeck[3].　　　[3] See note on xiii. 26. 1.
[4] vv. 3 ff.　　　[5] *O.R.F.* p. 248, Meyer[2].

vestrum' et 'contentione nostrum' dixit quaque
item ratione Quadrigarius in *Annali* undevicesimo
verba haec posuit: 'C. Mari, ecquando te nostrum
et reipublicae miserebitur!' Cur igitur Terentius
'paenitet nostri,' non 'nostrum,' et Afranius 'nostri
12 miseritus est,' non 'nostrum'? Nihil hercle," inquit,
"mihi de ista re in mentem venit, nisi auctoritas
quaedam vetustatis non nimis anxie neque super-
stitiose loquentis.   Nam sicuti multifariam scriptum
est 'vestrorum' pro 'vestrum,' ut in Plauti *Mostellaria*
in hoc versu:

Vérum illud esse[1] máxima[2] párs vestrorum in-
téllegit,

cum vellet 'maxima pars' dicere 'vestrum,' ita nonnumquam 'vestri' quoque dictum est pro 'vestrum.'
13 Sed procul dubio qui rectissime loqui volet 'vestrum'
14 potius dixerit quam 'vestri.' Et idcirco inportunis-
sime," inquit, "fecerunt, qui in plerisque Sallusti
exemplaribus scripturam istam sincerissimam cor-
ruperunt.   Nam cum ita in *Catilina* scriptum esset:
'Saepe maiores vestrum miseriti plebis Romanae,'
'vestrum' obleverunt et 'vestri' superscripserunt.
Ex quo in plures libros mendae istius indoles
manavit."
15   Haec memini mihi Apollinarem dicere, eaque tunc
ipsa, ita ut dicta fuerant, notavi.

---

[1] illud est, *codd. Plaut.*
[2] maxime, O[1]; maximum (maximam, *Plaut. B*) adeo,
Plaut.

---

[1] *Pro Planc.* § 16.   [2] *Div. in Caec.* § 37.

Cicero [1] *contentio vestrum,* and *contentione nostrum,*[2] and on the same principle Quadrigarius in the nineteenth book of his *Annals* wrote these words: [3] 'Gaius Marius, when pray will you pity us (*nostrum*) and the State?' Why then should Terence use *paenitet nostri,* not *nostrum,* and Afranius *nostri miseritus est,* not *nostrum*? Indeed," said he, "no reason for this occurs to me except the authority of a certain ancient usage, which was not too anxious or scrupulous in the use of language. For just as *vestrorum* is often used for *vestrum,* as in this line from the *Mostellaria* of Plautus,[4]

> The greatest part of you (*vestrorum*) know that is true

(where *vestrorum* is for *vestrum*), in the same way *vestri* also is sometimes used for *vestrum.* But undoubtedly one who desires to speak very correctly will prefer *vestrum* to *vestri.* And therefore," said he, "those have acted most arbitrarily who in many copies of Sallust have corrupted a thoroughly sound reading. For although he wrote in the *Catiline*: [5] 'Often your forefathers (*maiores vestrum*), pitying the Roman commons,' they erased *vestrum* and wrote *vestri* over it. And from this [6] that error has grown and found its way into more manuscripts."

This is what I remember hearing from Apollinaris, and I noted down his very words at the time, exactly as they were spoken.

---

[3] Frag 83, Peter².   [4] v. 280.   [5] xxxiii. 2.
[6] *Indoles* is perhaps "the nature of the error," *i.e.,* the disposition to make an error of that kind.

VII

Quam diversae Graecorum sint sententiae super numero
Niobae filiorum.[1]

1 MIRA et prope adeo ridicula diversitas fabulae
apud Graecos poetas deprenditur super numero
2 Niobae filiorum. Nam Homerus pueros puellasque
eius bis senos dicit fuisse, Euripides bis septenos,
Sappho bis novenos, Bacchylides et Pindarus bis
denos, quidam alii scriptores tres fuisse solos dixerunt.

VIII

De his quae habere συμπτωσίαν videntur cum luna iuvenescente[2] ac senescente.

1 ANNIANUS poeta in fundo suo, quem in agro
Falisco possidebat, agitare erat solitus vindemiam
2 hilare atque amoeniter. Ad eos dies me et quosdam
3 item alios familiaris vocavit. Ibi tum cenantibus
nobis magnus ostrearum numerus Roma missus est.
Quae cum adpositae fuissent et multae quidem, sed
inuberes macriusculaeque[3] essent: "Luna," inquit
Annianus, "nunc videlicet senescit; ea re ostrea
quoque, sicuti quaedam alia, tenuis exsuctaque est."
4 Cum quaereremus quae alia item senescente luna
tabescerent, "Nonne Lucilium," inquit, "nostrum
meministis dicere:

---

[1] *Lemma omitted by* ω; *supplied by* ς, *ι mitting* sint.
[2] iuvenescente, *suggested by Hosius, who writes* mansuescente
in his text; ansuescente δNΠ; anuescente (ac vescente, X),
OX; accrescente *or* adolescente, *Lion.*
[3] macriusculaeque, *Hertz*; macrae quaeque, NX; macrae-
que ΠX²; macrus queque, δ.

VII

How the opinions of the Greeks differ as to the number of
Niobe's children.

A STRANGE and indeed almost absurd variation is
to be noted in the Greek poets as to the number of
Niobe's children. For Homer says[1] that she had
six sons and six daughters; Euripides,[2] seven of
each; Sappho,[3] nine; Bacchylides[4] and Pindar,[5]
ten; while certain other writers have said that there
were only three sons and three daughters.

VIII

Of things which seem to have συμπτωσία, or "coincidence,"
with the waning and waxing moon.

THE poet Annianus owned an estate in the
Faliscan territory, where he used to celebrate the
vintage season with mirth and jollity. On one
occasion he invited me, along with some other
friends. As we were dining there one day, a large
quantity of oysters were sent from Rome. When
they were set before us and proved to be indeed
numerous, but neither rich nor very plump, Annianus
said: "Of course the moon is waning just now;
therefore the oyster also, like some other things, is
thin and juiceless." When we asked what other
things wasted away with the waning moon, he
answered: "Don't you remember that our Lucilius
says:[6]

---

[1] *Iliad* xxiv. 602.
[2] Frag. 455, N².
[3] Frag. 143, Bergk.
[4] Frag. 46, Blass².
[5] Frag. 65, Bergk.
[6] v. 1201, Marx.

> Luna alit ostrea et implet echinos, muribus fibras
> Et iecur addit?

5 Eadem autem ipsa quae crescente luna gliscunt, de-
6 ficiente contra defiunt. Aelurorum quoque oculi ad
easdem vices lunae aut ampliores fiunt aut minores.
7 Id etiam," inquit, "multo mirandum est magis, quod
apud Plutarchum in quarto *In Hesiodum Commentario*
legi : 'Cepetum revirescit et congerminat decedente
luna, contra autem inarescit adolescente. Eam causam esse dicunt sacerdotes Aegyptii, cur Pelusiotae
cepe non edint, quia solum olerum omnium contra
lunae augmenta atque damna vices minuendi et
augendi habeat contrarias.'"

IX

Qualibus verbis delectari solitus sit Antonius Iulianus, positis
in *Mimiambis* Cn.[1] Matii ; et quid significet M. Cato in
oratione quam scripsit de innocentia sua, cum ita
dictitat : "numquam vestimenta a populo peposci."

1 DELECTARI mulcerique aures suas dicebat Antonius
Iulianus figmentis verborum novis Cn. Matii, hominis
2 eruditi, qualia haec quoque essent, quae scripta ab eo
in *Mimiambis* memorabat :

> Sinuque amicam refice frigidam caldo,
> Columbulatim labra conserens labris.

[1] Cn. . . . quam *added by L. Müller.*

---

[1] Cf. Hor. *Serm.* ii. 4. 30, *lubrica nascentes implent conchylia
lunae* ; Cic. *de Div.* ii. 33.

The moon makes oysters fat, sea-urchins full,
And bulk and substance to the mussels adds ?[1]

Furthermore, those same things which grow as the moon waxes grow less as it wanes. The eyes of cats also become larger or smaller according to the same changes of the moon. This too," said he, "is much more greatly to be wondered at, which I read in the fourth book of Plutarch's *Commentary on Hesiod* :[2] ' The onion grows and buds as the moon wanes, but, on the contrary, dries up while the moon waxes. The Egyptian priests say that this is the reason why the people of Pelusium do not eat the onion, because it is the only one of all vegetables which has an interchange of increase and decrease contrary to the waxing and waning of the moon.' "

IX

A passage in the *Mimiambi* of Gnaeus Matius, in which Antonius Iulianus used to delight ; and the meaning of Marcus Cato in the speech which he wrote on his own uprightness, when he said : " I have never asked the people for garments."

ANTONIUS JULIANUS used to say that his ears were soothed and charmed by the newly-coined words of Gnaeus Matius, a man of learning, such as the following, which he said were written by Matius in his *Mimiambi* :[3]

Revive your cold love in your warm embrace,
Close joining lip to lip like amorous dove (*columbulatim*).

[2] Frag. 90, Bern.
[3] Frag. 12, Bährens (*F.P.R.* p. 282).

3 Item id quoque iucunde lepideque fictum dictitabat:

> Iam tonsiles tapetes ebrii fuco,
> Quos concha purpura imbuens venenavit.

. . .[1]

X

Quid vocabulum " ex iure manum consertum " significet.[2]

1 " Ex iure manum consertum " verba sunt ex anti-
quis actionibus, quae, cum lege agitur et vindiciae
contenduntur, dici nunc quoque apud praetorem
2 solent. Rogavi ego Romae grammaticum, celebri
hominem fama et multo nomine, quid haec verba
essent. Tum ille me despiciens: " Aut erras,"
inquit, " adulescens, aut ludis; rem enim doceo gram-
maticam, non ius respondeo; si quid igitur ex
Vergilio, Plauto, Ennio quaerere habes, quaeras
licet."
3 " Ex Ennio ergo," inquam, " est, magister, quod
4 quaero. Ennius enim verbis hisce usus est." Cumque ille demiratus aliena haec esse a poetis et haud
usquam inveniri in carminibus Ennii diceret, tum
ego hos versus ex octavo *Annali* absentes dixi, nam
forte eos tamquam insigniter praeter alios factos
memineram:

> Pellitur [3] e medio sapientia, vi geritur res;
> Spernitur orator bonus, horridus miles amatur.

---

[1] *Something is lacking, as the chapter-heading shows.*
[2] *Lemmata of X and XI omitted by ω.*
[3] Tollitur, *Cic. pro Mur.* 30.

---

[1] *Id.* 13.   [2] That is, the *murex* or " purple-fish."

And this also he declared to be charmingly and
neatly devised : [1]

The shorn rugs now are drunken with the dye
  With which the shell [2] has drenched and coloured
them. . . .

X

The meaning of the phrase *cx iure manum consertum.*

Ex iure manum consertum, or "lay on hands according to law," is a phrase taken from ancient cases
at law, and commonly used to-day when a case is
tried before the praetor and claims are made. I
asked a Roman grammarian, a man of wide reputation and great name, what the meaning of these
words was. But he, looking scornfully at me, said :
" Either you are making a mistake, youngster, or
you are jesting ; for I teach grammar and do not
give legal advice. If you want to know anything
connected with Virgil, Plautus or Ennius, you may
ask me."

" It is a question from Ennius then, master," said
I, " that I am asking. For it was Ennius who used
those words." And when the grammarian said in
great surprise that the words were unsuited to poetry
and that they were not to be found anywhere in the
poems of Ennius, I quoted from memory the following lines from the eighth book of the *Annals ;* for it
chanced that I remembered them because of their
particularly striking character : [3]

Wisdom is driven forth and force prevails ;
They scorn the speaker good, the rude soldier love.

[3] vv. 268 ff., Vahlen.

Haut doctis dictis certantes nec maledictis,
Miscent inter sese inimicitiam agitantes.
Non ex iure manum[1] consertum, sed magis ferro
Rem[2] repetunt regnumque petunt, vadunt so-
lida vi.

5 Cum hos ego versus Ennianos dixissem, "Credo,"
inquit grammaticus, "iam tibi. Sed tu velim credas
mihi, Quintum Ennium didicisse hoc non ex poeticae
litteris, set ex iuris aliquo perito. Eas igitur tu
quoque," inquit, "et discas unde Ennius didicit."

6 Usus consilio sum magistri, quod docere ipse de-
buerat a quo discerem praetermonstrantis. Itaque
id quod ex iureconsultis quodque ex libris eorum
didici inferendum his commentariis existimavi, quoniam in medio rerum et hominum vitam qui colunt
ignorare non oportet verba actionum civilium cele-

7 briora. "Manum conserere" . . . Nam de qua re
disceptatur in iure in re[3] praesenti, sive ager sive
quid aliud est, cum adversario simul manu prendere
et in ea re sollemnibus verbis vindicare, id est

8 "vindicia." Correptio manus in re atque in loco
praesenti apud praetorem ex *Duodecim Tabulis* fiebat,
in quibus ita scriptum est: "Si qui in iure manum

9 conserunt." Sed postquam praetores, propagatis
Italiae finibus, satis iurisdictionis[4] negotiis occupati,
proficisci vindiciarum dicendarum causa ad[5] longin-

---

[1] manum, *Cic. Fam.* vii. 13. 2 *and some MSS. of pro Mur.*
30; manu, ω.
[2] rem, *Cic.*; rei, ω.
[3] in iure in re, *Hertz*; in iure, N; in re, *early editors.*
[4] satis iurisdictionis, *Karlowa*; datis iur., *MSS.*
[5] ad *added by Oiselius*; in, *Carrio.*

[1] vi. 5.

Contending not with learning nor abuse,
They join in strife, not laying claim by law,
But, seeking with the sword both wealth and
    power,
With force resistless rush.

When I had recited these verses from Ennius, the grammarian rejoined : " Now I believe you. But I would have you believe me, when I say that Quintus Ennius learned this, not from his reading of the poets, but from someone learned in the law. Do you too then go and learn from the same source as Ennius."

I followed the advice of this teacher, when he referred me to another from whom I could learn what he ought to have taught me himself. And I thought that I ought to include in these notes of mine what I have learned from jurists and their writings, since those who are living in the midst of affairs and among men ought not to be ignorant of the commoner legal expressions. *Manum conserere,* " to lay on hands." . . . For with one's opponent to lay hold of and claim in the prescribed formula anything about which there is a dispute, whether it be a field or something else, is called *vindicia,* or " a claim." A seizing with the hand of the thing or place in question took place in the presence of the praetor according to the *Twelve Tables,* in which it was written : [1] " If any lay on hands in the presence of the magistrate." [2] But when the boundaries of Italy were extended and the praetors were greatly occupied with legal business, they found it hard to go to distant places to settle claims. Therefore it became

[2] Cf. xx. i. 48 ; see Allen, *Remnants of Early Latin,* p. 85.

quas res gravabantur, institutum est contra *Duodecim Tabulas* tacito consensu, ut litigantes non in iure apud praetorem manum consererent, sed "ex iure manum consertum" vocarent, id est alter alterum ex iure ad conserendam manum in rem de qua ageretur vocaret atque profecti simul in agrum de quo litigabatur, terrae aliquid ex eo, uti unam glebam, in ius in urbem ad praetorem deferrent et in ea gleba, tamquam in toto agro, vindicarent. 10 Idcirco Ennius significare volens gestum,[1] non, ut ad praetorem solitum est, legitimis actionibus neque ex iure manum consertum, sed bello ferroque et vera vi atque solida rem repeti dixit;[2] quod videtur dixisse, conferens vim illam civilem et festucariam, quae verbo diceretur, non quae manu fieret, cum vi bellica et cruenta.

XI

Quid sit "sculnae" verbum positum apud M. Varronem.

1 P. Lavini liber est non incuriose factus. Is in-
2 scriptus est *De Verbis Sordidis.* In eo scripsit "sculnam" vulgo dici, quasi "seculnam"; "quem qui elegantius," inquit, "loquuntur 'sequestrem' 3 appellant." Utrumque vocabulum a sequendo factum est, quod eius qui electus sit utraque pars fidem

---

[1] volens gestum, *Huschke*; volens bellum, N.
[2] rem . . . dixit *added by Boot.*

---

[1] *festuca*, "a stalk or stem," was used of the rod with
450

usual by silent consent, though contrary to the *Twelve Tables*, for the litigants not to lay on hands in court in the presence of the praetor, but to call for " a laying on of hands according to law " ; that is, that the one litigant should summon the other to the object in question, to lay hands on it according to law, and that they should go together to the field under dispute and bring some earth from it to the city to the praetor's court, for example one clod, and should lay claim to that clod, as if it were the whole field. Accordingly Ennius, wishing to describe such action, said that restitution was demanded, not by legal processes, such as are carried on before a praetor, nor by a laying on of hands according to law, but by war and the sword, and by genuine and resistless violence ; and he seems to have expressed this by comparing that civil and symbolic [1] power which is exercised in name only and not actually, with warlike and sanguinary violence.

XI

The meaning of the word *sculna*, used by Marcus Varro.

PUBLIUS LAVINIUS is the author of a carefully written book, entitled *On Vulgar Words*. In it he wrote that *sculna* was a colloquial form for *seculna*, " for which," says he, " more elegant speakers use *sequester*, or ' arbiter.' " Each of these words is derived from *sequor*, because both parties " follow " the decision of the arbiter who is chosen. Lavinius

which slaves were touched in the ceremony of manumission. Here *festucariam* (a ἅπαξ λεγόμενον) is extended in meaning to include any symbolic legal process.

451

4 sequatur. " Sculnam " autem scriptum esse in *Logistorico* M. Varronis, qui inscribitur *Catus,* idem
5 Lavinius in eodem libro admonet. Sed quod apud sequestrem depositum erat, " sequestro positum " per adverbium dicebant. Cato *De Ptolomaeo contra Thermum* : " Per deos immortalis, nolite vos atque . . . ."

reminds us in the same book that *sculna* was written
in the division of Marcus Varro's *Logistorica* entitled
Catus.[1]   But that which was deposited with the
arbiter they spoke of as *sequestro positum*, " deposited
for arbitration," using the adverb *sequestro*.   Cato,
in his speech *On Ptolemy against Thermus*, says:[2]
" By the immortal gods, do not . . . ."

[1] Frag. 37, Riese.   [2] x. 3, Jordan.

INDEX OF NAMES[1]

---

[1] L = Lemma, the headings of the various chapters of the twenty books. *Passim* usually indicates that the word occurs four times or more, ordinarily in L and in the first section. When a word occurs several times, but not in L or in the first few sections, f. and ff. are used. Titles of works of literature are put in italics. Explanations of names, and titles of collections of fragments, which are given in the Indices to Volumes i and ii are not repeated. Of the latter those numbered from 1 to 40 are in Vol. i, numbers 41 and 42 are in Vol. ii.

INDEX OF NAMES

---

[43] Th. Bergk,[4] *Poetae Lyrici Graeci*, Leipzig, 1882 (*B*[4]).

[44] A. Meineke, *Analecta Alexandrina*, Berlin, 1843.

INDEX OF NAMES

---

[45] F. G. A. Mullachius, *Fragmenta Philosophorum Graecorum*, Paris, 1860 (*F.P.G.*).

[46] F. Jacoby, *Apollodors Chronik* (Philol. Untersuchungen xvi), Berlin, 1902.

457

INDEX OF NAMES

INDEX OF NAMES

Athenae, i. 2. 1; ii. 2. 1; 12. 1; iii.
13. 3; vi. 5. 5; vii. 10. 2, 4 (*bis*);
13. 1; 17. 1 (*bis*), 2; x. 1. 1; xi.
9. 1; xii. 7. 5; 11. 1; xiii. 11. 3;
xv. 2. 1, 3; 20. 10; xvii. 8. 1;
20. 4; 21. 5, 7, 10, 19; xviii. 2. 1;
10. 3; 13. 1; xix. 1. 4; 6. 2; 8. 1;
12. 1.
Athenienses, ii. 1. 5; 12. 1; iii. 2. 4;
vi. 14. L, 8; vii. 10. 2; 17. 1; ix.
2. 10; xi. 18. 2, 4; xv. 17. L, 2;
20. 6, 10; xvii. 21. 4, 9, 12, 19, 23,
30, 48. *Atheniensis*, i. 3. 20; iii.
11. 6; xi. 18. L, 1; xv. 17. 1; xvii.
21. 18, 38.
Atheniensis populus, viii. 9; xi. 18.
L; xvii. 21. 9.
Atherbal, xviii. 12. 6. The name of
two Carthaginian commanders, one
in the first and one in the second
Punic war. Which is meant is
uncertain.
Athones, xvi. 9. 6. Plural of Athos,
the well-known mountain of Chal-
cidice in Macedonia, used by
Lucilius as typical of steep and
rugged country.
Atilius, xv. 24. A Roman writer of
comedy of the ante-classical period,
perhaps identical with the writer
of tragedy mentioned by Suetonius
(*Jul.* lxxxiv. 2).
Atilius, L., v. 17. 2. A Roman
senator.
Atilius Regulus, M., vii. 3; 4 *passim*.
Consul in 267 and 256 B.C.
Atilius Regulus, M., iv. 3. 2. Son
of the above, consul in 227 B.C.
with P. Valerius, and in 217.
(Atilius) Serranus, Q., xv. 28. 3. Con-
sul in 106 B.C.
Atinius, -a, -um, *adj.* to Atinius,
tribune of the commons in 197 B.C.;
plebiscitum, xiv. 8. 2; *lex*, xvii. 7.
L, 1.
Atreus, see L. Accius.
Atta, *see* Quinctius.
Attalus, xii. 13. 26. Attalus I, king
of Pergamum from 241 to 197
B.C.
Attica, Praef. 4; xv. 1. 6. *See also*
Attice.

Attice, xiv. 6. 4. Another form of
Attica.
Attice, xvii. 8. 7. *Adv.* to Atticus.
Attici, ii. 3. 2; xiii. 6. L.
Atticus, -a, -um, *adj.* to Attica:
ager, xviii. 10. 1; *homines*, v. 20. 3;
lingua, i. 2. 4; ii. 3. 1; *noctes*,
Praef. 4, 10; *puer*, xvii. 8. 4;
talentum, iii. 17. 3; *terra*, Praef. 4.
Atticum, Epistulae ad, see M. Tullius
Cicero.
Atticus, *see* Herodes.
Attius, iii. 16. 13, 14. *See* note.
Aufeia lex, xi. 10. 1. *See* C. Sem-
pronius Gracchus.
Augurinus, *see* Minucius.
Augurium Privatum, see Nigidius
Figulus.
Augustus, Caesar, ii. 24. 14, 15; vi.
8. 2; ix. 11. 10; x. 2. 2 (*ter*); 11. 5;
xiii. 6. 4; 12. 2; 21. 4; *Epistulae*,
x. 11. 5; 24. 2; *Epist. ad Gaium
Nepotem*, xv. 7. L, 3.
Aulus, xi. 8. 4. Refers to A. Postu-
mius Albinus.
Aulularia, see T. Maccius Plautus.
Aurelius Opilius : [13] *Indices Plauti*,
iii. 3. 1; *Musae*, i. 25. 17, 18 (cf.
Praef. 8).
Aurunci, i. 10. 1.
Auruncus, v. 12. 14.
Auspiciis, De, see Valerius Messala.
Auster, xvi. 11. 4, 6 (*bis*), 7. The South
Wind, personified.
Aventinus, *sc.* mons, xiii. 14. 4, 7 (*bis*).
Axium, ad Q., vi. 3. 10, 55. *See* M.
Tullius Tiro.

Babyloni, iii. 2. 5; xiv. 1. 11.
Bacchae, see Euripides.
Bacchylides,[47] xx. 7. 2.
Bagrada, also Bagradas, vii. 3.
Balbus, *see* Cornelius.
Bassus, *see* Ventidius.
Bello Carthaginiensi, De, see M. Porcius
Cato Censorius.
Bias, v. 11 *passim*.
Bibulus, *see* Calpurnius.
Bisaltia, xvi. 15. A country in Thrace
on the river Strymon.
Bithynia, xvii. 17. 2. A country in
the northern part of Asia Minor.

---

[47] F. Blass, *Bacchylidis Carmina*, Leipzig, 1899.

INDEX OF NAMES

INDEX OF NAMES

---

[48] See No. 17.

INDEX OF NAMES

" See No. 5.

INDEX OF NAMES

INDEX OF NAMES

INDEX OF NAMES

---

[50] R. Fuchs, De Erasistrato Capita Selecta, *Hermes*, xxix (1894), p. 171.

INDEX OF NAMES

INDEX OF NAMES

Graeciense scimpodium, xix. 10. 1.
Graecus and Graeci, Praef. 11; i. 7.
6, 17; 8. 4; 9. 6; 15. 17; 18. 2,
5; 20. 7; 22. 9; 25. 8, 11; ii. 7. 2,
18; 20. 4; 21. L, 4, 9; 22. 8, 10,
12; 23. 1; 26. 16, 19; 28. 1; iii.
9. 9; 10. 2; iv. 11. 1; 15. 6; v.
3. 2; 10. 1; 12. 10; 15. 5; 18. 8;
20. 4; vi. 3. 34; 6. 1; 9. 13; 11.
2; 12. 3; 14. 1; vii. 2. 1; 14. 4;
16. 11; viii. 2, 12; ix. 15. 6; 16.
L; x. 1. 11; 7. 1; 10. L, 1, 2;
12. 9; 18. 2; 24. 1; 25. 5 (*bis*);
xi. 7. 3; 15. 6; 16. 1, 9; xii. 5. 2;
6. 1; xiii. 6. L, 1; 9. 4 ff.; 11. 7
17. 1 (*bis*); 21. L; 22. 7; 23. 3,
9, 19; 30. 2; xiv. 3. 5; xv. 1. 7;
3. 8; 14. 4; 25. 1; xvi. 3. 9; 8. 9,
12, 13; 12. 1, 6; xvii. 2. 13; 3. 2,
4; 10. 13; 12. L, 1; xviii. 4. 10;
14. 1; xix. 1. 7; 2. 1, 2; 5. 5;
9. L, 7; 14. 8; xx. 6. 2; 7. L.
Graecus, -a, -um, *adj.* to Graecia, i.
8. 6; ii. 23. 22; 25. 8; 26. 8, 9;
ix. 9. 4; xix. 9. 10; *cognomentum*,
xi. 5. 1; *comoedia*, ii. 23. 19; *disciplina*, xiii. 25. 4; xv. 11. 3;
ἐνθυμημάτιον, xvi. 1. 1; *sc.*
ἐνθυμημάτιον, xvi. 1. 3; *sc. fabula*,
ii. 23. 3; *facundia* (*facundiae*), i. 2.
1; iii. 7. 1; ix. 2. 1; xiv. 1. 32;
xv. 2. 2; *figura*, xv. 14. 4; *grammatici*, ii. 25. 4; *historia* (*historiae*),
i. 11. 1; vi. 1. 1; x. 17. 1; 18. 2;
xvii. 15. 3; *homo*, ii. 21. 1; vii. 8.
1; *liber*, Praef. 2; ix. 4. 3; xvi. 8.
4; xviii. 2. 3; *lingua*, i. 18. 5;
ii. 22. 1; 26. 5, 7, 20; v. 20. 7;
xi. 1. 1; xiii. 9. 4 (*bis*); xv. 30. L;
xvi. 12. L; xvii. 17. L; xix. 13. 3;
sc. lingua, xviii. 14. 2; *litterae*, iii.
19. 1; xi. 16. 2; xiii. 9. 4, 5; 25.
4; *nomen*, ii. 10. 3; xi. 16. 8;
oratio, i. 2. 6; 7. 8; xi. 1. 1; 8.
L, 2, 3; xii. 1. 24; xvi. 3. 2;
xvii. 20. 7; xviii. 10. 11; xix. 1.
15; 12. 1; *oratores*, xiii. 25. 8;
sc. philosophi, i. 26. 11 (*bis*); *poema*,
ix. 9. 1; *poeta*, iii. 3. 15; xiii. 25.
8; xx. 7. 1; *praestigiae*, xiii. 24. 2;
proverbium, xiii. 29. 5; *ratio*, vi.
9. L; *res*, ii. 21. 3; v. 14. 1; xvii.
9. 18; xx. 1. 20; *scalae*, x. 15. 29;
scriptor, xi. 5. 6; *sententiae*, ix. 9. L;
sermo, ii. 26. 1; *sophista*, vi. 3. 34;

titulus, xiii. 9. 3; *tragoedus*, xi. 10.
6; *verbum*, i. 18. 2; ii. 26. 18;
viii. 13; x. 11. 5; xi. 16. L, 6;
xiii. 9. 4; xvi. 1. L; xvii. 5. 3;
xix. 13. 4; *versiculi*, xix. 11. 1;
versus, iv. 5. 7; ix. 9. 7; xiii. 18. 3;
vir, xvii. 21. L, 1; *vocabulum*, i,
18. 1, 2; ii. 26. L; v. 18. 7; 20. 3;
vi. 12. 2; ix. 5. 5; xi. 1. 1; xv.
30. 3; xvi. 7. 13; *sc. vocabulum*,
ii. 26. 8, 9; iv. 3. 3; *vox*, vii. 15. 6;
x. 4. 4; xi. 16. 2; xiii. 22. 5; xvhi.
9. 9; xix. 13. 5.
Grai, xiii. 8. 3.
Grammatici Commentarii, see Nigidius
Figulus.
Granius, iv. 17. 2.
Gratiae, xiii. 11. 2.

Hadrianus, Divus,[14] iii. 16. 12 (*bis*);
xi. 15. 3; xiii. 22. 1; *Oratio de
Italicensibus*, xvi. 13. L, 4.
Hamilcar, iv. 7. 2.
Hammon, *see* Iuppiter.
Hannibal, ii. 6. 7 (*bis*); (19. 9); iv. 7.
2 ff.; 18. 3; v. 5 (*passim*); vi. 1.
4; 2. 5 ff.; 18. L, 2; x. 3. 19 (*ter*);
(24. 6 ff.); xvi. 8. 7, 11.
Hariolus, see Naevius.
Harmodius, ix. 2. 10; xvii. 21. 7.
Harpalus, probably an error for Har-
pagus, x. 16. 4.
Hasdrubal, iv. 7. 2; xvii. 9. 16.
Hebdomades, see M. Terentius Varro.
Hector, xiii. 25. 18; xv. 6. 3, 4 (*bis*).
See also Ἕκτωρ.
Hectoreus ensis, xv. 6. 3.
Hecuba, xi. 4. 1.
Hecuba, see Ennius and Euripides.
Hegesias, ix. 4. 3.
Helicon, iii. 11. 3.
Heliconius Tripus, *see* Hesiodus.
Hellanicus, xv. 23 (*ter*). A writer of
history and chronicles; he was born
in Mitylene and was a contemporary
of Herodotus. *See also* Ἑλλάνικος.
Helvius Cinna, C., ix. 12. 12; xix. 9.
7; 13. 5.
Heraclides Ponticus, viii (end).
(Heraclitus), Praef. 12.
Herculaneum sacrificium, xi. 6. 2.
Herculanus pes, i. 1. 3.
Hercules, i. 1 (*passim*); iii. 9. 2; x.
16. 13; xi. 6. L, 1, 2; *Herculis
templum*, xix. 5. 4.

467

INDEX OF NAMES

INDEX OF NAMES

INDEX OF NAMES

INDEX OF NAMES

471

INDEX OF NAMES

INDEX OF NAMES

Megalenses ludi, ii. 24. 2 (see note); (sc. ludi), xviii. 2. 11.

Megara (-orum), vii. 10. 2, 4 (bis).

Megarenses, vii. 10. 3.

Melanippa, see Ennius.

Melicertes, xiii. 27. 2; *see also* Μελι-κέρτης.

Melicus, -a, -um, a dialectic form of Medicus, Medic: grues, vi. 16. 5.

Memmius, xix. 9. 7. Governor of Bithynia in 57 B.C., whom Catullus accompanied to his province.

Memnon, xix. 7. 6. Son of Aurora, an ally of Priam in the Trojan War; he was slain by Achilles.

Memoria, xiii. 8. L, 1, 3.

Memoriales Libri, Praef. 8.

Memorialia, see Masurius Sabinus.

Menander, ii. 23 (passim); xvii. 4 (passim); 21. 42; *Plocium*, ii. 23. 6 ff.; iii. 16. 3.

Menelaus, vi. 14. 7; xii. 2. 7.

Menenius Agrippa, xvii. 21. 13. Consul in 503 B.C. He persuaded the plebeians to return from the Sacred Mount in 493.

Menippeae Saturae, see M. Terentius Varro.

Menippus, ii. 18. 7.

Meropa, vi. 3. 28.

Messala, *see* Valerius.

Messana, x. 3. 12.

Metellus, *see* Caecilius.

Methymnaeus, xvi. 19. 3. An inhabitant of Methymna, a city of Lesbos.

Mettus Fufetius, *see* Fufetius.

Mevia, see L. Pomponius.

Milesii, i. 11. 7; xi. 9. 1 (quater); xv. 10. 2.

Milesius, -a, -um, *adj.* to Miletus: *legati*, xi. 9. L; *nomen*, xv. 10. 1; *virgines*, xv. 10. L.

Miletus, xi. 9. 1. A city in the northwestern part of Caria, in Asia Minor.

Milo, *see* Annius.

Milo, xv. 16. L, 1. The celebrated athlete of Crotona in southern Italy.

Milone, Pro, see M. Tullius Cicero.

Miltiades, xvii. 21. 9. An Athenian who became tyrant of the Chersonesus. Returning to Athens, he

became one of the ten generals of the State and commanded the army at the battle of Marathon in 490 B.C.

Mimas, ix. 12. 22.

Mimiambi, see Matius.

Minerva, x. 16. 14; xiii. 23. 4.

Minoia regna, vii. 6. 1.

Minos, xv. 21. 1. A mythical king of Crete, reputed to be the son of Zeus (Jupiter) and Europa. Probably a word meaning king or ruler, like the Egyptian Ptolemy.

Minucius Augurinus, C., vi. 19. 2.

Minucius Thermus, Q., x. 3. 17.

Mitridates, also Mithridates and Mithradates, xi. 10. 4; xv. 1. 4, 6; xvii. 16. 2; 17. L, 2. Mithridates VI, or the Great, king of Pontus from 120 to 63 B.C.

Mitridatios (sc. antidotus), xvii. 16. 6.

Mnesitheus, xiii. 31. 14.

Moera, iii. 16. 11.

Moles Martis, xiii. 23. 2; *see* note.

Molossus, *see* Alexander.

Morta, iii. 16. 11 (ter).

Mucius Scaevola, Q.,[4] iii. 2. 12; iv. 1. 17 (bis), 20; v. 19. 6; vi. 15. L; xi. 2. 4 (bis); xv. 27. 1; xvii. 7. L, 3; *De Iure Civili*, vi. 15. 2.

Mummius, L., x. 16. 17; xvi. 8. 10.

(Munatius) Plancus, L., i. 22. 19; x. 26. 1.

Musa, Praef. 19; iv. 3. 2; 10. 1; xiii. 11. 2; xvii. 21. 45; xviii. 9. 3. *See also* Μοῦσα.

Musae, Praef. 6; *see also* Aurelius Opilius.

Musonius,[32] v. 1. L, 1; ix. 2. 8 (bis); xvi. 1. L, 1; xviii. 2. 1.

Mycenae, x. 16. 14. The famous city in Argolis.

Mylattenses, i. 13. 11.

Mys, ii. 18. 8.

Naevius, Cn.,[3] i. 24. L, 1, 2 (bis); iii. 3. L; vii. 8. 5; viii. 14; xv. 24; xvii. 21. 45 (bis); epitaph of, i. 24. 1 ff.; *Bellum Punicum*,[51] v. 12. 7; xvii. 21. 45; *Hariolus*, iii. 3. 15; *Hesiona*, x. 25. 3 (bis); *Leon*, iii. 3. 15; *Triphallus*, ii. 19. 6.

---

[51] *Q. Enni Carminum Reliquiae. Accedunt Cn. Naevi Belli Poenici quae supersunt.* L. Müller, Leningrad, 1884. Also *F.P.R.*

INDEX OF NAMES

474

INDEX OF NAMES

---

[51] H. N. Fowler, *Panaetii et Hecatonis librorum fragmenta,* Bonn, 1885.

INDEX OF NAMES

INDEX OF NAMES

INDEX OF NAMES

---

[51] G. Meyer, *Publilii Syri mimi sententiae*, Leipzig, 1880.

INDEX OF NAMES

INDEX OF NAMES

INDEX OF NAMES

INDEX OF NAMES

---

[53] H. Kummrow, *Symbola Critica ad Grammaticos Lat.*, Berlin, 1880.

INDEX OF NAMES

---

[54] F. Wimmer, *Theophrasti Eresii Opera; III, Fragmenta,* Leipzig, 1862.

INDEX OF NAMES

10. 6; v. 6. 15; 8. 4; vi. 3. L, 8 (*bis*); 9. 15; x. 1. L, 7 (*ter*); 3. 1, 16; 20. 3; 21. L, 1, 2; 24. 1; xi. 11. 1; xii. 2, 2, 4 ff.; 3. 3; 12. L, 1, 4; 13. L, 29; xiii. 9. 1; xv. 3. 7; 6. 2, 4; xvii. 2. 5; 13. 2; xix. 8. 3; 14. L, 1; (*Brutus*), xi. 2. 4; *Orator*, ii. 17 (*passim*); xiii. 21. 24; xv. 3. L, 1, 2; xviii. 7. 8; *De Oratore*, i. 11. 15, 16; 15. 5, 6, 7; iv. 8. 8; xiii. 17. 2; *Orationes Antoninianae*, or *Philippics*, i. 16. 5; 22. 17; vi. 11. 3 ff.; xiii. 1 (*passim*); 22. 1, 6; *Pro Caecina*, vii. 16. 12; *Pro M. Caelio*, xvii. 1 (*passim*); *Pro Cluentio*, xvi. 7. 10; *Pro Milone*, i. 16. 15; *In Pisonem*, xiii. 25. 22 ff.; *Pro Cn. Plancio*, i. 4. L, 2 f., 6; ix. 12. 4; xx. 6. 11; *De Imperio Cn. Pompei*, i. 7. 16, 20; *De Provinciis Consularibus*, iii. 16. 19; xv. 5. 5 ff.; *Pro Quinctio*, xv. 28. 3 (*bis*), 6; *Pro C. Rabirio*, xii. 3. 1; *Pro Sex. Roscio*, ix. 14. 19; xv. 28 (*passim*); *Contra Rullum de Lege Agraria*, vii. 16. 7; xiii. 25. 4 ff., 27, 32; *Pro Sestio*, ix. 14. 6, 7; xii. 13. 25 ff.; *Pro Sulla*, vii. 16. 6; *In Verrem*: *Orat. de consist. Acc.*, or *Divinatio in Caecilium*, iv. 9. 7; xiii. 25. 9, 10; xx. 6. 11; *Actio II*, i. 7 (*passim*); ii. 6. 8; vii. 16. 13; x. 3. L, 7 ff., 12 ff.; xii. 10. 6; 13. L, 17, 19; xiii. 21. 15, 16 f., 22; *Contra Contionem Q. Metelli*, xviii. 7. 7, 9; *Epist. ad Atticum*, iv. 9. 6; *Epist. ad Fam.*, i. 22. 19 (*ad L. Plancum*); xii. 13. 21 (*ad Ser. Sulpicium*), 22; *Laelius sive de Amicitia*, i. 3. L, 13, 18; viii. 6; xvii. 5 (*passim*); *De Divinatione*, iv. 11. 3, 4; xv. 13. 7; *De Fato*, vii. 2. 15; *De Finibus*, xv. 13. 9; *De Officiis*, xiii. 28. 1; *De Republica*, i. 22. 8, 10; vii. 16. 11; xii. 2. 7; *Tusculanae Disputationes*, x. 18. 2; xvi. 8. 8; *De Gloria*, xv. 6. L, 1; *De Iure Civili in Artem redigendo*, i. 22. 7, 10; *Laus Catonis*, xiii. 20. 3, 4, 14; *Oeconomicus*, xv. 5. 8.
(*Tullium*) *Ciceronem, ad, De Analogia*, see C. Iulius Caesar.
(*Tullium*) *Ciceronem, ad, De Lingua Latina*, see M. Terentius Varro.

(*Tullium*) *Ciceronem, Epistula ad*, see Asinius Pollio.
Tullius Decula, M., xv. 28. 3. Consul in 81 B.C.
Tullius Tiro, M.,[29] iv. 10. 6 (cf. note on i. 7. 1); vi. 3. L, 8 ff.; xii. 3. L, 3, 4; xiii. 9 (*passim*); xv. 6. 2; *Epist.*, x. 1. 7, 8; *Epist. ad Q. Axium*, vi. 3. 10 ff.; Πανδέκται, xiii. 9. 3 ff. (cf. Praef. 7).
Tullus, *see* Hostilius.
Turio, L., *Pro, see* M. Porcius Cato Censorius.
Turius, L., xiv. 2. 26 (*quater*).
Turpilius, xv. 24. A Roman writer of comedy (*palliatae*), a younger contemporary of Terence.
Tusce, ii. 25. 8; xi. 7. 4.
Tusculanus -a, -um, *adj.*: *homo*, xiii. 24. 2; *fundum*, ii. 20. 3.
Tuscus, ii. 25. 8.
Tuscus, *see* Clodius.
Tyrii principes, ix. 9. 14.
Tyros, xiv. 6. 4. Tyre, a city of Phoenicia, at the eastern end of the Mediterranean.

Ulixes, i. 15. 3; ii. 26. 13; v. 1. 6; vi. 14. 7; ix. 12. 17 (*bis*); xi. 4. 2; xiv. 6. 3 (*ter*).
Umbri, iii. 2. 6.
Umbria, iii. 2. 6.
Usus, xiii. 8. L, 1, 3.
Utica, xiii. 20. 3, 11 ff.
Uticenses, xvi. 13. 4. The people of Utica.

Valerium Messalam, In, *see* Q. Caecilius Metellus Numidicus.
Valerius, xiii. 26. 2; xix. 14. 6; *Valeri* (vocative), xiii. 26. L, 1.
Valerius, L., v. 19. 9.
Valerius, Q., xvii. 21. 43. Consul in 239 B.C.
Valerius Aedituus,[3] xix. 9. 10, 11. A Roman writer of epigrams of the ante-classical period.
Valerius Antias,[7] i. 7. 10, 13; v. 21. 6; vi. 19. 8; vii. 8. 6; *Annales, Historia* or *Historiae*, iii. 8. 4; vi. 9. 9, 12, 17; vii. 7. 6.
(Valerius) Catullus, vi. 20. 6 (*bis*); vii. 16 (*passim*); xix. 9. 7.
Valerius (Flaccus), P., iv. 3. 2.

485

INDEX OF NAMES

INDEX OF NAMES

INDEX OF GREEK NAMES

---

[1] Lehrs, K., De Aristarchi Studiis Homericis,[3] Leipzig, 1882.

488

INDEX OF GREEK NAMES.

489

INDEX OF GREEK NAMES

---

[1] Wachsmuth, C., *Corpusculum Poesis Epicae Graecae Ludibundae*, Leipzig, 1885. *See also* note 43, p. 456.

INDEX OF SUBJECTS [1]

---

[1] This Index is not complete, but merely cites some of the many topics treated by Gellius. The categories necessarily overlap to some extent; for example Etymology and Lexicography. In such cases references are put under one of two or more such heads and, with a few exceptions, are not repeated. As a rule, references are given only to places where information is given in the text or in notes.

[2] These seem to have been the first days of the four seven-day phases of the moon; new moon, first quarter, full moon and last quarter.

INDEX OF SUBJECTS

INDEX OF SUBJECTS

---

[1] So Gellius; such forms are really of decl. IV.

[2] This and the following lists are not complete, and they do not always indicate the translator's opinion; they are limited for the most part to instances in which the word or phrase is characterized in the text as archaic (early), rustic, etc., and in some cases only a few specimens are given.

INDEX OF SUBJECTS

---

[1] Sometimes the derivation is given. A few phrases are included.

INDEX OF SUBJECTS

Greek and Latin writers, *see* Literary History.

Halcyon days, iii. 10. 5.

Hexameter, *see* Prosody and versification.

History and biography : chronological survey of Greek and Roman history, xvii. 21—Roman : Aemilius Lepidus, his reconciliation with Fulvius Flaccus, xii. 8. 5 ff.; Caedicius, heroism of, iii. 7; Caesar tries to silence Cato, iv. 10. 8; Sicinius Dentatus, his glorious career, ii. 11; Fabricius and the Samnites, i. 14; and Pyrrhus, iii. 8; and Rufinus, iv. 8; Manlius Torquatus, ix. 13; Regulus, vii. 4; Rome and Carthage as rivals, x. 27; Scipio Africanus, his self-confidence, iv. 18; marvellous tales about, vi. 1; his appeal to the tribunes, vi. 19. 2 ff.; his continence affirmed and questioned, vii. 8; his reconciliation with the father of the Gracchi, xii. 8. 1 ff.—Greek : Alexander and Bucephalas, v. 2; Croesus and his son, v. 9; Leonidas, honours paid to, iii. 7. 19—Alyattes, king of Lydia, i. 11. 7; Hannibal and Antiochus, v. 5; Mithridates as a linguist, xvii. 17. 2—History of Literature : Greek : Homer, birthplace of, iii. 11. 6 ff.; Homer and Hesiod, dates of, iii. 11. 1 ff.; Euripides, life of, xv. 20; prizes taken by, xvii. 4. 3; Hellanicus, Herodotus and Thucydides, dates of, xv. 23; Menander, number of his plays, xvii. 4. 4 f.; of his prizes, xvii. 4. 6; often defeated by Philemon, xvii. 4. 1 f.—Roman : Albinus rebuked by Cato, xi. 8; Ennius describes himself, xii. 4; his three languages, xvii. 17. 1; Laberius and Publilius Syrus, Caesar's estimate of, xvii. 14. 2; Naevius, Pacuvius and Plautus, epitaphs of, i. 24; Naevius writes plays in prison, iii. 3. 15; Nigidius and Varro, date of, xix. 14. 1; Pacuvius and Accius meet, xiii. 2; Plautus, early life of, iii. 3. 14; works of, iii. 3. 1 ff. *See also* Literary Criticism—History of

Philosophy : Aristotle and Alexander, xx. 5; Aristotle chooses his successor, xiii. 5; Aristotle and Plato buy books at high prices, iii. 17; Plato and Xenophon, alleged rivalry of, xiv. 3; Protagoras, how he became a philosopher, v. 3; Pythagoras, previous incarnations of, iv. 11. 14. *See also* Philosophy.

Law : aedile, improper conduct of an, iv. 14; adoption, methods of, v. 19; Areopagus, a difficult case referred to the, xii. 7; betrothal, law of, iv. 4; chattels, return of, iv. 2. 6 ff.; clients, obligations to, v. 13. 4 ff.; divorce and dowry, iv. 3; fines, xi. 1. 2 ff.; guardians, obligations of, v. 13. 4 f.; injuries, penalties for, xx. 1. 31 ff.; judge, duties of, xiv. 2; lex, privilegium and plebiscitum defined, x. 20; cf. xv. 27. 4; punishment, various reasons for, vii. 14; retaliation, xx. 1. 14 ff.; slaves, sale of, vi. 4; Solon, examination of a law of, ii. 12; sumptuary laws, ii. 24; xx. 1. 23; theft, definitions and penalties, vi. 15; xi. 18. 3, 6 ff.; xx. 1. 7 ff.; methods of detecting, xi. 18. 9; among soldiers, xvi. 4. 2; allowed in Egypt and Sparta, xi. 18. 16 f.; a discussion of the Twelve Tables, xx. 1; wills, xv. 27. 3; women, returnable if barren, iv. 2. 9 ff.; may not be adopted, v. 19. 10; must be abstemious, x. 23. 1 ff.; judged by husband, xx. 1. 23. 4 f.; a woman fined for unseemly language, x. 6.

Laws : Aebutian, xvi. 10. 8; Aemilian, ii. 24. 12; Antian, ii. 24. 13; Atinian, xvii. 7. 1 (Atinian plebiscitum, xiv. 8. 2); Aufeian, xi. 10. 1; Fannian, ii. 24. 3, 5, 7; xx. 1. 23; Licinian sumptuary, ii. 24. 7 ff.; xv. 8. L; xx. 1. 23; (of Licinius Stolo), vi. 3. 37; Porcian and Sempronian, x. 3. 13; Voconian, vi. 13. 3; xvii. 6. 1; xx. 1. 23. *See also* Decrees and Edicts.

Legal terms : actio in quadruplum, xi. 18. 10; actiones (cautiones) rei uxoriae, iv. 3. 1; adsiduus, xvi. 10. 5, 8, 15; agere ex sponsu, iv.

INDEX OF SUBJECTS

496

INDEX OF SUBJECTS

INDEX OF SUBJECTS

INDEX OF SUBJECTS

INDEX OF SUBJECTS